Overcoming Apartheid

Overcoming Apartheid

Can Truth Reconcile a Divided Nation?

James L. Gibson

Russell Sage Foundation
New York

FLIP

The Russell Sage Foundation

The Russell Sage Foundation, one of the oldest of America's general purpose foundations, was established in 1907 by Mrs. Margaret Olivia Sage for "the improvement of social and living conditions in the United States." The Foundation seeks to fulfill this mandate by fostering the development and dissemination of knowledge about the country's political, social, and economic problems. While the Foundation endeavors to assure the accuracy and objectivity of each book it publishes, the conclusions and interpretations in Russell Sage Foundation publications are those of the authors and not of the Foundation, its Trustees, or its staff. Publication by Russell Sage, therefore, does not imply Foundation endorsement.

Library of Congress Cataloging-in-Publication Data

Gibson, James L., 1951–
Overcoming apartheid : can truth reconcile a divided nation? / James L. Gibson.
p. cm.
Includes bibliographical references and index.
ISBN 0-87154-312-5
1. South Africa. Truth and Reconciliation Commission—History. 2. Apartheid—South Africa. 3. South Africa—Race relations—Government policy. 4. Human rights—Government policy—South Africa. 5. Amnesty—South Africa. 6. Reconciliation—Political aspects—South Africa. 7. Truth—Political aspects—South Africa. I. Title.

DT1974.2.G53 2004
323.168'09049—dc22 2003066879

The paper used in this publication meets the minimum requirements of American National Standard for Information Sciences—Permanence of Paper for Printed Library Materials. ANSI Z39.48-1992.

Text design by Suzanne Nichols.

RUSSELL SAGE FOUNDATION
112 East 64th Street, New York, New York 10021
10 9 8 7 6 5 4 3 2 1

This book is dedicated to the pillars of South Africa's truth and reconciliation process, Charles Villa-Vicencio, Alec Boraine, and Desmond Tutu, who accomplished far more for South Africa than even they dreamed possible.

CONTENTS

About the Author

James L. Gibson is Sidney W. Souers Professor of Government at Washington University in St. Louis, fellow at the Centre for International and Comparative Politics and Professor Extraordinary in Political Science at Stellenbosch University, South Africa, and Distinguished Visiting Research Scholar at the Institute for Justice and Reconciliation, South Africa.

Preface and Acknowledgments

While this book was being written, a low-scale civil war was taking place in American political science. Dubbed the "perestroika" movement, some academic political scientists were voicing a number of complaints against "scientific" political science. Many of these protestations were foolish and ill informed; some, however, were not.

Supporters of the perestroika movement argue that contemporary political science in the United States is too little concerned with politics. By this the critics mean that political scientists are too focused on methods and theory and have devoted too little attention to studying and analyzing the important political issues and controversies of our time. My own view is that it is impossible to expend too much effort on method and theory, given the range of unresolved methodological and theoretical problems characterizing our field. But at the same time, the complaint that politics is too often ignored has some validity. Consequently, this study is motivated in part by my desire to take important theories of political psychology and intergroup relations and advanced methodological techniques and marry them to what I judge to be one of the most important questions facing transitional polities: does truth lead to reconciliation?

This book therefore purports to contribute to both policy analysis and theory building and scientific hypothesis testing. The policy question is obvious: I seek to assess whether South Africa's truth and reconciliation process in fact achieved the goals it set for itself. In particular, I examine the degree to which South Africans are "reconciled," and then ask whether evidence exists to suggest that the truth and reconciliation process contributed to this reconciliation. Mine is not a strong research design from the point of view of policy analysis, since I am forced to rely on cross-sectional empirical evidence collected near the end of the truth and reconciliation process. But certainly one objective of this book is to draw some conclusions about whether the South African experiment ought to be attempted in other deeply divided societies. Generally, with some important caveats, I conclude that the process did indeed contribute to reconciliation and therefore that others may wish to borrow from the South African experience in trying to come to terms with their own repressive pasts.

In addressing the hypothesis that truth leads to reconciliation, I mobilize a body of social scientific theories in an attempt to give a full accounting of why some South Africans are reconciled and others are not. For instance, an important contribution of this book lies in its test of the so-called contact hypothesis. Social psychologists have long put forth the hypothesis that positive interracial attitudes emerge from interpersonal interactions between people of different races. This hypothesis has rarely been tested outside Western developed democracies; adding evidence from a multiracial political system like South Africa can contribute significantly to expanding the generalizability of the theory. This is just one example of the multiple ways in which theory is mobilized and tested in my attempt to understand individual-level reconciliation in South Africa.

My dual purposes—scientific hypothesis testing and policy evaluation—are not incompatible. The perestroika complaint that science ignores politics is a statement only about contemporary trends and says nothing about the inevitability of such a disjuncture. A central assumption of my research is that science must inform policy and that only through rigorous scientific inquiry can we begin to draw conclusions about a question as broad (and as profound) as that of whether truth is associated with reconciliation. Thus, my goal is to add something to our understanding of the policy issues surrounding reconciliation and transitional justice, while also making a contribution to several specific bodies of social scientific theory.

No research project of this scale is solely the product of the efforts of an individual scholar, and this one is no exception. Without the support of the Law and Social Sciences Program of the National Science Foundation (grant SES 9906576), this project could not possibly have been conducted.[1] I am especially indebted to program director Marie Provine for supporting this research. As

I have noted in other contexts, I admire no institution or agency more than I admire NSF. Its commitment to truth is as pure as any of which I am aware.

This project is a collaborative effort with Amanda Gouws of the Department of Political Science at Stellenbosch University. Since the day I first set foot in South Africa, Amanda has been an invaluable colleague and a dear friend. We do not see eye to eye on all issues of South African politics—what two strong-minded scholars would ever fulfill that condition?—but I have learned immeasurably from my association with Amanda, and for that I am deeply thankful. I also acknowledge my appreciation to the Department of Political Science at Stellenbosch University for naming me a "Professor Extraordinary in Political Science" while this research was being undertaken.

I also acknowledge my great debt to Chris Willemse. In addition to being a dear friend, Chris has given me a second set of eyes and ears when it comes to South African political history and contemporary affairs. Countless conversations with Chris have begun with the query "Chris, why is it that . . . ?" I have rarely encountered nonacademics with such keen insights. This project has profited immeasurably from his wisdom.

This project soon found its natural home at the Institute for Justice and Reconciliation (IJR) in Cape Town (where I am Distinguished Visiting Research Scholar). My association with the IJR is somewhat curious in that the institute has a policy-oriented action mission, while I consider myself nothing more or less than a scientist. Perhaps because we are so different, our collaboration has been so fruitful. I deeply admire the director of the institute, Charles Villa-Vicencio, whose strength of commitment and intensity of effort in building a multiracial and democratic South Africa has never failed to amaze me. I have learned profusely from my association with the institute. As a white person from outside South Africa, it is not always possible to understand the tragedy of apartheid from books, from statistics, or even from historical cinema and the arts. From my long and intense discussions with Charles and the institute staff, including Helen Macdonald, Paul Haupt, Nyameka Goniwe, Fanie du Toit, Erik Doxtader, and Zola Sonkosi, I have filled in at least some of the many gaps in my knowledge. For that, I am deeply appreciative.[2]

Most of the writing of this book took place while I was a visiting scholar at the Russell Sage Foundation in New York. I am first indebted to my university, and especially to executive vice chancellor Ed Macias for allowing me the opportunity to spend a year at the Foundation. Just as Manhattan is a special and unique place, so too is the Russell Sage Foundation. I have rarely encountered such a strong commitment to scholarship and such noble and well-meaning people.

Throughout my year at Sage I profited immensely from my discussions (not always or even usually on South Africa) with Jim Sidanius, John Hagan, Bob Hauser, Kay Deaux, Peter Katzenstein, and my many lunch companions over the year. I am especially indebted to Eric Wanner, president of the Russell Sage Foundation, for allowing me the chance to complete this book while in residence in one of the most wonderful cities in the world.

Portions of chapters 3 and 4 were presented in several different colloquia, including as a talk at Columbia University, Rutgers University, Fordham University, Indiana University, Rice University, City University of New York, the New York Law School, the University of Texas, the University of Colorado, and State University of New York at Stony Brook. Versions of this talk were also given at the New York Political Psychology Association (2002) and at the Sixth National Political Science Congress of the Chilean Political Science Association, held May 8–9, 2002, in Santiago. My paper "Does Truth Lead to Reconciliation? Testing the Causal Assumptions of the South African Truth and Reconciliation Process" is the recipient of the Sage Paper Award for the best paper in the field of comparative politics, presented at the annual meeting of the American Political Science Association in 2001 by the Comparative Politics Organized Section. A version of chapter 5 was presented to the sixtieth annual meeting of the Midwest Political Science Association, held April 25–28, 2002, in Chicago, as "Truth, Reconciliation, and the Creation of a Human Rights Culture in South Africa: An Investigation of the Effectiveness of the Truth and Reconciliation Process," and it is published as "Truth, Reconciliation, and the Creation of a Human Rights Culture in South Africa" in the 2003 issue of the *Law and Society Review* (vol. 38, no. 1). Chapter 7 of this book is drawn from Gibson (2002b). That paper is the 2003 recipient of the McGraw-Hill Award, awarded by the Law and Politics Organized Section of the American Political Science Association in recognition of the best journal article on law and courts written by a political scientist and published during the previous calendar year. In the original article, I acknowledged the contributions of a number of people, including those members of the IJR staff mentioned earlier and Eric Lomazoff, Marc Hendershot, and Christine Lamberson, who provided valuable research assistance on this project. I am also thankful to James Alt, Ronald Slye, and John T. Scott for comments on an earlier version of that article. Finally, I very much appreciate the advice and assistance provided by Kathleen McGraw on many aspects of that piece.

I also acknowledge and appreciate the comments of Steven Ellmann, New York Law School, and Anthony Marx, Columbia University, on the material presented in chapter 3.

Four people read the entire manuscript and offered copious suggestions for changes: Walter Murphy, Princeton University; Gunnar Theissen, Free University of Berlin; Alfred L. Brophy, University of Alabama; and Monika Nalepa, Columbia University. The care with which these friends read the manuscript improved it immeasurably. I have not always accepted the advice of my critics, but I nonetheless appreciate deeply every comment I received.

I am under no illusion that this book, even with its overall conclusion that truth does contribute to reconciliation, will change the politics of transitional societies. Much of the truth and reconciliation process in South Africa is perhaps unique to the conditions created by apartheid and to the specific individuals who directed the transition process. But if this book makes any contribution at all toward creating a world in which those who were formerly bitter political enemies become more reconciled with each other, I will be deeply gratified. Thus, the ultimate argument of this book is that truth is powerful and democracy will profit if we only (to paraphrase John Lennon) "give truth a chance."

James L. Gibson
Washington University in St. Louis

Chapter 1

Does Truth Lead to Reconciliation?

Perhaps no country in history has so directly and thoroughly confronted its past in an effort to shape its future as has South Africa. Working from the explicit assumption that understanding the past will contribute to a more peaceful and democratic future, South Africa has attempted to come to grips with its apartheid history through its truth and reconciliation process. This bold undertaking to mold the country's fate consumed much of the energy and many of the resources of South Africa during the initial days of its attempted transition to democracy.

The gargantuan task of addressing the past has been under the supervision of South Africa's Truth and Reconciliation Commission (TRC). Established in 1995, the TRC spent roughly five years examining and documenting atrocities committed during the struggle over apartheid.[1] At one level, the TRC was extraordinarily successful: it held countless hearings, interviewed thousands of victims of apartheid, granted amnesty to roughly 850 human rights violators, and produced a massive, five-volume *Final Report*.[2] And in terms of uncovering detailed evidence of what happened under specific circumstances—as in determining exactly what happened to the "Cradock Four"[3]—the TRC seems to have been effective as well (but see Jeffery 1999, who complains about numerous inaccuracies and bias in the TRC's history of several specific incidents). In many respects, and according to most observers, South Africa's truth and reconciliation process appears to have been phenomenally successful.

Indeed, the world has acknowledged the success of South Africa's TRC through the numerous attempts that have been made to replicate its truth and reconciliation process in other troubled areas of the globe. Truth commissions modeled on the South African experience have proliferated, and one of the leaders of South Africa's experiment has created a major institute in New York to assist countries in developing plans for reconciliation in the world's many festering hot spots. Perhaps the judgment that the TRC succeeded is based on nothing more than the simple (and simplistic) observation that South Africa appears to have made a relatively peaceful and quite unexpected transition from the apartheid dictatorship to a reasonably democratic and stable regime. Some surely attribute South Africa's transformation to its truth and reconciliation process. If a TRC "worked" in South Africa, perhaps it can work elsewhere.

South Africans themselves are not so sanguine about the process. Many complain that the TRC exacerbated racial tensions in the country by exposing the misdeeds of both the apartheid government and its agents and the liberation forces. Some vehemently reject the conjecture that "truth" can somehow lead to reconciliation, claiming instead that uncovering the details about the horrific events of the past only embitters people, making them far less likely to be willing to coexist in a new democratic regime (see, for example, Biko 2000). Indeed, based on my casual observations of the South African media, complaints and condemnations of the truth and reconciliation process seem to far outnumber laudatory assessments.

Social scientists must be more agnostic about the success of the truth and reconciliation process. Indeed, it is perhaps shocking to note how little systematic investigation has been conducted into the question of whether the truth and reconciliation process succeeded in its objectives. There are many who enumerate the objectives of the commission itself and document its activities, and there is no dearth of judges when it comes to evaluating the process (see, for example, Du Toit 2000), but no earlier research has treated the various components of the truth and reconciliation process as hypotheses subject to confirmation or disconfirmation through rigorous social science methods. To put it bluntly, we simply do not know even today whether (and to what degree) the truth and reconciliation process in South Africa succeeded in achieving any of its objectives.

Of course, assessments of "success" depend mightily on the specification of the goals of the process. Though the TRC was charged with conducting several types of activities (for example, granting amnesty to gross human rights violators), my central, uncontroversial contention in this book is that the objective of the truth and reconciliation process was to produce reconciliation in South Africa. This may not seem like a very rigorous or helpful specification of the country's aspirations, since "reconciliation" is one of the most ambiguous and abused words in the lexicon of South Africa. And others take a different tack, with some seeking to discover whether the process accurately discovered the truth of certain events (for example, Ignatieff 1996), others assessing whether the TRC maintained fidelity to the law that created it (see Jeffery 1999), and still others judging the process in terms of philosophical standards of justice (especially retributive justice; see Minow 1998).[4] But no prior investigation has squarely and systematically attacked the big question: *has truth led to reconciliation in South Africa?* Answering that question is the objective of this book.

This question is, without doubt, as complicated as it is important (or some might even say "intractable"). To begin, what is "truth"? What is "reconciliation"? Is it fanciful to think that such grand and amorphous concepts can be given rigorous empirical meaning? Can social science really say anything at all about a question as complicated as that of whether truth contributes to reconciliation?

A central contention of this book is that truth and reconciliation are concepts that can be (and should be) measured and assessed using rigorous and systematic social science methods. Just because these concepts are complex and complicated does not mean that they are impenetrable, or that hypotheses such as the one that truth causes reconciliation cannot be investigated. My efforts on this score will surely not please everyone. But throughout this analysis I assign "reconciliation" and "truth" concrete and unambiguous conceptual and operational meaning. At a minimum, those who disagree with my approach will know exactly what it is that they disagree with.

To assess the hypothesis that truth leads to reconciliation requires a careful plan of attack. The starting point in the analysis is the specification of the meaning of reconciliation. I contend that the construct refers to at least four specific and perhaps even independent subconcepts:

- *Interracial reconciliation*—defined as the willingness of people of different races to trust each other, to reject stereotypes about those of other races, and generally to get along with each other
- *Political tolerance*—the commitment of people to put up with each other, even those whose political ideas they thoroughly detest
- *Support for the principles (abstract and applied) of human rights*—including the strict application of the rule of law and commitment to legal universalism
- *Legitimacy*—in particular, the predisposition to recognize and accept the authority of the major political institutions of the New South Africa

This may well not be an exhaustive definition of reconciliation—perhaps there are other important components of the concept—but most objections to this list would surely be concerned with the need to include additional aspects of reconciliation rather than the question of whether these particular dimensions are central to the concept. A reconciled South African is one who respects and trusts those of other races, who is tolerant of those with different political views, who supports the extension of human rights to all South Africans, and who extends legitimacy and respect to the major governing institutions of South Africa's democracy. These are the dependent variables for this study, and each of these dimensions of reconciliation is considered in a separate chapter in the book.

It should be obvious by this point that I treat reconciliation as an attribute of individual South Africans. Perhaps a more conventional viewpoint considers reconciliation as a characteristic of societies or groups. While not denying that the degree to which an aggregate is reconciled is an interesting question (as in analyzing change in levels of reconciliation in a nation-state over time), my contention is that any understanding of reconciliation profits from beginning with an examination of the beliefs, values, and attitudes of ordinary people. If reconciliation means groups getting along together, then obviously reconciliation requires that individual South Africans eschew racism and embrace tolerance. A polity may be more than the sum of the individuals living within its territory, but it is impossible to understand a society without first understanding individual citizens—and in this case, the degree to which they are "reconciled."

Why is reconciliation important? For a political scientist interested in whether South Africa will be able to consolidate its attempted democratic transition, this question has an easy answer: reconciliation is hypothesized to contribute to democratization. Briefly put, a successful liberal democracy requires a sustaining and reinforcing "political culture." The beliefs, values, attitudes, and behaviors of ordinary citizens must be, at a minimum, not antithetical to the principles of democratic governance, and maximally they ought to favor and support the main institutions and processes of liberal democracy.[5] The most obviously relevant component of my approach to reconciliation is political tolerance, a concept that has been thoroughly analyzed in South Africa and elsewhere (see, for example, Gibson and Gouws 2003). For a liberal democracy to flourish, people must be willing to put up with political differences, in sharp contrast to the time-honored history in South Africa of killing one another over political disagreements (as in KwaZulu Natal). I also contend, however, that democracies work best when people are vigilant about human rights, and when they are unwilling to sacrifice law and legal process for expedient solutions to social problems (such as crime and terrorism). Further, political institutions need some "slack"—a reservoir of goodwill—if they are to function. Institutions that are supported only when they produce favorable policy outputs tend to be weak and ineffective. With a reservoir of goodwill, institutions command the political capital to go against public opinion in the short term—as in, for instance, protecting human rights against an outraged majority. And even interracial reconciliation contributes to democracy, since democracy requires coalitions built on similar interests, and racism and its cousins are inimical to the formation of such coalitions. For a political scientist, reconciliation is not an end in itself; instead, reconciliation is valuable because it contributes to the likelihood that South Africa will consolidate its democratic transition.

Indeed, South Africa's truth and reconciliation process is actually a mini-theory about the process of democratization, including an implicit causal model of how the truth and reconciliation process would contribute to the consolidation of democracy in South Africa. The theory posits that:

Amnesty → Truth → Reconciliation → Democratization

That is, the framers of the TRC accepted the hypothesis that when gross human rights violators are granted amnesty, they will come forward and tell the truth about their deeds. If a condition of receiving amnesty for gross human rights violations is full disclosure, South Africa could learn something about the black holes in its past by making amnesty available. Many believe that amnesty did indeed produce specific evidence of past transgressions that would have never come to light otherwise. These truths were then aggregated into a collective memory about the past.

In turn, understanding the past is hypothesized to contribute to reconciliation. Or to put the relationship somewhat differently, those who created the TRC assumed that understanding the truth about the struggle over apartheid was a necessary precondition to reconciliation. National unity and reconciliation could be achieved only, it was argued, if the truth about past violations became publicly known and acknowledged (see, for example, Truth and Reconciliation Commission 1998, vol. 1, ch. 4, p. 53). Truth might not *automatically* produce reconciliation, but without truth, reconciliation was thought to be highly unlikely. As Brandon Hamber and Richard Wilson (n.d.) put it:

> Thus a national process of uncovering and remembering the past is said to allow the country to develop a common and shared memory, and in so doing create a sense of unity and reconciliation for its people. By having this shared memory of the past, and a common iden-

> tity as a traumatised people, the country can, at least theoretically, move on to a future in which the same mistakes will not be repeated.

Finally, reconciliation is seen as a necessary condition for successful democratization. The theory here is not complicated: unless South Africans can agree to get along and refrain from killing each other, democracy in the country will fail. Such an assumption seems entirely reasonable.

This is a simple theory, although not simple to test. Many hope that the theory is empirically accurate, since South Africa has wagered a large part of its future on the veracity of these linkages.

The single most important purpose of this book is to test empirically the core hypothesis in this theory—that is, that truth leads to reconciliation. I refer to this as the "truth → reconciliation hypothesis" throughout this book. The four empirical chapters in which I test this hypothesis—once for each of the subdimensions of the overall concept—are the heart of this book.

One should not treat "truth" lightly, however, and I do not. Indeed, truth can be even more worrisome than reconciliation, especially since so many of us bridle (or should bridle) at even the intimation that "*the* truth"—official truth—exists. Whether one likes it or not, an explicit objective of the TRC was to produce a collective memory for South Africa. This is not just a chronicle of who did what to whom; instead, it is an authoritative description and analysis of the history of the country. Was apartheid a crime against humanity? Was the criminality of apartheid due to the missteps of a few rogue individuals, or was apartheid criminal by its very ideology and through its institutions? These are questions for which the TRC provided unambiguous and, by its accounting, definitive answers. My goal here is not to assess the historical accuracy of these claims but rather to determine the degree to which ordinary South Africans accept the truth as promulgated by the TRC—South Africa's "collective memory." When I consider the truth → reconciliation hypothesis, in every instance I am investigating the hypothesis that *those South Africans who accept the truth as documented by the TRC are more likely to be reconciled.* As I try to explicate more completely in chapter 3, "truth" here means the TRC's truth, nothing more.

Furthermore, factors other than truth can contribute to reconciliation. Indeed, social scientists have learned much about the various processes that undergird this hypothesis, and I would be foolish to ignore these important bodies of theory. For instance, one of the most venerable hypotheses of the literature on political psychology is that interracial contact contributes to interracial harmony. That hypothesis receives a great deal of scrutiny in this book. Other social science theories are carefully examined as well. My goal is to provide a comprehensive explanation of the variation in levels of individual reconciliation, as defined by the four dependent variables I identified earlier in this chapter.

Thus, my motives in writing this book are twofold: First, I hope to address the extremely important policy questions posed by the truth and reconciliation process and, most particularly, the hypothesis that truth leads to reconciliation. I hope that the results of this research will inform efforts to establish truth commissions elsewhere in the world.

Second, I hope to make a contribution to the social science of interpersonal and intergroup relations. Ultimately, reconciliation is about people getting along with and tolerating each other, and thus theories of political tolerance are directly relevant to this research. In addition to considering the standard hypotheses from the tolerance literature, I investigate the so-called contact hypothesis, as well as theories of collective memory and of the consequences of experiences with political repression. I realize that those who walk down the middle of the road often get hit by trucks traveling in both directions, but I try throughout this book to pursue both these policy and theoretical objectives. My hope is that those concerned with policy will come to appreciate the importance of theory, and that those mainly motivated by theory will see that it is important to try to address the policy issues at stake through rigorous social scientific inquiry.

To provide the context for this analysis, I begin with a brief overview of the truth and reconciliation process in South Africa, focusing in particular on the objectives assigned to the TRC by the legislation that created it.

Truth and Reconciliation in South Africa: History and Formal Objectives

Ending apartheid in South Africa came at considerable cost to those who had long struggled against the oppressive system. In South Africa, in contrast to other nations emerging from a tyrannical past (for instance, Argentina and Uganda), the ancien régime was not defeated.[6] This meant that the transition had to be brokered. One of the central issues in the talks over the transformation of the apartheid state was amnesty. The National Party and the leaders of other powerful white-dominated institutions (such as the security forces) made amnesty a nonnegotiable centerpiece of their demands (see Omar 1996). Without the promise of amnesty for the crimes (and criminals) of apartheid, the transition to democracy would have stalled, and the political violence that had been so widespread in the 1980s might have reemerged. The creation of the Truth and Reconciliation Commission, with the power to grant amnesty, was the price that the liberation forces had to pay to secure a peaceful transition to majority rule (Rwelamira 1996).

The Truth and Reconciliation Commission was provided for by the "Postamble/Endnote" to the Interim Constitution of 1993 and enacted by the new Parliament in 1995 as the Promotion of National Unity and Reconciliation Act (no. 34, 1995). That statute called for the establishment of the commission, with separate committees on human rights violations, amnesty, and reparations and rehabilitation. The TRC began functioning shortly thereafter.

The creation of the TRC was certainly controversial. Many parties, including Amnesty International, argued that international law and convention forbade granting amnesty for crimes against humanity, as well as for torture and similar offenses; the parties' slogan was: "No amnesty, no amnesia, just justice" (quoted in Verwoerd 1997).[7] Nonetheless, the South African Constitutional Court upheld the constitutionality of the act (*Azanian Peoples Organization [AZAPO] and others* v. *President of the Republic of South Africa and others*, CCT 117/96 [July 25, 1996]), and the TRC began functioning in 1995.[8]

The truth and reconciliation process was expected to last only two years. Instead, the TRC was in operation for six years. When President Thabo Mbeki dissolved the commission's amnesty committee, effective May 31, 2001, his proclamation also revived the TRC for another six months for the purpose of preparing two supplementary volumes to the *Final Report* (issued in 1998).[9]

Some evidence suggests that the truth and reconciliation process was deeply unpopular among South Africans of every color. For instance, a survey conducted in mid-1998 by *Business Day* (a reasonably well respected South African newspaper) found that nearly two-thirds of the public believed that the truth and reconciliation process had harmed race relations in South Africa (see Business Day Reporter 1998; see also Theissen 1997; Theissen and Hamber 1998; Gibson and Gouws 1999; and Macdonald 2000). Critics charge that the process has been characterized by little remorse or penance among the perpetrators, that not all of the guilty came forward to admit their crimes (for example, former state president P. W. Botha), and generally that whites have been unwilling to accept responsibility for apartheid. A host of other criticisms have also been laid against the details of the process employed by the TRC (see, for example, Jeffery 1999).

The TRC was established to achieve a general purpose as well as several specific objectives. According to the National Unity and Reconciliation Act, the goal "of the Commission shall be to promote national unity and reconciliation in a spirit of understanding which transcends the conflicts and divisions of the past" (sect. 3, 1). The specific means of achieving this goal were to include "establishing as complete a picture as possible of the causes, nature and extent of the gross violations of human rights which were committed during the period . . . including antecedents, circumstances, factors and context of such violations, as well as perspectives of the victims and the motives and perspectives of the persons responsible for the commission of the violations, by conducting investigations and holding hearings."

In calling for a "complete picture" of the past, the law specifically addressed the need to create a collective memory for South Africa. "A society cannot reconcile itself on the grounds of a divided memory. . . . Clearly, key aspects of the historical and ethical past must be put on the public record in such a manner that no one can in good faith deny the past. Without truth and acknowledgment, reconciliation is not possible" (Zalaquett 1997, 13).

A second mandate for the TRC involved "facilitating the granting of amnesty to persons who make full disclosure of all the relevant facts related to acts associated with a political objective and comply with the requirement of this Act." This objective obviously concerns the deeds of individual victims and perpetrators, but to many, over time, it came also to address the larger issue of apartheid itself. For instance, South Africa's Human Rights Commission declared on July 31, 1993, that "the enormity of the crime of apartheid as a system of social engineering must be revealed in all its nakedness, including the distortions wrought upon some of those who, in their fight against this evil, lost their way and engaged [in] the very human rights violations so systematically practised by their oppressors" (quoted in Hay 1998, 55).

The TRC was also charged with "establishing and making known the fate or whereabouts of victims and restoring the human and civil dignity of such victims by granting them an opportunity to relate their own accounts to the violations of which they are the victims, and by recommending reparation measures in respect of them." The purpose identified in this section is that of achieving reconciliation by restoring lost dignity to victims as well as providing them with compensation.

Finally, the TRC's fourth objective was to produce a report addressing the first three issues and making recommendations on how to develop a political culture in South Africa that would be respectful of the human rights of all citizens.

Thus, the most general goal of the truth and reconciliation process in South Africa has been to enhance the likelihood of reconciliation. Reconciliation was not given a great deal of specific content, although the framers of the process clearly sought to shape the views of individual South Africans—for instance, by getting them to accept the collective memory about the country's past and to endorse an expansive definition of human rights.

If reconciliation is to be turned into a concept amenable to empirical investigation, however, it must be given more specific and concrete meaning. I have already suggested that reconciliation is multidimensional, with four distinct aspects. It is useful now to consider these subdimensions more rigorously.

The Meaning of "Reconciliation"

Two themes dominate contemporary discussions of the truth and reconciliation process in South Africa. First, no one seems to know what "reconciliation" means. Mark Hay (1998, 13), for instance, calls "reconciliation" "one of the most abused words in recent history in South Africa." Indeed, Max du Preez (2001, 13), like some others, has gone so far as to claim that, "of course, reconciliation is a concept that cannot be measured." Du Preez apparently believes that this assertion is so self-evidently true that he judges it unnecessary to offer a defense of his point of view. Second, everyone is certain that reconciliation has failed in South Africa, or at least has not lived up to the expectations of most South Africans. People may not be able to define and measure the concept, but they seem to think they "know it when they see it"—or at least when they do not see it.[10]

But surely reconciliation means *something*. Indeed, the problem with the concept, according to some, is that it has *too many* meanings, not too few. For instance, Brandon Hamber and Hugo van der Merwe (1998) claim to have isolated five distinct ways in which reconciliation has been either implicitly or explicitly used. The problem with reconciliation is not that it is devoid of content; the problem is that reconciliation is such an intuitively accessible concept that everyone is able to imbue it with her or his own distinct understanding.

But perhaps reconciliation is not such a difficult and complicated concept after all. A great deal of complexity can certainly be attached to the idea, but it is also possible to distill the concept down to a few simple and specific elements. Reconciliation is often discussed as a relationship, either between victims and perpetrators or between beneficiaries and the exploited. The TRC *Final Report* refers to the following types of relationships: individuals with themselves, between victims, between survivors and perpetrators, within families, between neighbors, between communities, within different institutions, between different generations, between racial and ethnic groups, between workers and management, and, "above all, between the beneficiaries of apartheid and those who have been disadvantaged by it" (Truth and Reconciliation Commission 1998, vol. 5, ch. 9, pp. 350–51). To make the concept empirically manageable, I must first be clear about who is being reconciled with whom or what.

Discussions of reconciliation in South Africa typically refer to two distinct phenomena: dealing with the microtruth of what happened to specific loved ones, and dealing with the macrotruth about the nature of the struggle over apartheid. At the micro level, discussions often focus on the reconciliation of victims and perpetrators of gross human rights violations. This is the clearest meaning of the term "reconciliation," and it has been the subject of wide media coverage in South Africa. Stories about the most profoundly injured victims (or their families) granting forgiveness to their evil tormentors are the stuff of which soap operas are made, and they captured the fancy of the South African public, at least for a while.[11] When applied to victims and perpetrators, reconciliation typically means acceptance of blame, apology, and forgiveness. For many in South Africa, led by Desmond Tutu (see Tutu 1999), this type of reconciliation has deeply religious overtones, as in the third of the five definitions proposed by Hamber and van der Merwe (1998), which stresses a "strong religious ideology of reconciliation" based on identifying a "humanity" common to all groups in South Africa. Central to this definition is forgiveness, although Hamber and van der Merwe assert that "this perspective runs the risk of mistakenly equating forgiveness of past enemies with reconciliation."[12]

The larger South African society is the context for the second meaning of the term—reconciliation between the races and, closely related, between those who profited from apartheid and those who were injured by it. Dan Markel (1999, 407) refers to this as "the public reconciliative relationship" and asserts: "The TRC hoped to cultivate a broad-swathed public reconciliative role among and with the various racial and ethnic groups of South Africa, so that social groups would learn the skills necessary to cope with the pain experienced as a group in the past." This understanding of reconciliation has little to do with any specific human rights violation; rather, it involves coming to grips with (accepting responsibility and blame for) the subjugation of the black majority by the small white minority under apartheid. As Antjie Krog notes: "Reconciliation in this country is not between actual operators and victims, but between the beneficiaries (whites) and the exploited (blacks)" (quoted in Christie 2000, 147). This definition is similar to the first definition proposed by Hamber and van der Merwe (1998)—a "non-racial ideology of reconciliation," which is basically a condition in which South Africans live together as "non-racial citizens within a harmoniously integrated social setting." It is also similar to their second definition, which emphasizes "intercommunal understanding" and calls for "bridging the divide" between various distinct and generally separate racial communities. "From this perspective the TRC is considered to be a facilitator that can improve communication and mutual tolerance of diversity." As Kadar Asmal (2000, 1226) notes: "If you never pulled a trigger nor held a smoking gun, but yet you benefited from the societal system defended by the violence—if all you did was loaf around a poolside in an opulent white apartheid suburb—you still needed to be involved in the process [of transition and reconciliation]." My concern in this book is thus with these broader sociopolitical aspects of the reconciliation of all South Africans, not just victims and perpetrators. Reconciliation may be thought of as a continuum describing the relationship between those who were masters and slaves under the old apartheid system, not just the relationship between those who were victims or perpetrators of gross human rights violations.

In South Africa the groups that must reconcile are the four main racial groups in the country (see the appendix to this chapter)—whites, Africans, Colored people, and South Africans of Asian origin. The root cause of interracial alienation in South Africa was colonialism; the proximate cause was, of course, apartheid. The damage inflicted was inequality, loss of dignity, and untold violence and political repression. Whites treated Africans, Colored people,[13] and South Africans of Asian origin as if they were inferior in nearly every sense, including in the political and legal domains, and blacks were even expelled from their own country to the so-called Bantustans. The essential condition for reconciliation is therefore that South Africans of every race accept all other South Africans as equals and treat them as equal, extending dignity, respect, and cocitizenship to them. The TRC *Final Report* (Truth and Reconciliation Commission 1998, vol. 9, ch. 5, p. 425) asserts that reconciliation requires the recognition that "we are all in the same boat—we simply need to understand each other better and be more respectful of each other's culture." The report also concludes: "Reconciliation is based on respect for our common humanity" (435). Hay (1998, 14) defines reconciliation as "the establishing or recovery of human dignity and humanity of every person, rooted in human rights, and the acceptance of this by the individual and the society." When people talk about reconciliation, they often mean nothing more than the races getting along better—that is, a diminution of racial animosities. Accomplishing this aim requires that people come to interact with each other more (the breakdown of barriers across races) and communicate more, acts that in turn lead to greater understanding and perhaps acceptance and result in the appreciation and exaltation of the value of racial diversity and multiculturalism in the "Rainbow Nation."

Reconciliation also takes on three additional meanings beyond interracial reconciliation. The first is simply political tolerance, the willingness of South Africans to put up with their political foes.[14] South Africans may not be required to like or agree with each other, but many have expected the truth and reconciliation process to contribute to a sort of relatively peaceful coexistence. In its minimalist version, this means putting up with those who hold different or even repugnant ideas and viewpoints. In its maximalist rendition, tolerance means embracing one's former enemies, forgiving them, and perhaps even joining in political coalitions with them.

A third aspect of reconciliation has to do with the development of a political culture in South Africa that is respectful of the human rights of all people. The creation of a human rights culture was one of the explicit goals of the TRC. The *Final Report* (Truth and Reconciliation Commission 1998, vol. 5, ch. 9, p. 435) asserts: "Reconciliation requires that all South Africans accept moral and political responsibility for nurturing a culture of human rights and democracy within which political and socio-economic conflicts are addressed both seriously and in a non-violent manner." This conception is similar to the fourth definition of reconciliation proposed by Hamber and van der Merwe (1998). For South Africa's nascent democracy to prosper, the political culture must be one in which the universalistic application of the rule of law—and the rejection of the arbitrary exercise of governmental authority and power—is deeply valued and respected.

Finally, it is important as well to address the *institutions* that serve as the backbone of South Africa's new democracy, since democracy is both a set of formal institutions and a set of cultural values.[15] For instance, South Africans must come to tolerate each other, to be willing to countenance the expression of displeasing political ideas. But they must also come to support institutions that have the authoritative means of enforcing political tolerance as effective public policy. Just as the truth and reconciliation process sought to encourage respect for human rights in South Africa, it also implicitly sought support for the institutions charged with the protection of those human rights. If South Africans fail to extend legitimacy to the institutions of majority rule and the protection of minority rights, it would be difficult indeed to consider them reconciled with the nascent democratic system that has been implemented. To extend these institutions legitimacy is to accept at an elemental level South Africa's multiracial system of democratic rule and reconcile with the new political dispensation in the country. Reconciliation requires that all South Africans recognize the legitimacy of the political institutions created after the fall of apartheid.

Consequently, a "reconciled" South African is one who:

- eschews racial stereotyping, treating people respectfully as individuals, not as members of a racial group;
- is tolerant of those with whom he or she disagrees;
- subscribes to a set of beliefs about the universal application of human rights protections to all South African citizens; and
- recognizes the legitimacy of South Africa's political institutions and is therefore predisposed to accept and acquiesce to their policy rulings.

Thus, in this book I investigate reconciliation between *people*, among *groups*, with basic constitutional *principles*, and with the *institutions* essential to the new South African democracy.

Understanding Variation in Reconciliation: Testing Theory and Hypotheses

South Africans undoubtedly differ in the degree to which they hold reconciled attitudes. Since mine is a microlevel analysis, my overriding purpose is to account for the variability across individuals in these four aspects of reconciliation. Here I briefly introduce the theories that play a prominent role in my analysis.

Theories of Collective Memory

To speak of "truth" evokes the imagery of theories of collective memory. I contend in this book that the TRC attempted to assemble a collective memory of the apartheid past for South Africans, and this contention is unlikely to be controversial. What is perhaps novel in my analysis is the attempt to test the hypothesis that the degree of an individual South African's participation in the collective memory forged by the truth and reconciliation process is related to the degree to which that individual is reconciled. Thus, my findings have profound implications for those who would attempt large-scale attitude change through social persuasion, which is what the TRC sought to do—with at least a modicum of success.

Interracial Contact Theory

The contact hypothesis is one of the most venerable in political psychology, even if research has generated a variety of caveats to the simple idea that the more people interact, the more likely they are to accept each other. I rely heavily on the contact hypothesis as an explanation of the degree to which racial reconciliation has taken place in South Africa. Generally, racial isolation characterizes the country, but to the extent that people engage each other in circumstances of at least modest intimacy and a fragment of equality, reconciliation profits.

Theories of Political Tolerance

An impressive body of literature has emerged accounting for why some are tolerant of their political enemies and others are not. This literature has taught us, for example, about the crucial role that perceptions of threat play in shaping tolerance. In addition to investigating the conventional threat-centered explanations of intolerance, I focus here on the ways in which intolerance is connected to group identities. Intolerance is more than a matter of individuals not putting up with each other. It is also about intergroup conflict, and therefore social identity theory has much to say about political tolerance—a minimalist definition of reconciliation.

Experiences with Political Repression

Though no clear body of theory addresses the microlevel political consequences of having experienced political repression, I include this in my listing of theoretical approaches since it is so central to my analysis. Apartheid left deep scars on South Africa, and on South Africans, and individuals' experiences under apartheid no doubt have shaped their understandings of both truth and reconciliation. But not all South Africans were directly harmed by apartheid; not even all Black South Africans were directly injured by the repressive system.[16] One of the most unexpected findings from this research is that people fared so differently under apartheid. Consequently, the hypothesis that variation in experiences shapes levels of reconciliation is investigated across all four dimensions of reconciliation.

Legitimacy Theory

An important body of theory addresses the question of how institutions relate to the citizens they govern, and in particular how perceptions of institutional legitimacy contribute to compliance with unpopular political and legal decisions. I mobilize that body of theory in considering reconciliation with the new political dispensation in South Africa. To the extent that these new institutions suffer from a legitimacy deficit, they are unlikely to be effective agents of democratization.

Thus, my hope is that readers will find this analysis rich in terms of both the theory it addresses and the significance of the overall research question: does truth contribute to reconciliation?

The Plan of the Book

This book is structured around seven chapters in which empirical evidence is adduced to consider the hypothesis that the truth and reconciliation process has contributed to a more reconciled South Africa. These chapters all draw on a survey of South African opinion that I conducted in 2000 and 2001.

Chapter 2 is perhaps a somewhat unusual chapter for a book such as this, since it focuses on the independent variables used in the analysis rather than the dependent variables. I do this so as to set the context for my research on reconciliation, especially the context as defined by the relationship of contemporary South Africa to its apartheid past. Little rigorous research has been reported documenting how South Africans experienced apartheid, so I devote considerable effort to investigating how people believe they lived and their memories of the experiences they had under the old system. In general, many of my findings about apartheid are *entirely* unexpected, thereby justifying my examination of these results early in the book.

Chapter 2 also discusses group identities. This portion of the chapter is considerably less surprising, since I document that identities are important and that most South Africans view groups as continuing to be important in South African politics. These and the other indicators described in this chapter set the stage for testing hypotheses about variability in individual-level reconciliation.

In chapter 3, I analyze truth—or as I have noted, the truth as constructed by the truth and reconciliation process in South Africa. I begin the chapter by considering just what the TRC proclaimed about the country's apartheid past. Then I examine the degree to which ordinary South Africans accept this truth as the collective memory of the country, and I consider whether the activities of the TRC itself contributed to a common understanding of the nature of the country's apartheid past. My findings in this chapter are filled with unexpected nuggets, ranging from the widespread condemnation of apartheid among whites to the remarkable degrees to which Africans, Colored people, and those of Asian origin do *not* condemn apartheid. A multivariate analysis of truth acceptance reveals that group identities influence beliefs about the past, although not always in simple and direct ways. Perhaps the most important contribution of this chapter lies in documenting how collective memory can be rendered a rigorous theory and in suggesting how to analyze individual differences in acceptance of collective memories.

The first reconciliation-dependent variable for my analysis is investigated in chapter 4. There I test a variety of hypotheses about the factors that have contributed to interracial reconciliation among South Africans. For instance, I discover that interracial reconciliation is heavily dependent on interracial contacts. Not all contact has a salutary effect on racial attitudes—for instance, simply working with people of a different race has no positive consequences—but when South Africans interact in conditions of relative intimacy and equality, racial animosities decline. Most important, I make the bold claim in this chapter that, at least under some circumstances and with some groups, truth (as promulgated by the TRC) does indeed contribute to reconciliation. This is perhaps the most important chapter in the book, since it addresses one of the most fundamental aspects of reconciliation—the question of whether South Africans of different races can live peacefully and respectfully with each other.

In chapter 5, I analyze the second aspect of reconciliation—support for a human rights culture in South Africa, and in particular the universalistic rule of law. After discovering that support for the rule of law is not widespread in South Africa (although compared to such support in other established democracies, commitment to the rule of law in South Africa is *not* inordinately low), I report significant interracial differences in levels of commitment to this aspect of a human rights culture. Attitudes toward the rule of law are bound up in a larger set of beliefs about the rights and obligations of majorities and minorities in a liberal democracy, and these beliefs differ across the various racial groups in predictable ways. Finally, I produce evidence that the truth and reconciliation process may indeed have shaped (at least in part) the ways in which South Africans think about the rule of law and human rights.

Chapter 6 continues my concern with intergroup relations by focusing on political intolerance. Political tolerance is the minimalist form of reconciliation because it requires nothing more than that South Africans put up with their political enemies. Beginning the analysis with well-trodden theories of tolerance, I evaluate the hypothesis that intolerance is a function of the threats that people perceive from their political enemies. The hypothesis is confirmed, although it is interesting to note that sociotropic threats (threats to the country, to the South African way of life) are considerably more powerful predictors of intolerance than egocentric threats (threats to the individual himself or herself) or perceptions of the political power of the group. I also find that threat perceptions have abated somewhat since an earlier similar study conducted in 1996.

The most important contribution of this chapter is its investigation of the linkage between social identity theory and intolerance. Though the relationships are often complicated, the analysis establishes no significant connection between group identities and political intolerance. This finding represents an important challenge to those who see the roots of intergroup conflict in the group attachments of citizens.

In some respects, the analysis I report in chapter 7 is a digression, since I do not directly consider one of the four dimensions of reconciliation. Instead, this chapter addresses the question of how to compensate for the inherent injustice of granting amnesty to those who admitted gross human rights violations. The TRC awarded amnesties to more than one thousand miscreants, thereby creating a "retributive justice deficit." In this chapter, I report evidence that this justice deficit was in fact overcome by other aspects of the amnesty process. It will surprise few that distributive justice (compensation) can make up for some of the failure to achieve retributive justice. But the most important and interesting findings of this chapter are that two other forms of justice—restorative justice (apologies) and procedural justice (giving voice to the victims and their families)—contribute mightily to compensating for the inherent unfairness of granting amnesty to human rights violators. Though I explicitly do *not* claim that reconciliation requires the acceptance of the necessity of granting amnesties, I do conclude in this chapter that the amnesty component of the truth and reconciliation process did less damage to reconciliation than many believe, in large part because the process produced compensatory forms of justice.

In chapter 8, the final empirical analysis of reconciliation, I investigate the legitimacy that South Africans accord to the political institutions of the New South Africa. My central contention here is that reconciliation requires that South Africa's new Parliament and Constitutional Court be recognized as legitimate and authoritative and that, as a consequence, South Africans must accept the decisions of these institutions, especially the decisions of which they disapprove. This chapter relies heavily on legitimacy theory, which assigns a crucially important function to constitutional courts in liberal democracy: the need to overrule the actions of the majority when they infringe on the constitution, and especially on the rights of political minorities. In what is perhaps the most pessimistic portion of my analysis, I find that neither institution enjoys widespread and cross-racial legitimacy in contemporary South Africa. This lack of legitimacy is partly due to the failure of the Constitutional Court to establish a distinctly nonpolitical legal identity; as it is right now, views toward the court and the parliament are closely related and dependent as well on satisfaction with the short-term performance of the institution. Without a store of institutional legitimacy, South African institutions are dependent on pleasing their constituents if they are to gain acquiescence with their decisions. This does not bode well for the future, since these institutions must inevitably be able to make decisions that are displeasing to South Africans but pleasing to constitutional democracy when the two conflict.

The last chapter returns to the overarching question of whether truth actually leads to reconciliation, based on the empirical results of the five analytical chapters. I draw conclusions about the role that the truth and reconciliation process has played in the consolidation of South Africa's democratic transition. Though my most general conclusion is that the truth and reconciliation process has indeed contributed to reconciliation in South Africa, I nonetheless identify several ways in which the South African experience may not be generalizable to other transitional political systems.

Ultimately, however, democracy in South Africa has been well served by the efforts of the TRC and the many people who tried to create a truth for the country that would reconcile South Africa's many competing factions and interests.

Concluding Comments

This book's look at reconciliation from the viewpoint of the individual citizen is both the primary strength and weakness of this research. Individuals constitute the building blocks of a political system, and it is difficult to imagine how a society could be reconciled without individual members of that society also being reconciled. Thus, learning about levels of reconciliation among South Africans and discovering something about the causes of such reconciliation are crucial tasks to which this book purports to make an important contribution.

But not all questions of reconciliation can be understood in terms of the attributes of citizens. Groups are important, institutions are important, and some individuals (elites) are more important than others. Moreover, exogenous events (international terrorism, for instance) can play an enormous role in shaping how a society feels about difference and about those who are different. Thus, while my study here is concerned with a fundamentally important chapter in the larger book of South African reconciliation, the story I tell is a story of the beginning, not the end, of the process of reconciliation.

Appendix: Race in South Africa

Whatever one's preferences, no one can write about South African politics without writing about race. Since race is such a salient part of the South African context—and since race is such a contentious concept—I offer here my understanding of the meaning of the concept.[17]

It is common in South Africa to divide the total population into four racial categories for the purposes of research or to explain the demographic realities and/or socioeconomic conditions in the country, and I follow this practice throughout the analysis reported in this book. As Wilmot James and Jeffrey Lever (2000, 44) note: "The use of these categories is unavoidable given the fixity that they have come to acquire both in popular consciousness and official business." The use of these racial terminologies, however, differs from the way in which racial categorization may be understood in other societies. It is therefore important to understand the historical development of these categories, especially the legal boundaries imposed on racial groups by the apartheid government.[18]

The four racial groups are African, white, Colored, and South Africans of Asian origin (Indian). These groups are also often referred to as population groups, ethnic groups (although this term usually refers to African subcategories such as Xhosa or Zulu), or national groups. The African majority has been known by European settlers by different names over time, such as "native," "Bantu," or "Black," and some of these terminologies were later formalized by apartheid legislation. The Africans were the original inhabitants of the area now called South Africa; descendants of Iron Age farmers, they speak different variants of the Bantu languages spoken in sub-Saharan Africa, east of Cameroon (James and Lever 2000, 44). Generally, I refer to these people as Africans or blacks.

The white inhabitants of South Africa (formerly called Europeans) are descendants of Dutch, German, French (Huguenots who fled religious persecution in France), English, and other European and Jewish settlers. Though South Africa was colonized by the Dutch and the British in different historical periods, the British colonization caused English to become entrenched as a commonly spoken language.

"Colored" is considered a mixed-race category, although as James and Lever (2000, 44) argue, it is actually a residual category of people of quite divergent descents. "Colored" refers to the children of intermarriages between whites, Khoi-Khoi (commonly referred to as "Hottentots") and the San (commonly referred to as "Bushmen"), slaves from Malagasy and Southeast Asia (Malaysia), and Africans (Thompson and Prior 1982, 34).

The Indian population came to South Africa as indentured laborers to work on the sugar plantations in Natal in the late nineteenth and early twentieth centuries. They came from different regions in the Indian subcontinent, adhered to different religions, and spoke different languages, and so, like Colored people, they are not a homogeneous group. I refer to these people as South Africans of Asian origin, despite the fact that some Colored people are technically of Asian origin.

When the National Party came to power in 1948, it embarked on a legislative process aimed at securing white political power and keeping the white population group "pure." The Population Registration Act, 30 of 1950, and its various amendments legislated that all citizens of South Africa be classified according to racial or ethnic origins. Racial origin was determined by the natural father's classification. The policy was not consistently implemented, however, because when the father in a mixed-race marriage was African, the offspring was classified as African, but if the father was white, the offspring was classified as Colored (see Brookes 1968, 24). Additional criteria were acceptance in the community and appearance; a 1967 amendment added descent (Thompson and Prior 1982, 36). Very often mixed-race families were split up owing to the hues of their skin, causing immense suffering (Horrel 1982, 2).

The original act referred to the main groups as "white," "colored" and "Native." In 1951 the South African government replaced "Native" with "Bantu," and in 1978 it officially changed the term to "Black." The most commonly used term now for the original inhabitants of South Africa is "African," while "Black" is often used inclusively to refer to everyone who is not white. (The term originated as a negative reaction to references to groups other than whites as "nonwhites.") In this sense, "Black" is sometimes misleading, since it refers to Africans, Colored people, and those of Asian origin. ("Black" is rarely used in this way in this book.) The enforcement of the Population Registration Act was very important, since it was the foundation for the Group Areas Act, 41 of 1950 (legalizing separate neighborhoods for each racial group), and the Separate Amenities Act, 49 of 1953 (legalizing separate public facilities for the different racial groups).[19]

A direct response to the fixed racial categorization of the apartheid regime was the ideological endorsement of nonracialism by the African National Congress (ANC). This policy rejected race as a social construct and supported the underlying principle of equality for all, with appearance and descent playing no role. Yet the political and sociological realities created under apartheid—such as homogeneous neighborhoods and segregated schools—now coupled with political strategies such as affirmative action to undo past discrimination, still reinforce and politicize racial consciousness involving these specific categorizations (James and Lever 2000, 45). From the perspective of research on South Africa's political culture(s), it could therefore be justifiably argued that the subjective experience of these racial categorizations, the class positions, and the sociological and historical realities of their members justify the general practice of reporting these results separately by these racial groupings.

In earlier research (for example, Gibson and Gouws 2003; Gibson 2003), I have documented enormous differences across South

Africa's groups in terms of a wide variety of political attitudes. Consequently, it is essential that race be incorporated into the analyses in this book. To ignore race would be to fail to recognize that South African politics today continues to be shaped by its racist history. To incorporate race into this analysis is not to accept anything about apartheid but merely to acknowledge that apartheid shaped—and continues to shape—political reality in South Africa.

Chapter 2

Apartheid's Legacy in Contemporary South Africa: Experiences, Attributes, and Attitudes of the Sample

> Apartheid left its mark on three fundamental dimensions of the South African political system: its value systems, its structure and its political culture.
>
> —Willie Esterhuyse, "Truth as a Trigger for Transformation" (2000, 148)

> A lingering "apartheid memory" continues to restrict the development of trust and allegiance in the new political dispensation and its institutions.
>
> —Johnny de Lange, "The Historical Context, Legal Origins, and Philosophical Foundation of the South African Trust and Reconciliation Commission" (2000, 29)

The research on truth and reconciliation in South Africa reported in this book is based on a public opinion survey that I conducted in that country at the close of 2000 and beginning of 2001 (for technical details, see appendix A). The sample of over 3,700 South Africans we interviewed represents the entire South African population, with representative subsamples of each major racial, ethnic, and linguistic group in the country. Thus, it is entirely legitimate to draw inferences from the sample to the larger South African population of more than 43 million people. Few surveys have ever been conducted in South Africa that are of the technical quality of this one.

In the chapters that follow, I test a variety of hypotheses about the connections between truth and reconciliation. The central concern of this book is with the seemingly simple question of whether truth has contributed to reconciliation in South Africa. This question, however, is anything but simple if one wants to draw inferences about the causal connection between the two concepts. Truth may cause people to be reconciled, but complicating the causal flow, people with certain types of beliefs about South Africa's past may be more likely to be reconciled in the first place. Thus, *reciprocal causation* could reasonably be expected to characterize this relationship. Discerning the flow of causality is one of the most demanding tasks facing empirical social scientists, and one can virtually never do better than drawing probabilistic conclusions about causation.[1] Unfortunately for analysts, causality is of the utmost importance for understanding truth and reconciliation processes.

It is important to acknowledge at the outset that causal inferences are never perfect, even in the most "scientific" research. The basic limitation is that alternative explanations for social and political phenomena abound, rendering it difficult if not impossible to control for all possible rival hypotheses. The problem of discerning causality is compounded when concepts are measured at the same point in time, as they typically are in cross-sectional surveys such as this. Social scientists are good at determining what *goes with* what. Determining what *causes* what, and how, is a far more arduous and dicey process.

I shall have much more to say about the problem of causality throughout this analysis, since the question of what causes what has important implications for the analytical strategy of this book in general. I introduce the problem of causality at this point for two reasons. First, I want to encourage readers to think causally about all of the relationships considered in this analysis. Although social scientists are fond of asserting that "correlation does not imply causation" (things that go together do not necessarily cause each other), many of the linkages investigated here require some sort of conclusion about causality. Second, it is useful to introduce a variety of variables in this chapter that will be used as control variables in the substantive analyses throughout this book. These indicators, documented conceptually and operationally in this chapter, are used throughout my analysis as substantively interesting control variables. Consequently, I devote more space to presenting these variables than might otherwise be the case.

Another, less theoretical purpose is also served by addressing these descriptive data in this chapter. For many reasons, little is known about the structure of public opinion in South Africa. This lack of knowledge flows in part from the history of apartheid, but it is also attributable in part to the feeble support for the social sciences in South Africa and in part to ideology. (When one "knows" something, it is often unnecessary to bother with empirical evidence.) Because so little is understood, it is useful to begin the empirical portion of this study with a description of the sample, and hence of the South African population. The picture that emerges throughout the chapter is often startling and entirely unexpected. Because the evidence is so unforeseen, I establish here a context for public opinion in South Africa that is essential for understanding the remainder of the book. Many readers will find the South Africa depicted here to be quite at odds with the South Africa of their imagination, or even with the South Africa they think they know. I begin this discussion with a brief overview of the apartheid system that dominated South Africa until 1994.

A Brief History of Apartheid

Apartheid—which may be translated as "separateness"—swept South Africa as a consequence of the electoral victory of the National Party in 1948. Of course, the introduction of apartheid to South Africa was not the first appearance of racism and racial subjugation in the country—from the moment the Dutch colonists landed in 1652, the Europeans sought to implement a system based on racial hierarchy—but apartheid was a codification of racism that the world had never seen before. Apartheid was manifest in a body of legislation defining racial groups and delineating many of the crucial aspects of people's lives.[2] A full chronology of the statutory basis of apartheid was produced by the Truth and Reconciliation Commission (1998, vol. 1, ch. 13, pp. 448–97).

As a system based on racial hierarchy, apartheid naturally found it necessary to construct racial categories for all South Africans: blacks (or Africans), whites, Colored people, and those of Indian origin. The Population Registration Act of 1950 established these four racial groups. For example:

> A White person is one who is in appearance obviously white—and not generally accepted as Coloured—or who is generally accepted as White—and is not obviously Non-White, provided that a person shall not be classified as a White person if one of his natural parents has been classified as a Coloured person or a Bantu. . . . A Bantu is a person who is, or is generally accepted as, a member of any aboriginal race or tribe of Africa. . . . [A] Coloured is a person who is not a white person or a Bantu. (Truth and Reconciliation Commission 1998, vol. 1, ch. 2, sect. 26, p. 30)

One's rights and responsibilities under the apartheid system were defined by one's race, as established by law. Race was the defining characteristic of politics under the apartheid system established by the National Party. These categories, as noted in chapter 1, continue to dominate discussions of race in contemporary South Africa.

The aim of apartheid was the total separation of blacks and whites. To achieve this goal, South Africa established the so-called Bantustans as areas where blacks were allowed to reside. Apartheid never sought the expulsion of Colored people and those of Asian origin from the territory of the country, and indeed later reforms of the system provided for political representation for these two groups. (In 1983 separate parliamentary chambers were established for whites, Colored people, and those of Indian origin.) Perhaps the ultimate degradation of apartheid was to deny blacks citizenship in the country of their heritage and birth. T. R. H. Davenport and Christopher Saunders (2000, 398) describe the "Afrikaner Nationalist dream state" as "an independent white-dominated republic, surrounded by a cluster of economically dependent and therefore politically impotent black client states."

As was shown by the truth and reconciliation process, apartheid also had a dark, extralegal, and illegal side. The state engaged in systematic political repression against the liberation forces (see de

Kock 1998), with state-sponsored actions ranging from "dirty tricks" to the development of a vast system of informants, to assassinations and murders. The state also pursued a policy of "divide and conquer" against its adversaries through its (successful) efforts to foment political violence between the African National Congress (ANC) and the Inkatha Freedom Party (IFP). Apartheid is often defined as a system of laws, but in fact it was a conglomeration of legal and illegal means of separating blacks and whites and subjecting the former to subjugation and repression while providing vast subsidies to the small white minority.

When did apartheid end? Answering this question is more difficult than it might seem. Some believe today that an "apartheid mentality" is still pervasive in the country and therefore apartheid has not yet ended. The formal end of the apartheid system is perhaps best signaled by the ascension to power of the ANC as a result of the first democratic elections ever held in South Africa (in April 1994). But the undoing of apartheid actually began in late 1989 (when, for example, public beaches were desegregated) and was accelerated with the unbanning of the ANC (February 1990) and the release of the ANC leader Nelson Mandela from prison shortly thereafter.

A Demographic Profile of the Sample

At the time of the survey, *Statistics South Africa* (as reported in Forgey et al. 2001, 49) estimated that the population of South Africa was 77.6 percent African, 8.7 percent Colored, 2.5 percent Indian or Asian, and 10.3 percent white.[3] Thus, whites in South Africa are a small minority (smaller than the size of the African American population in the United States). South Africans of "minority" races constitute slightly less than one-fourth of the population.

The design of this survey takes into account the distribution of race in South Africa. Specifically, because a simple sampling design based on random selection would not generate sufficient numbers of Colored people, people of Asian origin, and whites for statistical analysis, the survey includes oversamples of these groups. Appendix A provides details on the sampling strategy, but I note here that the sample includes interviews with 2,004 Africans, 991 whites, 487 Colored people, and 245 South Africans of Asian origin. When I speak of the South African population, I of course weight the data appropriately so that the racial distribution in the sample approximates the population figures described in the last paragraph.

Race is more than a technical complication in sampling. Most research—including our own (for example, Gibson 2003; Gibson and Gouws 2003)—reveals deep divisions in South Africa according to race, and it is therefore always reasonable to hypothesize that racial differences exist in the variables considered in this book. That hypothesis is resoundingly reinforced throughout this analysis, so most of the statistical results reported herein are reported separately by these four racial groups.[4]

I believe that race is a social construct, not a biological one (as Colored people so amply demonstrate),[5] and therefore I do not treat race as some sort of determinant attribute of individuals.[6] Consequently, my analysis often begins with a simple description of how, and to what degree, the different racial groups differ. But the important, and difficult, task is to determine *why* racial differences exist. For example, an oft-tested hypothesis is that racial differences can be explained by reference to differences in the way the apartheid regime treated the four racial groups. I also typically ask whether racial differences are in fact reflections of differences in group economic positions within South Africa. Thus, race is omnipresent in the analysis that follows, but race rarely occupies serious conceptual status in my models. Race is almost always a surrogate for some other variable representing the experiences or attitudes of members of the group.

As the basic demographic figures reported here make plain, understanding race as a "black versus white" dichotomy is not particularly helpful. It is certainly true that the ideology of the liberation struggle joined Africans, Colored, and those of Asian origin in the single group "Blacks."[7] But whether these three groups share characteristics, experiences, and attitudes is an empirical question, and there are actually many good reasons to suspect that they may not be united. The analysis that follows does not prejudge the question

Table 2.1 Demographic Attributes of South Africa's Racial Groups

Attribute	African	White	Colored	Asian Origin
Gender				
Percentage female	50.1%	50.7%	49.3%	50.6%
Age				
18 to 30 years old	39.0	24.6	33.1	29.3
30 to 55 years old	48.2	49.2	79.7	53.7
56 years old and older	12.8	26.2	17.2	16.9
Level of education				
None or primary	32.2	.2	23.2	22.4
Secondary	61.4	59.5	64.3	67.8
Tertiary	6.3	40.3	12.5	9.8
Place of residence				
Percentage urban	40.3	84.3	59.5	84.1
Social class				
Upper or upper-middle	3.8	23.1	8.0	11.0
Middle or nonmanual	14.7	60.0	22.0	31.8
Manual or skilled, semiskilled	39.6	14.4	35.7	43.7
Manual, unskilled or unemployed	41.9	2.4	34.3	13.5
Unemployment				
Percentage unemployed	34.7	3.9	20.3	15.1
Opinion leadership				
Percentage opinion leaders	8.4	17.4	12.3	12.2
Home language				
Afrikaans	.1	52.9	78.6	2.9
English	.1	47.1	21.1	96.3
Xhosa	25.8	.0	.0	.0
Zulu	25.8	.0	.0	.0
Literacy				
Percentage literate	42.9	97.0	75.8	79.6
Religiosity				
Percentage attending religious services more often than monthly	64.0	54.3	71.8	70.6
Social class—ownership of goods				
Refrigerator and/or freezer	66.6	97.1	91.0	98.4
Electric floor polisher	2.0	27.3	14.8	14.7
Vacuum cleaner	4.3	86.1	33.5	44.5
Microwave oven	12.5	83.4	44.1	72.2
Hi-fi music center	59.1	87.5	66.5	77.6

Table 2.1 (Continued)

Attribute	African	White	Colored	Asian Origin
Automatic washing machine	6.8	88.8	56.7	56.7
Working telephone	18.7	81.5	55.4	77.1
Television set	73.8	95.1	90.8	95.9
Bank account	39.9	94.3	55.0	62.9
Pension fund	15.4	68.2	35.5	25.7
Automobile	9.7	85.0	36.8	48.6
Percentage owning none of these	10.6	.1	2.1	.8

Source: Author's compilation from the 2001 Truth and Reconciliation Survey.

of differences across these groups, and therefore I report most of the statistical results according to the four racial groups identified here.

Indeed, it is perhaps instructive to begin this analysis with a consideration of the basic socioeconomic differences across these various groups. Table 2.1 reports a panoply of information about the attributes of those we interviewed. Rather than address every piece of information in the table directly (a daunting task), I use these data to draw some general conclusions.

First, the sample clearly represents the diversity of the South African population. Unlike some earlier research, for instance, urban and rural residents are included in the survey. The diversity of home languages among whites and Colored people is noteworthy: the white portion of the sample is evenly divided between English- and Afrikaans-speakers; most Colored respondents speak Afrikaans, although a sizable minority speak English as their home language.

Note as well that the South African population is reasonably young, with between one-fourth and one-third of each racial group being thirty years old or younger. Consequently, a sizable portion of South Africans have never directly experienced the heavy boot of apartheid. Although it is difficult to identify a specific time at which apartheid ended, two dates mark important milestones: 1986, when the pass laws were abolished, and 1990, when the ANC was unbanned and Nelson Mandela was released from prison. If I (somewhat arbitrarily) split the difference in these figures and posit that apartheid ended in 1988, then 42.1 percent of the African respondents were eighteen years old or younger when it became defunct. One-third of the respondents were less than sixteen years old. Thus, upward of one-half of the black population in South Africa most likely never experienced apartheid directly, at least not as adults, the age when the full force of apartheid was felt. For a large percentage of Africans, these events took place in their childhood or early youth and were perhaps largely experienced by their parents, not by them.

Third, the sample amply documents the vast economic inequality of South Africans of different races. Consider unemployment first: while more than one-third of the African respondents report being unemployed and looking for work, this is true of only 3.9 percent of the whites.[8] The unemployment rate of Africans is twice that of Asian South Africans, and dramatically higher than that of Colored people. Class differences (as judged by the interviewer, and no doubt heavily reflecting employment status) are also staggering, with only 18.5 percent of the black respondents judged to be middle- or upper-class, compared to 83.1 percent of whites, 30.0 percent of Colored people, and 42.8 percent of the Asian respondents. Just what these class differences mean can be seen in the variables documenting the ownership of various goods. Many of the differences are enormous—85.0 percent of whites own an automobile, compared to 9.7 percent of Africans. Colored people and those of Asian origin appear to have a much higher economic standard of living than black South Africans. The data in this table provide stunning confirmation—if any is needed—of the vast economic inequality in South Africa.

Inequalities in education and literacy are also startling. Fewer than one-half of the African respondents are judged to be literate to the extent that they could read with ease the showcards used in the interview.[9] Nearly all white respondents are literate, as are large majorities of Colored people and those of Asian origin. Literacy rates reflect educational experiences: nearly one-third of the black respondents have little or no education, compared to 0.2 percent of the white respondents. The black-white differences in these data astound, but so too do the differences between whites and the other two racial minorities, as well as the differences between Africans and Colored people and those of Asian origin. For instance, compared to Africans, nearly twice as many Colored people and those of Asian origin are judged to be literate. These data strongly indicate just how different are the characteristics and experiences of Africans, Colored people, and those of Asian origin, the three groups often thought of as one group—"Black" South Africans.

These literacy rates have important implications for this survey. Though we tried to make our questions as simple as possible, the low level of literacy among some respondents surely caused them substantial difficulty in understanding some of the concepts about which they were queried. We anticipated this problem and made certain that virtually all of our questions had an explicit "don't know" or "uncertain" response available to the respondents, so as to minimize guessing and the fabrication of answers to our queries. One important negative consequence of illiteracy, however, is that the reliability and validity of the measures I employ here most likely vary according to the literacy of the respondent. Unfortunately, the problem is exacerbated by the unequal distribution of literacy across the groups. We must be sensitive to this limitation throughout the analysis that follows.[10]

The important conclusions of this section of my analysis are that (1) racial differences exist in a wide variety of social and economic attributes, with the result that (2) vast inequality exists among these groups. These conclusions must be borne in mind throughout this analysis.

I turn next to a consideration of South Africans' experiences with apartheid. Perhaps these differ as well across the various racial groups in South Africa.

Experiences Under Apartheid

The experiences that South Africans had with the apartheid system provide one of the most important independent variables considered throughout the book. As noted earlier in this chapter in the

Table 2.2 Racial Differences in Perceived Role Under Apartheid

	African	White	Colored	Asian Origin
Initial response				
Activist	5.4%	1.2%	6.2%	2.0%
Hero	1.4	.2	.2	.0
Victor	.7	.8	1.5	.4
Collaborator	1.5	3.0	1.1	.0
Sellout	.2	1.0	.4	.8
Bystander	17.1	25.1	21.6	23.3
Spectator	14.9	20.8	19.1	14.3
Inactive opponent	9.0	19.3	6.4	6.1
Victim	19.8	3.5	15.2	38.8
Slave	18.1	.0	3.9	2.0
Beneficiary	.4	6.0	2.1	1.6
None	.2	.0	.2	.0
Don't know	11.4	19.2	22.1	10.6
Any response				
Activist	7.4	1.7	7.5	2.0
Hero	2.0	.2	.6	.4
Victor	1.8	1.6	3.0	.8
Collaborator	3.0	3.6	1.5	.0
Sellout	.3	1.3	.9	.8
Bystander	23.3	34.1	29.8	33.1
Spectator	22.4	34.9	26.1	23.3
Inactive opponent	12.4	22.4	8.4	7.8
Victim	31.4	5.7	20.6	43.3
Slave	26.5	.3	6.0	3.3
Beneficiary	.6	8.4	2.6	2.0

Source: Author's compilation from the 2001 Truth and Reconciliation Survey.
Note: Entries are the percentage of all respondents of each race selecting the term.

discussion of the age distribution of the sample, a large percentage of the respondents were only youngsters when apartheid nominally ended. Thus, determining how apartheid treated each respondent is an important task for this analysis.

Table 2.2 reports our respondents' replies to what is a deceptively simple question: "People use many different words to describe their relationship with apartheid in the past. Which of the following best describes your role under apartheid?" The closed-end list consisted of eleven terms (reported in the table). These roles were constructed on the basis of the replies of the participants in our focus groups (for a discussion of the focus groups, see appendix A). Up to two responses were recorded.[11] The first portion of the table reports the initial self-characterization, while the second half of the table reports the percentages of respondents mentioning the term in either their first or second reply.

The terms most commonly chosen by the Africans in our sample are "victim" and "slave," selected by roughly 20 percent of the respondents as their initial characterization and by a majority of the respondents as one of their multiple responses. A second large group of Africans acknowledges that they were largely onlookers to apartheid (bystanders, spectators, or inactive opponents). It is perhaps surprising to note how few of the black respondents claim the term "activist": only 7.4 percent selected this as one of their two responses. (Another tiny percentage selected "hero," a possible synonym for activist.) Assuming that these respondents are being generous with themselves, the levels of self-characterized active opposition to apartheid seem remarkably low for what many perceive to have been a mass movement against apartheid.

Whites too are willing to describe themselves as not much involved with apartheid, with "bystander," "spectator," and "inactive opponent" attracting a large percentage of the white respondents. Virtually none of the whites in the sample claims to have been an activist.

Colored people are most likely to characterize themselves as bystanders (21.6 percent) or spectators (19.1 percent), with another 22.1 percent saying they do not know how to describe their role. A fairly small minority think of themselves as victims or slaves. These are important findings because they suggest that Colored people were especially disengaged from the struggle over apartheid. Being neither fully oppressed nor fully free, Colored people occupied an ambivalent position under the apartheid system.

The principal term embraced by the Asian respondents, "victim," was chosen by 38.8 percent of this group. This figure stands out as much larger than that for the other groups. South Africans of Asian origin may feel victimized by *both* apartheid and the struggle against it, although this cannot be clearly determined from these responses. That those of Asian origin are more likely to perceive themselves as victims than are Africans or Colored people is somewhat unexpected.

Three general conclusions emerge from this analysis. First, very small proportions of South Africans characterize themselves as having been actively involved in the struggle over apartheid. Fewer than 10 percent describe themselves as activists, and indeed it is perhaps a bit unanticipated that such a tiny fraction of the respondents embrace the term "victor."

Second, surprisingly few South Africans accept that they were victims of the apartheid system. All of these respondents were offered the term "victim" to describe their relationship to apartheid, but far fewer than half of the respondents (with the exception of those of Asian origin) see themselves primarily as victims. People may have been harmed by the system, but this apparently has not created a widespread sense of victimhood, even among black South Africans.

Finally, these data hint at substantial interracial differences in how people related to apartheid. Obviously, whites held a quite different position within the apartheid system, but it also appears that the experiences of black South Africans were not identical to the experiences of Colored people or those of Asian origin. We must be mindful in the analysis that follows that apartheid was not uniformly oppressive to all South Africans of color.

Harms and Benefits from Apartheid

We also sought more direct indicators of how South Africans were harmed by and benefited from apartheid. Table 2.3 depicts the respondents' self-reported experiences under the apartheid regime. The table entries are the percentages of each racial group claiming to have experienced each of the particular injuries. The data in the table demonstrate that apartheid left quite different scars, depending on one's race and perhaps on other factors as well.

Black experiences with apartheid varied considerably. At the two extremes, only a small proportion of these respondents were imprisoned by the authorities (9.9 percent), while 43.7 percent claim to have been harmed by not being permitted to associate

Table 2.3 Racial Differences in Harms Inflicted by Apartheid

Harms	African	White	Colored	Asian Origin
Required to move residence	17.2%	2.1%	16.3%	22.0%
Lost job	15.0	1.7	6.4	6.9
Assaulted by police	15.8	1.8	10.7	4.5
Imprisoned by authorities	9.9	.6	1.9	2.0
Psychologically harmed	15.6	4.1	11.1	6.9
Denied access to education	41.4	1.5	21.1	20.4
Unable to associate with other races	43.7	13.8	32.4	28.6
Had to use a pass to move about	35.3	.4	1.6	11.8
No injuries	39.4	82.3	57.7	51.0
Average—injuries index[a]	.24	.04	.13	.13
Standard deviation	.26	.09	.19	.18
Number of cases	2,003	986	485	245

Source: Author's compilation from the 2001 Truth and Reconciliation Survey.
Note: The question read: "Here is a list of things that happened to people under apartheid. Please tell me which, if any, of these experiences you have had."
[a]Cross-race difference of means: $p < .001$; $\eta = .39$.

with people of different races or colors.[12] Lack of access to education is another widely experienced harm. Still, it is noteworthy that a large minority of Africans (39.4 percent) claim no specific injuries from apartheid.[13] Indeed, only slightly more than one-third claim to have been subjected to the infamous pass laws.[14] These are perhaps surprising findings.

Whites, on the other hand, experienced very few injuries from apartheid.[15] Fully 82.3 percent of the white respondents claim to have been subject to no specific injury on this list, and only 13.8 percent felt harmed by their inability to associate with those of other races. Obviously, apartheid treated blacks and whites very differently.

As is often the case with this survey, Colored people and those of Asian origin had experiences that were somewhere between those of blacks and whites. A majority of Colored people and those of Asian origin identify no specific injury from apartheid. For instance, virtually no Colored people claim to have been subjected to the pass laws, and fewer than 12 percent of the Asian respondents say they had to have a pass to travel about. Surprising perhaps is the finding that South Africans of Asian origin are the most likely to report having had to change residences owing to apartheid (although the differences across these three groups are not statistically significant). Also unexpected is the small percentage of respondents claiming psychological injuries from apartheid: 11.1 percent and 6.9 percent, respectively, for Colored and Asian South Africans. Indeed, in answer to the general question asking respondents to compare the quality of life in 2001 with that under apartheid, a strong plurality of Colored people (39.5 percent) and those of Asian origin (43.9 percent) claim to have lived *better* under apartheid than at the time of the survey. Only 22.4 percent of Colored people and 26.2 percent of the Asian respondents report that they lived worse under the apartheid system (data not shown).

These data strongly reinforce the conclusion that South Africans of different races found different degrees and types of accommodation with the apartheid system. Apartheid did not uniformly terrorize blacks, Colored people, and those of Asian origin. Some—indeed, perhaps many—were able to escape the heavy boot of the apartheid system.

What of the benefits of the apartheid system? Do South Africans, especially whites, perceive themselves to have been the beneficiaries of apartheid? We asked the respondents to indicate whether they benefited from the apartheid system in a number of specific ways. The results are shown in table 2.4.[16]

Few black South Africans perceive themselves to have been beneficiaries of apartheid—fully three-quarters assert that they received none of these benefits. Indeed, despite the widespread perception of rampant crime at the time of this survey, few blacks see themselves as having profited from a relatively low crime rate under apartheid.[17] It seems that for most blacks crime has not exploded as a result of the demise of apartheid. Still, it is a bit surpris-

Table 2.4 Racial Differences in Benefits from Apartheid

Benefit	African	White	Colored	Asian Origin
Access to education	8.2%	64.2%	23.0%	54.3%
Cheap labor	11.7	42.1	12.3	45.7
Low crime rate	7.7	49.8	19.7	59.2
Access to jobs	12.6	58.7	25.3	56.3
Experienced no benefits	75.1	22.2	56.9	28.2
Experienced all four benefits	.7	25.3	3.0	30.6
Average—benefits index[a]	1.64	3.16	2.26	2.93
Standard deviation	.77	1.13	.97	1.27
Number of cases	2,002	981	466	245

Source: Author's compilation from the 2001 Truth and Reconciliation Survey.
Note: The question read: "Some people have told us that they benefited from the old system of apartheid. What about you—would you say you definitely benefited, probably benefited, probably did not benefit, or definitely did not benefit from . . .?"
[a]Cross-race difference of means: $p < .001$; $\eta = .58$.

ing that roughly one-fourth of black South Africans claim to have enjoyed some of these benefits under the apartheid system.

The level at which whites recognize that they were beneficiaries of apartheid is perhaps unexpected. A majority of whites assert that they profited from access to education and to jobs, and nearly a majority admit that they also benefited from a system that controlled crime in the white areas of the country. Puzzling as well is the comparatively small percentage of whites who acknowledge that they profited from the cheap labor provided by apartheid. This finding must surely represent the view that no direct benefit was provided to the respondent—perhaps it is these whites who had no housekeeper, gardener, or other staff—rather than rejection of the view that the price of fruits and vegetables and wine in the country had something to do with the wages paid to farm and vineyard workers under apartheid.[18] Still, fewer than one-fourth of the whites deny profiting at all from apartheid, while another one-fourth believe that they profited in all four ways (and perhaps in other ways as well). Most whites today accept that they did well under the apartheid system.

In general, Colored people claim not to have benefited from the apartheid system—56.9 percent assert that they received none of these benefits. Colored people are thus more likely than blacks to perceive themselves as having profited from apartheid, but less likely than whites or those of Asian origin to acknowledge any advantages from apartheid.

South Africans of Asian origin are quite similar to whites in recognizing myriad ways in which apartheid served them. For instance, in terms of access to jobs, over half of the Asian respondents acknowledge that they were favored under apartheid. The percentages perceiving no benefits and all four benefits differ insignificantly from the white percentages. Asians are the most likely of any of the four groups to assert that they gained from a depressed crime rate enforced by the apartheid state.

Thus, racial differences in both the perceived harms and perceived benefits of apartheid are enormous. As the eta coefficients in tables 2.3 and 2.4 reveal, racial differences in benefits are greater than racial differences in harms experienced under apartheid. This is largely because black perceptions of harm from apartheid do not diverge as much from white perceptions compared to the benefits variables.

It is useful to consider the *relative* costs and benefits of apartheid as well, not just the absolute levels of perceived costs and perceived benefits. The difference between benefits and costs is an interesting measure, since it represents the *net value of apartheid* to the respondent. I have calculated such a measure by subtracting the number of perceived costs from the number of perceived benefits (after standardizing the costs and benefits indices to a scale of 0 to 8). Those with a score of 0 are those whose costs and benefits are equal. Those with scores less than 0 are those who were net losers from apartheid; those with scores greater than 0 were net winners from apartheid. Of course, care must be taken not to interpret these percentages too literally. Rather, the index is simply an interval level measure of the relative benefits of apartheid to the respondent.

As figure 2.1 depicts, racial differences on the index are enormous (η = .63), with the means ranging from −1.1 among blacks

Figure 2.1 The Net Benefits and Costs of Apartheid, by Race

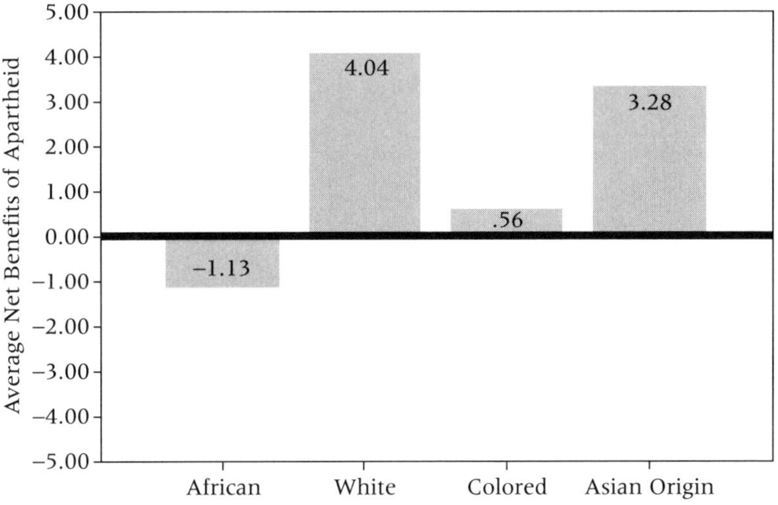

Source: Author's compilation from the 2001 Truth and Reconciliation Survey.
Note: The bars in this graph represent each racial group's average score on an index representing the net benefits of apartheid. The index is simply the difference between benefits and costs, and thus negative scores indicate that costs outweigh benefits (and vice versa). Cross-race difference of means: $p < .001$; $\eta = .63$.

to 4.0 among whites (with standard deviations in the range of about 2.5 to 3.8). Among blacks, 34.9 percent have a score of 0, while 14.2 percent were net beneficiaries of apartheid; among whites, for 20.3 percent apartheid was a wash on the factors considered here, while 76.7 percent see themselves as net beneficiaries (data not shown). Those of Asian origin tend to have profited from apartheid (69.8 percent), while Colored South Africans are almost equally divided in terms of having benefited, having been harmed, and coming out even from apartheid.[19] The old apartheid system meant quite different things for the different races in South Africa. Moreover, the groups conventionally classified as "Black" did not fare the same under apartheid.

Views of the Apartheid Past: Beliefs About the Importance of the Past

The process of addressing the abuses of the apartheid regime has been a painful one for South Africa.[20] The TRC's website reports full details of the crimes committed by those seeking amnesty; some hearings have revealed atrocities almost beyond belief (see, for example, de Kock 1998; Pauw 1997) and seem to have reopened many old wounds. Many South Africans have been appalled that such vicious perpetrators have received amnesty for their actions.[21]

How do South Africans feel in general about learning from their past? Our survey reveals that most hold ambivalent attitudes. For instance, virtually all South Africans agree that the past holds valuable lessons: when asked to react to the statement "When it comes to South Africa's past, we must learn from the mistakes that were made in order to avoid making the same mistakes again," virtually everyone agrees. But on the very next proposition, "It's better not to open old wounds by talking about what happened in the past," roughly three-quarters of whites, Colored people, and those of Asian origin agree with the statement. Nearly 60 percent of blacks also agree. Further, each racial group is evenly divided over whether they want their children "to learn about the horrific atrocities that were committed in the past." For instance, among the African respondents, 48.8 percent agree with that statement, but 50.0 percent do not. Black South Africans in general are more likely to accept that looking at the past is useful, although cross-race differences are relatively small. Thus, the past is not a simple matter for most South Africans; most hold complicated and perhaps even inconsistent views about the country's history.

Judging Contemporary Politics

Perceptions of the State of the Union

How do South Africans perceive the current state of affairs in their country? Many analysts and pundits paint the country as clouded by gloom and pessimism. We asked our respondents to rate the importance of thirteen social, political, and economic problems in South Africa, ranging from crime to HIV-AIDS, to "land ownership and redistribution." Among Africans, the problem judged most serious is unemployment, which is rated as "very important" (the highest importance on the response set) by fully 89 percent of the respondents (followed closely by poverty, rated as "very important" by 86 percent of the African respondents). Colored people also report that unemployment is the most important problem (91 percent). Among whites, crime receives the highest importance ratings, and among those of Asian origin unemployment and crime are rated at equal levels of importance. The issue most dividing South Africans by race is "finding the truth about the past." Though nearly one-half of the Africans (48 percent) rate this problem as very important, other South Africans judge it less so, with 11 percent, 33 percent, and 37 percent of whites, Colored people, and those of Asian origin, respectively, assigning the problem the highest priority. Interestingly, South Africans are least divided by race on the importance of "racism and discrimination," with 59 percent, 49 percent, 59 percent, and 60 percent of Africans, whites, Colored people, and those of Asian origin rating this problem as very important. That whites and Africans differ so little on the importance of race and discrimination is remarkable.[22]

Economic Perceptions and Expectations

We also presented the respondents with the standard battery of items measuring perceptions of the economy. They were asked to judge the country's economy as well as their own personal economic circumstances, and, as is conventional, we asked retrospective questions (comparison to the past) and prospective questions (expectations about the future). Table 2.5 reports the replies.

Consider first South Africans' views of their own economic circumstances. Compared to the recent past, a minority of South Africans are better off economically. Among Africans, only 4.3 percent claim to be doing a lot better economically, with another 22.8 percent asserting that they are at least a little better off than in the past. Thus, these data indicate that the economic circumstances of roughly one-fourth of the African population of South Africa are

Table 2.5 Racial Differences in Egocentric and Sociotropic Economic Perspectives

Economic Perceptions	African	White	Colored	Asian Origin
Egocentric prospective[a]				
Lot worse	10.1%	11.9%	4.9%	12.7%
Little worse	7.5	31.3	6.4	16.7
No change	20.9	32.4	22.2	26.5
Little better	33.9	15.6	38.9	25.3
Lot better	15.6	4.4	11.3	6.1
Don't know	12.0	4.3	16.3	12.7
Egocentric retrospective[b]				
Lot worse	15.7	16.7	14.2	14.7
Little worse	20.5	38.8	17.2	25.7
No change	36.1	33.8	38.4	40.4
Little better	22.8	8.4	23.2	13.5
Lot better	4.3	2.0	6.4	4.9
Don't know	.6	.3	.6	.8
Sociotropic prospective[c]				
Lot worse	15.8	28.4	12.1	25.3
Little worse	11.3	35.3	10.7	26.9
No change	19.1	16.5	20.5	13.9
Little better	30.3	14.2	31.4	22.4
Lot better	11.9	1.5	5.5	4.5
Don't know	11.6	4.0	19.7	6.9
Sociotropic retrospective[d]				
Lot worse	26.1	48.9	31.3	50.6
Little worse	24.0	33.6	24.7	28.2
No change	22.7	8.6	19.5	11.8
Little better	21.6	6.7	15.8	6.5
Lot better	2.7	.6	2.7	2.4
Don't know	2.9	1.7	6.0	.4
Worry about unemployment[e]				
Not at all	1.4	13.8	6.4	4.9
Not very	4.4	14.0	10.7	2.9
Worried a little	12.4	30.3	11.9	24.1
Very worried	77.1	40.4	69.2	66.1
Don't know	.2	.7	.6	.8
Unemployed	4.5	.7	1.2	1.2

Source: Author's compilation from the 2001 Truth and Reconciliation Survey.

[a]Egocentric prospective question: "And what about the next twelve months? How do you think your family's living standard will be *compared to now*? Would you say you and your family's living standard will be much worse, a little worse, nothing will change, a little better, or much better?"

[b]Egocentric retrospective question: "Compared with twelve months ago, would you say your family's living standards are much worse, a little worse, nothing has changed, a little better, or much better?"

[c]Sociotropic prospective question: "How do you think the economic situation in South Africa will change in the next twelve months? Will it get a lot worse, get a little worse, stay the same, get a little better, or get a lot better?"

[d]Sociotropic retrospective question: "How do you think the general economic situation in South Africa has changed over the last twelve months? Would you say it has got a lot worse, got a little worse, stayed the same, got a little better, or got a lot better?"

[e]Unemployment question: "How much does the thought worry you that, during the next twelve months, you or some member of your family might become unemployed? Are you not at all worried, not very worried, a little worried, or very worried?"

improving. On the other hand, 36.2 percent of the sample report being worse off at the time of the interview than in the past. Still, when we take into account those whose economic circumstances are not changing, a majority of black South Africans report that they are doing at least as well as they did in the recent past. The figures among Colored respondents are quite similar to those for the African portion of the sample.

Whites despair considerably more about their economic circumstances: only one in ten (10.4 percent) judge their economic situation to be improving, with a clear majority (55.5 percent) asserting that their status has declined. Those of Asian origin are not in as dire economic straits as whites, but they also seem to see themselves as doing considerably less well than do Africans and Colored people.

These economic perceptions should be understood not as indicating levels of economic accumulation but as perceptions of change in economic conditions. As was shown earlier in this chapter, whites command considerably more economic resources than Africans, even if they are more likely to perceive themselves as being on a downward trajectory.

In terms of optimism about the future, the data present a number of surprises. Nearly one-half of the Africans (49.5 percent) expect their economic circumstances to improve in the near future. Similar optimism characterizes the Colored respondents. Remarkably, only 17.6 percent of the African respondents and 11.3 percent of the Colored people in the sample project that they will be worse off economically in the future. These data thus reveal an unexpectedly high level of economic optimism among the majority in South Africa.

Whites hold quite different views about the future, with pessimism characterizing a large plurality (43.2 percent) of the white respondents. The respondents of Asian origin are not as pessimistic as the whites, but they are nonetheless considerably more downbeat than blacks or Colored people.

Thus, a strong contrast exists between the economic perceptions of black and white South Africans. Blacks not only perceive themselves as having done better economically, compared to whites, but they are also more optimistic about their own economic futures.

Whites, who are in fact decidedly better off than blacks, see their economic fortunes as having declined and as likely to decline in the future. Colored people are more like Africans in their views, and those of Asian origin are more similar to whites.

When it comes to the country's economy, the views of South Africans are similar to their assessments of their own personal economies. A considerable degree of optimism about the future characterizes Africans and Colored people, but whites and those of Asian origin are more pessimistic. Indeed, there is a closer connection between egocentric and sociotropic judgments than is ordinarily seen in survey data, suggesting that South Africans see their personal economic fate as linked to the country's economic performance to a fairly strong degree.

The last panel of table 2.5 provides an important corrective to the findings about economic optimism. Though many see their economic futures as being better, a very large majority of Africans (77.1 percent), Colored people (69.2 percent), and those of Asian origin (66.1 percent) report being "very worried" that they or some member of their family might become unemployed in the coming year. Whites are not nearly so concerned (40.4 percent). Thus, it appears that the key to economic success for most South Africans is keeping their jobs. For whites, job loss is much less of a concern. Of more importance is perhaps the deterioration of their economic circumstances due to a variety of factors, including the rising cost of labor, the decline of the value of the rand, and the failure to be able to command wage increases. White economic pessimism may also reflect views about their prospects in the long term in South Africa, not just in the next year or two.

It is easy to describe South Africa's economic situation as one of gloom and malaise, since this description does indeed characterize a portion of the population. But the survey data provide something of a contrary view. Perhaps most interesting is the degree to which the African majority express optimism about their own and their country's economic future.

Perhaps some portion of these findings can be explained by general perceptions of change. We asked the respondents a fairly simple question: "How much change do you believe there has been in

Table 2.6 Racial Differences in Perceptions of Change in South Africa

Perceptions of Improvement in Various Areas of Life Since 1994	African	White	Colored	Asian Origin
Ability to earn a living	47.9%	16.4%	45.0%	29.4%
Race relations	61.9	57.2	70.4	62.0
Personal freedom	75.8	45.3	81.6	51.4
Equality	63.4	55.1	68.5	50.2
Hope for the future	64.5	28.9	62.1	38.0

Source: Author's compilation from the 2001 Truth and Reconciliation Survey.
Note: The question read: "We are interested in your thoughts about how things might have changed since the election of 1994 and the end of apartheid in South Africa. Would you say the following have improved a great deal, improved somewhat, worsened somewhat, or worsened a great deal?"

South Africa since 1994?" The replies are highly instructive. Nearly two-thirds (64.7 percent) of the white respondents assert that things have changed a great deal (the most extreme point on the response set) since 1994, while fewer than one-fourth of the African, Colored, and Asian respondents judge that so much change has taken place. Perhaps the reality of post-apartheid South Africa is that whites have indeed experienced the greatest amount of change. Their position in society, their social status, their economic wealth, their political power, and their ability to determine the course of their own lives have all been altered rather dramatically since the black majority came to power in 1994. This is not necessarily to claim that all whites judge such change as unwelcome.

Table 2.6 reports the responses to five questions about whether change since 1994 has brought about improvements in various aspects of South African life. The data reveal some important interracial similarities as well as differences in perceptions of change. For instance, majorities of South Africans of each race agree that equality has improved in the country since 1994. Similarly, most agree that race relations have improved, although whites are slightly less likely to adopt this view and Colored people are slightly more likely to believe that race relations have gotten better. Still, there are some important interracial differences. Whites are far more likely to assert that the ability to earn a living has worsened (81.4 percent believe it has worsened at least somewhat—data not shown), and those of Asian origin are nearly as gloomy about economic changes. Whites and those of Asian origin are less likely to assert that their personal freedom has improved, probably because of their perceptions that crime rates have risen sharply. Perhaps the most disconcerting finding concerns hope for the future. Substantial majorities of African and Colored South Africans assert that hope has increased, while this view is held by a fairly small minority of whites and a (larger) minority of those of Asian origin. These data are compatible with the more general conclusion that optimism is more widespread among Africans than many might have expected, and that despair in the white community is fairly substantial.

Finally, we specifically considered the question of potential emigration, given the fairly common view that white flight from South Africa is substantial. We asked our respondents how likely it is that they will be living in South Africa in 2010.[23] Only slightly more than one-half of the white respondents (52.2 percent) say it is "extremely likely" that they will be living in South Africa in ten years (data not shown). To put the number in perspective, however, only 67.0 percent of the African respondents are certain that they will still be living in the country in 2010. Among Africans, 9.1 percent assert that it is not very likely or highly unlikely that they will be living in South Africa ten years hence; the comparable figure for whites is 14.2 percent. Indeed, the group with the strongest commitment to South Africa seems to be Colored people, most of whom are quite certain about continuing to live in South Africa (72.4 percent). Still, vast majorities of every racial group (80 percent or more) believe that it is either "extremely" or "quite" likely that they will be residents of the country in 2010. Despite the numerous difficulties facing South Africa—from poverty to crime to AIDS—most South Africans express reasonably strong commitments to the country and its future.

The picture painted by these data is not nearly as gloomy as is often portrayed in South Africa. Certainly white people are having some difficulty adjusting to the new economic and political realities in the country (and my own impression is that white people in South Africa are quite adept at complaining, if not whinging and whining). But most in South Africa express a remarkable level of optimism about the future. And the vast majority of people of all races seem committed to making their future in South Africa.

South African Group Identities

Much of the discussion in this chapter has focused on the nominal race of the respondents in the survey. As noted, race is largely a social construction, and indeed, more interesting than nominal race is the nature of the group affiliations that people embrace. Social identity theory, in its modern incarnation in the work of Henri Tajfel, provides a theoretical framework for understanding how identifications with groups shape a variety of political perspectives, including those under consideration in this book.[24] Following our earlier research in South Africa (Gibson and Gouws 2000), this section examines several attributes of the group identities that South Africans hold. I first consider the simple question of whether South Africans in fact identify with any ethnic, racial, or linguistic groups or with groups identified by other characteristics.

Table 2.7 reports the primary social identities of the four major racial groupings in South Africa. The respondents had little difficulty with this question, with virtually everyone accepting one of the offered terms as her or his social identity. Among black South Africans, the most attractive label is "African," claimed by 28.4 percent of the respondents. White South Africans are most likely to think of themselves primarily as "South Africans," as is true of Colored South Africans and South Africans of Asian origin. Very few whites are attracted to the term "White," although 26.1 percent of the Colored respondents claim the label "Colored," and 18.8 percent of the Asians select the term "Indian" (with another 9.0 percent identifying with "Asian"). Religious identities are surprisingly common, especially among whites, with 19.0 percent of the white respondents selecting "Christian" as their primary group identity. It is interesting to note that only very small percentages of nonblacks select the term "African" to describe their group identity.[25]

Generally, these identities are highly significant to the respon-

Table 2.7 Racial Differences in the Distribution of Primary Positive Social Identities

Primary Identity	All South Africans	African	White	Colored	Asian Origin
African	21.1%	28.4%	1.7%	4.5%	1.2%
South African	24.9	21.3	35.2	34.3	37.1
Black	9.4	12.5		1.6	
Zulu	6.6	8.8			
Christian	6.1	2.1	19.0	14.2	8.6
Xhosa	7.7	10.8			
Afrikaner	4.6		21.6	10.9	
Tswana	2.8	4.0			
North Sotho-Sepedi	2.4	3.2			
Colored	2.4			26.1	
South Sotho-Sesotho	3.2	4.5			
English	1.2		8.5		1.6
Muslim	.8			4.9	9.4
Tsonga-Shangaan	1.7	2.2			
White	1.0		6.3		
European	.4		2.6		
Boer	.5		3.0		
Hindu	.4				13.5
Indian	.6				18.8
Asian	.3				9.0
Brown	.2			1.4	
Other	1.6			1.0	
"South African"[a]	51.9	47.8	62.9	59.1	74.7
Number of cases	3,724	2,001	983	484	245

Source: Author's compilation from the 2001 Truth and Reconciliation Survey.
Note: Within the racial groups, only percentages greater than or equal to 1.0 percent are shown. For "All South Africans" the "other" category includes any group identity that was selected by fewer than 1.0 percent of any of the racial groups. The modal response within each group is highlighted in the table. χ^2 for differences across race = 4,954.5; $p < .001$.
[a]Percentage of respondents claiming "South African" identity as a primary *or* secondary identity.

dents. When asked to rate the importance of the primary identity selected, very large majorities (80 percent or higher) of Africans, Colored people, and those of Asian origin score the identity at the highest point on the scale ("very important"). Though whites are somewhat less likely to claim this highest level of importance, two-thirds nonetheless say that the group they selected is very important to them. The only primary identities for which fewer than half of the respondents rate the association as very important are English and European, although, in contrast, note that 76.9 percent of those selecting an Afrikaner identity rate it as very important.[26] Among those selecting South African as their primary identity, 81.8 percent claim it as very important to them. Clearly, we were successful in identifying group labels that are highly significant to most South Africans.

We coded multiple responses to this identity question, since most respondents give more than a single answer. At the bottom of table 2.7 are reported the percentages of respondents who selected South African as an identity in reply to either the primary question or the follow-up.

Though only one-fourth of the respondents select South African as their primary group identity, over one-half mention a national identity as one of their replies. Even though slightly fewer than one-half of the Africans select a South African identity, nearly three-fourths of South Africans of Asian origin identify themselves as South Africans. Claiming a national identity is also more common among white and Colored South Africans.

It is informative to compare these results with those from a similar survey conducted in 1996 (see Gibson and Gouws 2003). The comparison is particularly valid since the questions asked about social identities are identical. Perhaps the most interesting finding is that the percentage of the population identifying itself as South African has increased markedly. In the 1996 survey, 21.3 percent of the sample selected South African as a primary social identity, with 39.6 percent claiming the term as one of their identities (Gibson and Gouws 2003, 78). The comparable figures, for 1996 and 2001, respectively, for the various racial groups are:

African: 35.2 percent versus 47.8 percent

White: 53.0 percent versus 62.9 percent

Colored: 56.6 percent versus 59.1 percent

Asian origin: 53.0 percent versus 74.7 percent

Thus, national identities increased substantially for all except the Colored respondents, among whom national attachments did not diminish.

To consider further this issue of national identities, the 2001 survey included two statements specifically addressing feelings about being South African. Table 2.8 reports the results from these questions.[27]

Most South Africans assert that they are proud to call themselves South African, and most assert that their identity as a South African is very important to them. Some racial differences exist, with Colored people most likely to think of themselves in terms of the nation. This finding is perhaps unexpected in that the results from the identity question suggested that Colored people do not particularly identify with the nation.[28] It is also noteworthy that the greatest reticence about identifying with the country is among whites, although only a small proportion of whites reject a South African identity. To the extent that reconciliation implies that all South Africans express some degree of allegiance to the country, these data indicate a fairly high level of reconciliation.

These results also provide an important methodological lesson about the meaning of responses to essentially open-ended questions with a fixed number of possible replies. Consider the second statement in table 2.8, about the importance of "being a South African." Among those *not* selecting South African from the list, the proportions asserting that being a South African is very important are 83.9 percent of blacks, 74.5 percent of whites, 89.8 percent of Colored people, and 88.7 percent of those of Asian origin. Just because a respondent does not select a national identity from a list of terms does not necessarily mean that the identities *not* selected are *unimportant* to that person.

Group Versus National Identities?

Some research argues that national identities can serve as antidotes to the pernicious consequences of group identities. The theory here is that intergroup differences can be softened by a common national identity. South Africans may think of themselves as Zulus or Afrikaners, but if they also think of themselves as South Africans,

Table 2.8 South African National Identity and Pride, by Race

	Agree	Uncertain	Disagree	Mean	Standard Deviation	Number of Cases
"I am proud to be a South African."						
African	88.6%	7.4%	4.0%	1.62	.82	2,001
White	77.2	12.4	10.4	2.10	.93	983
Colored	93.0	3.7	3.3	1.62	.76	484
Asian origin	87.8	4.5	7.8	1.88	.86	245
"Being South African is an important part of how I see myself."						
African	87.1	7.5	5.4	1.68	.87	2,002
White	74.6	9.6	15.9	2.21	1.02	983
Colored	91.7	4.5	3.7	1.68	.76	484
Asian origin	89.4	2.4	8.2	1.87	.82	245

Source: Author's compilation from the 2001 Truth and Reconciliation Survey.
Note: The percentages are based on collapsing the five-point Likert response set (for example, "agree strongly" and "agree" responses are combined) and total to 100 percent across the three columns (except for rounding errors). The means and standard deviations are calculated on the uncollapsed distributions. Lower mean scores indicate more agreement with the statement. Cross-race difference of means: "It makes me proud to be called a South African": $\eta = .24$; $p < .001$. "Being a South African is a very important part of how I see myself": $\eta = .25$; $p < .001$.

then there is some basis for collaboration and coexistence. It is therefore useful to consider the relationship between national identities and group identities.

The conventional hypothesis is that the more one identifies with a subgroup, the less one identifies with the nation-state (see, for example, Sidanius et al. 1997). To test this hypothesis, we measured the strength of group identities by first allowing the respondents to identify the group with which they most strongly associate, and then asking them about the importance of this identity to them. These nominal group identities are reported in table 2.7. As noted earlier in this chapter, the importance of this identity was collected on a four-point response set: 78.7 percent of South Africans select the most extreme point on the scale ("very important").

The best way in which to test this hypothesis is to examine *within each identity group* the strength of the group identity and the responses to the two national identity statements. The conventional view is that these variables are negatively related: the more strongly one identifies with one's group, the more weakly one identifies with the nation. The data in table 2.9 report the correlations necessary to test this hypothesis. The first row of data indicates the correlations for those who select South African as their primary group identity. The table reports the correlations ranked by the number of respondents selecting each identity. Caution must be exercised in interpreting some of these coefficients, since some are based on relatively small numbers of respondents.

The data require that the hypothesis be unequivocally rejected. For nearly every group, the more one identifies with the group, *the more likely one is to hold a strong national identity*. For instance, consider those who select Zulu as their primary group identity. The greater the importance of Zulu identity, the more likely one is to assert that being South African makes one proud and the more important is a South African identity. These relationships are strong (r = .46 and .40, respectively). The magnitude of the correlations varies across identity, but in no instance is there a statistically significant or even nontrivial negative correlation between group identities and national identities. These data are important because they indicate that national and group identities are not

Table 2.9 The Relationship Between South African Group and National Identifications and Attitudes

	Correlation Between Strength of Group Identity and National Identity		
Identity	Proud to Be a South African	Being South African Is Important	Number of Cases
South African	.35***	.39***	1,031
African	.10**	.16***	610
Christian	.03	−.01	319
Afrikaner	.13*	.19**	263
Black	.25***	.29***	256
Xhosa	.20**	.18**	217
Zulu	.46***	.40***	177
Colored	.22*	.33***	126
English	.09	.10	90
South Sotho-Sesotho	.14	.36***	90
Tswana	.31**	.31**	80
North Sotho-Sepedi	.14	.13	63
White	.25*	.22	62
Muslim	.03	.16	50
Indian	.20	.47***	48
Tsonga-Shangaan	.29	.27	44
Hindu	.30	.28	34
Boer	.28	.24	30
European	−.08	.05	26
Asian	.29	.33	23
Ndebele	.01	.24	18
Other	−.05	−.21	15
Seswati-Swazi	−.03	.40	13

Source: Author's compilation from the 2001 Truth and Reconciliation Survey.
Note: Correlations are shown for groups with ten or more identifiers.
***$p < .001$; **$p < .01$; *$p < .05$

locked in a zero-sum tension with each other. Indeed, quite the contrary is true. South Africans seem entirely capable of holding multiple identities simultaneously and without apparent conflict.

Indeed, it seems possible that the opposite of group or national identity is in fact social isolation or atomization: the failure to identity with any group. Identity may reflect an enduring psychological attribute of individuals, with those able to identify with one group being better able to identify with other groups as well. Of course, I do not contend that this tendency toward joint identities applies to all groups—as, for instance, with groups that are in direct political conflict with one another. But in South Africa, identifying with the nation is not incompatible with identifying with one's group. In this sense, "tribalism" seems not to be inimical to asserting a strong national identity.

Anti-Identities

We also asked the respondents to identify the groups with which they most strongly do *not* identify. Only 5.5 percent claimed to have no "anti-identities"; 21.2 percent responded with more than a single anti-identity. Table 2.10 reports the distribution of the responses to this question.

Significant racial differences exist ($p < .001$; $\eta = .27$) in the willingness to declare an anti-identity: 23.8 percent of the Colored respondents asserted no anti-identity, but only 2.9 percent of the Africans and 7.2 percent of the whites were unable to identify a group with which they negatively associate.[29] Among black South Africans, the most common anti-identity was Boer, followed by Afrikaner, which is perhaps not surprising given that these are the ethnic terms associated with apartheid. Interestingly, white is not the primary anti-identity of Africans; instead, blacks focus on an ideologically defined subset of whites. Still, African anti-identities are strewn across the political landscape.

Whites are much more likely to focus on a single group with which they dis-identify—for over one-third of white South Africans, Black is their anti-identity. A plurality of Colored and Asian South Africans also dissociate with Black, but at rates roughly half that of whites. These distributions of identities and anti-identities suggest significant racial polarization in contemporary South Africa but also indicate that race in South Africa is clearly not simply a matter of "black" and "white."

The Psychological Benefits of Group Identities

Just because the respondents answered our questions about identity does not mean they vest these terms with psychological signifi-

Table 2.10 Racial Differences in the Distribution of Primary Negative Social Identities, 2001

Primary Identity	All South Africans	African	White	Colored	Asian Origin
African	2.1%	1.6%	4.4%	.6%	10.2%
South African	.4	.4	.5	.0	.4
Black	13.5	8.7	34.6	16.6	14.7
Zulu	3.0	3.1	2.7	1.4	8.2
Christian	.5	.4	.4	.4	3.3
Xhosa	1.2	1.0	1.7	2.9	.4
Afrikaner	13.9	17.5	3.0	4.7	12.2
Colored	2.7	2.6	.7	6.6	2.9
English	1.8	2.1	.5	1.4	.8
Muslim	4.4	2.8	9.8	7.2	5.3
Tsonga-Shangaan	1.1	1.3	.3	.4	.4
White	8.5	10.3	.3	5.1	10.6
European	4.0	4.9	.9	2.9	2.0
Boer	17.5	21.3	6.7	8.6	7.8
Hindu	3.1	2.8	5.1	2.1	4.9
Indian	3.6	4.8	1.2	1.6	.8
Asian	1.3	1.4	1.1	.8	.0
Brown	3.0	3.6	.3	3.1	3.3
Venda	1.1	1.3	.3	1.0	.8
Jewish	2.6	2.1	3.4	4.1	3.3
Other	5.0	2.8	14.7	4.5	5.3
None	5.5	2.9	7.2	23.8	2.4
Number of cases	3,724	2,003	990	487	245

Source: Author's compilation from the 2001 Truth and Reconciliation Survey.
Note: For "All South Africans," the "other" category includes any group identity that was selected by fewer than 1.0 percent of any of the racial groups. The modal response within each group is highlighted in the table. χ^2 for differences across race = 1445.4; $p < .001$.

cance. We therefore measured the psychic benefits that South Africans derive from their social identities by asking them whether they receive any security, importance, or self-esteem as a result of their group identifications.[30] Roughly two-thirds to three-fourths of the respondents claim to derive each of these psychic benefits, with 39.9 percent of the respondents asserting strong benefits of all three types. The measure of benefits received is fairly strongly correlated with the rated importance of the respondent's identity (r = .33).

Significant racial differences exist in the perceived value of group identifications, with whites substantially less likely to derive these benefits from their group identifications. For instance, while at least two-thirds of Africans, Colored people, and South Africans of Asian origin assert that they think better of themselves owing to their group identifications, fewer than half of the whites derive a similar benefit. On each of the three measures, nonwhite South Africans hold similar views; white South Africans stand out as being less likely to claim these psychic benefits as a result of their group memberships.

Beliefs About the Political Relevance of Groups

Finally, we asked the respondents to evaluate a series of statements about the political and personal significance of their group attachments. Their responses are reported in table 2.11.

South Africans clearly believe that their group attachments are important, as revealed in the responses to the third item in the table ("The group's fate affects me"). Very large majorities of every racial group agree with this statement. Nearly all South Africans also believe that their group should "stand together." Indeed, preferences for strong "group solidarity" can be seen throughout these data. For instance, the second proposition in the table asserts that individuals should subordinate their individual interests to the interests of the group. A large majority of South Africans proclaim the importance of following the group's view, even when it differs from the individual's view. Variability across racial groups in the responses to this proposition is not great ($\eta = .15$), with only a somewhat larger percentage of Asian respondents and a somewhat smaller proportion of whites asserting greater importance for the group than the individual. Overall, the data in table 2.11 reveal considerable perceived political significance of these group identities, with only small racial differences in these perceptions.

When the items in table 2.11 are subjected to factor analysis, two significant dimensions emerge.[31] The first factor, based on the first four statements in the table, clearly emphasizes the "group solidarity" items, while the second factor (based on the last two items) refers more to the political relevance of the group. Not unexpectedly, these two factors are strongly related ($r = -.68$), indicating that those who believe in greater group solidarity are much more likely to perceive greater political relevance for groups in South African politics (and, of course, vice versa). Racial differences on the group solidarity factor are significant, though small ($\eta = .17$, $p < .001$), while racial differences on the perceived political relevance of groups are even more trivial ($\eta = .12$, $p < .001$). The correlation between the two factors is similar for blacks, whites, and Colored people but slightly weaker among those of Asian origin ($r = -.59$). Generally, those who believe more strongly in group solidarity are also more likely to perceive that group identities are politically relevant.

There can be no doubt that group identities are important in South Africa—for all four racial groups. The importance of these associations is documented by the finding that people derive a series of psychic benefits from their identities. Given that group conflict has shaped much of the politics of the country for at least the last century, this finding should not surprise anyone.

National identities are fairly widespread and seem to be growing in South Africa. Large majorities of South Africans derive a sense of pride from being associated with their country. Most important, and contrary to some earlier findings, group identities are not inimical to national identities. Indeed, I have suggested that there may be a generalized propensity to identify with groups and that therefore the antithesis of identifying with groups or nations is social atomization. Being South African and being Zulu or Xhosa or even Afrikaner fit nicely together for most South Africans.

Finally, racial differences are smaller on these identity items than on most questions in the survey. All groups in South Africa draw benefits from their identities, in part because nearly everyone recognizes the political significance of groups in the politics of the country. Not many South Africans believe that groups can be ignored in contemporary politics. People do differ in their perceptions of the need for group solidarity—and that difference is important, as I demonstrate later in the book—but individual differences are much stronger than group differences.

Table 2.11 Attitudes Toward Groups and Social Identity, by Race

	Agree	Uncertain	Disagree	Mean	Standard Deviation	Number of Cases
"My group is best."[a]						
All South Africans	67.0%	12.4%	20.7%	2.24	1.17	3715
Black	68.7	11.3	19.9	2.19	1.18	2002
White	57.1	16.1	26.8	2.52	1.15	981
Colored	62.7	15.3	21.9	2.36	1.13	483
Asian origin	63.3	9.8	26.9	2.47	1.10	245
"I support my group's view."[b]						
All South Africans	73.6	11.5	14.9	2.14	1.05	3720
Black	74.3	11.4	14.3	2.10	1.06	2003
White	64.7	10.7	24.7	2.47	1.10	985
Colored	74.1	13.8	12.1	2.19	.98	486
Asian origin	81.6	5.3	13.1	2.11	.91	245
"The group fate affects me."[c]						
All South Africans	81.5	9.3	9.2	1.90	.96	3720
Black	81.1	9.9	9.0	1.87	.97	2003
White	82.1	7.9	9.9	2.01	.91	985
Colored	78.8	9.9	11.3	2.03	.97	486
Asian origin	89.0	2.9	8.2	1.83	.83	245
"The group should stand together."[d]						
All South Africans	82.1	8.7	9.2	1.83	.97	3724
Black	81.9	9.7	8.4	1.79	.96	2004

White	78.5	7.0	14.5	2.05	1.02	986
Colored	86.0	5.7	8.2	1.82	.91	487
Asian origin	86.1	2.4	11.4	1.94	.96	245
"I can't get much without the group."[e]						
All South Africans	46.0	22.0	32.1	2.75	1.22	3722
Black	46.2	21.0	32.8	2.75	1.27	2004
White	38.4	24.5	37.1	2.94	1.09	984
Colored	45.4	27.3	27.3	2.72	1.11	487
Asian origin	55.1	13.5	31.4	2.68	1.14	245
"Fate has to do with politics."[f]						
All South Africans	48.0	18.7	33.4	2.75	1.29	3720
Black	49.0	19.7	31.3	2.69	1.30	2003
White	42.8	13.6	43.7	2.99	1.24	987
Colored	44.6	23.8	31.6	2.81	1.12	484
Asian origin	43.3	10.6	46.1	3.08	1.27	245

Source: Author's compilation from the 2001 Truth and Reconciliation Survey.

Note: The percentages are based on collapsing the five-point Likert response set (for example, "agree strongly" and "agree" responses are combined) and total to 100 percent across the three columns (except for rounding errors). The means and standard deviations are calculated on the uncollapsed distributions. Lower mean scores indicate more agreement with the statement.

[a]"Of all the groups in South Africa, [my group] is best." $\eta = .13$; $p < .001$.

[b]"Even though I might sometimes disagree with the standpoint/viewpoint taken by [my group], it is extremely important to support [my group's] point of view." $\eta = .15$; $p > .001$.

[c]"What happens to [my group] in South Africa will affect my life a great deal." $\eta = .08$; $p < .001$.

[d]"When it comes to politics, it is important for all of [my group] to stand together." $\eta = .12$; $p > .001$.

[e]"Unless you are a member of a group like [my group], it is very difficult to get much out of South African politics." $\eta = .08$; $p < .001$.

[f]"The well-being of [my group] has more to do with politics than it does with our own hard work." $\eta = .12$; $p < .001$.

Concluding Comments

For two reasons, I have provided a considerable amount of information about the attributes of the South African population in this chapter. First, these data paint a sometimes startling picture of South Africa's political culture in the post-apartheid era. Second, many of the variables introduced in this chapter are key independent variables in the analyses that follow. Controlling for these variables (among others) strengthens my ability to make causal inferences about the origins of attitudes toward reconciliation.

Several broad conclusions stand out from the analysis:

- South Africa is a country characterized by vast inequality. Extreme differences persist between the small white minority and the large African majority, but so too are there great differences among those considered "Black" (Africans, Colored people, and those of Asian origin).

- South Africans experienced the apartheid system in different ways. Even so-called Black South Africans did not fare the same under the apartheid system. Because apartheid treated different groups differently, nostalgia about the old system is more commonplace than expected. Whites are surprisingly willing to admit that they profited in many important ways from the apartheid system.

- A heavy sense of gloom about the future does *not* characterize South Africans. Economic optimism is reasonably widespread, and the vast majority of each racial group express a commitment to continue living in South Africa. Certainly South Africans perceive many important social and economic difficulties for their country, contemporaneously and for the future. But most South Africans do not judge these problems to be insurmountable.

- South Africans derive significant psychic benefits from their associations with their groups. These groups are not always racial—whites are particularly likely to identify themselves in terms of their religious affiliations—but group identities are important to most people. This probably stems in part from the widespread perception that groups matter in South African politics, and that how well one does individually is at least in part a function of how well one's group does. Social or group identities are not a single, undifferentiated mass of beliefs but range from simple, nominal identities to complex beliefs about such factors as the need for group solidarity.

In sum, I find in contemporary South Africa an enduring legacy of apartheid (for an elaboration of this viewpoint, see Gibson 2003). That legacy is manifest most clearly in inequality and in the salience of group politics. It remains to be considered, however, how South Africans view their past, whether a collective memory about apartheid has yet emerged, and whether memory is dominated by race. That is the purpose of the next chapter.

Chapter 3

South African Collective Memories

> All that a truth commission can achieve is to reduce the number of lies that can be circulated unchallenged in public discourse.
>
> —Michael Ignatieff, "Articles of Faith" (1996, 113)

> Truth is truth. It is not, in and of itself, social reform, institutional transformation, or political reconciliation.
>
> —Charles Villa-Vicencio and Wilhelm Verwoerd, "Constructing a Report: Writing Up the Truth" (2000, 291)

A formidable literature on so-called collective memories exists that is of some direct relevance to this research. A collective memory is a "set of ideas, images, feelings about the past" (Irwin-Zarecka 1994, 4). Such memories are often socially constructed to meet contemporary social, psychological, and political needs. A collective memory thus represents a society's understanding of itself, especially its past. Generally, this body of research attempts to identify the central elements of the beliefs that people hold about the past, often with a focus on generational differences in memories.[1]

For instance, Howard Schuman and Amy Corning (2000) have investigated the knowledge and memories of a sample of Russians about a number of happenings from the past sixty years of Russian history. They not only document Russian beliefs about such events as the Cuban Missile Crisis but also investigate the influence of level of education and age on the acquisition of beliefs about these and other major aspects of Russian history (see also Jennings 1996; Schuman, Belli, and Bischoping 1997; and Schuman and Scott 1989). Similarly, Katherine Bischoping and Andrea Kalmin (1999, 503) analyze differences across individual Americans in the belief that the Holocaust was a unique historical event (a belief subscribed to by only a minority of the American population).[2] Though the empirical literature varies enormously in the degree to which concepts and indicators are defined systematically and rigorously,[3] as a heuristic, theories of collective memory provide an interesting way to think about the activities of truth commissions. Thus, it may be useful to consider whether the truth and reconciliation process was successful at creating a collective memory for South Africans.

The Truth and Reconciliation Commission itself thought it was engaged in a process of constructing a collective memory for South Africa. Although clearly rejecting the notion that it produced a single, official "truth," the primary authors of the commission's *Final Report* nonetheless believe that:

> contributing to the shared acknowledgment by all South Africans of what happened in the apartheid years, in both repression and resistance, as well as the recognition that humanity has the capacity to do it again (in one way or another), was surely among the most important legacies that the TRC could bequeath to the nation. This shared acknowledgment thus involves the public recognition of the painful truth about the past *and* about human nature. (Villa-Vicencio and Verwoerd 2000, 279, emphasis in original)

A "shared acknowledgment" is certainly a collective memory.

To date, however, no one knows whether the TRC succeeded at creating a commonly accepted view of South Africa's history. What South Africans believe about their past is an empirical question, answerable only through rigorous survey methods. Much supposition exists in South Africa concerning what ordinary people believe and whether their beliefs have been shaped by the TRC, but rigorous analyses of the nature of people's understanding of the country's past are practically nonexistent. Hence, I am concerned in this chapter with examining empirically the nature of South Africans' beliefs about apartheid and their country's past.

Though my research is certainly informed by the collective memory literature, I diverge from the conventional understanding of the concept in some important respects. First, I make no *assump-*

tion that anything about memory is "collective." That is, I treat the nature of the distribution of memories as an empirical question. It may well be that memory is in no sense collective or shared; it may instead be highly contested. Michael Ignatieff (1996, 111), for instance, is critical of Archbishop Desmond Tutu's view of the truth:

> Look at the assumptions he makes: that a nation has one psyche, not many; that the truth is one, not many; that the truth is certain, not contestable; and that when it is known by all, it has the capacity to heal and reconcile. These are not so much assumptions of epistemology as articles of faith about human nature: the truth is one and if we know it, it will make us free.

Those who study collective memory often treat memory as if it were consensually held—that is, subscribed to by nearly everyone in society—when in fact memories are typically constructed quite differently in different segments of the community, are often the subject of bitter political debate, and even if "collective," may be accepted by virtue of coercion and elite hegemony rather than by individual choice. Rather than referring to "collective" memories, it is perhaps more neutral to use the terms "social" or "historical" memory so as not to beg the empirical question of how widely such memories are accepted in a society. The degree to which South Africans endorse a collective memory about their past is an empirical question, as is the issue of whether different groups in society share similar or different conceptions of South African history.

"Memory" is sometimes used to indicate the ability to recall objective information about the past. This information is typically personal, as in the ability to remember exactly what one was doing at the moment New York's World Trade Center was attacked in 2001. Two aspects of this approach to collective memory are not very useful for my purposes. First, I am concerned with social, not personal, memory (although social memories are held by individuals). Social memories are memories of societal events rather than individual experiences. Second, my focus is not on objective, factual information but on subjective evaluations of the past. Social memories are important because they are often constructed by groups and shaped by group identities. Personal histories have limited political and social relevance; social histories can influence understandings and evaluations of contemporary events as well as motivate political action. Evaluation—not just documenting facts but explaining why things happened (as emphasized by Villa-Vicencio and Verwoerd 2000)—is important because historical facts cannot acquire meaning and sociopolitical relevance without normative assessments. For the purposes of this chapter, "memory" therefore refers to understandings and evaluations of apartheid and South Africa's history.

Despite my assertion that I am investigating subjective understandings of the past, "truth" is inevitably a loaded word, invoking the imagery of George Orwell's *1984* and the efforts of totalitarian systems to write and rewrite official histories. In this research, the phenomenon under investigation has to do with popular understandings and judgments about South Africa's past. I do not necessarily assume that there is an objective history of the past, although I do postulate that there is a view that has been constructed through the efforts of the truth and reconciliation process and subsequently proposed and endorsed by the TRC. The TRC had explicitly adopted as one of its missions the creation of a history of apartheid in South Africa and sought to encourage all South Africans to accept its version of that history.[4] Thus, in this research it is entirely unnecessary for me to construct an "accurate" version of South Africa's history, and the "truth" I investigate is the truth as proposed and endorsed by the TRC.

The purpose of this chapter is therefore to assess the degree to which South Africans accept the truth as promulgated by the Truth and Reconciliation Commission. I begin the analysis with a discussion of what constitutes the truth from the TRC's viewpoint. I next consider whether South Africans endorse this truth. The final portion of the chapter tests hypotheses that predict what type of person accepts the TRC's truth, focusing in particular on the influence of the TRC's hearings and activities and the experiences that people had under apartheid (as well as several other hypotheses and variables).

The TRC's View of the Truth About South Africa's Past

The Elements of the TRC's Truth

What did the TRC proclaim about South Africa's apartheid past? Whether one agrees with the findings or not, the central elements of the commission's understanding of the country's history include the following:

> *Apartheid was a crime against humanity and therefore those struggling to maintain that regime were engaged in an evil undertaking.*

There can be little doubt that the TRC judged apartheid a crime against humanity—as in the United Nations declaration to that effect[5]—and the commission's *Final Report* included an appendix specifically addressing this issue. The TRC asserted that "the Commission—as part of the international human rights community—affirms its judgement that apartheid, as a system of enforced racial discrimination and separation, was a crime against humanity. The recognition of apartheid as a crime against humanity remains a fundamental starting point for reconciliation in South Africa" (Truth and Reconciliation Commission 1998, vol. 1, p. 94; see also vol. 5, p. 222). Even the "minority position" issued with the report asserts that this section of the majority viewpoint "adequately addresses this issue," even as it tries to provide some additional context for why the South Africans acted as they did (vol. 5, pp. 448–50).

> *Both sides in the struggle over apartheid committed horrific offenses, including gross human rights violations.*

Again, this assertion hardly needs justifying. Indisputably, the TRC documented that numerous, gross human rights violations were committed by agents of the apartheid state, just as it documented gross human rights violations by the liberation forces. Indeed, the African National Congress itself has admitted that gross human rights violations were committed both in its camps in the border states and by ANC agents, and of course, the ANC established its own "truth commission" to investigate these atrocities (see Hayner 2002). Bishop Tutu asserts in the TRC's *Final Report*: "We believe we have provided enough of the truth about our past for there to be a consensus about it. There is a consensus that atrocious things were done on all sides" (Truth and Reconciliation Commission 1998, vol. 1, ch. 1, p. 18). For instance, the culpability of the ANC, the United Democratic Front (UDF), and Winnie Madikizela-Mandela is clearly discussed in the report (vol. 5, pp. 240–49). The TRC also takes the Inkatha Freedom Party (IFP) to task for committing gross human rights violations during the struggle over apartheid. The authors of the report are even more emphatic: "If the TRC ignored or failed to acknowledge the extent to which an individual, the state, or a liberation movement, either legally or illegally, deployed its resources systematically to violate the rights of others, it would have failed to give a full account of the past" (Villa-Vicencio and Verwoerd 2000, 286). Indeed, the TRC has even been accused of "poisonous evenhandedness" for its efforts to document abuses by both sides in the struggle.[6]

Apartheid was criminal because of both the actions of specific individuals (including legal and illegal actions) and the actions of state institutions.

The primary criminality of apartheid was its attempt to establish a state—even a state based to a limited degree on the rule of law—that did not treat its citizens equally, that denied full rights of political participation for the vast majority of the residents of the country, and that was grounded in an ideology (and religion) of racial superiority. To emphasize this point, the TRC held institutional and special hearings designed to show that the evil of apartheid was an evil of institutions as well as of individuals.[7] These hearings certainly did not attract the public attention commanded by the other activities of the commission, but they are no less important to its work, and the findings on this score consume considerable space in the *Final Report*. Furthermore, the *Final Report* often refers to the state as the "perpetrator" and specifically indicts the South African state for gross human rights violations (Truth and Reconciliation Commission 1998, vol. 5, p. 212).

Thus, whatever else may embellish South Africa's collective memory about its past, the criminality of apartheid and its institutions and the abuses by individuals on all sides during the struggle over apartheid were surely central elements in this history. As the TRC (1998, vol. 1, 111–12) proclaimed:

> One can say that the information in the hands of the Commission made it impossible to claim, for example, that: the practice of torture by the state security forces was not systematic and widespread; that only a few "rotten eggs" or "bad apples" committed gross violations of human rights; that the state was not directly and indirectly involved in "black-on-black" violence; that the chemical and biological warfare programme was only of a defensive nature; that slogans by sections of the liberation movement did not contribute to killings of "settlers" or farmers; and that the accounts of gross human rights violations in the African National Congress (ANC) camps were the consequence of state disinformation. Thus, disinformation about the past that had been accepted as truth by some members of society lost much of its credibility.

The truth promulgated by the TRC is very much the truth of discrete events. One approach to measuring truth acceptance among ordinary South Africans would therefore be to focus on whether people are aware of specific incidents and abuses. I have chosen not to take this tack, however, in part because it would be quite time-consuming to canvass knowledge of a wide variety of events and incidents, and in part because people most likely acquire specific information only on issues that are of some direct relevance or interest to them. Instead, I focus on the *lessons learned* from the revelations of the TRC. This is certainly what might be called an "interpretive" truth, but it might also be called "historical understandings." It seems obvious that the lessons the TRC wanted people to learn from its activities involve these broad understandings, not acceptance of its description and explanation of any given discrete event.[8] The TRC sometimes refers to this as understanding the "context" of these incidents, by which it means understanding the larger social and institutional forces that allowed a specific abuse to take place. To understand context is to provide an explanation for individual actions. The TRC clearly perceived its mandate in both these factual truth and explanatory truth terms (even if this mandate might have been self-assumed rather than delegated by the law establishing the commission). That apartheid was evil, that atrocities were committed by all sides in the struggle, that the evil of the system was an evil of institutions, not of individuals—these are the broad understandings of the past that the TRC sought to impart. These are the lessons the TRC wanted people to learn.

How Might the TRC's Truth Contribute to Reconciliation?

I also posit that it is precisely this sort of understanding of the past that contributes to reconciliation. Many doubt that specific information about atrocities leads to reconciliation of any sort. For instance, to learn that one's loved ones were informants and askari (spies) surely does not make reconciliation any easier or more probable. But that is not the type of learning that I (or the TRC) consider crucial from the point of view of societal reconciliation.

The lesson of the South African TRC was overwhelmingly that the struggle was justified by the evil of the regime, but that abuses were committed by all sides in the struggle. This message can contribute to reconciliation among both the oppressors and the oppressed under apartheid. For the oppressors, the revelations of the TRC make it absolutely incontrovertible that the regime engaged in illegal and inhumane actions against the liberation forces. Whites can no longer deny this, even if they try to diffuse responsibility by blaming individuals instead of institutions. The "truth" as promulgated by the TRC has surely contributed to some level of understanding among whites that apartheid was, or at least did, evil.

For the supporters of the liberation forces, the TRC's findings contribute to a more balanced view of those battling against apartheid, even if they continue to believe that the ANC fought a "just war."[9] The ANC, though undoubtedly essential to the liberation of South Africa, engaged in gross human rights violations of its own, including atrocities committed in its training camps (for which the ANC established its own truth commission). Perhaps more important, barbarous acts were undertaken in the name of the ANC as the organization lost control of many of its operatives in the late 1980s and early 1990s. It is difficult to treat the "necklacing" of individuals—a method of killing somebody by putting a tire around his or her neck and then setting it alight—as anything other than a gross human rights violation.[10] Moreover, black-on-black political violence during the struggle was often more widespread and vicious than anti-apartheid conflict (see Ellis 1998). I am not asserting that any degree of parity existed in the crimes committed in the name of or in opposition to apartheid, but it would be quite natural to come away from the truth and reconciliation process with the view that all sides in the struggle did some pretty horrible things.

The consequence of the "truth" as produced by the TRC is that it is now difficult for South Africans to characterize the struggle in terms of absolute good versus absolute evil. If one accepted the TRC's view of South African history, one would believe that the struggle against apartheid was just, though flawed, and that the struggle in defense of apartheid did horrible things, in part (but only in part) because specific individuals ran amok. A close reading of the TRC's record would lead to the view that the evil done by apartheid was to some degree an evil of specific individuals acting outside the law of the apartheid state. Both sides were compromised, even if it is still entirely reasonable to conclude that the struggle was justified. Information inevitably clouds simplistic understandings and judgments of history. As facts are assembled, juxtaposed, and sifted, perceptions of reality often lose their black-and-white character, taking on more subtle and nuanced shades. Even when no moral ambiguity or ambivalence arises, balanced evidence of abuses surely moderates views of the combatants in the struggle to at least some degree. This is most likely what the TRC sought to achieve.

It is difficult indeed to reconcile with ultimate evil.[11] It is less difficult to reconcile with more moderate evil, especially when one's own side is tainted as well. Moral relativism, I hypothesize, contributes to reconciliation. To the extent that the TRC's lesson portrayed a balanced view of good and evil, reconciliation may be less difficult to achieve.

I do not, by the way, claim that the product of truth commissions *always* has this effect. A different sort of truth might be produced under different historical circumstances. My argument goes specifically to the truth as promulgated by South Africa's TRC. Those who accept the TRC's truth, I hypothesize, will be more willing to compromise with, tolerate, and reconcile with their former enemies, in part because the TRC so self-consciously attempted to create a collective memory that could serve as an underpinning for reconciliation in South Africa.

Measuring Acceptance of the TRC's Truth

To what degree do South Africans accept the "truth" about the past? To provide empirical indicators of truth acceptance, we asked our respondents to judge the veracity of five statements about South Africa's apartheid past. These statements, and the position deemed to represent the conclusions of the TRC, are:

1. Apartheid was a crime against humanity. (True)
2. The struggle to preserve apartheid was just. (False)
3. There were certainly some abuses under the old apartheid system, but the ideas behind apartheid were basically good ones. (False)
4. The abuses under apartheid were largely committed by a few evil individuals, not by the state institutions themselves. (False)
5. Both those struggling for and those struggling against the old apartheid system did unforgivable things to people. (True)

These five statements are simple, widely accepted (at least throughout the world, if not necessarily in South Africa), and interrelated, and the veracity of the statements would undoubtedly not be controversial among the leaders of the truth and reconciliation process themselves.[12] As I have shown earlier, there is a close connection between these propositions and the conclusions of the TRC as chronicled in its *Final Report*.

One might expect that different groups in South Africa would judge the truth of these statements quite differently, for at least a couple of reasons. First, different groups held vastly different positions within South Africa's system of racial hierarchy. That is, apartheid treated the various racial groups in South Africa quite differently. Whites, of course, enjoyed a position of racial superiority, some degree of democratic government, within the context of a state that provided enormous subsidies and social benefits made possible by the exploitation of black labor. Colored people and those of Asian origin were denied the full benefits of citizenship that whites enjoyed but nonetheless were not always subject to the heavy boot of apartheid. The constitution of 1983, for instance, provided for political representation through a tricameral parliament with racially exclusive white, Colored, and Indian chambers. As Hein Marais (1998, 29–30) notes:

> The weight of the apartheid system was distributed unevenly among blacks (i.e., Africans, coloureds and Indians), as state budget allocation to housing, education and health departments showed. Along with white workers, Indians and coloureds predominated in the expanding sectors of the economy and were accorded some mobility within and between jobs. . . . By the 1970s there had developed in both "groups" a significant middle class, comprising mostly professionals and merchants. Although disenfranchised, these small minorities were deemed to be citizens of "white" South Africa.

Black South Africans reaped no benefits from the apartheid system.

Consequently, it would not be surprising to find that South Africans of different races had quite disparate relationships to apartheid. I consider more directly later in this chapter the evidence of the consequences of the costs and benefits that individuals experienced under apartheid (and see chapter 2), but for the moment it seems fair to assert that whites in general were extreme beneficiaries of apartheid; blacks were extremely oppressed, experiencing substantial costs but few benefits; and Colored people and those of Asian origin experienced both costs and benefits of apartheid.

Different groups most likely also have vastly different understandings and evaluations of the past. Whites, for instance, claim not to have known about the activities of rogue individuals (such as Eugene de Kock), but blacks are much more likely to be aware of what the state and its agents were doing to those who opposed apartheid. Apartheid was a daily reality for many black South Africans, one they could rarely escape. Thus, I hypothesize that strong racial differences exist in the degree of acceptance of the collective memory produced by the TRC and that these are to some degree related to individual experiences under apartheid.

The respondents' judgments of the veracity of these substantive statements about South Africa's past are reported in table 3.1.

Several of our propositions directly addressed apartheid: the first statement in table 3.1, for instance, states flatly: "Apartheid was a crime against humanity." This judgment turns out to be widely accepted among South Africans of every race, with large majorities of blacks, whites, Colored people, and those of Asian origin being willing to condemn apartheid. Still, whites are significantly less likely than others to judge the statement to be true: nearly one-fourth of the whites disagree with the proposition. (The cross-race difference of means test is significant at $p < .001$, $\eta = .32$.) Afrikaans-speaking whites are by far the most unwilling to accept that apartheid was a crime against humanity, with 29.7 percent rejecting this statement compared to only 16.2 percent of the English-speaking whites (data not shown). That only a relatively small minority of South Africans reject this conclusion about apartheid surely constitutes an important element of a collective South African memory shared by all racial groups.

But despite this apparent consensus condemning apartheid, a significant proportion of South Africans *of every race* also believe that the *idea of apartheid* was good, even if the implementation of the ideology was not. While this view characterizes a slim majority of whites (and 62.7 percent of Afrikaans-speaking whites), it is perhaps somewhat surprising that more than one-third of Africans, Colored people, and South Africans of Asian origin agree that, in principle, apartheid was a good idea. This is an entirely unexpected finding. How can we square these views with the belief that apartheid was a crime against humanity?

Reactions to this statement most likely reflect at least in part a reference to the "separate development" implications of apartheid,

Table 3.1 Acceptance of the TRC's View of South Africa's Past, by Race

	True	Not True	Don't Know	Mean	Standard Deviation	Number of Cases
Apartheid was a crime against humanity. (true)[a]						
Black	94.3%	4.5%	1.1%	4.54	.80	2002
White	72.9	23.4	3.8	3.75	1.31	984
Colored	86.4	7.6	6.0	4.30	1.05	485
Asian origin	89.0	8.6	2.4	4.27	.95	245
Despite abuses, apartheid ideas were good ones. (false)[b]						
African	35.5	58.7	5.8	3.44	1.52	2003
White	51.0	43.9	5.2	2.98	1.38	986
Colored	34.9	51.3	13.8	3.40	1.44	487
Asian origin	42.0	52.7	5.3	3.36	1.48	245
The struggle to preserve apartheid was just. (false)[c]						
African	39.4	57.3	3.3	3.33	1.59	2004
White	33.7	58.6	7.6	3.44	1.30	981
Colored	24.4	58.8	16.8	3.67	1.38	483
Asian origin	35.9	55.5	8.6	3.45	1.48	245
Those struggling for and against apartheid did unforgivable things. (true)[d]						
African	76.1	9.7	14.2	3.96	.98	2002
White	73.8	6.8	19.5	3.82	.81	986

Colored	66.0	6.2	27.7	3.72	.80	483
Asian origin	82.9	3.7	13.5	3.97	.68	245
The abuses of apartheid were due to evil individuals, not state institutions themselves. (false)[e]						
African	41.1	35.1	23.7	2.90	1.30	2003
White	43.2	28.1	28.8	2.81	1.03	987
Colored	28.2	35.3	36.5	3.06	1.03	482
Asian origin	46.5	34.3	19.2	2.83	1.15	245
Number of statements accepted[f]						
African	—	—	—	3.22	1.18	2003
White	—	—	—	2.76	1.40	988
Colored	—	—	—	2.96	1.46	487
Asian origin	—	—	—	3.14	1.23	245

Source: Author's compilation from the 2001 Truth and Reconciliation Survey.
Note: All variables are scored such that a high score indicates greater acceptance of the view shown in parentheses at the end of each statement. Responses were collected on a five-point response set.
[a]Difference of means test across race: $p = .001$; $\eta = .32$.
[b]Difference of means test across race: $p = .001$; $\eta = .14$.
[c]Difference of means test across race: $p = .001$; $\eta = .08$.
[d]Difference of means test across race: $p = .001$; $\eta = .10$.
[e]Difference of means test across race: $p = .002$; $\eta = .06$.
[f]Difference of means test across race: $p = .001$; $\eta = .15$.

rather than to the idea that a racial hierarchy is acceptable or desirable. Not only is apartheid a system of racial hierarchy, but it is also sometimes understood as a system of racial segregation and "separate development" ("aparte ontwikkeling").[13] This aspect of apartheid is compatible with some elements of black nationalism that emphasize the separation of races and the development of blacks apart from whites. For instance, the black consciousness movement (comprising organizations such as the South African Students' Organization, the Black People's Convention, and the Azanian People's Organization), in reaction to the levels of psychological abuse under apartheid, arose in South Africa under the leadership and influence of Steve Biko. The movement had as its main aim the psychological liberation of black people from feelings of inferiority and the restoration of their human dignity (see Leatt, Kneifel, and Nürnberger 1986, ch. 7; Sibisi 1991), and it rejected interracial integration as an important goal (at least in the short term). Similarly, the Pan-Africanist Congress (PAC) has never been interested in building a multiracial South Africa, so it seems quite likely that PAC supporters would favor at least some form of separate development. Thus, it is plausible that not all blacks in South Africa would view apartheid as a system of unequivocal evil.

Some empirical evidence on this matter is available. At a different point in the interview, we asked the respondents to judge the following statement (using a five-point Likert response set): "People should have the right to set up their own communities, and not allow those of a different race to live in their communities." Blacks are entirely divided on this issue, with 44 percent agreeing to the idea of separate communities and 46 percent disagreeing. Indeed, blacks are *more* likely than any other racial group in South Africa to agree to this form of racial segregation. Moreover, there is a reasonably strong relationship between favoring residential racial segregation and believing that the ideas behind apartheid are good ($r = .25$). Among those blacks favoring residential segregation, 48.4 percent claim that apartheid includes good ideas; among those disapproving of residential segregation this percentage falls markedly to 24.2 percent. Thus, at least some portion of the anomalous black approval of apartheid is surely a reflection of beliefs about the desirability of separate racial development. This evidence may not be definitive, but it is compatible with the view that those blacks who believe that apartheid ideas are good may have been reacting mainly to the idea of the physical separation of blacks and whites.

It is instructive to consider the replies to these two apartheid statements simultaneously, through a cross-tabulation of the data. A majority of black respondents (55.7 percent) hold consistent views—that is, they believe both that apartheid was a crime against humanity and that it is *not* true that apartheid was basically a good idea that was poorly implemented. These are steadfast opponents of apartheid. This view also characterizes a majority of those of Asian origin (51.0 percent) and nearly a majority of Colored people (46.2 percent), but only a minority of white people (36.8 percent). These people have no use for apartheid, either in the abstract or as it was implemented in South Africa.

Roughly one-third of each racial group believe that apartheid was criminal but that its criminality was associated with the implementation of the ideology rather than the ideology itself. Presumably, a variant of apartheid might be acceptable to these South Africans. A view also attractive to some whites (16.6 percent) is that apartheid was a good idea, not a crime, but that the ideas were poorly implemented, although this view does not characterize many in South Africa other than whites. (For example, 1.5 percent of the African respondents gave these replies.) Thus, most South Africans agree that apartheid was a crime, but disagreement is more widespread about whether separate development is a good idea. The only serious exception to this conclusion is found among whites, a minority of whom believe that the ideology is not criminal, even if the implementation of the ideology was less than satisfactory.[14] Thus, only a bare majority of blacks, Colored people, and South Africans of Asian origin unequivocally reject apartheid in principle and in practice.

In light of these ambivalent attitudes toward apartheid, it is not surprising to find that many South Africans believe that the struggle to preserve apartheid was just. It is unexpected, however, that *a greater proportion of blacks than whites hold this view*. Indeed, of all four racial groups, black South Africans are the *most likely* to assert that the struggle to preserve apartheid was just, although it should be noted that a majority of blacks do not subscribe to this view. Again, perhaps this indicates that people accept that each racial community has the right to a separate existence; if so, it follows that efforts to preserve separateness are legitimate. Still, it is important to acknowledge that a majority of South Africans of every race disagree that the struggle to preserve apartheid was just.

South Africans of every race accept what was probably one of the most important conclusions of the Truth and Reconciliation Commission—that both those who struggled for apartheid and those who struggled against it committed horrible abuses. The difference between blacks and whites on this issue is entirely insignificant, although Colored South Africans are slightly less willing to accept the veracity of this statement (owing to a higher percentage of respondents who are uncertain), while those of Asian origin are somewhat more likely to believe it to be true. It is noteworthy that, by implication, both blacks and whites endorse the view that "their side" in the struggle over apartheid engaged in horrible actions (although this should not be taken to mean that people believe that both sides did equally bad things or did them in equal numbers).

Considerable uncertainty exists about whether the failures of apartheid were a function of individuals or institutions, with uncharacteristically high levels of "don't know" replies appearing in the answers of each of the four racial groups. It is noteworthy that a plurality of blacks, whites, and those of Asian origin are willing to attribute the abuses *to individuals*, not to the state institutions themselves. This is consistent with the finding that many view apartheid as a good idea poorly implemented (perhaps because the institutions of apartheid were acceptable even if a handful of rogue individuals did horrific things in the name of apartheid). Colored South Africans are entirely divided on this question, with roughly equal proportions believing it to be true, believing it to be untrue, and being agnostic about its truth.

Because comparable survey data do not exist prior to the implementation of the truth and reconciliation process in South Africa, it is difficult to determine whether the TRC's activities contributed to the apparent willingness of many South Africans to blame individuals rather than institutions for the crimes of apartheid. My intuition is that the daily exposés of the actions of apartheid's rascals during the truth and reconciliation process may well have helped deflect blame away from the political system and focus it on specific individuals (an unintended consequence). That whites and blacks are equally likely to attribute the abuses to rogue individuals, not to apartheid institutions, may well be due to the TRC's revelations of the horrific deeds done by individual perpetrators (see, for example, de Kock 1998).[15] One consequence of focusing the truth and reconciliation process on the amnesty applications of individual actors and the victim statements of individual survivors is that institutional responsibility may have been diluted and diffused (despite the institutional hearings of the TRC), since, as a result of the TRC's revelations, blame for specific acts can so easily be attributed to individual actors. To the extent that the TRC sought to get people to understand that apartheid was a failure of the state and its institutions, not of specific individuals, it seems to have not been particularly successful.

An Index of Acceptance of the TRC's Truth

For purposes of hypothesis testing, it is useful to devise a summary index indicating the degree to which each South African accepts the truth as defined here. On the basis of the responses to these five statements, I calculated an index of truth acceptance. This summary score, which indicates the number of truths about apartheid endorsed by the respondent, is simply a count of the responses to the items, and hence it varies from 0 (rejecting all statements) to 5 (accepting the veracity of each one, that is, the two "true" responses and the three "false" responses).[16]

These five propositions refer to two different aspects of attitudes toward apartheid. Three items directly assess an individual's willingness to condemn apartheid: the belief that apartheid was a crime against humanity, that the ideas were not good ones, and that the struggle to preserve the system was not just.[17] The two remaining statements certainly offer judgments of apartheid but include as well beliefs about what happened during the struggle. Some believe that the evil of apartheid was in individuals, not in institutions, and some also believe that, even if apartheid was a desirable system, abuses were committed in its name (just as abuses were committed against it). Though all of these items are part of the TRC's collective memory package, the propositions represent a mixture of the attitudes and beliefs of the respondents.

This index of truth acceptance is therefore not identical to a simple measure of opposition to apartheid, although it is closely related. The single item on which a significant difference exists is on the assertion that both sides in the struggle committed atrocious acts. Some staunch opponents of apartheid would probably reject this statement (because the "just war" justified all acts), whereas those who accepted the collective memory as produced by the TRC would certainly accept the truth of this assertion. Thus, the TRC's truth is undoubtedly one condemning apartheid, even if it acknowledges that those struggling against the system occasionally used inhumane and unacceptable means.

Figure 3.1 reports the average scores on this index of the number of truths accepted for each of the four racial groups. Cross-race differences are statistically significant but far from large ($\eta = .15$). Not surprisingly, blacks are most likely to accept the veracity of these statements, whereas whites are least likely. However, the substantive differences are not nearly as great as one might have anticipated—the median number of items accepted for blacks, whites, Colored people, and those of Asian origin is three (data not shown).

On the other hand, considerable variability exists in how various ethnic, racial, and linguistic groups feel about the country's apartheid past. At one extreme, fewer than 10 percent of blacks speaking North Sotho and Shangaan accept the veracity of all of these statements, and only 5 percent of Afrikaans-speaking whites hold the same views (data not shown). At the other extreme are English-speaking Colored people, among whom fully 35 percent accept all five statements. Indeed, English-speaking Colored people are the most likely of any group to endorse these propositions—even more likely than black South Africans. Within groups, lan-

Figure 3.1 Acceptance of the TRC's Collective Memory—Average Number of Truths Accepted, by Race

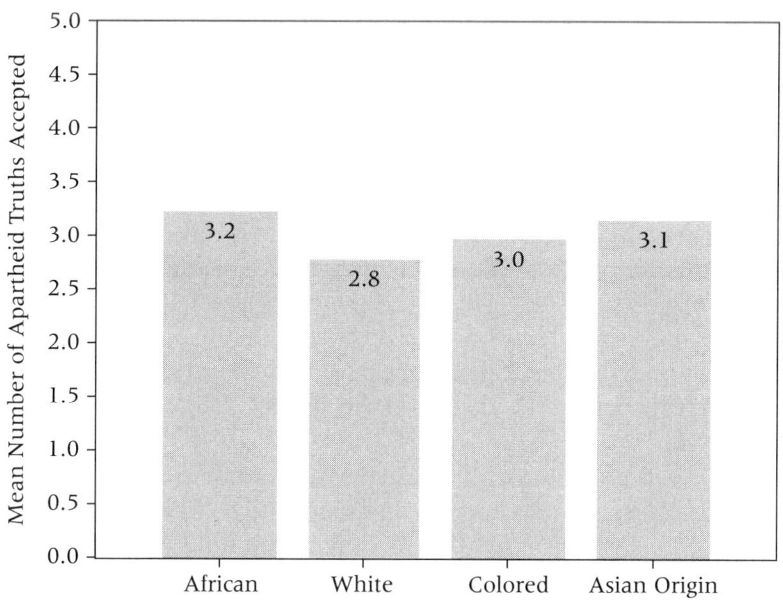

Source: Author's compilation from the 2001 Truth and Reconciliation Survey.
Note: Interracial difference of means: $p < .001$, $\eta = .15$.

guage does a reasonable job of differentiating among people in their views toward apartheid, as I demonstrate more rigorously later in this chapter.

This survey reveals that most South Africans of every race agree that apartheid as practiced in South Africa was a crime against humanity. Nonetheless, views about the country's apartheid past are complicated. In principle, apartheid is *not* perceived as inherently evil by everyone, even if most agree that apartheid ideas were implemented in South Africa in a criminal manner. Not surprisingly, whites are more forgiving of the failures of apartheid, but blacks, Colored people, and South Africans of Asian origin hold unexpectedly tolerant views of the country's apartheid past (most likely as it pertains to the idea of separate racial development, not racial hierarchy and domination). Generally speaking, the truth and reconciliation process seems to have been at least somewhat successful at exposing human rights abuses by all sides in the struggle over apartheid, thereby contributing to the country's collective memory about its apartheid past.

It is noteworthy that racial differences in truth acceptance are neither substantial nor particularly significant. Only on the question of whether apartheid was a crime against humanity do large racial differences exist, but even here it is a matter of the large white majority not being as big as the even larger black majority. On the number of truths accepted, racial differences are relatively small. Blacks, whites, Colored people, and those of Asian origin hold similar beliefs when it comes to the TRC's understanding of apartheid.

To this point I have established what South Africans believe about their past. I now turn to an investigation of the factors that may have led them to hold these views, beginning with the question of whether there is evidence that the TRC itself actually shaped contemporary understandings of the country's apartheid past.

Accounting for Variability in the Acceptance of the TRC's Truth

In measuring the degree to which each South African accepts the TRC's version of the truth about the country's apartheid past, I have reported results for the four major racial groups, because race seems inextricably related to understandings of the past. The last portion of this chapter changes tack and focuses instead on the theoretical factors that might account for this variability in truth acceptance.

This portion of the analysis begins with several conventional hypotheses. The first asserts that *those who were exposed to the activities of the TRC were more likely to accept its version of the truth.* Without doubt, the most rigorous way of ascertaining the impact of the commission on the thinking of South Africans would have been to do a survey panel, with interviews conducted both before the commission began its work and after that work was completed, but such a design has been lost to history.[18] Alternatively, I hypothesize that *those with more knowledge of the activities of the TRC are more likely to accept its truth about apartheid.*

For many South Africans, the revelations of the TRC—especially at the social and general levels considered here—were far from revealing. Those who lived under apartheid and were subject to its heavy boot no doubt harbored little uncertainty about whether the system was good or evil. Experience teaches. Thus, for many, exposure to the TRC was most likely of little consequence, since the information uncovered by the TRC was already known and understood to them.

This reasoning leads to the hypothesis that *experiences under apartheid are likely to predict truth acceptance.* Those who were harmed more and benefited less are more likely to condemn apartheid, irrespective of their exposure to the TRC. Though experiences under apartheid are surely closely related to race, using the direct measures available gives much better purchase on this hypothesis than treating race as a surrogate for apartheid experiences.

Following a long line of reasoning in the collective memory literature, I also hypothesize that *generational differences in attitudes toward apartheid are manifest within each racial group.* The youngest South Africans today have few direct experiences with apartheid and have been exposed during much of their lives to either a relatively benevolent white government or to the black leadership of the New South Africa. Older South Africans have had very different experiences. For this and many other reasons (for example, some older blacks were compromised by apartheid), I therefore expect young South Africans to be particularly critical of the country's apartheid past.

Some have speculated that what one believes about the past is connected to the social identity one adopts. For instance, Michael Ignatieff (1996, 114) argues that "truth is related to identity. What you believe to be true depends, in some measure, on who you believe yourself to be." Indeed, one way to think about race is to treat it as identity, substituting the subjective variable of group identification for the nominal variable of skin color. Since a number of different dimensions of group identity were measured in the survey (see chapter 2), I can consider the hypothesis that *group identity influences the degree to which the TRC's truth is accepted.*

Of course, these hypotheses cannot be tested rigorously without controls for a variety of other variables. For instance, an important cleavage even in contemporary South Africa is the divide between those dwelling in urban areas and their rural counterparts. At the close of this chapter, I examine in considerable detail a comprehensive account of the variance in the acceptance of the TRC's truth. Here I turn to the hypothesis linking exposure to the TRC with endorsement of its truth.

Accepting the Truth and the TRC

How much do these beliefs about South Africa's history reflect the influence of the activities of the TRC? This important question cannot, unfortunately, be answered definitively with the data at hand. Whether the TRC influenced attitudes is a question about *change,* and this survey could measure only attitudes at a single point in time. Therefore, any judgments about the causal influence of the TRC must be based on indirect evidence and inferential reasoning.[19]

One way of getting some purchase on the question of change is to begin from the hypothesis that two simple factors contributed to the ability of the TRC to convince South Africans of its version of the truth. First, to be effective, *the TRC had to capture the attention of people.* This leads to the expectation that those with more awareness of the TRC's activities are more likely to accept its truth.[20]

The second factor has to do with confidence, which is not the same variable as attentiveness. Some South Africans paid attention to the TRC precisely because they distrusted it so much. Whites in particular feared that the TRC was engaged in a witch hunt, and therefore they may have monitored the commission's actions to determine whether white interests were being unduly harmed. Thus, a second hypothesis is that *the TRC has had its greatest influence among those who were the most trustful of it.*

Both attentiveness to and confidence in the TRC are related to the race of the respondent, although at quite different levels. Modest differences exist across the four racial groups in knowledge of the activities of the TRC ($\eta = .13, p < .001$).[21] The group primarily contributing to this difference, however, is Colored people, who are significantly more likely to report knowing little or nothing about the commission. Figure 3.2 displays the percentage of respondents who claim virtually no knowledge of the activities of the TRC. Though the TRC passed by few black, white, and Asian South Africans, fully one-third of Colored people claim to be unaware of the commission's activities. Perhaps this reflects the perception among some Colored people that the events and history addressed by the TRC are not of much relevance to them.

When it comes to confidence in the TRC, racial differences are far more substantial ($\eta = .48, p < .001$). Figure 3.3 reports the percentage of respondents expressing either "a great deal" or "quite a lot" of confidence in the commission.[22] Approximately two-thirds of the African respondents express high levels of confidence in the TRC, whereas fewer than one in five whites is of a similar opinion. Roughly one-third of Colored people and of those of Asian origin trust the commission. Thus, we see from the data in these two figures that the TRC has attracted a great deal of attention from the African majority in South Africa and that, unlike their fellow South Africans, most blacks have considerable confidence in the TRC. This finding will surely surprise many observers of the truth and reconciliation process, even if the finding of white displeasure with the TRC is entirely expected.

In light of these interracial differences, it is natural to observe quite different relationships across the four racial groups between confidence in the TRC and attentiveness to its activities. At one extreme, knowledge and confidence are very strongly related: the correlation among Colored respondents is .56. At the other extreme, among whites the two variables are only weakly correlated ($r = .11$), although it is noteworthy that the relationship is positive, not negative (more knowledge is associated with greater confidence). For black and Asian South Africans, the correlations are positive and moderate ($r = .26$ and $.24$, respectively). Though I

Figure 3.2 Lack of Awareness of the Activities of the TRC, by Race

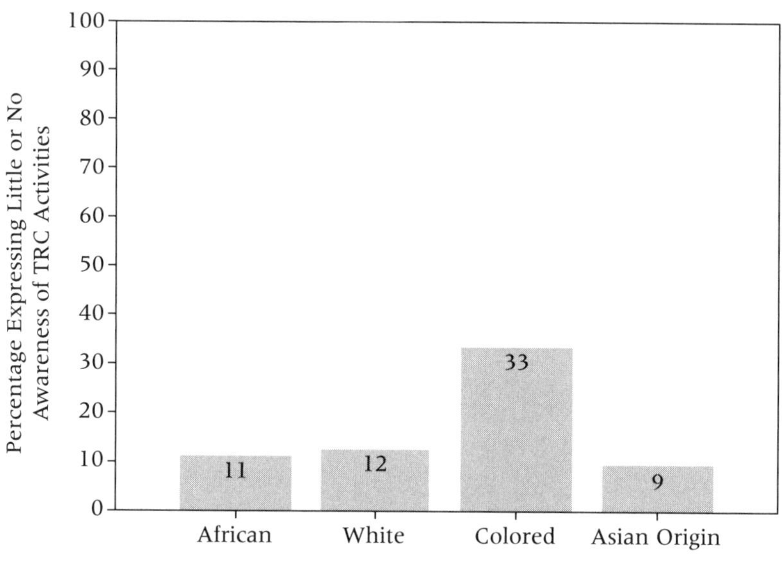

Source: Author's compilation from the 2001 Truth and Reconciliation Survey.
Note: The interracial differences on the full awareness measure are as follows: $p < .001$, $\eta = .13$.

cannot definitively judge the direction of causality here, it seems that in general paying more attention to the TRC may have made South Africans of every race at least somewhat more confident in the commission.[23] Those who are least confident are those who have been least attentive to the activities of the TRC.

But a central question of this research is whether knowledge of the TRC's activities translates into agreeing with the TRC's truth. For many South Africans, knowing more about the TRC is indeed associated with greater acceptance of the truth. The hypothesis is supported for all but black South Africans ($r = -.04$). Among whites, Colored people, and South Africans of Asian origin, greater attentiveness to the activities of the TRC is related to greater acceptance of the truth about the country's apartheid past, with respective correlations of .12, .23, and .12. These relationships are not

Figure 3.3 Confidence in the TRC, by Race

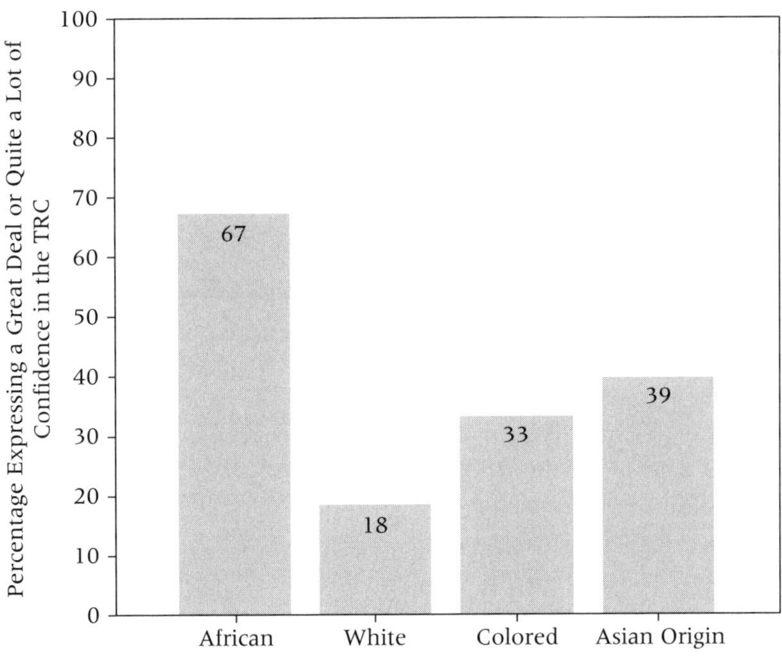

Source: Author's compilation from the 2001 Truth and Reconciliation Survey.
Note: The interracial differences on the full confidence measure are as follows: $p < .001$, $\eta = .48$.

particularly strong, but these data indicate that it is plausible that the activities of the TRC contributed to truth acceptance among nonblack South Africans. What people believe about the country's past seems to reflect at least in part what they learned from tending to the activities of the TRC.

Perhaps another factor involved in these relationships is source credibility—that is, confidence in the TRC itself. Many South Africans are deeply distrustful and critical of the TRC, ranging from some blacks who are angry with the commission for its "poisonous evenhandedness" (in seeming to equate atrocities committed by those struggling against apartheid with those committed by people struggling to defend apartheid) to whites who criticize what they see as a strong pro-ANC bias in the process. It may well be that confidence moderates the relationship between attentiveness to the TRC and acceptance of the truth.

Among whites and Colored people, confidence does indeed have a direct effect on truth acceptance: as confidence in the TRC increases, so too does acceptance of the truth. Among blacks and those of Asian origin, however, no such relationship exists, and indeed, I found slight *negative* relationships (among blacks, $r = -.10$; among South Africans of Asian origin, $r = -.06$). That the relationship between confidence and truth acceptance would be negative adds to the puzzle (even if these coefficients are so small as to be virtually trivial).

The most interesting hypothesis is that confidence interacts with attentiveness, serving in effect as a weight attached to attentiveness. *When confidence is high, I hypothesize that attentiveness readily translates into truth acceptance. But when confidence is low, attentiveness should have few consequences for truth.* This hypothesis can be tested using an interactive equation incorporating the linear effects of attentiveness and confidence and the conditional effect of the multiplicative term between the two variables.

The hypothesis receives some support, but only among white South Africans (a group among whom confidence is generally low).[24] When confidence in the TRC is low, attentiveness contributes nothing to truth acceptance ($b = .03$). When confidence is high, however, attentiveness does indeed seem to influence acceptance ($b = .21$), just as hypothesized. Among Africans and Colored people there is some weak indication of a significant interactive relationship, but the sign of the coefficient is in the wrong direction. Thus, among whites, confidence in the commission seems to be a necessary condition for influence. This seems not to be so among other South Africans.

When it comes to black South Africans, the connections between confidence, awareness, and truth acceptance offer many intriguing puzzles, especially as concerns the basic finding that knowledge of the TRC and its activities is unrelated to acceptance of the TRC's truth. This result is particularly enigmatic since black South Africans not only are highly aware of the TRC but express high levels of confidence in it as well (although there is considerable variability among blacks on both of these measures).

To investigate further these puzzling findings about black South Africans, it is useful to return to the individual components of the truth acceptance index. I hypothesize that *where the TRC has been effective at communicating its message, there is relatively widespread agreement with the TRC's viewpoint, and knowledge of and trust in the TRC are related to truth acceptance*. That is, TRC success should be indicated by agreement with the commission's viewpoints and with high levels of awareness and trust. Table 3.2 reports the evidence necessary for testing these hypotheses.

Table 3.2 reports quite a lot of information about the nature of black beliefs about the TRC's truth. The first column is simply the percentage of Africans accepting the view of the TRC. The second column shows the degree of variability in truth acceptance, with high scores indicating greater disagreement over the TRC's conclusion. Columns 3 and 4 report the bivariate correlation coefficients between truth acceptance and knowledge of the activities of the TRC and confidence in the commission itself. If the TRC has had an impact on black attitudes, these coefficients would most likely be positive. The two columns reporting multivariate significance refer to an equation in which both knowledge and confidence are predictors of the responses to the individual truth statements. The coefficients reported are probabilities from a test of statistical significance in which the null hypothesis is that confidence and awareness are each unrelated to truth acceptance (that is, that the regression coefficient is indistinguishable from zero). These significance tests must be understood in conjunction with the signs of the coefficients. In nearly every instance, the sign of the multivariate regression coefficient is the same as the sign of the bivariate coefficient.[25] In interpreting these coefficients, one should bear in mind that the correlation between confidence and knowledge among blacks is .26 (as reported earlier in this chapter).

Table 3.2 Knowledge of and Confidence in the TRC and Acceptance of the TRC's Truth Among Black South Africans

			Knowledge of the TRC		Confidence in the TRC	
	Accepting TRC's Truth	Variance (σ^2)	Bivariate Correlation	Multivariate Significance	Bivariate Correlation	Multivariate Significance
Apartheid was a crime against humanity. (true)	94.3%	.80	.03	n.s.	.06**	.008
Despite abuses, apartheid ideas were good. (false)	58.7	1.52	−.07***	.054	−.11***	.000
The struggle to preserve apartheid was just. (false)	57.3	1.59	−.10**	.004	−.16***	.000
Both sides did unforgivable things. (true)	76.1	.98	.08***	.010	.10***	.000
Abuses were due to individuals, not institutions. (false)	35.1	1.30	.01	n.s.	−.07***	.000

Source: Author's compilation from the 2001 Truth and Reconciliation Survey.
Note: For the multivariate analysis, probabilities are shown if they are less than .10.
n.s. = not statistically significant at $p \geq .10$.
***$p < .001$; **$p < .01$; *$p < .05$

Among black South Africans, the strongest evidence of an influence of the TRC can be found on the statement that both sides in the struggle did horrible things. This is the one "truth" that may not have been widely accepted prior to the revelations of the TRC. This conclusion is now fairly widely endorsed among blacks (76.1 percent), and relatedly, there is not a great deal of divergence of opinion in the black community (σ^2 = .98). Both greater knowledge of the TRC and confidence in the TRC contribute (and do so independently) to acceptance of the view that both sides committed abuses during the struggle (both of the multivariate coefficients are highly statistically significant). These relationships are not particularly strong—for instance, while 72.6 percent of Africans with no confidence in the TRC accept that both sides in the struggle engaged in human rights abuses, 79.2 percent of those with a great deal of confidence in the commission hold the same view (data not shown)—but they do constitute the best evidence of an influence of the TRC on the beliefs of black South Africans about the past.[26]

A few of the coefficients for black South Africans are unexpectedly negative. For instance, those who paid more attention to the TRC and trusted it more are *less likely* to believe it to be false that the struggle to preserve apartheid was just (r = −.10 and −.16, respectively), just as they are more likely to accept the contention that some of the ideas of apartheid were good (r = −.07 and −.11, respectively). This suggests that some may have learned a lesson from the TRC that was contrary to its intention (since the commission's conclusions roundly condemned apartheid).

If I understand the causality correctly here, it seems that blacks who paid more attention to the TRC came to understand something about the legitimacy of apartheid and its defense, irrespective of whether that was the intent of the TRC. Indeed, if we reconsider the data in this table from the point of view of substantive opinions (rather than simple acceptance or rejection of the TRC position), black South Africans who know and trust the TRC more are:

- more likely to accept that the ideas behind apartheid were good;
- more likely to believe that the struggle to preserve apartheid was just; and

- more likely to believe that both sides in the struggle did horrible things.

And those with more confidence in the TRC are slightly more likely to believe that:

- apartheid was a problem of people, not institutions; and
- apartheid was a crime against humanity.

Thus, in almost every instance, greater awareness of and confidence in the truth and reconciliation process is associated with *more moderate attitudes among Africans toward apartheid* and its people and institutions. This finding is perhaps somewhat contrary to the intentions of the TRC itself. Many believe that the revelations of the TRC hardened attitudes toward apartheid and the past. These data seem to indicate otherwise. This is an important finding that must be borne in mind throughout the analysis reported in this book.

These findings strongly suggest that the activities of the TRC did indeed contribute to greater acceptance of the truth about the country's apartheid past among whites, Colored people, and those of Asian origin. The more one knows about the affairs of the TRC, the more likely one is to accept the TRC's truth. These findings are of themselves significant for reconciliation in South Africa. It seems that the TRC was successful in getting some South Africans to moderate their views about apartheid by accepting that many horrific things were done in the name of racial separation. For many, the TRC seems to have challenged the basic legitimacy of apartheid, thereby moderating their views of the past.

Black South Africans are another matter. Here there is no clear evidence that the TRC's activities shaped views about the country's apartheid past. Indeed, the data seem to suggest that, among blacks, the TRC's lessons may have been badly misunderstood. Final conclusions should not be drawn prior to the multivariate analysis considered later in this chapter, but from these data, the TRC seems not to have done much to build its version of a collective memory among the African majority in South Africa.

Indeed, once we recall how similar white and black opinions are today (at the time of the survey) on many of these issues, it is reasonable to suggest that the process moved blacks and whites in opposite directions, away from their historical positions as polarized enemies, *bringing them closer together in their views about South Africa's apartheid past.* If this is so, then the truth and reconciliation process contributed to reconciliation in South Africa by constructing a collective memory—a moderate view of apartheid—that is shared by blacks and whites alike. This is a finding of considerable importance.

One obvious explanation for the weak relationships between attentiveness to the TRC and beliefs about the past among black South Africans is that blacks did not need to learn of the country's experience with apartheid from the TRC, since they were already painfully aware, through their own experience, of what apartheid had done to the country. The TRC's exposés of gross human rights violations were perhaps new information for many in South Africa, but not for most Africans, who learned these lessons simply from living every day under apartheid. Thus, it is essential that I consider carefully the influence of experience on the ways in which South Africans understand their country's past.

The Influence of Apartheid Experiences on Truth Acceptance

As noted in some detail in chapter 2, apartheid did not treat all South Africans equally. For instance, 37.7 percent of our black respondents claim to have lived a little or a lot better under apartheid than at the time of this survey. It may well be that personal experience makes acceptance of the truth about apartheid more likely. Consequently, I hypothesize that *those harmed by apartheid are more willing to endorse a truth that is critical of the country's past.* This hypothesis requires that I rely on the measures of experiences that South Africans have had with apartheid that were developed and discussed in chapter 2.

Do these experiences under apartheid shape views of the truth of South Africa's past? Since the TRC's truth strongly condemns apartheid, I expect that those who were harmed by apartheid accept that truth and that those who were not harmed tend to reject it. Similarly, those who benefited from apartheid are unlikely to endorse the TRC's truth. It would be unusual for those who were the beneficiaries of the old system to accept that apartheid was a crime against humanity, that the struggle to preserve it was unjust, and so on.

Testing this hypothesis using the experiential variables should also provide a better understanding of the racial differences in truth acceptance identified earlier. With race, we must always ask *exactly what it is about race* that accounts for observed differences. Race can be a surrogate for many other variables (such as social class or experiences). In this instance, I hypothesize that *most racial differences in accepting the truth about the past are associated with how well one fared under the apartheid system.*

Table 3.3 reports the results of two regressions. The index of truth acceptance is first regressed on the degree to which the respondent was harmed by apartheid, and then on the degree to which the respondent benefited from apartheid. The second regression is based on the index of the net benefits of apartheid (as discussed in chapter 2). Both regressions are reported so as to determine whether absolute or relative experiences are more consequential for understanding apartheid attitudes.

Among black South Africans, suffering harms under apartheid is indeed associated with greater acceptance of the TRC's truth. Those who benefited more from apartheid, on the other hand, are less likely to participate in the truth, although this relationship is not particularly strong. In general, blacks who are net beneficiaries of apartheid are less likely to accept the TRC's truth, although, not unexpectedly, the driving force in this relationship seems to be harms, not benefits (on which there is considerably less variance). In this sense, experiences under apartheid continue to have an influence over blacks today.

Among whites, the relationships are not entirely the same. Like blacks, whites who were harmed more are more likely to accept the truth about apartheid. Of course, the harm that whites experienced was not from blacks (most likely) but instead from the apart-

Table 3.3 The Effect of Apartheid Experiences on Truth Acceptance, by Race

	Degree of Acceptance of the TRC's Truth
Harms from apartheid	
African	.14***
White	.23***
Colored	.22***
Asian origin	.03
Benefits from apartheid	
African	−.07***
White	.08*
Colored	−.15***
Asian origin	−.29***
Harms minus benefits from apartheid	
African	−.13***
White	.06
Colored	−.22***
Asian origin	−.31***

Source: Author's compilation from the 2001 Truth and Reconciliation Survey.
Note: The coefficients for harms and benefits are from a multiple regression analysis including both independent variables. The coefficients reported are standardized regression coefficients (β).
The coefficients for the "harms minus benefits" variable are also standardized regression coefficients, resulting from regressing each of the dependent variables on a single variable indicating the differences between the benefits and harms experienced under apartheid. This variable is coded such that higher scores indicate greater net benefits from apartheid.
***$p \leq .001$; **$p \leq .01$; *$p \leq .05$

heid system itself, so the harm variable takes on a somewhat different meaning for whites as compared to blacks. Perceived benefits have little to do with white attitudes, perhaps because to the extent that whites view themselves as beneficiaries of apartheid, they view their *group* (white people in general) as having benefited rather than accept that they *individually* profited from apartheid, thereby reducing the impact of this attitude. Net experiences with apartheid have little impact on white attitudes toward blacks, perhaps because the variable is so strongly skewed in the direction of net benefits (see chapter 2).

The pattern of relationships is different among Colored people as well. Like blacks and whites, Colored people who were harmed more by apartheid are more likely to endorse the truth about it. But unlike whites and blacks, a substantively significant relationship exists between benefits and attitudes, with those benefiting more being less likely to accept the TRC's truth, perhaps because many Colored people report that they were beneficiaries of the apartheid system (thereby contributing to greater variance in the independent variable). The "net benefits of apartheid" variable consequently predicts truth acceptance fairly strongly, with net beneficiaries of apartheid being less likely to condemn the old system.

A final pattern emerges with South Africans of Asian origin, among whom being injured by apartheid has nothing to do with beliefs about the past. But, like Colored South Africans, those who accept that they benefited from apartheid are considerably less likely to subscribe to the truth about the past. Because they benefited, they are less likely to condemn the apartheid past. The net benefits of apartheid thus strongly predict acceptance of the truth.

Apartheid experiences were varied, and consequently it is not particularly surprising that apartheid left different attitudinal residues, depending on one's race. Except for whites—most of whom admit being beneficiaries of the apartheid system—those who were net beneficiaries of apartheid tend not to accept the truth about the past. Not all of these relationships are strong—and indeed, some may be obliterated in the multivariate analysis later in this chapter—but experiences do seem to have something to do with contemporary attitudes toward South Africa's past.

Unraveling the Puzzle of Black South Africans' Views of the Past

The findings seem to indicate that the attitudes of black South Africans are shaped more by their experiences with apartheid than by their exposure to the activities of the TRC. Still, the puzzle remains that large percentages of blacks do not uniformly condemn apartheid (as shown in table 3.1). Further, on some aspects of the truth, negative relationships between exposure to the TRC and acceptance of its truth exist. Because several of the findings from my analysis of black South Africans do not seem to be internally consistent, and because the question of the direction of the causal flow is still quite unsettled for black South Africans, additional analysis must be conducted.

The truths about apartheid, as I have identified them, actually represent two different kinds of truth. Three of the statements I put to the respondents are directly and strongly critical of apartheid. The remaining two statements, in contrast, tend to exculpate apartheid, in part by asserting that abuses were committed by all sides and in part by blaming atrocities on institutions rather than individuals. As I have noted, the TRC sought to get South Africans to accept a balanced view of the past rather than a one-sided and dogmatic view that everything about apartheid was horrible and everything about the liberation forces was wonderful. To understand more clearly African views of the past, it is perhaps useful to separate these two types of viewpoints. Thus, for the following analysis, I have created a three-item index of attitudes toward apartheid based on the propositions that apartheid was a crime against humanity, that apartheid ideas were bad, and that the defense of apartheid was unjustifiable.

Reversing the causality, it may well be that those blacks who are less likely to condemn apartheid *in the first place* were more likely to pay attention to the TRC and have confidence in it. The logic of this causal argument goes something as follows. If the TRC influenced attitudes toward apartheid, those who were more knowledgeable about the activities of the TRC would be more likely to condemn apartheid because that is the position the TRC took. That more knowledge is associated with a less negative attitude toward apartheid may well mean that those who were more accepting of apartheid in the first place were the most likely to pay attention to the activities of the commission. The TRC by its very existence represented a compromise with apartheid; the most hardened anti-apartheid activist is hardly likely to have been an enthusiastic supporter of the commission (even if some activists were indeed reluctant supporters). Thus, there is an appealing logic to reversing the causal flow: attentiveness to the TRC sprang from attitudes toward apartheid rather than vice versa.

But it is perplexing that not all of the relationships between exposure to the TRC and acceptance of each truth are of the same nature. If we speculate about the causal structure underlying these relationships, especially by adding a dynamic dimension, the following story might be constructed.

- Those who were harmed more by apartheid judge the system more negatively. The correlation among Africans between the amount of harm experienced and a three-item index of opposition to apartheid is .11.
- Those holding more negative attitudes toward apartheid are less likely to pay attention to the truth and reconciliation process and to acquire information from it. The correlation between apartheid attitudes and attentiveness to the TRC is −.09.
- Attentiveness to the TRC, however, is *positively* correlated with the belief that both sides in the struggle committed atrocities ($r = .08$).
- On the other hand, this belief that both sides were culpable is negatively related to overall judgments of apartheid: the more one opposes apartheid, the less likely one is to accept the view that human rights abuses were engaged in by all sides in the struggle ($r = -.11$).
- Thus, as a dynamic process, there is some tendency for preexisting attitudes to influence attentiveness toward the TRC proceedings, but learning from the activities of the TRC changes attitudes as well, particularly attitudes regarding the culpability of both sides in the struggle.

I cannot emphasize too strongly that these relationships are quite weak, that my understanding of these relationships is conjectural, and that the findings are perhaps compatible with other causal processes. But they are also compatible with the processes just outlined. The TRC seemed to attract the attention of black South Africans already predisposed not to judge apartheid harshly, but it then contributed to these moderate views by convincing blacks that both sides in the struggle did things for which they should be blamed. The relationship between exposure to the TRC and attitude change is reciprocal: each caused each. Thus, this analysis has adduced important evidence that the TRC actually influenced the collective memory of Africans and that perhaps its influence was mainly to moderate beliefs about the evils of apartheid.

Age Differences in Accepting the Truth

The literature on collective memories devotes considerable attention to generational differences in beliefs about the past, typically under the assumption that learning about political events during the early stages of one's life cycle has a more enduring impact on beliefs and attitudes than learning at later points in the cycle. The most obvious example is the age cohort defined by an event, such as the Vietnam War generation in the United States.

Not all empirical evidence, however, supports the view of generational differences. For instance, Schuman and Corning (2000, 951) believe that when collective memory is measured in terms of the spontaneous remembrances of respondents, age has much to do with the results. But when more objective measures of memory are considered, the influence of age is markedly weaker. They conclude: "Thus, personal memories may refer back primarily to experiences during one's adolescence or early adulthood, while objective knowledge more easily spans all the events experienced over a lifetime, as well as reaching backward to a past not directly experienced by the individual." Since apartheid was not a discrete event, and since it was an overbearing fact of daily life for all South Africans, generational differences in beliefs about the country's past should be expected to be minimal.

Among black South Africans, age has nothing to do with acceptance of the truth about apartheid. I find neither a linear effect of the continuous age variable nor a monotonic effect associated with age categories. Nor do the youngest blacks hold distinctive attitudes (defining the young as those born between 1975 and 1983). Finally, even atheoretical curvilinear effects (as indexed by the curvilinear correlation coefficient, η) are trivial. I can conclude with great confidence that age and participation in the collective memory about the past are unrelated among black South Africans.

Pretty much the same is true of white South Africans. Truth acceptance declines ever so slightly with age ($r = -.07$), and nearly all of the effect is linear. The weakness (or even triviality) of this relationship is demonstrated by the average number of statements about the past accepted by the youngest and oldest groups: 2.7 and 2.8, respectively (with standard deviations of approximately 1.4). The youngest whites thus differ insignificantly from their older counterparts. The most reasonable conclusion from these data is that age and generation matter little among whites in terms of their relationships with the past.

The conclusion for Colored South Africans is similar to that for whites. Linear, nonlinear, and monotonic effects are small, if not trivial, and they are statistically insignificant. Nor are Colored young people distinctive in their attitudes toward apartheid.

South Africans of Asian origin are another matter. Here I observe a reasonably strong linear effect of age ($r = -.23$), and young South Africans of Asian origin are certainly distinctive in their greater acceptance of the truth about apartheid. The youngest cohort endorses on average 3.6 of the statements; the oldest cohort accepts only 2.6 of them. This is a highly significant difference. The number of cases available for analysis is small, but age seems to matter considerably for those of Asian origin (and the effect of age can be captured in a linear, continuous variable).

For the vast majority of South Africans, acceptance of the truth about South Africa's apartheid past is associated with neither age nor generation. Surely this is because apartheid had such a pervasive impact on South African society, and because I am analyzing broad understandings and evaluations of history rather than remembrances of specific happenings. The uprising in Paris in 1968 was an event that was not of equal salience to all French (or American) people, and as a consequence generational differences emerged. But apartheid was not an "event" with generation-specific meaning (except perhaps for those of Asian origin), and therefore the collective memory about apartheid in South Africa is a memory shared or not shared irrespective of age.

Social Identities and Truth Acceptance

The exact nature of the hypotheses linking group identities and truth acceptance requires some additional elaboration. Among Africans, Colored people, and those of Asian origin, I hypothesize that stronger group identities are associated with more acceptance of the TRC's truth. The logic here is that the TRC largely condemned apartheid, and those identifying more strongly with "Black" groups are also more likely to condemn apartheid.

Among whites, however, I expect that stronger group identities are associated with *rejection* of the TRC and its truth. This hypothesis is based in part on the supposition that whites were generally opposed to the truth and reconciliation process and mainly thought of its inquiries as contrary to their interests (see Gibson and Macdonald 2001). Certainly the TRC itself was quite critical of whites as a group. Consequently, the more whites identify with their groups, the more likely they are to reject the truth as promulgated by the TRC. Table 3.4 reports the empirical evidence relevant to these hypotheses.

The strongest and clearest finding in this table has to do with attitudes toward the political relevance of groups in South Africa. For those of every race, people who believe that groups are highly important in South African politics are quite a bit less likely to accept the TRC's truth. This finding means that those who still believe that South African politics is the politics of group struggle are less likely to accept the TRC's position on apartheid. One might have expected exactly the opposite relationship—that those more strongly attached to their group would be more likely to accept the TRC's truth since it strongly condemns apartheid. Such is not the case. And to reiterate, this relationship characterizes all South Africans, irrespective of race. This finding is important and requires further explication.

Perhaps those who believe in the relevance of groups hold more benign attitudes toward apartheid because they accept the legitimacy of group segregation. For instance, of the Africans agreeing that groups are necessary to getting something out of South African politics, 46 percent also agree that the ideas behind apartheid

Table 3.4 Racial Differences in the Impact of Social Identities on Truth Acceptance

Social Identity Dimension	African	White	Colored	Asian Origin
Existence of South African identity				
b	.01	.22	.09	−.02
Standard error	.03	.05	.06	.10
β	.00	.14***	.07	−.01
Strength of South African identity				
b	−.02	−.04	−.07	.14
Standard error	.02	.03	.04	.06
β	−.02	−.04	−.07	.16*
Strength of primary identity				
b	.03	−.05	−.01	−.06
Standard error	.03	.04	.06	.09
β	.03	−.05	−.01	−.05
Psychic benefits of identity				
b	.12	−.07	−.09	−.05
Standard error	.02	.03	.04	.07
β	.13***	−.07*	−.10*	−.06
Any anti-identity				
b	−.06	−.15	.24	.14
Standard error	.09	.09	.07	.28
β	−.02	−.05	.15***	.03
Group solidarity				
b	.03	−.12	.14	.09
Standard error	.03	.04	.05	.08
β	.04	−.14**	.17**	.10
Political relevance of groups				
b	−.26	−.18	−.28	−.24
Standard error	.03	.04	.06	.08
β	−.32***	−.18***	−.30***	−.25**
Intercept	3.40	3.74	3.93	3.22
Standard error	.15	.19	.45	.45
R-squared	.10***	.14***	.10***	.07**
Standard deviation—dependent variable	.70	.73	.67	.68
Standard error of estimate	.67	.68	.65	.67
Number of cases	1,991	946	472	245

Source: Author's compilation from the 2001 Truth and Reconciliation Survey.
Note: The dependent variable in this analysis is the degree of acceptance of the TRC's truth.
***$p \leq .001$; **$p \leq .01$; *$p \leq .05$

were basically good ideas (data not shown). In contrast, only 23 percent of those disagreeing that groups are important endorse the ideas behind apartheid.[27] What these data seem to suggest is that those who believe in the political relevance of groups also tend to approve of the separation of groups and therefore do not uniformly condemn apartheid. When groups are deemed to be relevant, then it follows that groups have the right to organize and protect themselves and to separate from others. This finding comports with my earlier conclusion that how Africans feel about apartheid depends in part on their perception of the legitimacy of racial segregation.

One other finding pertains to South Africans of all races: the strength of one's primary group identity has *nothing* to do with one's beliefs about the past. This is consistent with our earlier research in South Africa indicating that group identities per se have few direct consequences for attitudes (see, for example, Gibson and Gouws 2003). Rather, it is the attitudes that are sometimes (but not inevitably) associated with identities that are consequential.

Few other findings in table 3.4 consistently characterize South Africans of all races. For instance, strong national identities influence only whites (their nominal identity with South Africa) and Colored people (the strength of their national identities). For Africans and Colored people, commitments to South Africa have no consequences for understandings of the past. These identities may be more significant for whites and those of Asian origin, since in principle at least some members of these two groups have divided national loyalties. Colored people and Africans generally have no national connections other than to South Africa. Before trying to interpret these group-specific findings further, it is useful to consider whether the relationships persist in a multivariate analysis.

Multivariate Analysis

To this point, I have examined the correlates of truth acceptance individually and without extensive control variables. I have taken this analytical approach so as to explicate as clearly as possible some of the most common hypotheses in the literature, such as the age-memory connection.[28] More definitive and comprehensive consideration of the origins of beliefs about the country's past obviously requires multivariate analysis.

Table 3.5 reports the results of regressing the measure of truth acceptance on a variety of predictor variables, ranging from those discussed earlier in this chapter to a series of control variables. The table is complicated, in part because it is necessary to report the results separately for each of the four major racial groups in South Africa. The predictors in the table include those connected to the TRC (for example, knowledge of the TRC), the group identity measures, as well as indicators of cognitive mobilization (for example, media consumption) and a number of conventional control variables (such as size of place of residence—see chapter 2 for a discussion of these variables).

I must note initially that, in general, the equations do a reasonable job in predicting who is and who is not likely to accept the TRC's truth, even if the amount of variance explained by the equation varies somewhat, from a low of 14 percent among Africans to a high of 26 percent among Colored South Africans.[29]

Second, the degree to which black South Africans accept the truth about apartheid depends mainly on their beliefs about the political relevance of groups in South African politics, the degree to which they benefited from apartheid, and the extent to which they derive psychic benefits from their group identifications. Thus, the identity variables provide considerable purchase on why some endorse the TRC's truth and others do not. The black South Africans most likely to agree with the TRC's version of the truth are those who reject group-based politics, but who nonetheless find group identity to be significant (they derive some benefits from their group identifications), and who were harmed by apartheid. The factors that do not predict black attitudes toward the truth are also important: for instance, there is a complete lack of relationship between truth acceptance and size of place of residence, age, gender, or class. Reactions to the TRC's truth do not vary by the conventional sources of disagreement within the black community such as class and gender.

Among whites, acceptance of the truth is more common among

those whose home language is English, not Afrikaans (the strongest relationship) and who have more contact with blacks, express more confidence in the TRC, are of a higher social class, and believe in the importance of group solidarity.[30] It should be reiterated that these are all independent effects, such that the influence of home language, for example, is independent of the respondent's social class and group attitudes. Perhaps the most interesting findings here are that contact with black South Africans contributes to accepting the truth about the past, as well as the rather dramatic independent effect of being Afrikaans. Whites who speak Afrikaans as their home language are substantially less likely to participate in South Africa's collective memory, ceteris paribus. Further, those whites motivated to seek out interracial interactions are more likely to accept the TRC's condemnation of apartheid. Generally, the identity variables have rather weak influences on truth acceptance among white South Africans.

Among Colored people, four variables stand out as particularly strong predictors of truth acceptance. Most important, Colored South Africans who believe strongly in the relevance of groups in politics are less likely to accept the TRC's truth. In addition, better-educated Colored people and those who were harmed under apartheid are more likely to endorse the TRC's view of South African history. More moderate but still highly significant effects can be seen for gender, home language, and interest in politics. Those who reject the collective memory tend to be less interested in politics, speakers of Afrikaans, and women.

The degree to which South Africans of Asian origin accept the truth is very much a function of their relationship to apartheid (whether or not they were beneficiaries), their age, and their beliefs about the political relevance of groups. In addition, endorsement of the TRC position is more likely among those who have adopted a strong national identity, those who live in rural areas, those from a higher social class, and females.

Across all South Africans, the best predictor of views about the apartheid past is attitudes toward the political relevance of groups. For all except whites, those who see groups as having greater political relevance are less likely to accept the truth (and even among

Table 3.5 Multivariate Determinants of Truth Acceptance by South Africans

	Africans				Whites			
	b	Standard Error	β	r	b	Standard Error	β	r
Interracial contact	.01	.02	.01	.05	.09	.02	.14***	.27
Net benefits of apartheid	−.04	.01	−.14***	−.13	−.00	.01	−.00	.05
Knowledge of the TRC	−.03	.02	−.03*	−.05	.03	.03	.03	.12
Confidence in the TRC	−.07	.02	−.09***	−.10	.09	.03	.10**	.19
Strength of South African identity	−.01	.02	−.01	−.03	−.01	.03	−.02	−.16
Psychic benefits of identity	.12	.02	.13***	.13	−.04	.03	−.04	−.18
Group solidarity	.04	.03	.05	−.17	−.10	.04	−.11**	−.30
Political relevance of groups	−.26	.03	−.31***	−.29	−.08	.04	−.09*	−.28
Media consumption	.06	.02	.08**	.08	.05	.03	.06*	.07
Interest in politics	.01	.02	.01	.02	.00	.03	.00	.06
Opinion leadership	−.07	.06	−.03	.00	.02	.06	.01	.05
Level of education	.03	.02	.04	.05	.06	.02	.08**	.21
Illiteracy	.03	.02	.04	−.01	−.03	.10	−.01	−.07
Afrikaans language	—	—	—	—	−.28	.05	−.19***	−.33
Age	−.00	.00	−.02	−.01	−.00	.00	−.05	−.09
Social class	−.00	.02	−.00	−.04	−.10	.03	−.10**	−.18
Size of place of residence	−.00	.01	−.01	−.06	−.04	.02	−.07*	−.13
Gender	−.02	.03	−.01	−.03	.07	.04	.05	.04
Intercept	3.33	.17			3.33	.22		
Standard deviation—dependent variable	.71				.73			
Standard error of estimate	.66				.64			
R-squared			.14				.25	
Number of cases	1,950				924			

Table 3.5 (Continued)

	Colored South Africans				South Africans of Asian Origin			
	b	Standard Error	β	r	b	Standard Error	β	r
Interracial contact	−.02	.02	−.03	.06	−.04	.04	−.06	.02
Net benefits of apartheid	−.04	.01	−.16***	−.22	−.05	.01	−.27***	−.31
Knowledge of the TRC	.00	.04	.00	.21	.06	.07	.06	.11
Confidence in the TRC	−.01	.04	−.01	.11	−.06	.05	−.07	−.05
Strength of South African identity	−.04	.04	−.04	−.08	.12	.07	.14	.13
Psychic benefits of identity	.00	.04	.00	−.13	−.00	.06	−.00	−.02
Group solidarity	.13	.05	.15**	−.07	.05	.08	.06	−.05
Political relevance of groups	−.26	.05	−.27***	−.22	−.20	.07	−.22**	−.21
Media consumption	.04	.03	.06	.23	.00	.06	.00	.03
Interest in politics	.08	.04	.12*	.28	.06	.05	.07	.14
Opinion leadership	−.17	.09	−.08	.02	.10	.13	.05	.14
Level of education	.12	.04	.18**	.31	−.04	.06	−.05	.14
Illiteracy	−.01	.05	−.02	−.20	.07	.08	.07	−.02
Afrikaans language	−.23	.09	−.14**	−.27	—	—	—	—
Age	.00	.00	.03	−.01	−.01	.00	−.19**	−.16
Social class	.06	.04	.08	−.17	−.08	.05	−.11	−.18
Size of place of residence	−.03	.02	−.08	−.21	.06	.03	.12	−.02
Gender	−.19	.06	−.14**	−.18	−.14	.09	−.10	−.11
Intercept	3.48	.32			3.80	.44		
Standard deviation—dependent variable	.68				.69			
Standard error of estimate	.60				.63			
R-squared			.26				.22	
Number of cases	447				241			

Source: Author's compilation from the 2001 Truth and Reconciliation Survey.
Significance of standardized regression coefficient (β): ***p ≤ .001; **p ≤ .01; *p ≤ .05.

whites, the weak coefficient achieves statistical significance). As I noted earlier in the chapter, this most likely means that those who accept the legitimacy of group difference and separation are less likely to condemn apartheid unequivocally. The second best predictor is the measure of the net benefits of apartheid. Again, except for whites, those who were beneficiaries of apartheid are less likely to adopt the TRC's view. Where relevant (that is, among white and Colored people), Afrikaans-speakers generally are quite a bit less likely to accept the truth, and this finding holds even within the quite comprehensive statistical analysis (that is, even after controls for level of education, age, size of place of residence, and so on). The effects of all of the other variables are limited in their generalizability. (For example, Colored and Asian women, but not African and white women, are less likely to accept the truth.)

It is important to reiterate that how South Africans judge the past is to a considerable degree related to how they experienced that past. Those who did well under apartheid tend to be less critical of it and therefore also tend to reject the TRC's strong condemnation of the apartheid system. This finding should surprise no one. However, that so many South Africans fared well under apartheid, including blacks, Colored people, and those of Asian origin, is surprising and adds pungency to this finding. Nearly everyone believes that apartheid was a crime against humanity, but considerable disagreement exists on just how bad apartheid was, and in general, South Africans' participation in South Africa's collective memory about apartheid reflects how well each of them managed under that system.

Concluding Comments

This survey supports a variety of conclusions about the production of a collective memory about apartheid for South Africans.

The TRC and its activities captured the attention of large segments of the South African population. Moreover, Africans in particular expressed considerable confidence in the commission. If salience and trust are necessary conditions for the TRC to have shaped South Africa's collective memory, then it is entirely possible that the TRC influenced beliefs about the past.

Some beliefs about the past are very widely shared within South Africa. For instance, most South Africans of every race believe that apartheid was a crime against humanity. To at least some degree, a common understanding of the country's past has emerged. If one thinks of reconciliation as nothing more than people sharing common understandings of the apartheid past (a view that I do not endorse—see chapter 1 on the meaning of reconciliation), then reconciliation is fairly widespread in South Africa.

Still, *many aspects of the past are contested.* Especially significant is the resistance of Afrikaans-speakers—white and Colored—to the view that apartheid was an evil system. However, even among black South Africans, many see the apartheid past equivocally, as a mixture of good and bad.

The TRC seems to have had some influence in creating a South African collective memory. Not all of the viewpoints of the commission are widely accepted, but I adduce empirical evidence suggesting that the TRC was successful in getting many to accept its view of the country's apartheid history.

Because the TRC's truth is a balanced truth, condemning to at least some degree all participants in the struggle over apartheid, the influence of the commission has been to moderate views of the past. As a result of the revelations of the TRC, many whites seem to have been convinced to abandon the view that those struggling to preserve the apartheid state were noble and that those challenging the state were vile. Many blacks, on the other hand, learned from the TRC that the liberation forces also committed heinous acts, just as they were shown that at least some of the worst abuses of apartheid were associated with rogue individuals. If nothing else, the TRC seems to have laid to rest some of the fictions that each side in the struggle mobilized to defend its positions and legitimacy. The effect of the TRC seems to have been to move blacks and whites closer together in their understandings of the country's past. As a consequence, racial differences in participation in the TRC's collective memory are *not* great.

Some more general lessons about collective memory emerge

from this analysis. First, *collective memory can be measured in a rigorous fashion*. This analysis has benefited from the explicit efforts of the TRC to fashion a collective memory, but systematic empirical methods have been used to assess the degree to which South Africans participate in the country's collective memory.

My analysis has shown that *group identities matter for participation in the country's memory, but not always in direct and simple ways*. Simply having a group identity, even a strong one, is not strongly connected to beliefs about the past. Instead, the most significant aspect of identity concerns beliefs about the political relevance of groups. A theme that recurs frequently throughout this book is that many South Africans accept, perhaps as a result of the experience of apartheid, the legitimacy of group difference and separation and consequently do not roundly condemn all aspects of apartheid. Identity per se does not shape apartheid beliefs, but the collateral values that sometimes flow from identity do indeed have considerable relevance for acceptance of the TRC's collective memory.

Finally, some may consider acceptance of the TRC's truth as one form of reconciliation. I do not, however. Instead, I give quite different meaning to the concept of reconciliation (as already noted) but then hypothesize that those who accept the TRC's truth are more likely to be reconciled. For instance, the next chapter considers the hypothesis that endorsing the truth is connected to interracial reconciliation. It is to the assessment of the truth → reconciliation hypotheses that I now turn.

Chapter 4

Interracial Reconciliation

We are all in the same boat—we simply need to understand each other better and be more respectful of each other's culture.

—Truth and Reconciliation Commission (1998, vol. 9, ch. 5, p. 425)

Perhaps no meaning of "reconciliation" is as intuitively obvious as that people of different races in South Africa must be able to get along with each other. Without interracial reconciliation, South Africa cannot survive as a multicultural polity. Reconciliation may mean more than people of different races putting up with each other, but interracial reconciliation is perhaps the bedrock without which all other forms of reconciliation are devoid of meaning.

In this chapter, I therefore examine the nature of the attitudes that South Africans hold toward their fellow citizens of different races. I refer to this as "interracial reconciliation"—by which I mean trust, rejection of stereotypes, and respect for those of other races. The central questions addressed here are: To what degree are South Africans reconciled with those of other races? And why are some South Africans more reconciled than others? Answering these questions can provide useful insights into how a more racially harmonious South Africa can be built.

The problem of racial attitudes is of course one that has attracted the attention of scholars for quite some time. In the United States the problem has been subject to the intense scrutiny of social scientists at least since World War II. Therefore, I rely heavily on existing theories of racial attitudes to try to explain why some South Africans hold positive attitudes toward those of other races, but others do not.

No theory of interracial attitudes has received more attention than the so-called contact hypothesis. This hypothesis states that the key to positive racial attitudes is interaction. Without contact, people of different races can successfully harbor suspicions and fears about those who are different. My research provides a telling test—one of the few ever conducted outside the confines of Western developed democracies—of whether interracial contact in South Africa has contributed to interracial reconciliation.

Just what is interracial reconciliation, and how reconciled are South Africans? The survey data have much to say about these questions.

Conceptualizing Racial Reconciliation as Interracial Respect and Understanding

An essential element of post-apartheid reconciliation is that South Africans of every race accept all other South Africans as equals and treat them as equal, extending dignity and respect to them. When people talk about reconciliation, they often mean nothing more than a diminution of racial animosity—that is, that the races should get along better with each other. This probably means that people are reconciled when they come to interact with each other more (barriers across races break down) and communicate more, perhaps ultimately gaining greater understanding and perhaps even acceptance, which result in their appreciation and exaltation of the value of racial diversity.

Thus, an elemental component of reconciliation is mutual respect, and a fundamental ingredient in mutual respect is the willingness to judge people as individuals rather than brand them with group stereotypes.[1] A more reconciled society is one in which people understand, accept, and even appreciate differences in groups other than their own. To the extent that South Africans do not respect and understand the various racial groups making up their country, are fearful of them, and subscribe to negative racial stereotypes, reconciliation has not been achieved. Thus, as an empirical matter, it is necessary to consider how ordinary people in South

Africa feel about their fellow citizens of other racial groups. The questions used to measure interracial reconciliation, therefore, ask South Africans about their assessments of members of the "opposite race."

Selecting Members of the Opposite Race

In principle, it would be desirable to ask members of each major racial grouping about their attitudes toward all other groups—to ask blacks, for instance, to evaluate whites, Colored people, and those of Asian origin. In practice, such a strategy would require dozens of individual questions, which would simply consume too much of the available interview time and would also be quite taxing on the respondents. Since that approach was not practical, I found it necessary to adopt an alternative measurement scheme.

The optimal strategy for black and white respondents was not difficult to identify: we asked black respondents their views of whites, and white respondents their views of blacks. To ask those who were clearly superordinate and subordinate under apartheid about each other makes perfect sense from the point of view of the future of interracial reconciliation in South Africa.

More complicated calculations were involved in selecting the optimal group about which to ask Colored and Asian respondents. Given the geographic concentration of Colored people in the Western Cape and those of Asian origin in KwaZulu Natal, I felt it unreasonable to query respondents from these two groups about each other. The choice then boiled down to whether to ask them about whites or blacks.

The ideology of the liberation struggle asserted that Africans, Colored people, and Indians (those of Asian origin) were united in a common fight against apartheid. It was therefore very much in the interest of those struggling against apartheid to dismiss differences and discount conflicts among these three groups.[2] From the point of view of this ideology, no interracial reconciliation is necessary among those oppressed by apartheid. Consequently, it might make sense to ask these respondents about their views of whites.

I chose instead to ask Colored and Asian respondents about their opinions of the black majority. I made this decision not because I think there is no need for interracial reconciliation between whites and Colored people and between those of Asian origin and whites. Nor do I believe that white racism is confined to attitudes toward black South Africans. Instead of emphasizing historical relationships among South Africa's four main racial groupings, I chose instead to focus on the contemporary relationships between each of the racial minorities and the black majority.[3] As blacks move into positions of economic, social, and political power within South African society—as they surely must and will—the question of whether there can be reconciliation between the racial minorities and the racial majority will be of considerable importance. By asking about the interracial reconciliation of these groups, I do not presuppose (or even hypothesize) that levels of reconciliation will be low. Indeed, perhaps one of the least investigated issues from an empirical viewpoint is whether those who were "Black" under the old system of apartheid are now sufficiently reconciled to unite in a political coalition.

This decision to ask Colored people and those of Asian origin about black South Africans was based in part on the interracial conflict manifest in the focus groups we held. Both the Colored focus group (held in Cape Town) and the Indian group (held in Durban) exposed substantial antipathy toward black South Africans. Among Colored people, this conflict seemed to focus on affirmative action and other means by which black South Africans were able to gain economic advantage over Colored people (for example, the job requirement that an employee speak Xhosa). One participant exclaimed:

> I thought that if the ANC takes over they will make everybody's lives a better life—white, black, Colored. But it seems now that it's the same like in the past where the whites have everything and now the Africans—not all the Africans but most of them—they have everything and we still . . . they treat us as Africans but we're not actually Africans. We the Colored people still have to look for jobs. My sister has been looking for a job for so long now and it's always, "Sorry, you must be black," or, "You don't speak Xhosa, so there's no job for you."

I do not deny that there is substantial conflict between Colored people and whites, especially over jobs (and that conflict was clearly manifest in the focus group). But since the possibility of significant interracial antipathy between Colored and black people exists and may be exacerbated by economic competition, my survey questions explore this possibility.

Similar remarks during the Indian focus group contributed to the decision to focus on Indian-African relations. Many of the Indian participants in the focus groups expressed a keen awareness of the history of conflict in Africa between Indians and blacks. For instance, one focus-group participant made the following observation:

> Look at all the African states [where] nobody has become successful. Look at Rhodesia, they kicked us out, everywhere. It's frightening. That is the attitude that the blacks have there (and abroad), and this is how they want [it]—you're white, you don't belong here, you're Indian, you don't belong here. This is an African country, it's ours, and we'll live the way we want.

Another respondent asserted with regard to black South Africans:

> This is their country. Just a point that I want to make to add to what the two speakers have already said, is that—and I remember quite well, I was a teenager at the time—when Buthelezi, the IFP [Inkatha Freedom Party] guy, said (. . . and it made a hit in the newspaper about fifteen, twenty years ago) . . . , "All Indians must go back to India, this is no place for you here." So the message was put across.

Thus, it seemed reasonable to explore the degree of racial reconciliation between black South Africans and those of Asian origin.

Most extant literature on intergroup conflict would predict that economic and political competition between groups like Coloreds, Indians, and blacks would be fairly substantial, especially in times of economic scarcity and retrenchment (as was true at the time of the survey). Colored people may see blacks as profiting unfairly from affirmative action and Indian people may believe that blacks do not accept that Indians achieved their position of relative economic superiority through hard work and fair economic practices. Were there not at least some conflict among these groups, it would be surprising.

To reiterate, in an ideal world with unlimited resources (including the resource of respondents' patience in answering our questions), all South Africans would have been asked about the three "opposite" racial groups. By asking Colored and Asian respondents about black South Africans, I am making no ideological statement. Nor am I prejudging anything about the findings or presupposing that Colored and Asian attitudes toward whites are harmonious and free of antipathy and ill will (and vice versa). Politically, black South Africans are dominant in South Africa, as befits a group comprising 78 percent of the population. The questions therefore asked the ethnic and political minorities about their relations with the African majority.

Indicators of Interracial Reconciliation

Table 4.1 reports the replies to nine questions about the opposite racial group. These statements represent people's feelings about the opposite race as well as their willingness to accept stereotypes about the other group. Thus, for instance, the first item in the table asked black respondents to agree or disagree with the statement: "I find it difficult to understand the customs and ways of white people." (A five-point Likert response set was used to collect the replies to these queries.)

If reconciliation requires interracial understanding, then a majority of South Africans of every race are not reconciled. For instance, over two-thirds (68.0 percent) of the African respondents say they find it hard to understand white people, while a majority of Colored people and those of Asian origin (and nearly a majority of whites) claim that they find it difficult to understand the customs and ways of black people. It is particularly striking that fewer than one-fourth of the African respondents assert that they are generally able to understand whites (by virtue of disagreeing with the statement that they do not understand whites).

Table 4.1 Cross-Racial Understandings and Misunderstandings of the "Opposite Race", by Race

	Agree	Uncertain	Disagree	Number of Cases
It is difficult to understand their customs and ways.				
African	68.0%	9.5%	22.5%	2,004
White	48.6	10.5	40.9	992
Colored	50.3	8.0	41.6	485
Asian origin	54.3	4.5	41.2	245
They are untrustworthy.				
African	56.0	23.1	20.9	2,002
White	33.4	20.7	46.0	983
Colored	26.6	23.4	50.0	482
Asian origin	41.6	16.7	41.6	245
I often don't believe what they say.				
African	44.5	23.5	32.0	1,999
White	35.9	17.7	46.4	988
Colored	29.5	20.1	50.4	482
Asian origin	40.8	12.2	46.9	245
I feel uncomfortable around them.				
African	46.8	12.3	40.9	2,004
White	34.7	12.5	52.8	989
Colored	24.3	8.7	67.0	485
Asian origin	36.7	6.5	56.7	245
They are more likely to engage in crime.				
African	40.7	31.1	28.3	2,000
White	59.2	10.7	30.1	989
Colored	40.2	20.5	39.2	482
Asian origin	59.2	11.4	29.4	245
They are selfish and only look after their group interests.				
African	68.9	15.7	15.3	2,001
White	45.3	18.3	36.4	986
Colored	40.1	19.8	40.1	479
Asian origin	45.7	11.8	42.4	245
I could never imagine being in a party made up mainly of them.				
African	58.5	20.1	21.4	1,999
White	42.1	17.8	40.1	980

(Table continues on p. 124.)

Table 4.1 *(Continued)*

	Agree	Uncertain	Disagree	Number of Cases
Colored	19.5	19.7	60.8	472
Asian origin	29.8	15.1	55.1	245
It is hard to imagine ever being friends with one of them.				
African	52.7	13.1	34.2	2,004
White	18.5	12.9	68.6	987
Colored	12.8	10.3	76.9	485
Asian origin	19.2	1.6	79.2	245
South Africa would be a better place without any of them.				
African	19.4	18.5	62.1	2,001
White	19.1	16.6	64.2	973
Colored	5.7	15.1	79.2	477
Asian origin	14.7	9.0	76.3	245

Source: Author's compilation from the 2001 Truth and Reconciliation Survey.
Note: All cross-race differences are statistically significant at $p < .001$.

Without understanding, it is perhaps not surprising that levels of interracial trust are not particularly high. A majority (56.0 percent) of blacks believe that whites are untrustworthy, while one-third of whites believe that blacks are untrustworthy (with another 20.7 percent being uncertain whether blacks can be trusted). Uncertainty on this item is particularly noteworthy (perhaps because some respondents believe that some are trustworthy but others are not, and they did not know how to fit that view into the available responses to this question).[4] Still, it is perhaps a bit surprising that nearly one-half of the white respondents (46.0 percent) reject the view that blacks are untrustworthy, while only 20.9 percent of the black respondents reject the stereotype of white untrustworthiness. A (bare) majority of Colored people repudiate the stereotype about blacks, as do about four in ten of the respondents of Asian origin.

This lack of trust is also manifest in an unwillingness to believe what members of the opposite racial group say—a plurality of blacks assert that whites are not to be believed. Levels of trust and willingness to believe blacks are higher among our white, Colored, and Asian respondents.

Perhaps as a consequence of this lack of trust, nearly a majority of blacks are uncomfortable around whites, while a majority of whites, Colored people, and South Africans of Asian origin do not claim to feel uncomfortable around blacks. If "not uncomfortable" is the same thing as "comfortable," then it is perhaps encouraging for reconciliation that a majority of the racial minorities in South Africa feel at ease in the presence of members of the black majority.

A few of these questions directly address prejudicial stereotypes, such as the belief that certain groups are likely to engage in crime. As the data indicate, a plurality of each group assert that the opposite race is likely to engage in crime (although the relatively high percentage of blacks unable to judge whites should be noted). A majority of whites and those of Asian origin believe that blacks are more likely to commit crime, although this belief is not shared by a majority of Colored people. It is noteworthy that blacks are also concerned about the criminality of whites—40.7 percent agree that whites are more likely than others to engage in crime. Only a minority of respondents reject this racial stereotype.

Another stereotype has to do with the selfishness of the group. Here we find that blacks are quite willing to ascribe selfish motives to whites (68.9 percent), while only a plurality of whites (45.3 percent) hold similar views of blacks. Colored people and those of Asian origin are equally divided on the veracity of this stereotype.

The next item is of particular importance for the politics of South Africa since it refers to the possibility of a multiracial political coalition. Only a small minority of blacks (21.4 percent) assert that they might consider being in a political party made up mainly of whites. With respect to a party made up mainly of blacks, the figures climb to 40.1 percent for whites, 55.1 percent for those of Asian origin, and 60.8 percent for Colored South Africans. Most of the black majority see little reason why they should become a minority in a white-dominated party; the minority racial groups find the possibility of being a minority member in a black party much more acceptable—perhaps because this scenario is more likely if these groups are to acquire any political power in South Africa.

Imagining being friends is less objectionable than imagining being in a political party together. Still, a majority of blacks assert that it is difficult to envisage being friends with a white person. The percentages of whites, Colored people, and South Africans of Asian origin who find interracial friendships unimaginable are quite small—in every case this negative view is limited to no more than one in five respondents.

Finally, on whether a racially homogeneous South Africa is desirable, few South Africans would prefer to see members of the opposite racial group vacate the country. Substantial majorities of each racial group do not agree that South Africa would be a better place without people of other races. Blacks and whites are perhaps slightly less committed to a multiracial country than are those of Asian origin and especially Colored people, but generally little support exists for this form of ethnic homogeneity and uni-culturalism.

Thus, attitudes toward racial reconciliation vary considerably depending on the particular question. At one extreme, few South Africans believe their country would be better off were it racially homogeneous. At the other extreme, most find it difficult to understand those of other races, and many believe that those of the opposite race are selfish. Still, it is clear from these data that unreconciled attitudes do *not* dominate in South Africa: only a handful of the percentages in the "Agree" column in table 4.1 (the response indicating an unreconciled viewpoint) exceed 50 percent (a majority of the respondents). On the other hand, few of the percentages in the unreconciled ("Disagree") column exceed 50 percent either. Not surprisingly, people in South Africa have fairly complicated and ambivalent views toward those of the opposite race.

To get a better purchase on the nature of these attitudes toward racial reconciliation, it is useful to construct an index of reconciliation. Such an index is especially valuable because it increases both the validity and reliability of measurement and because it eliminates overreliance on interpreting the responses to any given question in the set of indicators.[5]

This set of items is reasonably reliable, with the alpha coefficients varying from .79 (those of Asian origin) to .88 (whites). It appears that attitudes toward racial reconciliation are internally consistent and hence reliable.

Do these various attitudes all represent a single coherent view of those of the "opposite race"? One way in which this question can be addressed involves a factor-analysis of the responses to these nine items. I hypothesize that *each of these specific beliefs about those of the opposite race stems from a more general and global attitude* and therefore I expect that these items will be shown to be uni-dimensional by factor analysis.

Among black and white South Africans, a strongly uni-dimensional structure emerges from the factor-analysis of these items. Among Colored people, a second significant factor exists (using oblique rotation), although the eigenvalue just barely exceeds the 1.00 threshold ($\lambda = 1.05$) and the factor accounts for a trivial amount of the pooled variance (11.7 percent, as compared to 48.4 percent explained by the first factor). Among South Africans of Asian origin, a second, substantively significant factor exists ($\lambda = 1.23$), although these two factors are strongly intercorrelated ($r = .5$). In conjunction with the evidence on reliability reported earlier, it seems fair to conclude that attitudes toward racial reconciliation are dominated by a single, internally consistent attitude toward those of the opposite race.

I have created a reconciliation index from the responses to these nine items. The index is simply the number of "reconciled" responses minus the number of "unreconciled" answers. This index has several desirable properties (for example, it is not related to the number of "uncertain" or "don't know" responses to these items [$r = .02$]), and it is sensitive to the fact that many people hold mixed views toward those of the opposite race. The index varies from -9 (all responses expressed racial intransigence) to $+9$ (all responses were reconciled). Table 4.2 reports racial differences in this index of reconciliation attitudes. For ease of interpretation, I have also reported a trichotomous version of the continuous variable (based on collapsing the responses, as reported in note b in the table).

On balance, only black South Africans hold negative views toward the opposite racial group. The mean for our African respon-

Table 4.2 Racial Differences in Levels of Interracial Reconciliation

	African	White	Colored	Asian Origin
Reconciliation index				
Mean[a]	−1.78	.88	2.54	1.27
Standard deviation	4.80	5.41	4.86	4.82
Number of cases	2,004	988	485	245
Reconciliation trichotomy[b]				
Less reconciled	49.1%	32.4%	19.0%	22.9%
Mixed	30.5	23.1	27.8	34.7
More reconciled	20.5	44.5	53.2	42.4

Source: Author's compilation from the 2001 Truth and Reconciliation Survey.
[a]Difference of means, across race: $F = 138.29$, $p < .001$. $\eta = .32$.
[b]This index is based on the following categorization of the reconciliation index:
−9 to −3 = less reconciled
−2 to 2 = mixed
3 to 9 = more reconciled

dents is −1.78, which means that, on average, blacks gave more unreconciled replies than reconciled ones when asked these questions about whites. In contrast, our Colored respondents were much more positively oriented toward blacks, with a tendency (on average) to give more reconciled than unreconciled responses. Racial differences on this index are highly statistically (and substantively) significant.[6]

The reconciliation trichotomy highlights these interracial differences in racial reconciliation. Nearly half of the black respondents are scored as "less reconciled" (by virtue of giving at least three more unreconciled than reconciled responses), while roughly one-third of the whites are less reconciled. Again, our Colored respondents were the most likely to hold racially reconciled attitudes, while a plurality of whites and those of Asian origin expressed more reconciled viewpoints.

Within each racial group, there are some differences in racial reconciliation based on language and ethnicity. Among blacks, although not a great deal of variability in degrees of racial reconciliation can be found according to ethnicity or language, a couple of exceptions are significant. Africans who speak North Sotho tend to hold considerably more negative attitudes toward whites than other blacks—only 12.0 percent are classified as "more reconciled" (data not shown). Perhaps the same is true of those speaking South Sotho, although the differences are not so great. Among whites, those who speak Afrikaans are considerably less reconciled than English-speakers: 41.3 percent of Afrikaners are relatively less reconciled, compared to only 22.4 percent of white English-speakers. And though the numbers are small, a similar language-based difference exists among Colored people. Of the 382 Colored respondents who speak Afrikaans as their home language, only 48.4 percent hold more reconciled attitudes, compared to 70.6 percent of the 102 English-speaking Colored respondents. (Since the overwhelming majority of South Africans of Asian origin speak English at home, no division of that sample by language is possible.) Based on the uncategorized responses on the racial reconciliation index, blacks who speak North Sotho are the most unreconciled group in South Africa, and English-speaking Colored people are the most reconciled.

It is important to place these results in perspective in order to distinguish between empirical findings (facts) and explanations or justifications of the findings. One response to the evidence that blacks tend to hold less reconciled attitudes than others in South Africa is to attempt to explain and justify those attitudes with reference to apartheid and the history of racial repression in the country. Such an apology would not be difficult to construct. I have no objection to such an effort, and indeed, I suspect that the hypothesis is largely correct. But a fact and the explanation of the fact should not be confused. The fact is that blacks in South Africa are the most likely to hold unreconciled racial attitudes, whatever the explanation or justification may be. Discovering the explanation of this fact is the most important objective of the empirical analysis reported later in this chapter.

Social Desirability and the Honesty of Survey Responses

A possible explanation of the finding that whites hold more racially reconciled attitudes than blacks has to do with social desirability—the unwillingness of whites to express openly the negative views they hold of black South Africans. In the United States it has become quite difficult to measure racial attitudes among whites owing to strong social pressures against explicit expressions of racism.[7] Could it be that these South African findings are biased by the tendency of whites to censor their negative attitudes toward blacks? Several logical and empirical tests suggest otherwise.

It must first be noted that if self-censorship explains white attitudes, then pressure to give socially desirable replies is perhaps even more common among our Asian and Colored respondents, since their revealed attitudes are even more reconciled than those of whites. It seems doubtful that this is the case in contemporary South Africa.[8]

I included in the survey a test of the willingness of the respondents to fabricate views when in fact they had none. The "fictitious group" experiment asked the respondents their opinions about "the Mishlenti Society"—a nonexistent group.[9] Though this is not exactly the same thing as self-censorship of views for fear of portraying oneself unfavorably, it is generally accepted that opinion fabrication is a response to perceived social desirability—in this case, the desirability of being informed (see, for example, Schuman and Presser 1981). The preface to the question explicitly encouraged the respondents to indicate when they had no view toward a group about which we were asking. Table 4.3 indicates how well the subjects followed these instructions.

Large majorities of South Africans of every race correctly respond that they have "no opinion" toward the Mishlenti Society. When an opinion is expressed, it tends to be a negative one, with only a tiny proportion of the sample voicing positive views toward this fictitious group. Most important, racial differences in opinion fabrication are *entirely trivial.* Certainly, there is no evidence here that whites are more likely than other South Africans to try to portray themselves in a positive light by fabricating responses to our questions.

Moreover, a vast majority of the white respondents were willing to express at least some negative views toward blacks, with nearly 82 percent of the white respondents voicing at least one pejorative attitude toward blacks. The average number of negative responses

Table 4.3 Attitudes Toward the Mishlenti Society (a Fictitious Group), by Race

	No Opinion[a]	Dislike	Like	Number of Cases
African	73.2%	22.2%	4.6%	1,994
White	76.0	23.6	.4	985
Colored	80.9	17.0	2.1	482
Asian origin	73.5	22.0	4.5	245

Source: Author's compilation from the 2001 Truth and Reconciliation Survey.
[a]Cross-race differences on a dichotomous measure of opinionation: $\eta = .06$; $p = .004$.

is 3.4, with a median of 3.0 (53.3 percent of the white respondents gave three or more unreconciled responses toward blacks). These data indicate that the overwhelming majority of whites feel no need to disguise at least some of their negative attitudes toward black South Africans.[10] Thus, there is little evidence to suggest that white racial attitudes are anything but sincere.[11]

Although many South Africans hold ambivalent views on racial reconciliation, it seems that these attitudes are relatively coherent and meaningful to the respondents. Statistically, they are quite reliable, among South Africans of every race. Substantial racial differences exist in average levels of reconciliation, with Colored people exhibiting the most racially reconciled attitudes and blacks holding the least reconciled views. Generally, however, racial reconciliation in South Africa is perhaps more common than might be expected in light of the country's history of racism and racial separation and domination.

Is Truth Associated with Reconciliation?

It is of course extremely difficult to test the *causal* hypothesis linking truth acceptance and reconciliation, since truth may contribute to reconciled attitudes, but reconciled attitudes may also make it easier to accept the truth about the past. So, while deferring the question of causality to the last portion of this chapter, I here consider the degree to which acceptance of the truth and reconciled attitudes "go together," the degree to which they are interrelated. If no such relationship is found, then the two attitudes are not

Table 4.4 The Effect of Truth Acceptance on Racial Reconciliation

Truth Acceptance → Racial Reconciliation	African	White	Colored	Asian Origin
Intercept (standard error)	−2.52 (.57)	−11.76 (.71)	−6.12 (1.19)	−3.33 (1.63)
b	.21	3.76	2.37	1.29
standard error	.15	.21	.32	.45
β	.03	.51***	.33***	.18***
Standard deviation—dependent variable	4.81	5.42	4.88	4.82
Standard error of estimate	4.81	4.67	4.62	4.75
R-squared	.00	.26***	.11***	.03***
Number of cases	1,958	958	457	241

Source: Author's compilation from the 2001 Truth and Reconciliation Survey.
Note: Significance of standardized regression coefficients (β): ***p < .001, **p < .01; *p < .05.

likely to be causally connected. If connected, then the question of causality arises and must be systematically addressed.

The results of regressing attitudes toward racial reconciliation on acceptance of the truth about apartheid are startling (see table 4.4). For black South Africans, those who accept more truth are no more or less likely to hold racially reconciled attitudes than those who accept less truth (β = .03). But among whites, Colored people, and those of Asian origin, the relationships are both statistically and substantively significant (β = .51, .33, .18, respectively). Indeed, among whites in particular, the relationship is remarkably strong.

It is useful to illustrate just how substantial this relationship is among whites. Note first that the index of racial reconciliation varies from −9 to +9, and that the truth acceptance indicator varies from 0 to 5. According to the equation in table 4.4, when a white South African accepts none of these propositions about the truth, the expected score on the reconciliation index is −4.1—a not very reconciled state indeed. The effect of accepting one additional statement about apartheid is to increase racial reconciliation by 1.8 units (which is nearly two of the nine statements). Thus, the predicted reconciliation index score of one who accepts all five statements is +4.9 (−4.1 + 9.0), which is a relatively high level of racial reconciliation. The difference between holding predominantly unreconciled views (−4 on the index) to mainly reconciled views (+5) is highly significant substantively and has important political implications. Thus, the connection between truth and reconciliation among whites is substantial and of considerable import.

The influence of truth on reconciliation among Colored people and those of Asian origin is smaller, with regression coefficients roughly half the size of the white coefficient. Nonetheless, those accepting all five statements about the apartheid past are expected to hold quite reconciled attitudes toward their black fellow citizens, especially in contrast to those who reject these statements about the truth. Truth seems to contribute to reconciliation to at least a moderate degree.

The puzzle in table 4.4 is black South Africans—acceptance of the truth has virtually no impact on black attitudes toward whites.[12] The contrast between the black and white coefficients is stark indeed (b = .21 versus 3.76). The lack of relationship among blacks requires further consideration.

One possibility is that all blacks accept the truth about apartheid, and therefore the variability in reconciliation cannot be attributed to the "constant" truth. (It is axiomatic in statistical analysis that constants cannot account for the variation in variables.) This explanation must be rejected, however.

In terms of the variable indicating the number of truths accepted, the observed range among the black respondents is from 0 to 5, with a mean of 3.2 statements accepted (standard deviation = 1.2) and a median of 3.0. For whites, the range is from 0 to 5, the mean is 2.8 (standard deviation 1.4), and the median is 3.0. Neither distribution exhibits any degree of skewness (which might make the means less useful as a summary of the distribution), although more whites are at the lower extreme than blacks (5.4 percent of blacks accept none or only one of the statements; the figure for whites is 20.3 percent). There certainly appears to be enough variance in the index that a statistical relationship could be manifest among blacks were there in fact one.

Another possibility is that the relationship between truth and reconciliation varies across different segments of the black South African population. To consider this hypothesis, I have examined the correlation between truth and reconciliation by dividing the black respondents by many different variables that I hypothesize might affect the truth → reconciliation relationship.[13] Generally, the relationship between truth and reconciliation does not vary in meaningful ways (that is, there are no sensible and monotonic changes in the regression coefficients) when blacks are divided by gender, age categories, level of education, opinion leadership, literacy, size of place of residence, social class, or interest in politics. Some differences exist on the basis of home language, but among Xhosa- and Zulu-speakers the coefficients are indistinguishable from zero, and within other language groups no ready interpretation of the coefficients exists (for example, a significant negative relationship is found among Tswana-speakers). With one exception, I have found no meaningful distinctions among blacks in the nature of the relationship between perceptions of truth and acceptance of racial reconciliation.

The exception to these null findings, however, is quite revealing. I divided the black sample according to the frequency of church attendance, dichotomizing the variable between those who attend church at least monthly and those who attend less frequently (about 30 percent of black South Africans).[14] The data indicate that, among relatively less religious blacks, greater acceptance of the truth contributes to racial reconciliation; among the relatively more religious, truth and reconciliation are unconnected. The regression equation for these two groups are:[15]

Infrequent attenders: Reconciliation $= -5.80 + .99 \times$ Truth Acceptance

Frequent attenders: Reconciliation $= -1.16 - .13 \times$ Truth Acceptance

The coefficient for infrequent attenders is highly statistically significant, while the coefficient for the frequent attenders is entirely trivial. (The respective standardized coefficients are .15 and −.02.)

This finding is quite intriguing and perhaps unanticipated in light of the religious veneer often associated with the truth and reconciliation process.

Note that the intercept for more religious blacks is considerably higher than that for less religious blacks (although the bivariate correlation between the religiosity dichotomy and reconciliation is only .06, which barely achieves statistical significance).[16] Religious blacks start with a somewhat higher level of reconciled attitudes, and greater appreciation of the truth contributes *nothing* to increments in reconciliation. Among the relatively less religious, acceptance of the truth makes a substantial difference in reconciliation.

It may well be that among religious blacks, reconciliation is largely a nonpolitical, otherworldly process and thus is immune to influence by understandings of the facts about the country's apartheid history. Put another way, the basis of being reconciled differs between religious and irreligious blacks. Among the former, perhaps reconciliation depends on the acceptance of certain religious teachings (or other unknown factors). Among the irreligious, reconciliation may turn on understandings of life on earth, not in the hereafter. Thus, at least with this portion of the black population, truth is indeed connected to reconciliation.[17]

The finding that truth makes a contribution to reconciliation among all South Africans except fairly religious blacks will surely be surprising to those in South Africa who are skeptical about whether truth and reconciliation have anything to do with one another. Still, the strength of the *causal* inference connecting truth and reconciliation is weak, since I have established only that truth and reconciliation covary together. To parse out the causality more clearly, it is necessary to develop a more comprehensive understanding of the origins of truth acceptance and of racial reconciliation.

Alternative Explanations of Truth and Reconciliation: The Contact Hypothesis

I have established to this point that participation in the truth is related to racial reconciliation, at least for some South Africans. Since causality is a crucial issue here, and since there are alternative explanations of both truth acceptance and racial reconciliation, this interrelationship must be considered within a broader understanding of the origins of both truth and reconciliation.

A formidable literature exists on the question of whether interracial contact enhances racial harmony. "In its simplest form, this hypothesis states that contact, particularly close and sustained contact, with members of different cultural groups promotes positive, tolerant attitudes. By contrast, the absence of such contact is believed to foster stereotyping, prejudice, and ill will toward these groups" (Ellison and Powers 1994, 385, citations omitted). The process is straightforward:

> According to proponents of the contact hypothesis, interracial contact provides direct information regarding the values, life-styles, behaviors, and experiences of other racial groups. When information about other groups is gained through long-term interactions with coworkers, neighbors, and others, the acquired information is likely to be relatively accurate and largely favorable in content. This positive first-hand information may then be generalized into positive perception of the group(s) as a whole. In the absence of such first-hand information, however, individuals may be unable to counter unfavorable impressions and stereotypes of other racial and cultural groups. In addition, individuals may be influenced by slanted media images of other racial groups, as well as by selected public statements of racial and ethnic group leaders and other indirect (and often inaccurate) sources of information about these groups. (385–86)

Or as Lee Sigelman and Susan Welch describe it (1993, 781): "Adherents of the contact hypothesis view racial segregation as a source of ignorance and ignorance as a breeding ground for derogatory stereotypes and racial hostility. If stronger social bonds could be forged between blacks and whites, they contend, racial attitudes would improve dramatically."

The contact hypothesis is not invariably supported by the empirical literature, but considerable evidence confirms the view that increasing interracial contact contributes to reconciliation, at least under some circumstances (see, for example, Sigelman and Welch 1993; Ellison and Powers 1994; Sigelman et al. 1996; see generally

Pettigrew 1998 and Pettigrew and Tropp 2000). The circumstances that seem to make interracial contact especially effective at dispelling prejudice include: equal status (the expectation and perception by the parties of equality in the interaction); common goals (sharing a common objective, as in athletics or the military); intergroup cooperation (interactions based around cooperative rather than competitive circumstances); and support from authorities, law, or custom (the presence of authoritative norms encouraging acceptance) (see Pettigrew 1998). Or as Mary Jackman and Marie Crane (1986, 461) more simply summarize the literature: "First, the contact should not take place within a competitive context. Second, the contact must be sustained rather than episodic. Third, the contact must be personal, informal, and one-to-one. Fourth, the contact should have the approval of any relevant authorities. Finally, the setting in which the contact occurs must confer equal status on both parties rather than duplicate the racial status differential." Jackman and Crane point to social equality in particular as a crucial attribute of social interactions if salutary effects on racial attitudes are to be realized.

Interracial understanding and trust are often the focus of those who study the influence of contact on racial attitudes. For instance, Christopher Ellison and Daniel Powers (1994) consider three indicators of the attitudes that black Americans hold toward whites: disapproval of interracial dating, skepticism regarding the motivations of whites, and perceptions of improvement in the racial climate in the United States. Sigelman and Welch (1993) analyze perceptions of hostility between racial groups and preferences for close social ties between the two races. Jackman and Crane (1986) employ a multidimensional dependent variable, ranging from "cognitive differentiation between blacks and whites" to "affective differentiation," to "social predispositions toward blacks," as well as policy attitudes on social issues. These authors are studying what may readily be understood as "racial reconciliation." Thus, extant research propounds the hypothesis that racial reconciliation will be more common among those who have greater contact with people of a different race. This hypothesis has rarely if ever been systematically investigated outside the context of Western industrialized societies.

Table 4.5 Interracial Interactions Among South Africans

	African	White	Colored	Asian Origin
Contact at work				
A great deal	7.0%	42.3%	35.0%	39.2%
Some	10.4	21.7	17.3	14.7
Not very much	15.0	11.5	9.7	6.9
Hardly any	11.9	9.5	8.0	3.3
No contact at all	55.6	15.0	30.0	35.9
Number of cases	1,991	989	486	245
Contact outside work				
A great deal	2.1	11.7	21.5	15.1
Some	8.4	31.5	20.0	28.2
Not very much	13.0	23.5	15.1	28.2
Hardly any	16.2	19.7	13.6	18.0
No contact at all	60.4	13.5	29.5	10.6
Number of cases	2,000	990	484	245
Eaten a meal together				
Quite often	3.3	17.3	24.7	21.2
Not very often	15.7	37.2	35.2	43.7
Never	81.0	45.5	40.1	35.1
Number of cases	2,004	991	486	245
"True" friends				
Quite a number	1.5	6.6	17.7	19.2
Only a small number	17.6	28.7	30.0	45.3
Hardly any	24.4	26.9	20.2	20.0
None	56.4	37.8	32.1	15.5
Number of cases	2,002	988	486	245

Source: Author's compilation from the 2001 Truth and Reconciliation Survey.

I have measured levels of interracial contact using four different indicators. The extant literature suggests that different forms of experience have different effects, so a global measure of interactions is less useful at this point in the analysis than a set of items indicating different types of relationships. Table 4.5 reports the frequency of different types of interracial contact.

It is perhaps not surprising that the racial minorities—whites, Colored people, and South Africans of Asian origin—report more contact with the black majority than blacks report contact with whites.[18] Only 7.0 percent of the African respondents report having a great deal of contact with whites, while 42.3 percent of the whites claim to have a great deal of contact at work with blacks. It is noteworthy that a majority of Africans report no contact at all with whites at work.

In every instance, interracial interactions outside work are even less common. For example, the white figure for quite frequent contacts with blacks plummets from 42.3 percent to only 11.7 percent. Similar declines characterize Colored people and those of Asian origin. Few blacks have regular contact with whites either at home or at the workplace. Of course, one must be cautious in judging the nature and quality of this contact—white reports, for instance, may be based on nothing more than hierarchical interactions with their black housekeepers. At this point, these data should be understood only as indicating some form of interaction; whether the interaction has any salutary effects can be judged only at the hypothesis-testing stage of this analysis.

A potentially more intimate form of interaction involves sharing a meal. Such interaction, however, is even rarer. Fully four of five blacks report that they have never shared a meal with a white person. Colored people are most likely to report sharing a meal with blacks, but even here only one-fourth (24.7 percent) claim to eat together quite often.

It is therefore not surprising that few South Africans report having very many friends of the opposite race. Virtually no blacks have quite a lot of white friends, and only a tiny proportion of whites (6.6 percent) have quite a number of black friends. A majority of black South Africans have no white friends at all. Interracial friendships are more common among Colored people and blacks, however, as well as among those of Asian origin and blacks.

The picture that emerges from these data is one of substantial racial isolation, especially among black South Africans. Obviously, it is more difficult for blacks to interact with whites, given the simple demographics of the South African population. But for most black South Africans, the world in which they live daily is devoid of significant numbers of white people. Whites are far more likely to interact with blacks, although white-black friendships are fairly uncommon (especially if we treat the "hardly any" response on the

Table 4.6 The Effect of Interracial Contact on Racial Reconciliation Among South Africans

	African	White	Colored	Asian Origin
Contact at work				
b (standard error)	.15 (.10)	−.17 (.11)	.13 (.15)	.22 (.17)
β	.04	−.05	.04	.08
r	.19	.19	.28	.24
Contact outside work				
b (standard error)	.28 (.13)	.51 (.14)	.63 (.18)	.64 (.26)
β	.07*	.12***	.20***	.16*
r	.22	.35	.38	.36
Eaten a meal together				
b (standard error)	1.18 (.27)	2.53 (.24)	.81 (.39)	.29 (.45)
β	.12***	.35***	.13*	.05
r	.24	.47	.37	.31
"True" friends				
b (standard error)	.71 (.15)	1.21 (.19)	.54 (.27)	1.70 (.36)
β	.12***	.21***	.12*	.34***
r	.23	.42	.36	.46
Intercept (standard error)	−2.87 (.14)	−2.81 (.34)	−.33 (.37)	−3.70 (.64)
Standard deviation—dependent variable	4.79	5.42	4.85	4.82

Source: Author's compilation from the 2001 Truth and Reconciliation Survey.
Significance of standardized regression coefficient: ***p < .001; ** p < .01; *p < .05.

friendship question as essentially "none," as it most likely should be understood).

A key question for this analysis is whether contact increases racial reconciliation. Table 4.6 reports the answer, based on regressing the index of racial reconciliation on the four measures of interracial contact.

The first thing to consider in this table is the bivariate correlation coefficients (r). These statistics indicate the *total* relationship between the variable and reconciliation. Since the contact variables are themselves interrelated, the total effect and the *independent* effects are often quite different. Nonetheless, all of the bivariate correlations are correctly signed (as contact increases, reconciliation increases). All of the correlations are reasonably strong, and some are quite strong. Some tendency can be observed for the coefficients for blacks to be smaller than the coefficients for the other groups, perhaps in part owing to restricted variance in the contact measures for blacks (that is, blacks experience greater racial isolation). In general, the effect of greater interracial interaction is to enhance racial reconciliation.[19]

It is also noteworthy that a considerable amount of variance is accounted for by this simple equation. The R-squared coefficients indicate that about one-quarter of the variance in racial attitudes can be explained for whites and those of Asian origin, about one-fifth of the variance among Colored people, and 8 percent among blacks. Again, because blacks have fewer interactions with whites, the statistical effect of contact is diminished.

The specific contact variable that best predicts racial reconciliation varies, with one important exception: *contact at work has no significant effect for any of the racial groups in terms of producing more reconciled racial attitudes.* Surely the quality of the contact in the workplace—often based on a hierarchical relationship—is such that people learn very little about each other. If contact makes a difference, it is interaction of a different sort.

Sharing a meal together enhances racial understanding and reconciliation for blacks, white, and Colored people, but not for those of Asian origin. For Asians, the key factor seems to be contact of an even more personal nature—having a friendship with a black person. Perhaps this reflects the importance of meals within different cultures: dining together may provide more of an opportunity for social engagement within some cultures than in others. Hence, the variable has a more powerful effect on racial attitudes.

It is important to emphasize that racial isolation impedes racial reconciliation within each racial group. The intercepts report the expected value for racial attitudes in the absence of any form of interracial contact. Only for Colored people is the intercept close to zero, and none of the coefficients is greater than zero (indicating a balance of more reconciled attitudes). Increased contact nearly always contributes to greater racial reconciliation. Though the effects are weaker for blacks, they are nonetheless statistically and substantively significant for each racial group.[20] Racial reconciliation is difficult to achieve without interracial interaction. Such interactions do not necessarily produce more reconciled attitudes, but they certainly make them possible.[21]

In light of the strong interrelationships among the contact variables, I have created a single summary index of the degree of interracial interactions. Since contact within the workplace seems to play no role in creating more reconciled racial attitudes, I have excluded that variable from the index. To ensure against unequal weighting of the various components of the index, I standardized each of the variables to a range from 0 to 4. Thus, a 0 on the index is substantively important—it means no contact with those of the opposite race outside work, no shared meals, and no friends of the opposite race. This index is strongly related to racial reconciliation: the correlations for blacks, whites, Colored people, and those of Asian origin are, respectively, .28, .52, .43, and .47. These are substantial relationships indeed. These South African findings thus add weight to the conventional view of the salutary effects of interracial interaction.[22]

Multivariate Analysis

I have established to this point that participation in the TRC's truth is related to racial reconciliation, at least for some South Africans. Since causality is such an important issue, and since I have hypothesized alternative explanations of both truth acceptance and racial reconciliation, it is necessary to consider this interrelationship within a broader understanding of the origins of both truth and reconciliation. In the multivariate analysis, the principal hypotheses I test include:

> *Hypothesis 1*: Based on the contact hypothesis, I expect that more interracial contact is associated with more reconciliation, although not necessarily with greater acceptance of the TRC's truth.

Hypothesis 2: Experiences under apartheid influence the degree to which an individual participates in the TRC's collective memory. Those who benefited from apartheid are expected to be less likely to judge it harshly, but more likely to be reconciled with South Africans of other races.

Hypothesis 3: If the truth and reconciliation process had anything to do with the attitudes that South Africans hold, then knowledge of and confidence in the TRC should contribute to greater endorsement of the commission's truth. However, the direct effect of these variables on interracial reconciliation should be minimal.

Hypothesis 4: More generally, those who are more engaged in public affairs (cognitively mobilized) are expected to be more likely to embrace the TRC's truth, although the effect of most of these variables is probably mediated through knowledge of the activities of the TRC.

Hypothesis 5: Since apartheid was the creation of Afrikaners, I expect that those who speak Afrikaans as their home language are less accepting of the TRC and less likely to engage in racial reconciliation.

In this analysis, I also control for a variety of demographic attributes of the respondents.

Table 4.7 reports the results of regressing the measures of truth and reconciliation on these predictor variables. The table is complicated, in part because it shows the results for each of the four major racial groups in South Africa, with blacks split by whether they are religious or not, and in part because the results for two dependent variables are reported.

Consider the determinants of truth acceptance first, and start by noting that the amount of variance explained by the equation varies substantially, from a low of 4 percent among religious Africans to a high of 22 percent among white and Colored South Africans. In general, levels of truth acceptance among black South Africans are not particularly well predicted by this equation.

(Text continues on p. 148.)

Table 4.7 Multivariate Determinants of Truth Acceptance and Racial Reconciliation Among Four Racial Groups

	Truth Acceptance				Racial Reconciliation			
	b	Standard Error	β	r	b	Standard Error	β	r
Colored South Africans								
Interracial contact	−.01	.02	−.02	.06	1.40	.16	.38***	.45
Net benefits of apartheid	−.04	.01	−.18***	−.23	−.20	.07	−.12**	−.23
Knowledge of the TRC	−.00	.04	−.01	.22	.18	.27	.04	.32
Confidence in the TRC	.01	.04	.01	.12	.40	.26	.08	.24
Media consumption	.05	.03	.08	.24	.24	.23	.05	.16
Interest in politics	.08	.04	.12*	.29	.67	.24	.14**	.32
Opinion leadership	−.19	.09	−.09*	.03	.74	.60	.05	.14
Level of education	.14	.04	.20***	.32	.18	.26	.04	.22
Illiteracy	.01	.05	.01	−.20	.27	.33	.04	−.13
Afrikaans language	−.24	.08	−.15**	−.26	−1.88	.56	−.16***	−.21
Age	.00	.00	.02	−.01	−.03	.01	−.09*	−.11
Social class	.06	.04	.08	−.17	.23	.26	.04	−.15
Size of place of residence	−.03	.02	−.07	−.21	−.12	.12	−.05	−.15
Gender	−.19	.06	−.14**	−.19	.93	.40	.10*	−.06
Intercept	3.19	.27			−1.22	1.78		
Standard deviation—dependent variable	.68				4.88			
Standard error of estimate	.61				4.08			
R-squared			.22***				.32***	
Number of cases	457				457			
South Africans of Asian origin								
Interracial contact	−.05	.04	−.07	.02	1.82	.28	.40***	.47
Net benefits of apartheid	−.05	.01	−.28***	−.31	−.08	.08	−.06	−.09
Knowledge of the TRC	.05	.07	.05	.11	.53	.46	.08	.26

Confidence in the TRC	−.05	.06	−.06	−.05	.35	.35	.06	.13
Media consumption	.00	.06	.01	.03	.30	.37	.05	.16
Interest in politics	.03	.05	.04	.14	−.13	.35	−.02	.16
Opinion leadership	.16	.13	.08	.14	−.99	.84	−.07	.02
Level of education	.02	.06	.02	.14	1.18	.39	.23**	.30
Illiteracy	.08	.08	.08	−.02	.74	.50	.10	−.12
Age	−.01	.00	−.17*	−.16	3.73	1.66	.13*	.15
Social class	−.09	.06	−.12	−.18	−.01	.02	−.02	−.13
Size of place of residence	.04	.03	.08	.02	.14	.35	.03	−.17
Gender	−.12	.09	−.09	−.11	.30	.19	.09	.01
					−.79	.56	−.08	−.17
Intercept	4.14	.39			−8.64	2.47		
Standard deviation—dependent variable	.69				4.82			
Standard error of estimate	.64				4.12			
R-squared			.17***				.31***	
Number of cases	241				241			
Irreligious Africans								
Interracial contact	.01	.04	.01	.05	1.21	.23	.23***	.30
Net benefits of apartheid	−.05	.01	−.17***	−.14	.29	.07	.16***	.17
Knowledge of the TRC	−.08	.04	−.09*	−.05	.38	.24	.07	.15
Confidence in the TRC	−.09	.03	−.12**	−.12	−.29	.20	−.06	−.05
Media consumption	.11	.04	.15**	.15	.42	.22	.09	.20
Interest in politics	.02	.03	.02	.04	−.00	.21	−.00	.09
Opinion leadership	−.02	.11	−.01	.03	.49	.66	.03	.09
Level of education	.07	.04	.10	.13	.18	.26	.04	.17
Illiteracy	−.01	.04	−.01	−.08	−.05	.26	−.01	−.17
Age	−.00	.00	−.03	−.05	.01	.02	.04	−.06
Social class	.03	.04	.03	−.04	.09	.26	.02	−.12
Size of place of residence	−.00	.01	−.00	−.06	−.09	.08	−.05	−.15
Gender	−.01	.07	−.01	−.05	−.14	.44	−.01	−.06

(Table continues on p. 146.)

Table 4.7 (Continued)

	Truth Acceptance				Racial Reconciliation			
	b	Standard Error	β	r	b	Standard Error	β	r
Intercept	3.44	.29			−4.43	1.80		
Standard deviation—dependent variable	.72				4.64			
Standard error of estimate	.70				4.35			
R-squared			.08***				.14***	
Number of cases	578				578			
Religious Africans								
Interracial contact	.02	.02	.03	.05	1.34	.16	.24***	.28
Net benefits of apartheid	−.04	.01	−.13***	−.13	.21	.05	.11***	.12
Knowledge of the TRC	−.03	.03	−.03	−.04	.06	.17	.01	.10
Confidence in the TRC	−.08	.02	−.11***	−.10	−.15	.14	−.03	.01
Media consumption	.05	.02	.06*	.05	−.06	.16	−.01	.11
Interest in politics	.00	.02	.00	.01	.10	.15	.02	.09
Opinion leadership	−.06	.07	−.02	−.01	−.01	.47	−.00	.04
Level of education	.02	.03	.02	.01	−.17	.17	−.04	.16
Illiteracy	.04	.03	.06	.03	−.92	.19	−.19***	−.22
Age	−.00	.00	−.03	.01	.01	.01	.03	−.07
Social class	−.01	.03	−.02	−.03	.03	.17	.01	−.10
Size of place of residence	−.01	.01	−.05	−.06	−.07	.06	−.03	−.12
Gender	−.00	.04	−.00	−.02	.09	.27	.01	−.02
Intercept	3.69	.18			−.12	1.17		
Standard deviation—dependent variable	.70				4.87			
Standard error of estimate	.69				4.60			
R-squared			.04***				.12***	
Number of cases	1,380				1,380			

Whites								
Interracial contact	.11	.02	.16***	.27	2.32	.15	.45***	.52
Net benefits of apartheid	.00	.01	.01	.05	−.05	.05	−.03	.01
Knowledge of the TRC	.03	.03	.03	.13	.30	.21	.04	.18
Confidence in the TRC	.11	.03	.12***	.20	1.16	.20	.16***	.26
Media consumption	.06	.03	.07*	.09	.06	.18	.01	.07
Interest in politics	−.02	.03	−.03	.06	−.16	.19	−.03	.09
Opinion leadership	.03	.06	.01	.06	−.43	.39	−.03	.04
Level of education	.07	.02	.10***	.20	.32	.14	.07*	.17
Illiteracy	−.03	.10	−.01	−.06	−1.10	.69	−.04	−.11
Afrikaans language	−.36	.05	−.25***	−.33	−1.42	.31	−.13***	−.25
Age	−.00	.00	−.04	−.07	.01	.01	.03	−.03
Social class	−.12	.03	−.11***	−.18	−.17	.22	−.02	−.10
Size of place of residence	−.04	.02	−.07*	−.13	.03	.12	.01	−.03
Gender	.08	.04	.06	.03	.57	.30	.05	.02
Intercept	3.19	.19			−3.74	1.30		
Standard deviation—dependent variable	.73				5.42			
Standard error of estimate	.65				4.46			
R-squared			.22***				.33***	
Number of cases	958				958			

Source: Author's compilation from the 2001 Truth and Reconciliation Survey.
Significance of standardized regression coefficient (β): ***p ≤ .001; **p ≤ .01; *p ≤ .05.

Irrespective of whether they are religious or not, the degree to which black South Africans accept the truth about apartheid depends on how much they benefited from apartheid and their confidence in the TRC. Those who were hurt most by apartheid are most likely to accept the truth about the country's past. As I noted earlier, however, greater confidence in the TRC is weakly associated with *less* acceptance of the truth. Moreover, in this multivariate analysis, more knowledge of the TRC is associated with less acceptance of the truth. Perhaps this is because attentiveness to the TRC led blacks to focus on individuals and apartheid rather than on the broader apartheid system. Reflecting the fact that irreligious blacks base their opinions about the past more on earthly affairs, the degree of media consumed also predicts their truth acceptance, whereas the relationship among religious Africans is trivial. The factors that do not predict black attitudes toward the truth are also important—such as the complete lack of relationship between size of place of residence and truth acceptance.

Among whites, acceptance of the truth is more common among those who speak English, not Afrikaans (the strongest relationship), and are in greater contact with blacks, more confident in the TRC, of higher social classes, and better educated. It should be reiterated that these are all independent effects, such that the influence of home language, for example, is independent of social class and level of education. Perhaps the most interesting findings here are that contact with black South Africans contributes to accepting the truth about the past, as well as the rather dramatic effect of being Afrikans. Whites who speak Afrikaans as their home language are substantially less likely to participate in South Africa's collective memory, ceteris paribus.

The equation for Colored people is similar to that for whites, with some important exceptions. Interracial contact matters little, but the perceived benefits from apartheid matter considerably: those who benefited more are substantially less likely to accept the truth. A strong effect of education is also apparent, as is a moderate influence of home language.

The degree to which South Africans of Asian origin accept the truth is very much a function of their relationship to apartheid (whether or not they were beneficiaries), age, and social class (but not level of education). Interracial contact plays only a small role in their truth acceptance.

In terms of racial reconciliation, one important finding characterizes all five groups. First, in every instance, interracial contact contributes to reconciliation. The relationships are weaker among blacks but are nonetheless substantial and highly significant. This is a telling confirmation of the conventional hypothesis, since a host of additional variables are controlled in these equations. The strong influence of contact is the primary reason why racial reconciliation is better predicted than truth acceptance for every group.

The effect of benefiting from apartheid is also interesting, since among blacks, beneficiaries are more likely to be reconciled, but among Colored South Africans, beneficiaries are less likely to be reconciled. It is important to reiterate that the target of reconciliation differs here—the questions for blacks refer to whites, and for Colored respondents the questions refer to blacks—so in fact these findings may not be as contradictory as they first seem. Whether one was a net beneficiary from apartheid does little to predict the attitudes of whites and South Africans of Asian origin.

Among religious Africans, the strong influence of illiteracy is worthy of note. Those who are illiterate are much less likely to hold reconciled attitudes toward whites, even despite controlling for level of education, and so on, since they are held constant in the equation. Moreover, the effect of illiteracy has nothing to do with attentiveness to the TRC (since attentiveness is controlled in the equation). This influence is also independent of contact with whites. Furthermore, it does not pertain to irreligious blacks, among whom illiteracy has no predictive power.

Several of these findings on the determinants of reconciliation attitudes mirror those from the truth acceptance equation. For instance, whites and Colored people who speak Afrikaans as their home language are considerably less likely to hold reconciled racial attitudes. Among whites at least, the effect of language on reconciliation is somewhat smaller than on truth acceptance, although it is still substantial.

Finally, the influence of level of education is quite limited in these equations. Only among those of Asian origin is there an effect on attitudes toward racial reconciliation.

These findings provide some clues as to why truth and reconciliation are not related among black South Africans. Those blacks who benefited from apartheid do not hold hostile views toward apartheid, and consequently they are more likely to react positively toward whites. Thus, these blacks score low on truth but high on reconciliation. On the other hand, blacks who fared poorly under apartheid tend to score high on truth acceptance but low on reconciliation. Putting these two groups together, the correlation between truth and reconciliation should be approximately zero. In fact, it is.

I shall not pursue these multivariate relationships further, since the primary objective of this chapter is to investigate the causal connection between truth and reconciliation. To assess the causal hypothesis, a different form of statistical analysis is required, one that builds on the equations reported in table 4.7.

The Causal Connection Between Truth and Reconciliation

To establish strong causal inferences linking truth acceptance and reconciliation, a complex, longitudinal (and probably experimental) research design would be necessary. In the absence of such a design, a statistical technique is available that provides at least some purchase on the causal relationship between truth and reconciliation. Two-stage least squares yields estimates of the influence of truth on reconciliation and the effect of reconciliation on truth (on two-stage least squares, see Berry 1984; Hanushek and Jackson 1977).

The first stage in the regression involves the creation of instrumental variables through the regression equations reported in table 4.7. Unfortunately, the results in table 4.7 indicate that the variance in truth acceptance among Africans is insufficiently well understood to continue with the two-stage least squares. For the other three groups, however, the first-stage equations provide useful instrumental variables for both truth and reconciliation.

For the second-stage regression, my hypotheses identify three types of variables: factors influencing truth acceptance but not reconciliation (experiences under apartheid, knowledge of and confidence in the TRC, media consumption, interest in politics, and illiteracy); factors influencing reconciliation but not truth acceptance (interracial contact); and control factors hypothesized to affect both truth acceptance and reconciliation. In the second-stage regression, each endogenous variable is modeled as a function of the instrument representing the other endogenous variable, and *only* the exogenous variables are hypothesized to have direct effects on the endogenous variable. The coefficients of greatest interest from this analysis concern the effects of truth on reconciliation and, estimated independently, the influence of reconciled attitudes on truth acceptance. Table 4.8 reports the two-stage least squares results for whites, Colored people, and those of Asian origin.

Truth and Reconciliation Among Colored South Africans Among Colored people, acceptance of the truth and racial reconciliation are related: r = .33. But does this mean that acceptance of the truth leads to reconciliation or that those who were already reconciled found the truth acceptable? The second-stage equation yields strong support for the inference that truth acceptance does indeed cause racial reconciliation. The unstandardized coefficient for the equation in which reconciliation causes truth is −.05; for the equation in which truth causes reconciliation, the coefficient is +5.29. The former coefficient is of course trivial and statistically insignificant; the latter coefficient is neither. Clearly, among Colored people, greater appreciation of the truth about apartheid leads to greater racial reconciliation (and not vice versa). In light of the advanced statistical analysis, the inclusion of essential control variables, and the strength of the empirical evidence, the inference that truth causes reconciliation is clearly supported.

Table 4.8 also reconfirms the strong influence of interracial contact on racial reconciliation: those who have more (and more significant) interactions with Africans are more likely to hold reconciled attitudes. In addition, Colored women are significantly more reconciled with Africans than Colored men.

(Text continues on p. 155.)

Table 4.8 Two-Stage Least Squares Analysis of Truth Acceptance and Racial Reconciliation Among Three Racial Groups

	Truth Acceptance			Racial Reconciliation		
	b	Standard Error	β	b	Standard Error	β
Whites						
Truth acceptance	—			6.11	1.36	.82***
Interracial contact	—			1.68	.23	.33***
Racial reconciliation	.05	.01	.36***	—		
Net benefits of apartheid	.00	.01	.02	—		
Knowledge of the TRC	.02	.03	.02	—		
Confidence in the TRC	.06	.03	.06*	—		
Media consumption	.05	.02	.06*	—		
Interest in politics	−.01	.03	−.02	—		
Illiteracy	.02	.09	.01	—		
Size of place of residence	−.04	.02	−.07**	—		
Opinion leadership	.05	.05	.02	—		
Level of education	.05	.02	.08**	−.06	.18	−.01
Afrikaans language	−.29	.05	−.20**	.97	.62	.09
Age	−.00	.00	−.05	.02	.01	.06
Social class	−.11	.03	−.10**	.49	.29	.06
Gender	.06	.04	.04	.19	.33	.02
Intercept	3.38	.17		−24.53	4.69	
Standard deviation—dependent variable	.73			5.42		
Standard error of estimate	.60			4.68		
R-squared			.25***			.30***
Number of cases	958			958		

Colored South Africans						
Truth acceptance	—			5.29	1.26	.73***
Interracial contact	—			1.59	.17	.44***
Racial reconciliation	−.01	.02	−.05	—		
Net benefits of apartheid	−.05	.01	−.19***	—		
Knowledge of the TRC	−.00	.04	.00	—		
Confidence in the TRC	.01	.04	.02	—		
Media consumption	.05	.03	.08	—		
Interest in politics	.09	.04	.13*	—		
Illiteracy	.01	.05	.01	—		
Size of place of residence	−.03	.02	−.08	—		
Opinion leadership	−.18	.09	−.09*	—		
Level of education	.14	.04	.21***	−.42	.35	−.09
Afrikaans language	−.25	.09	−.15**	−.76	.70	−.06
Age	.00	.00	.02	−.03	.02	−.09*
Social class	.06	.04	.09	−.11	.28	−.02
Gender	−.18	.06	−.13**	1.70	.52	.17***
Intercept	3.18	.27		−17.20	4.42	
Standard deviation—dependent variable	.68			4.88		
Standard error of estimate	.61			4.55		
R-squared			.22***			.26***
Number of cases	457			457		
South Africans of Asian origin						
Truth acceptance	—			2.29	1.16	.33*
Interracial contact	—			2.04	.28	.45***
Racial reconciliation	−.03	.03	−.22	—		
Net benefits of apartheid	−.05	.01	−.27***	—		
Knowledge of the TRC	.08	.08	.09	—		
Confidence in the TRC	−.05	.06	−.05	—		

(Table continues on p. 154.)

Table 4.8 *(Continued)*

	Truth Acceptance			Racial Reconciliation		
	b	Standard Error	β	b	Standard Error	β
Media consumption	−.01	.06	.01	—		
Interest in politics	.04	.06	.05	—		
Illiteracy	.10	.08	.10	—		
Size of place of residence	.05	.03	.11	—		
Opinion leadership	.10	.14	.05	—		
Afrikaans language	.57	.30	.14	—		
Level of education	.05	.07	.07	1.04	.35	.20**
Age	−.01	.00	−.17*	.02	.02	.05
Social class	−.10	.06	−.12	.48	.38	.09
Gender	−.14	.09	−.10	−.44	.59	−.05
Intercept	3.88	.41		−15.87	5.37	
Standard deviation—dependent variable	.69			4.82		
Standard error of estimate	.67			4.19		
R-squared			.17***			.28***
Number of cases	241			241		

Source: Author's compilation from the 2001 Truth and Reconciliation Survey.
Significance of standardized regression coefficient (β): $***p \le .001$; $**p \le .01$; $*p \le .05$.

Among Colored people, truth acceptance is not related to reconciliation but is instead a function of level of education, experiences under apartheid, being an Afrikaans-speaker, and, to a lesser degree, gender and interest in politics. Perhaps the most interesting finding from this analysis has to do with the independent influence of speaking Afrikaans. Colored people who speak the language of apartheid are less likely to accept the truth than English-speakers. And of course the impact of this variable is entirely independent of level of education, knowledge of the TRC, and even net benefits experienced under apartheid. However, the direct effect of speaking Afrikaans on reconciliation is trivial, since the influence of the variable flows entirely through truth acceptance. Being a Colored Afrikaans-speaker shapes one's understanding of the truth about apartheid, and consequently one's level of reconciliation with the African majority.

Truth and Reconciliation Among South Africans of Asian Origin Among South Africans of Asian origin, truth and reconciliation are related at r = .18 (p = .004); truth acceptance is associated with reconciliation (at least weakly and significantly). According to the two-stage least squares model, truth directly contributes to reconciliation (b = 2.29), but reconciliation does not influence truth acceptance (b = −.03). Contact with Africans also strongly shapes the racial attitudes of those of Asian origin, just as experiences under apartheid shape their views of the truth about apartheid. But the most important finding is that, among South Africans of Asian origin, those who have come to accept the truth about apartheid tend to be substantially more reconciled.

Truth and Reconciliation Among White South Africans The analysis for white South Africans is problematical, since truth and reconciliation are so strongly correlated with each other (r = .51). Under such conditions, two-stage least squares has difficulty partitioning the reciprocal causation into individual components. In fact, that is exactly the conclusion of the analysis: truth does lead to reconciliation (b = 6.11), but reconciliation also leads to truth (b = .05). Both coefficients are highly statistically and substantively significant. Thus, while there is strong evidence that accepting the TRC's truth leads to reconciliation among whites, it is also true that those who come to accept the TRC's truth are to some degree already reconciled with their African fellow citizens.

Similar to Colored South Africans, being Afrikans directly shapes understandings of the past but does not influence reconciliation directly. Because Afrikaans-speaking whites tend to reject the TRC's truth, they also tend to be less reconciled with the African majority.

Interracial contact also strongly influences racial reconciliation among whites. Indeed, none of the other independent variables has any significant direct effect on white racial attitudes. In terms of truth acceptance, only home language and reconciliation attitudes have strong direct influences on levels of participation in the country's collective memory.

Three conclusions about the causal link between truth and reconciliation emerge from my analysis:

- Among South Africans of Asian origin and Colored South Africans, accepting the truth about the past seems to cause people to be more reconciled.
- Among white South Africans, truth leads to reconciliation, but those more reconciled are also more prepared to accept the truth. Thus, truth and reconciliation go together, but the causal relationship appears to be reciprocal. Still, among whites, accepting the truth does indeed contribute to reconciliation.
- Among blacks, truth does not lead to reconciliation; nor does reconciliation lead to truth acceptance.

Conjectures About the Processes by Which Truth Leads to Reconciliation

To get some additional purchase on the processes of attitude change that may have resulted from South Africa's truth and reconciliation process, it is necessary to move beyond the available data, which, after all, are drawn from a single point in time. I begin by imagining what interracial attitudes might have been like under apartheid.

The decade of the 1980s was a period of low-scale civil war in South Africa. The ANC had launched a campaign to make the country "ungovernable," and it succeeded to a remarkable degree. The apartheid regime was forced to declare a state of emergency, and urban terrorism became fairly commonplace. This was a time of intense political conflict between the forces of apartheid and the forces of liberation.

It is easy to imagine that racial attitudes were extremely polarized as a result of the struggle. The views of white South Africans toward blacks were most likely heavily tinged by the historical racism that had dominated most of their lives under apartheid. Moreover, whites viewed the liberation movement as the spearhead of a Communist threat, believing the ANC to be a stooge of worldwide communism. Not only were the liberation forces dominated by Communists, but they were godless as well. Urban terrorism petrified whites. Some whites imagined that their black housekeepers would rise up in revolution, perhaps even poisoning their families while serving one of the daily meals. Enforced racial segregation made anything but pro forma interracial contact unlikely, and what contact took place was inevitably grounded in inequality. It is easy to suppose that most whites, even those who did not strongly support apartheid, viewed the liberation movement as a movement dominated by evil. The war against the liberation forces was therefore a "just war." Reconciliation under such circumstances was extremely improbable (to say the least).

Black attitudes toward whites were unlikely to have been any more favorable. Among a majority of blacks, whites were probably viewed as irretrievably racist, irrevocably committed to apartheid, and willing to deal with blacks only when forced to. Because apartheid was a "crime against humanity," those who benefited from apartheid were criminals themselves. Contacts with whites were rare, and those that did take place were often dehumanizing. Many black South Africans were forcibly removed from their places of living, and some were banished to the so-called Bantustans. Resentment and outrage against the white system were widespread.

For many blacks, apartheid was the source of all that was wrong with South Africa. The war against the apartheid state was therefore a "just war."

If I am correct about the nature of attitudes prior to the transition, then strong impediments to reconciliation existed. Both blacks and whites most likely understood and trusted each other very little, rarely interacted, held vicious stereotypes about each other, and disliked and were highly threatened by those of other races. This is almost certainly the landscape that faced the TRC when it began its efforts at creating a more reconciled South Africa.[23] An exogenous force was necessary to open the door to a change in attitudes.

The primary way in which the truth and reconciliation process could induce attitude change was through the creation of cognitive dissonance. To get South Africans to change their attitudes toward those of other racial groups, it was essential that the cognitive basis of racial beliefs be shaken up. Change in racial attitudes is often difficult to achieve because exogenous forces capable of generating widespread dissonance rarely occur naturally, and most people are able to fend off a trickle of unwelcome information as it filters into their consciousness. As figure 4.1 depicts, the truth and reconciliation process may have changed the way South Africans think about each other by creating cognitive dissonance and by mitigating cognitive dogmatism. In short, the truth and reconciliation process may have created uncertainty and doubt among South Africans about the goodness and morality of their own cause. Virtually all parties in South Africa—from the African National Congress to the National Party—condemned the TRC's *Final Report*. The truth exposed by the TRC included atrocities that might have made people less likely to reconcile. But because the TRC documented atrocities on all sides in the struggle over apartheid, many South Africans became less certain about the purity of their side in the struggle and were forced to acknowledge that the "other side" might also have been unfairly victimized. Sharing responsibility, blame, and victimhood evens the score ever so slightly, providing a basis for dialogue. When people are no longer dogmatically attached to a

Figure 4.1 Processes by Which "Truth" Leads to Attitude Change

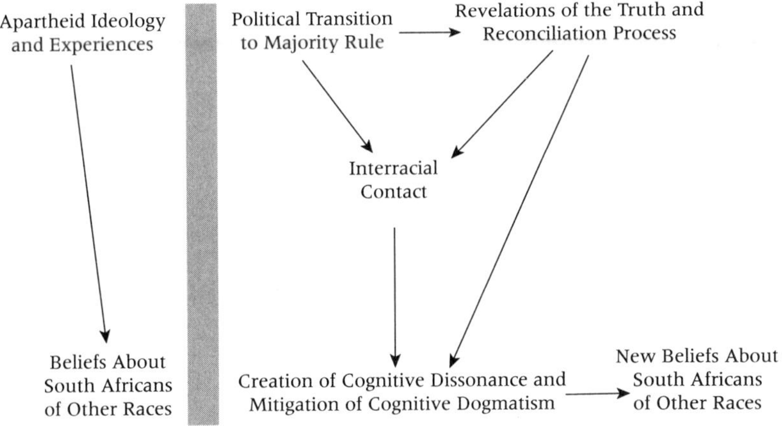

Source: Author's compilation from the 2001 Truth and Reconciliation Survey.

good-versus-evil view of the struggle, a space for reconciliation can be opened.

In its attempts to reshape South Africa's understanding of its apartheid past, the truth and reconciliation process is a force perhaps capable of getting people to rethink their attitudes. If the TRC was successful in stimulating South Africans to reevaluate their understandings of race and racial conflict in South Africa, perhaps it was capable of creating enough attitudinal dissonance to provide an engine for change in racial attitudes.

How might the truth and reconciliation process have created this dissonance? Perhaps the most important lesson of the TRC was that both sides in the struggle did horrible things. How might this finding of the TRC have affected white and black attitudes?

White people could have learned from the truth and reconciliation process that the defense of the apartheid state involved numerous indefensible actions. Many of the atrocities unearthed by the TRC involved the state's acts of extreme excess in the political repression of dissidents. Whether they should have known or not, many white South Africans claim to have been shocked by these revelations and to have never imagined that the state would go as far as it did to crush resistance to apartheid.[24] For instance, when asked about this in one of our focus groups, a group of white South Africans had the following conversation:

> "Yes, all these things when they came out at the TRC, I thought, 'My God, where was I living? Was that in South Africa?'"
>
> "It's a very good point."
>
> "The whites, you didn't know any of that was going on. You looked on apartheid and you were comfortable, because you could go to the shops and go where you liked."
>
> "It was a very clever system."
>
> "It was wonderful, but I didn't know these things were happening. I was shocked to learn what was going on. But that was the government we were living under."
>
> "I remember having arguments with my father. He was saying, 'Don't believe everything you get told.' I'm telling him, 'This is happening to my friends,' and he kept saying they were Communists. . . ."
>
> "That's it, you see! Because that is what the justification for all this was, to us."
>
> "It was the brainwashing."

When the interviewer asked the members of this group whether they were actually aware of the atrocities committed by the state, they responded:

> "I think we were aware of people being separated, separate toilets, buses, you know this."
>
> "The superficial things."
>
> "But, in my opinion . . . I can remember growing up, hearing drums on the farm, having a wonderful time, and to me that was some of their choice."
>
> "They were happy living in these. . . . "
>
> "Yes, they were happy. We were ignorant in a sense of knowing what actually really went on."

Perhaps some whites, even those who still cannot accept that apartheid was a crime against humanity, have come to view the implementation of apartheid, or at least its defense, as criminal. At a minimum, it seems quite unlikely that the defenders of apartheid were as heroic and legitimate after the revelations of the truth and reconciliation process. The "just war" in defense of apartheid seems less just after the exposés of the TRC.

White South Africans have also learned that liberation does not lead to communism. The TRC did not have to teach whites this lesson; history was sufficient. With the breakdown of the worldwide Communist movement, with the moderation of both the Mandela and Mbeki governments, few whites today would equate ANC rule with the rule of godless Communists.

Whites cannot have helped but be impressed by the magnanimity and graciousness of Nelson Mandela during the early days of the transition. Mandela's continual pleas for tolerance and reconciliation—not to mention his well-publicized donning of a rugby shirt (the sport of choice among whites)—undoubtedly contributed to more benign racial attitudes among whites.

Whites may also have come to accept some of the guilt and blame for the benefits they enjoyed under apartheid and for the costs that the system imposed on the vast majority of South Africans. Though some whites may have been unaware of the atrocities committed by their state against the liberation forces, no whites could claim to be unaware of the enormous subsidy that apartheid provided for their standard of living.

Thus, whites who were attentive to the truth and reconciliation process learned that their side was less than noble in creating and defending apartheid, that they had been duped and lied to by their own leaders, and that the opposition was perhaps less radically evil in its efforts to create a new system in South Africa.

The truth and reconciliation process may have contributed as well to attitude change among blacks, although because the revelations of the process were often not news to blacks, attitude change may not have been as radical or as widespread.[25] Prior to the TRC, blacks in South Africa were entirely aware of the evil of apartheid, and the TRC did little to dispel this knowledge. But the truth and reconciliation process may have also taught blacks that horrible things were done—against other blacks as well as against whites—

in the name of liberation. In many respects, the campaign of ungovernability in the 1980s turned blacks against blacks; there were great pressures toward conformity (reinforced by the horrific crime of "necklacing"), and some degree of gangsterism occurred under the guise of the struggle (see, for example, Marks 2001; see also Gobodo-Madikizela 2003, 147). We asked the members of one of our African focus groups what they thought of the revelation that both those struggling against apartheid and those defending it had done terrible things. The moderator's comments are in italics.

> "It's very true, both sides have blood on their hands."
>
> "Even the so-called liberators had very inhumane methods that they used when they wanted to put through a message—in camps abroad and within the country. A lot of people were hurt in the townships. If you were successful you were accused of selling out."
>
> "We as blacks don't empower our people; whites lift each other up. When we blacks get to the top, we forget our own."
>
> "It's true, both sides did bad things."
>
> *"You only mention the liberation movements. Why not the white regime?"*
>
> "That is obvious—with them we don't even need to mention it, because we know exactly what happened."
>
> *"But was it justified for both camps to do what they did?"*
>
> "Not at all."
>
> "But in those days there was no time to think about whether the actions were justified or not."
>
> *"So both sides did wrong?"*
>
> "Yes."
>
> "Two wrongs don't make a right."

The truth and reconciliation process was also important for blacks because it often confirmed what many had earlier regarded as "disinformation" created by the apartheid regime. In the 1980s one never knew what to believe. Some Africans were also no doubt moved by the revelations of terrorism directed against innocent white civilians. Many black South Africans most likely came away from the truth and reconciliation process believing that the struggle against apartheid was indeed a "just war" but that many unjust and inhumane actions were taken in the name of liberation.

Moreover, black South Africans have surely learned that apartheid is not the sole source of the myriad problems they face. Perhaps it is true that apartheid caused poverty, which in turn causes AIDS (as President Mbeki argues), but few in South Africa accept this linkage today. The end of apartheid offered little immediate relief to the millions of South Africans living in abject poverty.

Thus, one can imagine that reconciliation with whites began to look possible when Africans were encouraged to rethink the view that apartheid was a system of infinite evil that was brought down by a movement of ultimate good.

Furthermore, with the fall of the forced segregation of apartheid has come at least some increase in interracial interactions in South Africa. We must be careful not to overstate the point, but whites encountering blacks in situations of social equality was very rare before 1994 and has become less rare since 1994. Not only has the frequency of intergroup contact surely increased since the transition, but so too has the quality of the interaction, especially in terms of formal equality (and to a lesser degree, power). The opportunity for blacks and whites to get to know each other has blossomed since the transition (even if taking advantage of the opportunity has been unevenly distributed). These changes probably contribute to greater possibilities for reconciliation.

Thus, the effect of the truth and reconciliation process may have been to get people to question their beliefs about good and evil in the past and present in South Africa. As the Truth and Reconciliation Commission (1998, vol. 1, pp. 111–12) proclaimed:

> One can say that the information in the hands of the Commission made it impossible to claim, for example, that: the practice of torture by the state security forces was not systematic and widespread; that only a few "rotten eggs" or "bad apples" committed gross violations of human rights; that the state was not directly and indirectly involved in "black-on-black" violence; that the chemical and biological warfare programme was only of a defensive nature; that slogans by sections of the liberation movement did not contribute to killings of "settlers" or farmers; and that the accounts of gross human rights violations in the African National Congress (ANC) camps were the consequence of state disinformation. Thus, disinformation about the

> past that had been accepted as truth by some members of society lost much of its credibility.

Those who accepted the positions of the TRC might have come to see the struggle over apartheid as one of pretty good good against pretty bad bad, not as absolute good versus infinite evil. As noted earlier, it is hard to reconcile with infinite evil; it is perhaps easier to reconcile with bad that is not entirely evil (especially if there is some degree of repentance). Truth may have opened the door to reconciliation by encouraging people to abandon their view that South Africa is populated by people with worldviews so distant that they are unreconcilable. The revelations of the truth and reconciliation process may have encouraged self-reflection and self-criticism, thus moderating the views of the adversaries in the struggle. As Gobodo-Madikizela (2003, 119) asserts, to demonize one's enemies as monsters is too easy—it lets them off too easily; further, "to dismiss perpetrators simply as evildoers and monsters shuts the door to the kind of dialogue that leads to an enduring peace" (125). Continuing, she argues:

> Daring, on the other hand, to look the enemy in the eye and allow oneself to read signs of pain and cues of contrition or regret where one might almost have preferred to continue seeing only hatred is the one possibility we have for steering individuals and societies toward replacing long-standing stalemates out of a nation's past with genuine engagement. Hope is where transformation begins; without it, a society cannot take its first steps toward reconstructing its self-identity as a society of tolerance and coexistence. (125–26)

In general, strong impediments exist to new information generating attitude change. However, the information provided by the truth and reconciliation process had several attributes that made it more likely to be influential. First, the information was widely accessible, not only in terms of quantity—which by all accounts was absolutely overwhelming—but also in terms of the type of information broadcast. The South African media focused overwhelmingly on the human interest side of the TRC's activities, in contrast to the commission's broader ideological and intellectual goals. South Africans learned of the suffering of ordinary people through the TRC. What they learned was often extremely graphic—as in Policeman Benzein's demonstration of his notorious "wet bag" method of torture, broadcast widely throughout South Africa. This type of fare was often addictive to ordinary people, and few in South Africa could have escaped exposure to the reports of the activities of the truth and reconciliation process.

The information typically had no conspicuous ideological content; no obvious message was being sold. Consequently, reports on the TRC did not necessarily raise the sort of defensive alarms that often make new information impotent to bring about attitude change. The lack of ideological content flowed in part from the human interest dimensions of the reports, but also in part from the TRC's conscious desire to reach all segments of society. Surely the truth and reconciliation process was used by some to launch ideological attacks on either the apartheid system or the liberation movement, but much of what the TRC put before the South African people was simple and subtle; it had to do with bad guys hurting good guys.[26] Without an obvious and explicit ideological veneer, many of the messages and stories of the TRC were attractive and palatable to South Africans of many different ideological persuasions.

The information presented to South Africans by the TRC was also typically unrebutted, in part because miscreants were coming before the TRC to admit their crimes and be awarded amnesty. Certainly there was occasional conflict—for example, some victims would challenge the motives of the perpetrators, arguing, for instance, that they were economic, not political, and therefore not covered by the amnesty legislation. But generally the intense denials that often cloud political controversies were limited in South Africa's truth and reconciliation process.

Thus, many of the factors that usually contribute to persuasion in fact reinforce the possibility that the truth and reconciliation process may have created attitude change. The information was salient and interesting, subtle in its messages, and largely not greeted by counterarguments. And it did not invoke defense mechanisms, since it was not threatening, as it might have been. These are just the conditions likely to give rise to social persuasion.

Concluding Comments

In this chapter, I have addressed three issues: Do truth and reconciliation go together (covary)? If so, in what direction is the relationship (positive or negative)? And did one cause the other? My analysis has answered the first and second questions with considerable certitude: in no instance is truth associated with a lack of reconciliation, and among whites, Colored South Africans, and those of Asian origin, a substantial positive relationship is revealed in the data. For these three groups, I also adduce evidence that truth may cause reconciliation, although given the constraints of these data, considerably less confidence in this causal conclusion is warranted. Thus, the minimalist conclusion of this research is that the truth and reconciliation process has done little to harm race relations in South Africa; the maximalist conclusion is that the truth process has actually caused a salutary change in racial attitudes.

Among black South Africans, truth seems to contribute little to reconciliation. This is perhaps a disappointing finding, although it should be strongly emphasized that truth does not contribute to a lack of reconciliation either. Many feared that the revelations of the TRC would harden black attitudes toward whites, making coexistence in the New South Africa even more difficult. That the truth and reconciliation process seems not to have had a negative influence among Africans, while having positive impacts on whites, Colored people, and those of Asian origin, indicates that the process has clearly been a net benefit to South Africa.

My consideration of alternative hypotheses has also led to some important discoveries, the most significant of which has to do with the contribution of racial interactions to reconciliation. South Africans who interact with those of other races tend to understand and trust them more and to reject racial stereotypes. This finding is neither trivial nor tautological—under many conditions, interracial interactions exacerbate racial tensions rather than calming them. And not all types of interracial interaction produce this salutary effect in South Africa—for instance, the data clearly demonstrate that interracial interactions in the workplace have no such influence. In general, racial isolation seems to make racial reconciliation much more difficult.

The truth and reconciliation process in South Africa is grounded in a set of assumptions and hypotheses that are much in need of additional empirical investigation. At many points in my analysis I have suggested that longitudinal data are essential to unravel complex patterns of causality. "Truth" and "reconciliation" are empirical concepts that can indeed be measured, and future research should focus on the collection of longitudinal data so that change over time can be rigorously assessed. It may already be too late to collect the necessary data connecting the activities of the TRC with truth acceptance, but reconciliation is an ongoing process in South Africa, so it is crucial that regular efforts to measure the degree of reconciliation be mounted.

My analysis supports a rather complex view of the nature of reconciliation in contemporary South Africa. From the point of view of a society that formally abandoned apartheid less than a decade ago—and a society in which civil war was a very real possibility in the not-too-distant past—the levels of racial reconciliation discovered in this survey are remarkable. Few observers of South African politics would have anticipated the findings reported here.

Still, racial reconciliation among the black majority in South Africa poses some unique challenges. Most obviously, blacks bore the brunt of the repression under the apartheid system created by the whites, so it is not at all surprising that their feelings toward their white fellow citizens are not particularly charitable. But several other factors seem to contribute as well to negative racial attitudes among blacks. Perhaps most important is that blacks rarely have any meaningful interaction with whites; as a result, interracial understanding is difficult at best. Also significant is the fact that greater education does *not* contribute to greater reconciliation among blacks; nor are young blacks any more likely to be reconciled than older blacks. Perhaps my most hopeful finding is that reconciliation is more likely within the black community as memories of experiences under apartheid fade, but several of these results are not so encouraging.

Note should also be made of Afrikaans-speaking whites, a group notable for its distinctive rejection of racial reconciliation. Unfortunately, this research offers few suggestions for how Afrikaans-speakers can become more accepting and trustful of their black fellow citizens.

Has the truth and reconciliation process contributed to democratization in South Africa? To answer this question in any meaningful way requires more investigation than is possible with these survey data. But this analysis suggests that the truth and reconciliation process has had some positive influences, at least for some South Africans. Among whites, for instance, greater attention to and confidence in the TRC is associated with greater acceptance of the truth about apartheid, and consequently with greater racial reconciliation. This has been especially true for English-speaking whites. The causality involved in these relationships may be somewhat ambiguous, but these data are strongly compatible with the conclusion that whites learned something from the TRC and that what they learned made them better able to get along with their black fellow citizens. If so, then this is a very important contribution of the truth and reconciliation process to the consolidation of democratic reform in South Africa.

Appendix

Social Desirability: Voting for the National Party

Another way in which I got some purchase on the degree to which whites may have misrepresented their views on race was to ask them about their support for the National Party (NP). It is common in South Africa today to wonder how the National Party could have ruled the country for so long when so few whites, it is supposed, say that they ever supported it. Our data provide some concrete evidence on this score. We directly asked our respondents whether they had ever voted in favor of or supported the National

Table 4A.1 Racial Differences in Admitted Support for the National Party

"Before Nelson Mandela was elected in 1994, did you ever vote in favor of or support the National Party?"	African	White	Colored	Asian Origin
Yes	.7%	54.4%	21.4%	15.1%
No	54.5	34.4	53.3	16.3
Did not vote	44.3	10.2	24.5	67.3
Don't know	.4	.9	.9	1.2
Number of cases	2,001	958	458	245

Source: Author's compilation from the 2001 Truth and Reconciliation Survey.

Party. If whites are answering our questions by trying to make themselves appear in a favorable light, then we would expect that few would be willing to assert that they supported the party of apartheid. Table 4A.1 reports the replies to the question: "Before Nelson Mandela was elected in 1994, did you ever vote in favor of or support the National Party?"

As it turns out, it is fairly common for white South Africans to admit to having supported or voted for the National Party, with a majority of whites (54.4 percent) confessing to having been in the NP camp. Large differences exist between English and Afrikaans-speaking whites, with roughly two-thirds of the latter acknowledging their allegiance to the NP (data not shown). And indeed, when we implement a control for the age of the respondent (recognizing that many of the respondents in the survey in fact had few if any opportunities to vote for the NP since they were too young), we find that almost two-thirds of white South Africans above the age of thirty-four assert that they supported the NP at some point prior to the transition. Surely some whites disguised their true feelings during the interview, but it seems from all the available evidence that this was not very common among the white respondents.

Support for the NP was not as widespread among Colored South Africans, although neither was the level of support trivial. Perhaps the most interesting finding concerning those of Asian origin is their low level of (reported) voting: two-thirds of the Asian respondents claimed not to have voted under the old system.

Table 4A.2 The Connection Among White South Africans Between Supporting the National Party and Apartheid

"Was your vote based on the National Party's position on apartheid?"	"Did you ever vote for the National Party?"	
	Yes	No
Yes		
Because I supported apartheid	24.8%	
Because I opposed apartheid		31.9%
No	72.2	62.0
Don't remember	3.1	6.1
N	521	329

Source: Author's compilation from the 2001 Truth and Reconciliation Survey.

Voting for the NP may not be exactly the same as supporting apartheid. We therefore asked the respondents whether their support for the NP was due to its position on apartheid and, conversely, whether their choice not to support the NP was due to apartheid. Table 4A.2 reports the results for the white respondents in the sample.

It is true that only one-fourth of the whites in the sample claimed to have supported the National Party owing to its policies on apartheid. This figure may underestimate the truth, because whites are reluctant to acknowledge their own support of apartheid. But it is also evident that whites do *not* assert that they *opposed* the NP owing to apartheid. Indeed, the percentage of NP supporters and opponents who based their support on the party's apartheid position is roughly equivalent. If whites are not clearly overstating their opposition to apartheid, then perhaps neither are they understating their support for it.

Finally, table 4A.3 reports the interviewer assessments of the honesty of the respondents they interviewed. Recall that nearly all blacks and whites were interviewed by interviewers of the same race, and that same-race interviews were conducted with a large majority of Colored people and those of Asian origin. Generally, an impressive majority of the respondents were judged to be reasonably honest. To the extent that there is an exception to this finding,

Table 4A.3 Racial Differences in Perceived Honesty of Replies

Interviewer Judgment	African	White	Colored	Asian Origin
Not as honest	21.6%	7.2%	17.0%	11.3%
As honest as most	61.5	80.8	74.7	74.8
Somewhat more honest	10.6	8.8	4.7	8.4
A great deal more honest	6.3	3.1	3.6	5.5
Number of cases	1933	953	470	238

Source: Author's compilation from the 2001 Truth and Reconciliation Survey.

it is among black respondents, not whites. Only a very small percentage of whites were gauged by the interviewers to be not very honest.

No analysis such as this can ever provide definitive evidence that survey respondents were absolutely honest in their replies to questions. But the evidence adduced here does *not* set off alarm bells about the possibility of strong social desirability influences in the data. It appears that the climate of race in contemporary South Africa allows most people to voice their true views, for better or worse, at least in private, to a same-race interviewer.

The Causal Connection Between Contact and Interracial Reconciliation

A major contention of this chapter is that interracial contact contributes to more salutary racial attitudes. The opposite direction of causality—tolerant racial attitudes lead to more contact—is not implausible and therefore deserves some additional consideration.

Data can rarely reveal causality; rather, causality comes from theory, and the only thing data can do is make us more or less confident of our causal inferences. This assertion is generally true, but it is especially the case with cross-sectional data. Unraveling the causality of two variables that occur at the same point in time is challenging, to say the least, and this problem afflicts every type of political science. Unfortunately, however, we care about making inferences about causality.

How might the nature of a causal structure be discerned? There are three possibilities. First, one might conduct a logical analysis to determine causality. For instance, contact involving no choice on the part of the individual (forced interaction) cannot be said to be a function of the preferences of the individual. Second, extant literature addresses this question to at least some degree, so it is useful to review what earlier scholars have concluded. Finally, some statistical and methodological approaches yield a basis for making strong inferences about the direction of causality. I consider each of these, in reverse order.

Statistical Solutions Two types of methodological approaches to establishing causality are prominent in the literature: efforts to disentangle cross-sectional data with advanced statistical techniques and longitudinal studies that take advantage of the presumption that causes exist prior to effects. Both of these approaches have been applied to the contact hypothesis.[27]

In this instance, longitudinal approaches are obviously not useful, since these are cross-sectional data. The ability to apply the advanced statistical techniques is dependent on finding an "instrument" for contact—variables that predict contact but are not related to truth or reconciliation. Though I made a great effort to find a predictor of contact unrelated to reconciliation, I failed. This problem is exacerbated by the fact that, at the bivariate level, contact and reconciliation are strongly intercorrelated. Thus, with these data, I cannot draw a conclusion based on statistical analysis about the structure of the causality involved.

One bit of revealing statistical analysis is available, however. Thomas Wilson's approach to the question of causality (as in, for example, his 1996 analysis of the General Social Survey data) is to make use of the assumption that personality attributes are relatively obdurate and therefore unlikely to change as a result of interracial contact. Formed early in life, personality attributes precede contact in the causal sequence, even if contact is in part a function of such characteristics. If contact is still related to interracial attitudes even controlling for personality attributes, then we are entitled to conclude that contact does in fact contribute to salutary racial views.

Using a measure of *xenophobia*, which is commonly assumed to

Table 4A.4 The Impact of Contact on Reconciliation

	Coefficient Without Control	Coefficient with Xenophobia Control
Blacks	.28	.27
Whites	.52	.49
Colored people	.43	.43
Asian origin	.47	.47

Source: Author's compilation from the 2001 Truth and Reconciliation Survey.

be a personality characteristic (Cloninger, Svrakic, and Przybeck 1993), I discover the results reported in table 4A.4 on the relationship between contact and interracial reconciliation:

Thus, these results (standardized regression coefficients), after controlling for the personality attribute that might well predispose one toward interracial contact, add considerable weight to the claim that contact shapes racial attitudes.

Of course, I recognize that this test is not perfect because it is highly contingent on the assumption that xenophobia is a personality trait that is inculcated early in life and fairly resistant to change (or at least resistant to change through interactions with other people). Wilson (1996, 56) defends this approach, asserting:

> This conclusion and the analysis leading to it rest heavily [on the assumption] that diffuse prejudice toward other minorities, used here as an indicator of personality based prejudice, is unaffected by contact with Blacks. If this assumption is wrong, then this study's procedure of using diffuse prejudice as a control for self-selection is clearly inappropriate. However, this assumption has a firm theoretical basis in Allport's (1954) account of contact's effect on prejudice and in his view that personality-based prejudice is highly resistant to change.

Thus, at least some theory and statistical evidence support the causal structure I propose in this chapter.[28]

Extant Research What does the literature tell us about the nature of the relationship between contact and racial attitudes? The contact literature is vast and has taught us several things.

Interracial contact definitely contributes to more positive racial attitudes. Pettigrew and Tropp (2000, 94) have recently reported a major meta-analysis of the contact literature, based on 203 individual studies with 313 independent samples and 746 separate tests and involving 90,000 subjects from 25 different nations. They conclude: "*Overall, face-to-face interaction between members of distinguishable groups is importantly related to reduced prejudice.* Of the 203 studies, 94% found an inverse relationship between contact and prejudice" (109, emphasis in original). I do not think there is any doubt whatsoever that it is reasonable to expect that contact shapes attitudes.

Generally, levels of interracial contact are not greatly dependent on attitudes. Pettigrew and Tropp (2000, 100) directly consider the problem of the causal sequence, concluding that studies based on longitudinal designs, advanced statistical techniques, and what they term "no-choice studies" (studies in which subjects have little discretion as to whether to engage in contact)[29] reveal that "contact as the cause of reduced prejudice is more important than the selection-bias possibility that prejudiced people avoid contact." Because of its relevance to my study, their conclusion on the results from statistical studies of causality is also important: "These methods reveal that prejudiced people do indeed avoid intergroup contact. But the path from contact to reduced prejudice is even stronger. . . . Thus, these methods suggest that, while both sequences operate, the more important effect is intergroup contact reducing prejudice" (99). Let me continue with the Pettigrew and Tropp conclusions: "Further, this solid link cannot be explained by selection and retrieval biases. Bigoted people do avoid contact with the scorned group, but the causal sequence from contact to diminished prejudice is stronger" (109). Thus, from their analysis, I am not entitled to claim that attitudes have no impact on contact, but it is reasonable to conclude that the causal sequence I postulate in this chapter is more probable than positing the opposite sequence (and the statistical results I report show that contact has an independent impact even controlling for the personality attributes likely to give rise to interracial contact in the first place). Thus, the results I report here are entirely consistent with the practices and findings of extant literature.

Logical Analysis Can a logical structure be built in favor of one of the hypothesized causal flows? Perhaps.

In South Africa, since 1994, it is likely that interracial contact has changed more readily than have racial attitudes, since racial attitudes are generally assumed to be rather resistant to change and thus to evolve quite slowly. With the fall of apartheid, opportunities for interracial contact increased dramatically. Moreover, South Africans have less choice in whether or not they will mix with people of other races, since some degree of integration has been mandated in the schools, in housing, in the workplace, and in public places. Further, the quality of such contact has surely increased as blacks have been released from a subservient and subordinate position in South Africa. This is somewhat similar to Pettigrew and Tropp's (2000, 99) "no-choice studies." If racial attitudes change slowly, and if interracial contact in South Africa has increased rather substantially and is to some degree involuntary, then it seems plausible that contact causes attitudes.

Chapter 5

Truth, Reconciliation, and the Creation of a Human Rights Culture

> Reconciliation requires that all South Africans accept moral and political responsibility for nurturing a culture of human rights and democracy within which political and socio-economic conflicts are addressed both seriously and in a non-violent manner.
>
> —Truth and Reconciliation Commission (1998, vol. 5, ch. 9, p. 435)

South Africa's truth and reconciliation process was surely the most ambitious the world has ever seen. Not only was the Truth and Reconciliation Commission charged with investigating human rights abuses and granting amnesty to miscreants, but the process was expected as well to contribute to a broader "reconciliation" in South Africa (the "reconciliation" half of the truth and reconciliation equation). In a country racked by a history of racism and racial subjugation, and one just emerging from fifty years of domination by an evil apartheid regime, doing anything to enhance reconciliation between the masters and slaves of the past is a tall order indeed.

As the epigraph to this chapter illustrates, however, the truth and reconciliation process was also given another task: building a political culture in South Africa that would be respectful of human rights. The process was expected to be backward-looking, in the sense of documenting and dealing with the gross human rights violations of the past, as well as forward-looking in trying to prevent future tyranny. Its assignment was to nurture a human rights culture that would serve as a prophylactic against rights abuses in the future.

In an effort to address this mandate, the *Final Report* of the TRC includes in its recommendations a section on the "promotion of a human rights culture" (Truth and Reconciliation Commission 1998, vol. 5, ch. 8). Most of the recommendations concern actions to be taken by the government (for example, recommending that the government recommit itself to regular and fair elections), but the TRC also urges that its report be made widely available, presumably under the assumption that those who read the report will adopt certain attitudes and values. "Culture," as apparently understood by the TRC, largely refers to institutional actors but may also include the beliefs, values, and attitudes of ordinary citizens.

Many political scientists take culture very seriously and carefully distinguish between institutions and cultural values. Within our theories of democratic consolidation, establishing a culture that is respectful of human rights involves the creation of a set of political values and attitudes favoring human rights. A human rights culture is one in which people value human rights highly, are unwilling to sacrifice them under most circumstances, and jealously guard against intrusions into those rights. Such a culture may stand as a potent (but not omnipotent) impediment to political repression.

The charge to the truth and reconciliation process to address South Africa's culture of human rights is also a charge to social scientists to consider several important theoretical and empirical questions. Has South Africa made progress in developing a culture supportive of human rights? How widespread are such values? Are they concentrated within any particular strata within the South African population? How have these values changed? Why have they changed? Did the truth and reconciliation process itself have anything to do with how ordinary South Africans judge and value basic human rights?

These microlevel questions are all central elements of prominent theories within political science. In essence, the question is one of social learning and cultural change. Presumably (because rigorous data on the matter are not available), in the old South Africa human rights abuses were tolerated, if not accepted. Conceivably, this view characterized both the defenders *and* opponents of apartheid, in the sense that a struggle against a system as radically evil as apartheid might well have seemed to justify deviations from the strict observance of human rights. The TRC was expected to change people's attitudes and values, to teach them that human rights must be inviolable, and to frame human rights as an issue essential to successful democratization. Though those who wrote the enabling legislation may not have had large-scale cultural engineering in mind when they spoke of creating a human rights culture in South Africa, social science theories certainly endorse the importance of such a culture and offer at least some clues about how it might be created.

Thus, this chapter has several purposes. First, I ask whether the contemporary political culture of South Africa is supportive of human rights. Second, I then investigate the distribution of support for human rights, beginning with the always important racial differences. Race, however, is never a very satisfactory explanation of social and political attitudes and values, so I turn to more theoretically grounded explanations of variability in stances toward human rights. I assess whether there is any evidence that the truth and reconciliation process itself had an impact on support for human rights in South Africa, especially since awareness of the TRC's activities seems to have penetrated all corners of South African society. Finally, I examine a variety of additional hypotheses—ranging from historical and contemporary experiences to interracial attitudes, to preferences for different aspects of democracy—as possible explanations of the value that South Africans attach to human rights. Throughout this analysis, I focus on one particular aspect of human rights: commitment to universalism (versus particularism) in the application of the rule of law. In the end, I draw the conclusion that, even though South Africa has far to go in becoming a culture in which human rights are highly regarded among all segments of the mass public, the truth and reconciliation process may well have contributed to creating a human rights culture in the country.

The Meaning of a Human Rights Culture

What those who wrote the law creating the TRC meant by the term "human rights culture" is not entirely clear, primarily because so many different meanings are packed into the term. The values incorporated within the concept "human rights" seem to include: political tolerance, rights consciousness, support for due process, respect for life, deference to the rule of law, and even support for democratic institutions and processes more generally. An appropriate apothegm for the meaning of a human rights culture in South Africa is perhaps everything that the apartheid regime was not.

Social scientists must of course take the concept more seriously and treat it more systematically and rigorously. One simple distinction, hinted at already, is that human rights can be enhanced by certain institutional structures (such as an independent judiciary) *and* by certain political attitudes and values held by ordinary people within the polity. Institutions and cultures are two separate entities, and the question of whether one reinforces and supports the other is a vital empirical question (see Ibhawoh 2000).[1]

Some who have written about human rights in South Africa emphasize the institutional underpinning of such a culture. Jeremy Sarkin (1998), for instance, discusses the panoply of institutions connected to the enforcement of human rights in South Africa (for example, the Constitutional Court, the Human Rights Commission, the Commission on the Restitution of Land Rights) in an article that refers to "culture" in its title. Sarkin's concern is determining whether there are institutional mechanisms that contribute to the widening and deepening of human rights protections. The institutional infrastructure necessary to create and defend human rights in South Africa is surely crucial for this purpose, but most political scientists would treat culture and institutions as fairly distinct phenomena, each worthy of its own detailed investigation.

Indeed, political scientists have used the term "culture" to refer to the politically relevant beliefs, values, attitudes, and behaviors of ordinary citizens. Democracy—and human rights—is about more than just institutions. "The transformation of democratic *forms* into democratic *norms* . . . is crucial for democracy to take root" (Hoffmann 1998, 148, emphasis in original). Larry Diamond (1999, 65) concurs, noting that the consolidation of democratic reform is only possible when

> political competitors . . . come to regard democracy (and the laws, procedures, and institutions it specifies) as "the only game in town,"

> the only viable framework for governing the society and advancing their own interests. At the mass level, there must be a broad normative and behavioral consensus—one that cuts across class, ethnicity, nationality, and other cleavages—on the legitimacy of the constitutional system, however poor or unsatisfying its performance may be at any point in time.

Exactly the same may be said about the value ascribed to human rights within a culture.[2] For instance, Bonny Ibhawoh (2000) cites the importance of the "cultural legitimacy of human rights" for establishing respect for human rights in practice in Africa. Thus, one way of looking at the question of whether South Africa has developed a culture respectful of human rights is to examine the attitudes and values of ordinary South Africans. How much value do ordinary people attach to human rights?

Before answering these questions, we should first ask: what exactly are the attitudes and values that are central to human rights? We can imagine a long list of values, but surely that enumeration would include:

Support for the rule of law: A preference for rule-bound governmental and individual action

Political tolerance: The willingness of citizens to "put up with" their political enemies

Rights consciousness: The willingness to assert individual rights against the dominant political, social, and economic institutions in society

Support for due process: Commitment to non-arbitrary, explicit, and accountable procedures governing the coercive power of the state

Commitment to individual freedom: A basic dedication, undergirding all of these values, to anything that enhances the ability of individuals to make unhindered choices

Commitment to democratic institutions and processes: A recognition that human rights—the rights of both majorities and minorities—are essential to making liberal democracy function effectively

These grand concepts provide some guidance for an empirical inquiry into attitudes toward human rights, but each of course requires a great deal more consideration and explication.

In this chapter, I focus on support for the rule of law. I do so because a cardinal foundation of human rights is the idea that authority must be subservient to law. Law certainly does not "guarantee" human rights—rights are often lost through entirely "legal" means, and legal "guarantees" may ultimately depend on political forces—but without law, citizens must rely on the beneficence of authorities. Unless South Africa can develop a culture respectful of the rule of law, it is difficult to imagine that human rights will prosper.[3]

The rule of law is a concept subject to various definitions and interpretations. Therefore, before proceeding any further, it is worthwhile to consider in some detail the meaning of the concept from a more theoretical perspective.

The Meaning of Support for the Rule of Law

According to extant research on public attitudes toward the rule of law (see, for example, Gibson and Caldeira 1996), the essential ingredient of this construct is *universalism*—the belief that law ought to be universally heeded, that is, obeyed and complied with. To the extent that law generates an undesirable outcome, law ought to be changed through established procedures rather than manipulated or ignored. Thus, willingness to abide by the law is pivotal to the concept.

The antithesis of universalism is *particularism*, based typically on either expedience or on the substitution of some sort of moral judgment for legality. Some may feel that law should be set aside (or bent) in favor of solving problems quickly or efficiently, while others may be unwilling to accept legal outcomes that, by some standards, are "unjust."[4] To the extent that people are willing to follow the law *only* if it satisfies some external criterion, the rule of law is compromised. Respect for the rule of law thus means that following the law (universalism) is accorded more weight than other values that might trump legality, such as expediency or even fairness.

"The rule of law" is a concept typically applied to the state. For instance, Grazyna Skapska (1990, 700) defines the rule of law as "the legal control of anyone who wields power, . . . the strict observance of formal law by the authorities." For the rule of law to prevail, there must be the "subordination of all political authorities and state officials to the law, setting limitations to their power, guaranteeing civil rights and liberties and principles of due process. The stress, next to the division of powers, [should be] put on the independence of the judiciary, on the nonpolitical character of the courts, and on the judicial control of governmental decisions."

But the referent for the rule of the law need not be limited to the state; the concept refers to *both* the citizen and the state. Just as the authorities ought to be constrained by legality in a law-based regime, individual citizens must respect the rule of law in their own behavior.

Violations of the rule of law do not necessarily go against the perceived self-interests of the majority. For instance, Peter Solomon (1992) points to instances in the former Soviet Union in which ordinary citizens *demanded* that the authorities dispense with the rule of law in dealing with suspects in notorious criminal cases. There were many instances in which "people's justice" had little to do with the rule of law (and perhaps not that much to do with justice either). It is easy to imagine that runaway crime is a case in which many are willing to sacrifice the rule of law for more expedient remedies.

Many have argued that a rule-of-law state (a "Rechtsstaat") is a necessary condition for democratic governance (see, for example, Rose, Mishler, and Haerpfer 1998, 32–33). By this they mean that the state must be bound by law and should not act arbitrarily or capriciously. As Seymour Martin Lipset (1994, 14) notes:

> Where power is arbitrary, personal, and unpredictable, the citizenry will not know how to behave; it will fear that any action could produce an unforeseen risk. Essentially, the rule of law means: (1) that people and institutions will be treated equally by the institutions ad-

> ministering the law—the courts, the police, and the civil service; and (2) that people and institutions can predict with reasonable certainty the consequences of their actions, at least as far as the state is concerned.

Authoritarian regimes are notorious for their antipathy to the rule of law. Solomon (1992, 260) asserts: "Soviet officials and politicians were not used to subordinating their interests to law. Many of them treated the law as an instrument to be embraced when useful and ignored when expedient. In short, their actions reflected the syndrome known as 'legal nihilism.'" The "telephone justice" of socialist legal practice in Central and Eastern Europe and the former Soviet Union emphatically represents the antithesis of the rule of law (see Markovits 1995).

I must acknowledge, however, that freedom is often lost under the mantle of law and that not all authoritarian governments necessarily reject the rule of law. As Martin Krygier (1990, 641) reminds us: "There was, after all, a Nazi jurisprudence, and it was a horrible sight." Much of the early Nazi attack on German Jews was accomplished under the authority of law. And of course few governments today would repudiate the rule of law openly, since the rule of law is a powerful and seemingly universal means of legitimizing authority. Legality can serve tyrants nearly as well as democrats.

Thus, I contend that the rule of law is a continuum bounded by universalism and particularism. Though the concept usually is applied to the state, it is equally apposite to the behavior of individual citizens. Further, though the rule of law is most likely *necessary* for democratic government, it certainly is not *sufficient*. The rule of law may be enlisted by both dictatorial minorities and tyrannical majorities. Finally, the rule of law has meaning as an attribute of institutions, of cultures, and of the belief systems of ordinary citizens.

The Rule of Law Under Apartheid

There has been some debate about whether the apartheid regime in South Africa was based on the rule of law. Certainly many of the repressive actions taken against the "Black" majority were grounded in laws properly adopted by the parliament—after all, apartheid itself was a comprehensive legal edifice. Indeed, in its *Final Report* 1998 (vol. 4, ch. 4, p. 101), the TRC found that: "Part of the reason for the longevity of apartheid was the superficial adherence to 'rule of law' by the National Party (NP), whose leaders craved the aura of legitimacy that 'the law' bestowed on their harsh injustice."

But the government also seemed to follow the law only when it was expedient to do so; no elemental and principled commitment to a law-based state characterized apartheid. Revelations from the hearings of the TRC make absolutely plain that the rule of law was frequently suspended by the apartheid authorities as they became increasingly threatened by the liberation forces during the 1980s.[5] The suspension of law was manifest in the various declarations of states of emergency (accomplished through legal procedures), but more significant was the widespread, lawless repression apparently authorized and paid for by the state (for example, the Civil Cooperation Bureau—see Pauw 1997; de Kock 1998). Thus, the historical legacy of apartheid is not one that contributes much to the rule of law.

Nor were all elements of the liberation forces particularly devoted to the rule of law. The ANC, though undoubtedly essential to the liberation of South Africa, committed gross human rights violations of its own, including atrocities in its training camps (whose abuses were investigated by the ANC's own "truth commission"; see Hayner 2000). Perhaps more important, barbarous and lawless acts were committed in the name of the ANC as the organization lost control of many of its operatives in the late 1980s and early 1990s.[6] For example, it is difficult to treat the vigilante justice of the townships in the 1980s as having anything to do with the rule of law. Though the liberation forces were not as cavalier as the apartheid state when it came to setting law aside, the rule of law was often a casualty of the liberation struggle.

The TRC was presented with the difficult task of building a human rights culture respectful of the rule of law, but little in South Africa's past suggested that the rule of law would become a deeply cherished value. Thus, one of the most important definitions of "reconciliation" is support for a human rights culture in South Africa. More specifically, I contend that support for a human rights culture requires support for the rule of law. Whether a culture favorable to the universal application of the rule of law exists in South Africa is the central question addressed in the empirical portions of this chapter. In the analysis that follows, I use the term "rule of law," but in every instance I mean legal universalism—the belief that law ought to prevail, even if "there are severe exigencies to the contrary," and that the law is not "something to be manipulated or ignored in pursuit of one's own self interests (variously defined)" (Gibson and Caldeira 1996, 60).

The Nature of South African Support for the Rule of Law

I asked the South African respondents to express their agreement or disagreement with four statements measuring support for the rule of law (with the response supportive of the rule of law following in parentheses).

1. Sometimes it might be better to ignore the law and solve problems immediately rather than wait for a legal solution. (disagree)
2. It's all right to get around the law as long as you don't actually break it. (disagree)
3. In times of emergency, the government ought to be able to suspend law in order to solve pressing social problems. (disagree)
4. It is not necessary to obey the laws of a government that I did not vote for. (disagree)

Each of these statements juxtaposes a value against strictly following the law. For example, the first item asks the respondent to make a choice between expediency and adherence to the rule of law. Table 5.1 reports the responses to these four measures of support for the rule of law.

These measures do not of course represent all possible facets of

Table 5.1 Support for the Rule of Law, by Race

	Agree—Do Not Support	Uncertain	Disagree—Support	Mean	Standard Deviation	Number of Cases
1. "Sometimes it is better to ignore the law and solve problems immediately."						
All South Africans	44.7%	14.5%	40.8%	2.93	1.31	3,726
African[a]	48.8	14.4	36.8	2.82	1.34	2,003
White	31.6	13.1	55.3	3.29	1.20	991
Colored	35.3	17.5	47.2	3.18	1.20	487
Asian origin	44.1	8.6	47.3	3.02	1.20	245
2. "It's okay to get around law if you don't break it."						
All South Africans	51.6	14.4	34.0	2.76	1.28	3,724
African[b]	57.3	15.2	27.4	2.58	1.25	2,002
White	29.0	10.4	60.6	3.45	1.15	990
Colored	44.4	15.8	39.8	2.99	1.22	487
Asian origin	64.9	6.9	28.2	2.58	1.12	245
3. "In times of emergency, the government should be able to suspend law."						
All South Africans	58.9	19.2	21.9	2.48	1.18	3,724
African[c]	61.2	19.5	19.3	2.39	1.18	2,003
White	49.2	17.7	33.1	2.81	1.17	990
Colored	56.3	21.0	22.7	2.61	1.08	485
Asian origin	59.0	11.1	29.9	2.70	1.12	244

4. "It is not necessary to obey the laws of a government I didn't vote for."						
All South Africans	27.6	10.9	61.6	3.46	1.31	3,716
African[d]	33.0	11.7	55.3	3.31	1.38	2,002
White	8.3	4.3	87.4	4.06	.86	988
Colored	19.4	15.0	65.6	3.56	1.11	479
Asian origin	21.6	6.5	71.8	3.62	1.11	245
Average support for the rule of law						
All South Africans	—	—	—	2.91	.82	3,727
African[e]	—	—	—	2.77	.80	2,004
White	—	—	—	3.40	.74	991
Colored	—	—	—	3.08	.75	487
Asian origin	—	—	—	2.98	.68	245
Average number of items endorsed						
All South Africans	—	—	—	1.58	1.16	3,727
African[f]	—	—	—	1.39	1.08	2,004
White	—	—	—	2.36	1.15	991
Colored	—	—	—	1.74	1.23	487
Asian origin	—	—	—	1.77	1.13	245

Source: Author's compilation from the 2001 Truth and Reconciliation Survey.

Note: The percentages are calculated on the basis of collapsing the five-point Likert response set (for example, "agree strongly" and "agree" responses are combined) and total across the three rows to 100 percent (except for rounding errors). The means and standard deviations are derived from the uncollapsed distributions. Higher mean scores indicate greater support for the rule of law.

[a] $p < .000; \eta = .16$.
[b] $p < .000; \eta = .30$.
[c] $p < .000; \eta = .16$.
[d] $p < .000; \eta = .25$.
[e] $p < .000; \eta = .33$.
[f] $p < .000; \eta = .34$.

the rule of law. Earlier research has shown, however, that many components of the concept evoke consensus from ordinary people (Gibson and Caldeira 1996). For instance, it is a waste of survey items to ask whether the government ought to be allowed to govern arbitrarily, setting the law aside whenever necessary or expedient, or whether courts ought to be subservient to politicians. Contrariwise, the results in table 5.1 reveal that people do indeed differ in the strength of their commitments to the universalism of law and legality.

The first thing to note about this table is that generally support for the rule of law is *not* widespread in South Africa. A majority of South Africans believe it is okay to get around the law so long as the law is not broken (item 2) and that in an emergency the law should be suspended in order to solve social problems (item 3), and a plurality would ignore the law if necessary to solve problems immediately (item 1). Only on the issue of whether one should obey a law passed by a government that one did not vote for (item 4) does a majority in support of the rule of law emerge. In general, the respondents are quite divided in their judgments of the importance of the rule of law, and we see that South Africans strongly committed to legal universalism constitute a minority in their country.

The table also documents significant racial differences in the responses to each proposition. Based on the mean replies, black South Africans are in every instance the least likely to support the rule of law. Conversely, whites are the most likely to endorse the rule of law. The differences are in some instances quite substantial, as in the statement that it is okay to get around the law if you do not actually break it: 60.6 percent of the white respondents disagree with this statement, while only 27.4 percent of the black Africans are similarly inclined. On most items, Colored people and those of Asian origin hold attitudes similar to those of Africans. In terms of the number of these rule-of-law propositions endorsed, whites express support for 2.4 statements, those of Asian origin support 1.8 statements, Colored people support 1.7 statements, and Africans on average voice support for the rule of law in only 1.4 of these propositions. These are fairly large and substantively significant racial differences. (See the eta statistics summarizing the extent of interracial differences in the responses to these questions.) It is particularly troubling that support for the rule of law is so limited among the African majority.

Cross-National Comparisons

It appears that South Africa is some distance from being a culture based on widespread support for the rule of law. But to gain better perspective on these South African results, it is useful to compare them to surveys conducted in other countries. Fortunately, some of these same statements have been put to representative samples in a number of European countries and the United States.

In 1995 our Survey of Legal Values was conducted in seven countries.[7] Several propositions measuring support for the rule of law were included on that survey, based on the same conceptualization as used in the South African study (that is, some alternative value is juxtaposed against strictly following the law). Two of the items are identical to statements used in the 2001 South African survey. In table 5.2, I report the responses to both of the items for each country.

The starkest conclusion from these data is that Americans exhibit an unusual degree of attachment to the rule of law. For instance, consider the first item in table 5.2: an overwhelming majority of Americans disagree with the statement that it may sometimes be better to ignore the law and solve problems immediately rather than wait for a legal solution, thereby expressing their commitment to the rule of law, in contrast to only 40.8 percent of the South Africans. Moreover, nearly twice as many Americans as South Africans believe that it is improper to bend the law, even for good reason. South Africa and the United States stand out in sharp contrast in the data in this table.

There can be no doubt that South African political culture is characterized by less support for the rule of law than American culture, but the South Africans are *not* particularly distinctive in their rejection of the rule of law, especially when compared with Europeans. Indeed, on both of these statements, the South Africans reject the rule of law at approximately the same level as the

Table 5.2 Cross-National Comparisons of Attitudes Toward the Rule of Law, 1995 and 2001

	Agree—Do Not Support	Uncertain	Disagree—Support	Mean	Standard Deviation	Number of Cases
1. "Sometimes it is better to ignore the law and solve problems immediately."						
Bulgaria	32.3%	30.7%	37.1%	3.08	1.26	1,184
France	50.8	18.8	30.4	2.73	1.31	762
Hungary	34.1	23.4	42.5	3.13	1.16	783
Poland	27.4	26.7	45.9	3.28	1.22	813
Russia	34.3	39.4	26.4	2.90	.90	759
Spain	35.3	15.8	49.0	3.18	1.10	768
United States	21.7	7.6	70.7	3.60	1.00	806
South Africa, 2001	44.7	14.5	40.8	2.93	1.31	3,726
2. "It's okay to get around law if you don't break it."						
Bulgaria	40.5	26.3	33.2	2.90	1.28	1,188
France	51.4	14.8	33.8	2.83	1.27	757
Hungary	36.9	24.7	38.4	3.05	1.18	784
Poland	49.8	18.4	31.8	2.74	1.33	815
Russia	36.2	28.8	35.0	2.98	.96	760
Spain	39.1	22.8	38.2	3.00	1.00	768
United States	29.0	10.2	60.8	3.42	1.07	807
South Africa, 2001	51.6	14.4	34.0	2.76	1.28	3,724

Source: Author's compilation from the 2001 Truth and Reconciliation Survey.
Note: The percentages are calculated on the basis of collapsing the five-point Likert response set (for example, "agree strongly" and "agree" responses are combined) and total across the three rows to 100 percent (except for rounding errors). The means and standard deviations are derived from the uncollapsed distributions. Higher mean scores indicate greater support for the rule of law.

French. (Francophone cultures generally seem not to hold law in particularly high regard.)

From these data, it appears that a culture deeply respectful of the rule of law has not yet been established in South Africa, although it must be said that it may not have been established in some mature democracies as well. Perhaps most important, large racial differences exist in attitudes toward law.

Support for the Rule of Law and the Truth and Reconciliation Process

To what degree are contemporary attitudes toward the rule of law related to the activities of the truth and reconciliation process? This question is of course quite difficult to answer definitively without longitudinal data on how attitudes have changed. The ideal research design has been lost with the passage of time, since such a design would have involved interviewing the same people before and after exposure to the activities of the process. In the absence of such data, I pursue two approaches to answering this question. First, I consider whether support for the rule of law in the aggregate has increased, based on a comparison between these 2001 data and an earlier, comparable survey conducted in South Africa in 1996. Second, I investigate whether the cross-sectional evidence is compatible with the conclusion that the truth and reconciliation process has shaped attitudes toward the rule of law.

Change in South African Attitudes Toward the Rule of Law

Because these same statements were put to a representative sample of South Africans in 1996, I can compare the responses in 2001 to those five years earlier. One might hypothesize that two factors have contributed to an increase in respect for the rule of law. First, the lawmaking institutions of the New South Africa have far more legitimacy than those of the apartheid era, at least among Africans and probably among Colored people and those of Asian origin as well. Laws in South Africa today are made within an institution (Parliament) that is politically accountable to the (black) majority.

Second, greater experience with democratic governance and procedure may have enhanced respect for the rule of law. In many respects, law serves the interests of the majority today, rather than repressing that majority and denying it rights and liberties. Thus, a reasonable expectation would be that *support for the rule of law is more widespread in 2001 than in 1996*, when the vestiges of apartheid were more widespread and salient.

On the other hand, I should note that whatever the objectives of the truth and reconciliation process, many aspects of the process may well have contributed to *undermining* respect for the universal application of the rule of law. An obvious example is amnesty—extending freedom from prosecution to those who admitted horrific violations of South African laws is probably not a formula for enhancing respect for law. Moreover, the defense that amnesty was necessary to avoid civil war in essence asserts that expediency, albeit an extremely significant expediency, should trump law. Even the departures from legalistic procedures in the hearings of the TRC, as well as the condemnation by the Constitutional Court of at least some of the most egregious deviations from due process, cannot have taught South Africans the value of strict adherence to the law. Thus, there are many good reasons for suspecting that the truth and reconciliation process in South Africa actually had exactly the opposite effect than was intended by those who created it. The data in table 5.3 allow this hypothesis to be assessed.

Nothing in table 5.3 supports the conclusion that the rule of law has become more firmly established in contemporary South Africa. In nearly every instance, the mean scores in 1996 and 2001 are quite similar. Indeed, from a statistical point of view, the proper conclusion is that there has been little change in attitudes toward the rule of law between 1996 and 2001.

These data suggest that the truth and reconciliation process has had limited influence on attitudes toward the rule of law among ordinary people in South Africa. The data are not dispositive, however, in that aggregate-level change (such as that reported in table 5.3) can (and often does) mask substantial microlevel change. If those who are becoming more sympathetic toward the rule of law are counterbalanced by those who are becoming less sympathetic,

Table 5.3 Change in Support for the Rule of Law, 1996 and 2001

	Agree—Do Not Support	Uncertain	Disagree—Support	Mean	Standard Deviation	Number of Cases
1. "Sometimes it is better to ignore the law and solve problems immediately."						
1996	36.4%	16.9%	46.6%	3.18	1.27	2,559
2001	44.7	14.5	40.8	2.93	1.31	3,726
2. "It's okay to get around law if you don't break it."						
1996	48.4	16.7	34.9	2.89	1.25	2,560
2001	51.6	14.4	34.0	2.76	1.28	3,724
3. "In times of emergency, the government should be able to suspend law."						
1996	51.2	24.9	23.9	2.66	1.14	2,560
2001	58.9	19.2	21.9	2.48	1.18	3,724
4. "It is not necessary to obey the laws of a government I didn't vote for."						
1996	30.2	13.0	56.8	3.40	1.33	2,560
2001	27.6	10.9	61.6	3.46	1.31	3,716

Source: Author's compilation from the 2001 Truth and Reconciliation Survey.
Note: The percentages are calculated on the basis of collapsing the five-point Likert response set (for example, "agree strongly" and "agree" responses are combined) and total across the three rows to 100 percent (except for rounding errors). The means and standard deviations are derived from the uncollapsed distributions. Higher mean scores indicate greater support for the rule of law.

the overall appearance may be one of stasis when in fact considerable change is taking place. For the moment, however, these data yield little evidence indicating that the truth and reconciliation process has contributed to more widespread support for the rule of law in South Africa.

The Influence of the TRC

In order for the truth and reconciliation process to influence attitudes toward the rule of law, people must have been attentive to the commission and acquired some awareness of its activities. A necessary condition for influence may be awareness.[8] In addition, it is reasonable to hypothesize that *those with greater confidence in the TRC are more likely to endorse the rule of law.* Finally, we would expect that *more steadfast supporters of legal universalism will be found among those who accept the findings of the TRC*—the "truth" or collective memory produced by the TRC (see chapter 3 for measurement details).

To test these hypotheses, I have regressed rule-of-law attitudes on three indicators of the respondent's understanding of the TRC: awareness of its activities, confidence in the commission, and acceptance of the TRC's truth about South Africa's apartheid past. I have also included two control variables—the extent of media consumption and interest in politics in general—so as to pinpoint more carefully the influence of the truth and reconciliation process itself, as compared to more general media use and political awareness. I expect that support for the rule of law will be more common among those who are aware of the TRC, who trust it, who accept its truth, who are more attentive to the media in general, and who are interested in politics. Table 5.4 reports the results of this regression.

The most important conclusion from this table is that, in general, those who accept the truth as produced by the TRC are more likely to support the rule of law. The statistical relationships are quite substantial for Africans ($\beta = .25$), whites ($\beta = .28$), and Colored people ($\beta = .23$). Among those of Asian origin, the coefficient is positive ($\beta = .07$), but not statistically significant, so it is not clear that truth acceptance and the rule of law actually go to-

Table 5.4 The Influence of the Truth and Reconciliation Process on Support for the Rule of Law

Predictor	b	Standard Error	β	r
Africans				
Knowledge of the TRC	.05	.02	.05*	.02
Confidence in the TRC	−.09	.02	−.10***	−.11
Acceptance of the TRC's truth	.28	.03	.25***	.26
Media consumption	.04	.02	.05*	.06
Interest in politics	−.02	.02	−.02	.00
Intercept	1.78	.11		
Standard deviation—dependent variable	.80			
Standard error of estimate	.77			
R-squared			.08***	
Number of cases	1,999			
Whites				
Knowledge of the TRC	−.03	.03	−.03	.06
Confidence in the TRC	.09	.03	.10**	.16
Acceptance of the TRC's truth	.28	.03	.28***	.31
Extent of media consumption	.02	.03	.03	.07
Interest in politics	.08	.03	.09**	.11
Intercept	2.26	.12		
Standard deviation—dependent variable	.74			
Standard error of estimate	.69			
R-squared			.11***	
Number of cases	975			
Colored people				
Knowledge of the TRC	−.08	.05	−.10	.04
Confidence in the TRC	−.01	.04	−.01	.03
Acceptance of the TRC's truth	.26	.05	.23***	.26
Media consumption	.01	.04	.01	.09
Interest in politics	.14	.04	.18***	.20
Intercept	2.08	.19		
Standard deviation—dependent variable	.75			
Standard error of estimate	.72			
R-squared			.09***	
Number of cases	479			
Asian origin				
Knowledge of the TRC	.04	.07	.04	.02
Confidence in the TRC	−.07	.06	−.08	−.09

(Table continues on p. 196.)

Table 5.4 (Continued)

Predictor	b	Standard Error	β	r
Acceptance of the TRC's truth	.07	.07	.07	.07
Media consumption	.02	.06	.03	.02
Interest in politics	−.03	.05	−.04	−.02
Intercept	2.77	.29		
Standard deviation—dependent variable	.68			
Standard error of estimate	.68			
R-squared			.01	
Number of cases	244			

Source: Author's compilation from the 2001 Truth and Reconciliation Survey.
***$p < .001$; **$p < .01$; *$p < .05$

gether. *But for the vast majority of South Africans, endorsing more of the TRC's truth is related to a stronger acceptance of the need for universalism in law.*

This finding requires further explication. What specifically is the connection between accepting the TRC's truth and valuing the rule of law? The two variables are no doubt linked by the commission's insistence on applying rules and principles of human rights equally to all combatants in the struggle over apartheid. It is the TRC's insistence on universalism (judging all sides in the struggle according to the same criteria) and its unwillingness to accept arguments to the effect that ends justify means (that a "just war" can excuse violations of the rule of law) that probably cemented relationship between the truth and legal universalism. Causality is always difficult to establish (especially with cross-sectional data), but the TRC's lesson was that law (human rights) must be respected by all, and those accepting that lesson are more committed today to universalism in the application of the rule of law in South Africa.

Still, it is debatable whether the activities of the TRC actually *caused* these attitudes, since the coefficients for knowledge and confidence in the TRC are weak or trivial for all of the groups. Perhaps we would not expect the multivariate effects of knowledge and confidence to be very strong—since their influence on support for the rule of law should be mediated through endorsement of the TRC's truth—but the bivariate relationships (representing the total effects of the variables—r) are generally weak as well. In no instance is greater awareness of the activities of the TRC significantly related to attitudes toward the rule of law.

Understanding the coefficients linking confidence in the TRC to rule-of-law attitudes presents some challenges. For whites, greater confidence is related to more support for the rule of law, as predicted. For Colored people, no significant relationship exists. And for the African majority, the relationship is negative: those who express more confidence in the TRC are *less* likely to support the rule of law. Though the coefficient is, strictly speaking, indistinguishable from zero, the same may be true for those of Asian origin as well. The inverse relationship presents a conundrum for the hypothesis.

Perhaps for some Africans the TRC itself actually represents a violation of the rule of law.[9] After all, the TRC's main job is to override the traditional criminal law that would have punished people for their criminal deeds. The TRC may therefore be understood as abrogating law instead of enforcing it. One who believes that law ought to be universally applied, irrespective of the consequences, would surely find it difficult to support letting some of South Africa's most notorious criminals go free after admitting their heinous crimes. Perhaps the meaning of this coefficient among Africans is that those predisposed toward the universal application of law found it difficult to have confidence in the TRC, even though they paid attention to the activities of the commission and accepted some of its conclusions about South Africa's apartheid past.

It is noteworthy, however, that whites seem not to be influenced by the same processes, since commitment to the rule of law is *positively* (and significantly, although quite weakly) related to confidence ($\beta = .10$). This is all the more surprising once the stronger commitment of whites to the rule of law is recalled. Perhaps whites who express confidence in the TRC do so in part because they view the commission as legally constituted and, in the end, at least somewhat rule-bound in its proceedings (even if occasionally forced to adopt such rules by litigation and court judgments). Still, many whites condemned the TRC for engaging in a "witch hunt" (whatever the truth of the matter), so we might have expected this coefficient to be negative, with the rule-of-law supporters expressing less confidence in the TRC. Though the relationship is quite weak, the data seem to indicate otherwise.

Political interest and media consumption do not affect attitudes toward the rule of law among Africans or those of Asian origin. Among whites and Colored people, greater interest in politics is associated with greater support for the rule of law. It is difficult to understand all of these individual coefficients. The important thing to note, however, is that the effects of the variables concerning the TRC are not dependent on a person's level of interest in politics and the magnitude of her or his media consumption.

Thus, I have unearthed some evidence that the truth and reconciliation process might have shaped attitudes toward the rule of law in South Africa. Those who accept the truth about South Africa's past as promulgated by the TRC are more likely to endorse the rule of law. For three of the four groups (and thus for the vast majority of South Africans), these relationships are reasonably strong. The causal processes involved remain a bit murky, as they almost always are with cross-sectional analysis. But at a minimum, I confidently conclude that truth acceptance and respect for law go together in South Africa. And even if the truth and reconciliation process did not enhance support for human rights, little evidence indicates that the process significantly undermined respect for the rule of law.

Multivariate Analysis: Other Processes That Contribute to Support for the Rule of Law

Factors other than the activities of the truth and reconciliation process may well have shaped South Africans' attitudes toward the rule of law. In particular, I consider several hypotheses:

> *Experience*: Here I include historical experiences with apartheid and contemporary perceptions of the seriousness of the crime problem in South Africa. Since some South Africans fared better under apartheid than others, it is reasonable to hypothesize that

those victimized more under apartheid are more likely to hold the rule of law in low regard.[10] In addition, the perceived escalation of crime since the demise of apartheid, especially among whites, may have eroded support for legal universalism.

Racial reconciliation: Attitudes toward the rule of law may reflect perceptions of who will benefit from law—the white minority or the "Black" majority. Among some Africans, "rights" have long been synonymous with "white rights." As Heinz Klug (2000, 76) observes: "Even John Dugard, a long-standing supporter of a bill of rights for South Africa, expressed concern that those 'who have suffered long outside the protection of the law are now unwilling to see their oppressors brought within the protection of the law.'" Consequently, I hypothesize that *racial animosity influences attitudes toward legal universalism and those who feel more positively about South Africans of other races are more likely to support the rule of law.*

Strong majoritarianism: The rule of law is sometimes portrayed as a means of constraining the will of the majority.[11] In a sense, the rule of law is the antithesis of power; it requires the majority not to act on the mere basis of the power of its majority status but instead to act legally. In a liberal democratic polity, the legal process typically extends some power to political minorities through promises of minority rights. Thus, I hypothesize that *those who believe strongly in the rights of the majority are less likely to support the rule of law.*

Individualism: Similar reasoning applies to beliefs about the importance of the individual. The rule of law is often seen as a means of protecting individuals (perhaps only temporarily) from the wrath of the group. For instance, Ibhawoh (2000, 853) sees a "fundamental conflict between the implicit individualism of human rights and the importance of collectivism and definitive gender roles in most African cultures." Thus, I expect that *those who value individuals more highly in general are more likely to support universalism in the application of the rule of law.*

Ideology and political preferences: The governing majority in South Africa is of course the African National Congress. The rule of law has often been bound up in ideological debates about race and rights in South Africa, especially during the constitutional construction process of the mid-1990s. Rights and law are viewed by some as a means of constraining the power of the ANC to bring about social change, especially changes that might be contrary to the interests of whites.[12] I therefore consider the hypothesis that *attitudes toward law are a function of ideological commitments and preferences,* as in the hypothesis that supporters of the ANC are less enthusiastic about the rule of law because the constraints of law are most likely to be applied against the governing majority. If people judge the rule of law in terms of whether their side profits from it or not, then attitudes toward the ANC should predict preferences for legal universalism. Because the Inkatha Freedom Party has traditionally held such a strong position in KwaZulu Natal, I also include a measure of affect for the IFP as a predictor of support for the rule of law.[13]

Control variables: South Africa is characterized by sharp cleavages along many different lines. I therefore include a variety of control variables for class, gender, urban-rural differences, and literacy and education. I also incorporate the controls for media consumption and interest in politics considered earlier. Finally, I use a measure of opinion leadership to test the elitist hypothesis that *opinion leaders are more committed to the rule of law than ordinary people.*

The appendix to this chapter addresses the measurement of the various predictors. Table 5.5 reports the results of the separate regressions for each of the four racial groups.

A remarkable degree of similarity characterizes the findings across the four racial groups. In each instance, those more strongly committed to majoritarianism are less likely to support the rule of law. These relationships are reasonably robust. *For South Africans of every race, law seems to be perceived as a mechanism for preventing the majority from getting what it wants.* Those who believe in strong majoritarianism are much less likely to believe in legal universalism.

Attitudes toward South Africans of other races also influence

Table 5.5 Multivariate Determinants of Support for the Rule of Law Among Four South African Racial Groups

	b	Standard Error	β	r
Africans				
Acceptance of the TRC's truth	.23	.03	.20***	.26
Knowledge of the TRC	.04	.02	.04	.03
Confidence in the TRC	−.05	.02	−.06**	−.10
Injuries from apartheid	.02	.07	.01	−.01
Perceived seriousness of crime	−.04	.03	−.04	−.02
Perceived increase in crime	−.02	.01	−.05*	−.03
Racial reconciliation	.02	.00	.13***	.18
Support for strong majoritarianism	−.24	.02	−.25***	−.30
Support for individualism	.11	.03	.08***	.16
Affect for the African National Congress	−.03	.01	−.09***	−.12
Affect for the Inkatha Freedom Party	.02	.01	.05*	.10
Media consumption	.03	.02	.04	.07
Interest in politics	−.00	.02	−.00	.01
Opinion leadership	−.05	.06	−.02	−.02
Level of education	−.04	.02	−.05	.04
Illiteracy	−.06	.02	−.07	−.07
Afrikaans language	.42	.52	.02	.01
Age	.00	.00	.02	−.01
Social class	.01	.02	.01	−.04
Size of place of residence	.01	.01	.03	−.03
Gender	.07	.04	.04	.01
Intercept	3.04	.23		
Standard deviation—dependent variable	.80			
Standard error of estimate	.72			
R-squared			.19***	
Number of cases	1,944			
Whites				
Acceptance of the TRC's truth	.15	.04	.15***	.30
Knowledge of the TRC	−.05	.03	−.05	.06
Confidence in the TRC	.04	.03	.04	.15
Injuries from apartheid	−.50	.25	−.06*	.05
Perceived seriousness of crime	.01	.06	.01	−.00
Perceived increase in crime	−.03	.02	−.06*	−.13
Racial reconciliation	.03	.01	.21***	.35
Support for strong majoritarianism	−.23	.03	−.23***	−.28
Support for individualism	.00	.04	.00	.05

(Table continues on p. 202.)

Table 5.5 (Continued)

	b	Standard Error	β	r
Affect for the African National Congress	.03	.01	.08*	.30
Affect for the Inkatha Freedom Party	−.00	.01	−.01	.10
Media consumption	.01	.03	.01	.06
Interest in politics	.04	.03	.05	.10
Opinion leadership	.01	.06	.01	.04
Level of education	.03	.02	.04	.16
Illiteracy	.02	.10	.01	−.04
Afrikaans language	.13	.05	.09**	−.04
Age	.00	.00	.03	.04
Social class	−.05	.03	−.04	−.15
Size of place of residence	.01	.02	.02	.02
Gender	.04	.04	.03	.04
Intercept	3.34	.36		
Standard deviation—dependent variable	.73			
Standard error of estimate	.65			
R-squared			.23	
Number of cases	957			
Colored people				
Acceptance of the TRC's truth	.20	.06	.18***	.27
Knowledge of the TRC	−.09	.05	−.12*	.05
Confidence in the TRC	−.01	.04	−.01	.03
Injuries from apartheid	−.07	.19	−.02	.12
Perceived seriousness of crime	−.01	.09	−.01	.03
Perceived increase in crime	−.03	.02	−.08	−.06
Racial reconciliation	.02	.01	.11*	.23
Support for strong majoritarianism	−.27	.04	−.27***	−.29
Support for individualism	.09	.06	.06	.13
Affect for the African National Congress	.02	.01	.07	.07
Affect for the Inkatha Freedom Party	.00	.01	.01	.07
Media consumption	−.01	.04	−.01	.09
Interest in politics	.11	.04	.14**	.20
Opinion leadership	.11	.10	.05	.08
Level of education	.01	.04	.01	.16
Illiteracy	.00	.06	.00	−.09
Afrikaans language	−.05	.10	−.03	−.16
Age	.00	.00	.00	−.02
Social class	−.06	.04	−.08	−.14

Table 5.5 (Continued)

	b	Standard Error	β	r
Size of place of residence	−.00	.02	−.00	−.08
Gender	.06	.07	.04	−.03
Intercept	3.21	.53		
Standard deviation—dependent variable	.75			
Standard error of estimate	.68			
R-squared			.21	
Number of cases	467			
Asian origin				
Acceptance of the TRC's truth	.05	.06	.05	.06
Knowledge of the TRC	.03	.07	.03	.00
Confidence in the TRC	−.06	.06	−.07	−.07
Injuries from apartheid	.21	.26	.06	−.01
Perceived seriousness of crime	−.04	.11	−.02	−.04
Perceived increase in crime	.03	.03	.07	.03
Racial reconciliation	.04	.01	.25***	.23
Support for strong majoritarianism	−.27	.06	−.28***	−.32
Support for individualism	.27	.08	.22***	.23
Affect for the African National Congress	.00	.02	.02	−.01
Affect for the Inkatha Freedom Party	−.04	.02	−.13*	−.08
Media consumption	.01	.06	.01	.00
Interest in politics	−.07	.05	−.09	−.03
Opinion leadership	−.12	.13	−.06	−.06
Level of education	−.07	.06	−.09	.05
Illiteracy	.03	.08	.03	.01
Afrikaans language	−.07	.26	−.02	−.04
Age	−.00	.00	−.03	−.02
Social class	.06	.05	.07	.04
Size of place of residence	.00	.03	.00	.02
Gender	−.13	.09	−.10	−.05
Intercept	3.26	.69		
Standard deviation—dependent variable	.68			
Standard error of estimate	.62			
R-squared			.23	
Number of cases	241			

Source: Author's compilation from the 2001 Truth and Reconciliation Survey.
***p ≤ .001; **p ≤ .01; *p ≤ .05

attitudes toward law for all four groups, although the strength of the relationship varies somewhat across the groups. Generally, those who hold more conciliatory racial attitudes are more likely to support the rule of law.

The effect of these two variables—racial reconciliation and majoritarianism—may indicate that commitments to the rule of law are to some degree instrumental rather than principled. I have no direct way of measuring whether the respondent believes he or she directly profits from the strict enforcement of the law, but it seems that attitudes toward law are bound up with beliefs about the conflict (historical and contemporary) between the majority and the minority in South Africa. Those reconciled with the opposite race are perhaps less threatened and therefore feel less need for the protection of law, just as those who support strong majority rule seem not to want strong constraints from legality. The rule of law seems to be associated with the interests of the minority (however that minority is defined), presumably because the majority can protect itself with power and has little need for recourse to law.

The finding that acceptance of the TRC's truth influences legal attitudes is unshaken by the multivariate analysis. Except for South Africans of Asian origin, those who accept more of the TRC's truth about the country's apartheid past are more likely to support the rule of law. Perhaps these people learned from the TRC's revelations the terrible consequences of lawlessness and therefore place their hopes on the constraints associated with the rule of law.

Just a handful of the other variables have any influence at all on attitudes toward the rule of law. South Africans of Asian origin who are more strongly committed to individualism support law more, although individualism has little impact on most South Africans. Similarly, Asian women are less likely to support the rule of law, but only slightly, and generally this view does not characterize most South African females. Perhaps the most interesting and idiosyncratic finding is that Asian South Africans who are more favorable toward the IFP are less likely to support the rule of law, even though their attitudes toward the ANC are unrelated to legal preferences. Perhaps this relationship is better put in the negative: Asian South Africans who harbor more antipathy toward the IFP are more likely to support the rule of law. This no doubt has something to do with the history of intense political conflict (indeed, at some recent points, warfare) involving the IFP in KwaZulu Natal (the home of most of the Asian respondents).

It is worth noting that many factors have no influence whatsoever on attitudes toward the rule of law. Particularly interesting is the finding that having been harmed by apartheid has no effect on legal attitudes. When put together with the evidence that accepting the TRC's truth *does* shape attitudes, this seems to suggest that attitudes have been shaped more by *learning* about the past than by *experiencing* it. This possibility is in part surely a function of the fact that, for many, apartheid is becoming a distant memory, but it also gives greater credence to the claim that the TRC's revelations had some independent influence on attitudes toward law.

Also surprising is the finding that perceptions of crime have little if any influence on attitudes toward the rule of law. Few would have predicted this result. Perhaps this reflects an ambivalence about law and crime. Some of those fearful of crime surely want strict enforcement of the law, but others may prefer getting around legal constraints in order to crack down on crime. Given this mixture of views, the coefficients linking crime concern and support for legal universalism would be trivial, as they are. It seems from these data that fear of crime in South Africa is not inimical to the rule of law.

A host of demographic variables have little or no influence on legal attitudes. Urban-rural differences, social class, age, opinion leadership, and education and literacy generally have very small effects at best. Particularly noteworthy is the lack of influence of social class, as is the weak relationship between level of education and legal attitudes. At least a portion of these findings have to do with the fact that these background variables are related to the attitudes that predict support for the rule of law; once those attitudes are controlled, socioeconomic differences have no residual influence.

One background factor poorly understood in this analysis is race, since the data in table 5.5 analyze differences *within*, not across, races. One further analytical step is therefore necessary to combine the effects of these substantive variables and race.

To address more comprehensively the influence of race, I regressed rule-of-law attitudes on three sets of variables: substantive variables (truth acceptance, racial reconciliation, and support for strong majoritarianism);[14] three racial dummy variables (distinguishing Africans from whites, Colored people, and South Africans of Asian origin); and interaction terms (the interactions among the three substantive and three dummy variables). I then performed hierarchical regressions, adding the interactive terms separately for each set of substantive attitudes and then adding all interactive terms to the equation simultaneously. The hypotheses considered under this analysis are (1) that the intercepts differ across races (the groups differ in levels of support for the rule of law) and (2) that the slopes for each of the substantive independent variables differ across race (the factors shaping attitudes toward legal universalism vary by race).

The regression analysis is absolutely unambiguous with regard to attitudes toward majoritarianism and racial reconciliation: the slopes across the four racial groups differ *insignificantly*. The influence of these two variables of substantive interest is not dependent on the respondent's race.

The influence of truth acceptance (as represented in the regression coefficients for the various interactive terms) does seem to vary across race, but not greatly. Among South Africans of Asian origin, whether one accepts the truth about the past has less influence on attitudes toward the rule of law ($b = -.22$, $p = .002$), and acceptance of the truth has little influence within this group ($b = (.25 - .22) = .03$). The effect of truth on attitudes toward law is slightly diminished among whites ($b = -.08$, $p = .052$), although the resulting coefficient is not reduced to insignificance ($b = (.25 - .08) = .17$).

The effect of race on the intercepts, however, is quite different. Even within the full equation (the equation with all interaction terms), the dummy variable for whites is highly significant ($p < .000$), with whites, ceteris paribus, substantially more committed than Africans to the rule of law ($a = (2.83 + .73) = 3.56$). Black and Colored South Africans do not differ in their attitudes ($p = .235$), but there is a substantial difference between Africans and those of Asian origin ($p = .007$, $a = (2.83 + .93) = 3.76$). Thus, even when we take into account feelings about majoritarianism, truth acceptance, and racial reconciliation, whites and South Africans of Asian origin are more strongly committed than are Africans to the rule of law.

Concluding Comments

Several important conclusions emerge from this analysis. First, South Africans are not inordinately supportive of the rule of law, even if their lack of support is not unusual in comparison with the levels of support in some established European democracies. Second, strong racial differences exist in commitments to law, with Africans and Colored people exhibiting much weaker support for legal universalism. Third, I have adduced some evidence that the TRC had an influence on attitudes toward the rule of law through its exposure of the abuses of law under the apartheid regime and its demonstrated commitment to the universal application of principles of human rights. Finally, attitudes toward the rule of law have much to do with beliefs about the relationship between majorities and minorities in South Africa. Supporters of the rule of law seem to endorse weaker forms of majoritarianism and stronger forms of minoritarianism and to hold more tolerant attitudes toward South Africans of different races.

This last point deserves considerable emphasis. Rather than reflecting concrete experiences—either contemporaneous experiences with crime or historical experiences with apartheid—attitudes toward the rule of law instead flow from more basic democratic values. Those who have not learned the complex lessons of democracy have also failed to learn about the importance of the rule of law. This seems to imply that, for some, law is politicized in South Africa. Rather than being a means of protecting all South Africans from arbitrary and abusive action, law may be seen as a means of protecting the privileged minority. I suspect that some South Africans view law as a means by which whites maintain their hegemony in South Africa. If so, this is an important, and ominous, finding, to the degree that democratization and reconciliation depend on legal universalism.

It may well be that since South Africans have had little experience with legal universalism, they have yet to learn of its value. The TRC seems to have had some influence on attitudes toward law, although I admit that the evidence of causality is not as strong as it might be. By exposing people to the consequences of arbitrary government not constrained by law and by judging all sides in the struggle according to the same criteria, the truth and reconciliation process may have deepened and widened respect for law.

One of the "negative" findings of this analysis also warrants emphasis: support for the rule of law is not related to perceptions of crime and criminality in South Africa. Many have feared that the demand to "do something" about crime would result in the undermining of law in the country. In fact, that seems not to be the case, at least from the point of view of ordinary South Africans. Perhaps South Africans know all too well the consequences of extending unrestrained power to the country's security forces.

Nor are attitudes toward the rule of law related to experiences under apartheid. This is an important finding because it indicates that, at least on this issue, the legacy of apartheid may be fading.

This analysis has not addressed all of the important issues related to the rule of law. For instance, these data say little about tolerance of corruption or willingness to make courts subservient to politics or the substance of the law that legal universalism would enforce. Nor have I investigated other by-products of the truth and reconciliation process, such as the legitimacy that the process seems to have extended to expectations of amnesty for wrongdoings of every sort (fixing cricket matches, for instance) and to the relaxation of due process constraints on hearings of various sorts. These are all important omissions, and care must be taken not to overgeneralize from these findings to broader conclusions about the future of the rule of law and the consolidation of democracy in South Africa.

Nonetheless, a central problem of all new democracies, South Africa included, is minoritarianism. South Africans are deeply intolerant of political differences (Gibson and Gouws 2003); many have not accepted the virtues of the liberal half of the liberal democracy equation (majority rule plus minority rights). Still, it is perhaps surprising that the rule of law is associated with minoritarianism—one might have guessed that the universalism of law would be attractive to everyone. Instead, it seems that intolerance, strong majoritarianism, and disregard for the rule of law go together in the minds of many South Africans. This is not a formula for the successful consolidation of democracy and the protection of human rights.

South African democracy is still in its infancy. A decade ago the country was racked by political violence more widespread and severe than it had ever experienced during the heyday of apartheid. South African political culture was deeply scarred by apartheid, and the vestiges of antidemocratic attitudes and practices will take generations to overcome. Whites have surrendered only a small portion of their privileges, and they continue to dominate economically and socially, if not politically. Thus, from this perspective, it is perhaps extraordinary that so many South Africans hold law in any regard at all and that they are willing to set their immediate interests aside and accept legal processes and outcomes. Broadening and deepening the respect of ordinary South Africans for the law should be among the highest priorities for those committed to a more democratic future for the country.

Appendix: Measurement of Independent Variables

Experience I developed a measure of the degree to which each respondent believes he or she was harmed by apartheid. The index is simply the average number of harms experienced. Details on this measure are provided in chapter 2.

Two indicators of perceptions of crime are included:

> There has been some talk recently about crime in South Africa. In terms of how it affects you personally, would you say that in

the last year the level of crime has got worse, has not changed, or has got better?

1. Got better
2. Has not changed
3. Got worse

[*If respondent chose "Got worse"*] Would you say that crime has got a great deal worse, moderately worse, or only a little worse in comparison to last year?

1. Got a great deal worse
2. Got moderately worse
3. Got only a little worse

Please tell me how important each of the following problems is to you personally—very important, important, not very important, or not important at all.

Level of crime

Racial Reconciliation The respondents were asked nine questions about members of the "opposite race"—that is, Africans were asked the questions in reference to whites, and all other respondents were asked the questions using blacks as the reference group. The index employed is the balance of reconciled to unreconciled responses (see chapter 4 for additional details).

Strong Majoritarianism The index is the average response to the following items:

1. The party that gets the support of the majority ought not to have to share political power with the political minority. (agree)

2. The constitution is just like any other law; if the majority wants to change it, it should be changed. (agree)
3. If the majority of the people want something, the constitution should not be used to keep them from getting what they want. (agree)
4. Voting in South African elections should be restricted to those who own property. (disagree)

Individualism The index is the average response to the following items:

1. People should go along with whatever is best for the group, even when they disagree. (disagree)
2. It is more important to do the kind of work society needs than to do the kind of work I like. (disagree)
3. People have to look after themselves; the community shouldn't be responsible for the actions of each citizen. (agree)
4. The most important thing to teach children is obedience to their parents. (disagree)

Ideology and Political Preferences Affect toward the ANC and IFP was measured with the following questions:

> And now I'd like to ask you about your attitudes toward some groups of people. I am going to read you a list of some groups that are currently active in social and political life.
>
> Here is a card showing a scale from 1 to 11. The number 1 indicates that you *dislike* the group very much; the number 11 indicates that you *like* the group very much. The number 6 means that you neither like nor dislike the group. The numbers 2 to 5 reflect varying amounts of dislike toward the group, and the numbers 7 to 10 reflect varying amounts of like.
>
> The first group I'd like to ask you about is Afrikaners. If you have an opinion about Afrikaners, please indicate which figure

most closely describes your attitude toward them. If you have no opinion, *please be sure to tell me*. What is your opinion of:

Supporters of the African National Congress?

Supporters of the Inkatha Freedom Party?

For a substantive discussion of the results of these questions, see chapter 6.

Chapter 6

Tolerance: The Minimalist View of Reconciliation

> You don't get reconciled with someone you agree [with]. You get reconciled with someone with whom you disagree; otherwise there would be no point in having reconciliation. You do not reconcile with someone whom you have no discordance with.
>
> —Archbishop Desmond Tutu, Truth and Reconciliation Commission (1998, vol. 5, ch. 9, p. 412)

I argued in chapter 1 that "reconciliation" is a word capable of taking on many different meanings. One understanding of reconciliation is that people come to accept and perhaps even embrace each other. Desmond Tutu, for instance, often seems to subscribe to this theory of reconciliation, which he has been quite active in promoting. In response, some have criticized this approach to reconciliation, arguing that it undermines the liberal portions of liberal democracy by tending to delegitimize strong conflict and disagreement (Marx 2002), and even that to ask victims to reconcile with perpetrators in this way is yet another crime against them. Clearly, many in South Africa seek a form of reconciliation short of the Christian ideal of universal brotherhood, redemption, and forgiveness (see, for example, Wilson 2001).

An alternative view is that reconciliation requires far less than embracing one's political opponents. Instead, reconciliation demands that South Africans do nothing more than *put up with* those whom they oppose. Tolerance is a minimalist definition of reconciliation, albeit one that was recognized by the participants in the truth and reconciliation process as crucial to reconciliation. To reconcile in South Africa may not require that people respect or accept each other's point of view but rather that they *tolerate* each other. Reconciliation requires that South Africans stifle the urge to repress those on the opposite side of political debates and struggles.

Defining reconciliation in terms of tolerance fits well with extant thinking on the requisites of democracy. Democracies unquestionably require certain types of political institutions, such as institutions of majority rule and institutions designed to protect political minorities from the wrath of the majority. But democracies also require (or at least profit from) a tolerant citizenry. When citizens are unwilling to put up with each other, then the marketplace of ideas becomes unduly constrained and narrowed and cannot function the way it must if democracy is to flourish. Unless people feel free to express their viewpoints, majority opinion may monopolize public debate (on the so-called spiral of silence; see Noelle-Neumann 1984), drowning out minority viewpoints. Tolerance is an endorphin for the contentious body politic; it makes open debate over political differences less painful. Tolerance is thus an essential palliative for the ailments that are inevitable in democratic politics.

Consequently, the question of how tolerant South Africans are must be answered if reconciliation is to be fully understood. In this chapter, I address several questions:

How much do South Africans dislike those of differing political viewpoints? What is the structure of political antipathy in the country? Does group antipathy, for instance, parallel race?

Is antipathy associated with perceptions that one's political foes are threatening? To the extent that antipathy and threat go together, a volatile mix of attitudes is created.

How tolerant are South Africans of those with whom they disagree? Is intolerance narrowly focused on particular political enemies, or is it instead dispersed across a broad ideological landscape? This is an important distinction, since narrowly focused intolerance is typically considered to be especially pernicious.

Does truth acceptance affect any of these processes? That is, are those who accept the TRC's truth less likely to dislike other political groups, less likely to see the groups as threatening, and more likely to be willing to tolerate the groups?

What role do group identities play in shaping threat perceptions and political intolerance? The conventional wisdom of social identity theory is that strong group identities breed intolerance, which is worrisome if group attachments are relatively obdurate.[1]

Answering these questions will take us some distance toward an understanding of whether South Africa will be able to accommodate its citizens' vast ideological differences.

This chapter differs from the others in some important respects. Instead of merely analyzing the nature of contemporary South African tolerance, I make explicit comparisons to earlier findings. In particular, I compare the 2001 data with a nearly identical study (Gibson and Gouws 2003) that was based on surveys conducted in 1996 and 1997 in South Africa. Because the two projects are so similar in both their conceptualization and their operationalization of tolerance, strong comparisons can be made, putting the 2001 data in the more revealing context of change.

Because such strong theories about the structure of intolerance exist, I also consider the question of whether South African intolerance has the characteristics that are likely to make it consequential for the manner in which politics is played out in South Africa. For instance, to the extent that intolerant South Africans perceive others as intolerant as well, they may become emboldened and their attitudes are potentially more pernicious. If intolerance is focused in South Africa—in the sense of a consensus about the sort of groups that constitute the dominant threat in the country and therefore should not be tolerated—then intolerance carries more repressive potential than if the groups deemed to be threatening are dispersed across the ideological landscape. Moreover, to the extent that intolerance is grounded in group identities, which tend to be relatively obdurate, efforts to convert intolerance to tolerance are likely to be met with strong resistance and little success. Finally, I address the crucial hypothesis that accepting the TRC's truth about the country's apartheid past contributes to greater political tolerance. I investigate these and other questions in this chapter with an eye toward drawing conclusions about the likely consequences of intolerance for intergroup reconciliation and the further democratization of the South African political system.

The Significance of Political Tolerance for Reconciliation and Democratization

The literature on political tolerance is vast and includes our own recent major study of intolerance in South Africa (Gibson and Gouws 2003). Most scholars argue that tolerance and liberal democracy go hand in hand, since the political discussion, debate, and competition essential to effective democracy is stifled without widespread political tolerance. Intolerance breeds majority tyranny; since the majority has the power to protect its own right to speech, the rights of minorities (political, ethnic, and so on) to democratic freedoms are threatened if a country's political culture does not endorse political tolerance.

In few countries is this theory more relevant than in South Africa, where political cleavages are deep and historically rooted. Such divisions have often produced intense conflict and political violence, including the violence of the recent transitional period. Not only is the country divided by race, but ethnic and language divisions are of great significance as well. To the extent that political ideologies align with fixed characteristics such as race, ethnicity, and even class, coalitions based on political, economic, or social interests are more difficult to form. Without interactions and coalitions, few forces are available to break down historical animosities. Further, as greater political equality has come to South Africa, class conflict has become more significant and substantial and often intermingles with racial cleavages. Thus, to the extent that intolerance is grounded in group politics—and especially identity politics—intolerance in South Africa is more tenacious, more difficult to tame, and more pernicious, and reconciliation is therefore imperiled.

The TRC recognized intolerance as an important impediment to reconciliation in South Africa, as Archbishop Tutu's statement at the beginning of this chapter makes plain. Moreover, the leaders of the TRC often spoke of the need for political tolerance, as when they equated reconciliation with "respect for the rights and legitimacy of political opposition groups" (Villa-Vicencio 2000, 208). Thus, it is important to investigate tolerance as an agent of reconciliation. I begin the analysis with empirical consideration of the structure of intergroup political animosities.

The Structure of Antipathy in South Africa: Who Hates Whom?

South Africa was obviously badly divided under apartheid, and not just between blacks and whites. Political violence in KwaZulu Natal, for instance, claimed the lives of thousands of black South Africans, many if not most of them killed by other black South Africans (whose actions were sometimes instigated, it should be noted, by agents of the white apartheid state). Bitter divisions have often characterized whites as well, especially between English- and Afrikaans-speakers. If South African political culture is characterized by broad and intense political hatred—and if that hatred is group-based—then reconciliation will be difficult indeed.

We queried our respondents about the degree to which they like or dislike various South African groups, using a scale ranging from disliking the group a great deal (a score of 1) to liking the group a great deal (11). The groups we asked about varied from mainstream political parties like the African National Congress and the Inkatha Freedom Party to more extreme political movements like PAGAD (People Against Gangsterism and Drugs).[2] Table 6.1 reports the results.[3]

The most disliked group among South Africans is clearly the Afrikaner Resistance Movement (Afrikaner Weerstandsbeweging, or AWB), which is hated by nearly three-fourths of South Africans.[4] The next most hated group is PAGAD, followed closely by Afrikaners and the IFP. The most liked group on the list is the ANC, followed by trade unionists. Of course, the data in table 6.1 charac-

Table 6.1 The Distribution of Affect Toward Political Groups in South Africa

	Dislike Very Much	Mean[a]	Standard Deviation	Number of Cases	Interracial Differences—η[b]
Afrikaners	47.7%	3.89	3.23	3716	.77
African National Congress	11.2	8.02	3.32	3707	.70
Afrikaner Resistance Movement (AWB)	74.6	2.10	1.82	3712	.34
South African Communist Party	21.8	5.47	2.96	3713	.59
Pan-Africanist Congress	21.2	5.29	2.82	3708	.51
New National Party	34.8	4.25	2.75	3713	.51
Democratic Party	27.8	4.81	2.97	3713	.62
Inkatha Freedom Party	41.9	3.77	2.64	3711	.17
One-party state advocates	24.4	5.25	3.04	3708	.35
PAGAD	52.4	3.23	2.51	3714	.14
Trade unionists	9.7	6.74	2.72	3710	.45
Muslims	25.8	4.63	2.57	3710	.29

Source: Author's compilation from the 2001 Truth and Reconciliation Survey.

[a]High scores indicate greater positive affect.

[b]This statistic indicates the degree of racial polarization in affect ntoward these groups. All cross-race differences in means are statistically significant at $p < .001$.

terize all South Africans and thus tend to reflect the views of the African majority.

These data can provide a picture of how much political antipathy exists in South Africa and whether antipathy is related to race. Of the twelve groups we asked about, the average number of groups rated as extremely disliked is 3.9 (median = 4.0).[5] As an empirical matter, the racial groups do not differ greatly in the number of groups on this list that they dislike. The average number of groups rated to any degree negatively by blacks is 7.0; for whites, Colored people, and those of Asian origin, the averages are 7.1, 6.2, and 6.6, respectively. These differences are statistically significant, but they are also quite small (η = .12). Perhaps most important, since the average scores for blacks and whites are the same, it appears that there was no apparent bias in the list presented to the respondents. All South Africans seem to have had a roughly equal chance to express their displeasure toward their relevant political opponents. In general, South Africans tend to feel quite negatively toward their political foes.

Similarly small differences exist in the number of groups liked by each of the racial groups. The average number of groups rated positively are 3.4, 2.9, 3.5, and 3.6, for blacks, whites, Colored people, and those of Asian origin, respectively. Apparently, whites found slightly less to like on the list we read to them, but again, while statistically significant, the cross-race differences are actually quite small (η = .13).

Though overall quantities of sympathy and antipathy seem similar across the different racial groups, in fact, *whom one dislikes* depends heavily on race. The statistic eta, also reported in table 6.1, is a measure of the degree to which South Africans of different races rate these groups differently.

I refer to large racial differences in affect for these groups as "racial polarization" in group antipathy. The largest such polarization is found in reactions to Afrikaners (η = .77), followed closely by the ANC (η = .70) and the Democratic Party (η = .62). Interestingly, very low racial polarization in affect is found when it comes to the IFP (η = .17) and PAGAD (η = .14). These groups are widely disliked, irrespective of race.[6] In general, racial differences in attitudes toward these groups are fairly strong and highly statistically significant.

It is informative to consider in more detail racial polarization in attitudes toward Afrikaners and the ANC. Among black South Africans, 63.7 percent like the ANC very much, with another 23.7 percent expressing some degree of positive affect toward the party. Attitudes toward Afrikaners are virtually the mirror image: 62.5 percent dislike Afrikaners a great deal, with another 28.0 percent expressing some negative views toward Afrikaners. On the other hand, among whites (both English- and Afrikaans-speakers), positive affect toward Afrikaners is widespread—41.7 percent like Afrikaners a great deal, and 35.6 percent like them to some degree—and negative affect toward the ANC is widespread, with 43.2 percent disliking the ANC a great deal and 28.4 percent disliking it to some degree. Only 9.4 percent of whites express *any degree of positive feelings* toward the ANC; only 4.5 percent of Africans hold *any positive views at all* toward Afrikaners. This is a very high degree of racial polarization in feelings toward these two groups, a finding suggestive of fairly intense political animosity and conflict between these groups.

Table 6.2 examines the complete structure of group sympathy and antipathy among the four racial groups. I report in this table the groups that half or more of the respondents in each racial group rated as disliked or liked. For instance, the first row indicates that 90.5 percent of the African respondents and 69.0 percent of those of Asian origin judge Afrikaners negatively, but that fewer than half of the white and Colored respondents are negatively oriented toward Afrikaners (indicated by the absence of any figures in the table for these cells). The darkly shaded groups are those toward whom there is a consensus of opinion across the four races; lightly shaded entries indicate the agreement of three or more groups. Thus, more than half of whites, Colored people, and those of Asian origin are negatively predisposed toward the South African Communist Party; Africans, however, do not share this opinion.

Three groups draw the antipathy of South Africans of every race: the AWB, the IFP, and PAGAD. Large majorities of each racial

Table 6.2 Group Sympathy and Antipathy, by Race

Groups	African	White	Colored	Asian Origin
Disliked by one-half or more				
Afrikaners	90.5%			69.0%
African National Congress		71.6%		
Afrikaner Resistance Movement	95.5	77.9	92.1%	89.0
South African Communist Party		88.0	65.6	68.6
Pan-Africanist Congress		81.6	63.8	67.3
New National Party	80.4			
Democratic Party	76.3			
Inkatha Freedom Party	75.3	56.2	67.2	71.0
Supporters of a one-party state		76.9	51.7	
PAGAD	75.8	84.1	70.8	71.4
Trade unions		60.8		
Muslims	59.6	61.4		
Liked by one-half or more				
Afrikaners		77.4	54.5	
African National Congress	87.4			
Afrikaner Resistance Movement				
South African Communist Party				
Pan-Africanist Congress				
New National Party			50.7	54.7
Democratic Party		77.1	51.5	62.0
Inkatha Freedom Party				
Supporters of a one-party state				
PAGAD				
Trade unions		62.0		
Muslims				54.7

Source: Author's compilation from the 2001 Truth and Reconciliation Survey.
Note: Only percentages greater than or equal to 50 percent are shown in this table. Thus, fewer than half of the African respondents dislike the ANC.

group express hostility toward these groups. For whites, Colored people, and those of Asian origin, there is also agreement on antipathy toward the South African Communist Party and the PAC. No interracial consensus exists on groups that are liked, although all except Africans are favorably predisposed toward the Democratic Party.

Our African respondents are by far the most favorably oriented toward the ANC, a not-too-surprising finding. Fully 87.4 percent of the black respondents rate the ANC positively. The only other group even approaching the popularity of the ANC among blacks is unions, positively rated by 62.0 percent of the respondents. The group rated most negatively is also not a surprise—95.5 percent of black South Africans express antipathy toward the AWB. In addition, more than half of the blacks in the sample hold negative views toward Afrikaners, the New National Party, PAGAD, the IFP, and even Muslims. Black intergroup animosity thus ranges quite widely.

Whites give their most positive ratings to Afrikaners, followed closely by the Democratic Party: 77.4 percent rate the former favorably, while 77.1 percent give positive scores to the latter. Large majorities of white South Africans rate the Communist Party, the PAC, PAGAD, the AWB, supporters of a one-party state, and the ANC unfavorably, and smaller but still substantial majorities dislike Muslims, trade unionists, and the IFP. Whites too find much on our list of groups to which to object.

For Colored people, the poles of sympathy and antipathy are defined by Afrikaners (54.5 percent positive) and the AWB (92.1 percent negative). Colored people do not dislike the ANC as whites do and are not as antagonistic toward trade unionists and Muslims. Still, six of the groups attract antipathy from a majority of Colored people.[7]

For those of Asian origin, a majority are favorably predisposed toward the Democratic Party, the New National Party, and Muslims. In terms of groups disliked by those of Asian origin, two findings are worthy of emphasis: significant majorities express antipathy toward Afrikaners and toward the IFP.

Thus, while different racial groups direct their antipathy in somewhat different directions, there is strong agreement on the undesirability of groups like the AWB, PAGAD, and the IFP. Perhaps one of the strongest cross-race conflicts is represented in the finding that majorities of whites, Colored people, and those of Asian origin think favorably of the Democratic Party, while a substantial majority of Africans perceive the party negatively. Thus, there is a considerable degree of political animosity in South Africa, and in many instances it is closely connected to race.

Least Liked Groups

For the purposes of measuring political intolerance, it is necessary to determine which of these groups the respondent dislikes the most, since tolerance is a concept that applies only to groups or objects that are disfavored or disagreeable (see, for example, Sullivan, Piereson, and Marcus 1982; Gibson and Gouws 2003). Table 6.3 reports the so-called least-liked method of assessing attitudes toward these groups. The respondents were asked to identify the groups they dislike the most, using the list of groups we provided or citing any other group they wished to add to the list.[8] The selection of the least liked (that is, the most disliked) group is important because it is a precursor to the questions about perceptions of threat and political intolerance. We asked the respondents to rank the four groups they dislike the most. As can be seen in table 6.3, some portion of the sample has difficulty identifying more than two groups they dislike a great deal, even if virtually all respondents can name a most disliked and second most disliked group.

Among all South Africans (who are of course dominated by black South Africans), the single most disliked group is the AWB, with 36.7 percent of the respondents naming this group as their most disliked. Across all four disliked nominees, nearly three-fourths of the respondents put the AWB among their most hated political enemies (see column 1). From the remaining entries, the impression is that group hatred is dispersed over the political landscape, with not much agreement among South Africans on who their prime political enemy is.

The impression of dispersed antipathy is still supported when these data are broken down by the race of the respondent, as they

Table 6.3 The Distribution of Disliked Groups

Group	Among Most Disliked	Most Disliked	Second Most Disliked	Third Most Disliked	Fourth Most Disliked
Afrikaners	36.1%	19.1%	14.3%	8.3%	4.2%
African National Congress	20.1	7.1	2.6	2.1	1.8
Afrikaner Resistance Movement	74.7	36.7	27.6	9.4	5.6
South African Communist Party	24.9	3.3	5.5	4.2	2.5
Pan-Africanist Congress	23.7	2.4	4.8	5.9	4.0
New National Party	27.0	4.3	9.8	12.3	7.3
Democratic Party	18.1	1.9	4.8	8.6	7.1
Inkatha Freedom Party	36.5	8.7	10.3	13.5	8.6
Advocates of a one-party state	14.4	2.5	2.6	3.1	2.0
PAGAD	47.5	10.4	10.8	11.7	11.1
Trade unionists	5.2	0.4	0.7	1.2	1.4
Muslims	14.1	1.7	2.7	3.9	4.4
Other	6.4	1.5	2.3	1.6	1.6
None	—	.0	1.5	14.2	38.4
Number of cases		3,660	3,660	3,660	3,660

Source: Author's compilation from the 2001 Truth and Reconciliation Survey.
Note: The percentages for the most disliked, second most disliked, third most disliked, and fourth most disliked groups total to 100 percent down the columns (except for rounding errors).

are in table 6.4. That table shows that a large majority of Africans name the AWB as among their most disliked group, but that no other group attracts a supermajority from Africans, and only Afrikaners draw strong antipathy from a majority of the African respondents. Even the IFP, which in 1996 was named as among the most disliked groups by fully 77.5 percent of the African respondents (Gibson and Gouws 2003, 54), is listed as among the most disliked groups by fewer than half of the African respondents. These data suggest that African political animosity is dispersed across a number of groups, even if it is concentrated on those groups representing mainly white interests (such as the National Party and the Democratic Party). Among Africans, there are three significant

Table 6.4 The Distribution of Disliked Groups, by Race

Named as Among Most Disliked	African	White	Colored	Asian Origin
Afrikaners	59.4%	.8%	13.4%	32.7%
African National Congress	4.1	46.7	27.1	28.6
Afrikaner Resistance Movement	86.8	45.6	83.4	77.6
South African Communist Party	3.9	60.5	34.8	33.1
Pan-Africanist Congress	6.9	51.3	35.4	26.5
New National Party	43.2	3.5	15.6	12.7
Democratic Party	28.9	1.2	11.3	11.8
Inkatha Freedom Party	47.5	15.4	32.8	39.6
Advocates of a one-party state	3.8	34.2	17.3	15.5
PAGAD	39.2	57.5	55.7	58.8
Trade unionists	1.4	12.9	4.1	6.9
Muslims	10.6	23.4	11.3	11.0
Other	8.0	5.7	2.3	4.9

Source: Author's compilation from the 2001 Truth and Reconciliation Survey.
Note: Entries are the percentages of each racial group naming the political group as among their most disliked groups. All cell entries greater than 50.0 percent are shaded.

changes since the comparable survey conducted in 1996: a substantial increase in animosity toward Afrikaners (42.5 percent versus 59.4 percent named them as among the four most disliked groups, in 1996 and 2001, respectively); the substantial decline in animosity toward the IFP; and the rise of ill feelings toward PAGAD (which was not among the most disliked groups in 1996).

A majority of whites list Communists, PAGAD, and the PAC as among their most disliked groups, while Colored people focus on the AWB and PAGAD, as do those of Asian origin. Otherwise, political animosity is dispersed across numerous groups. Among whites, there are three significant changes since 1996: a decline in animosity toward the Communists (perhaps under the theory that the Communists are now less powerful and relevant to South African politics), toward the PAC, and toward trade unionists; a slight rise in animosity toward the ANC; and of course the dramatic increase in hatred for PAGAD. For Colored people, there are two significant changes: declines in animosity toward the PAC and IFP and the growth of anti-PAGAD feelings. Finally, within our Asian sample, anti-Afrikaner sentiment grew, anti-PAC and anti-IFP feelings declined, and anti-PAGAD views blossomed. Across all groups, the most significant finding from the 2001 survey is the rather substantial decline in animosity toward the Inkatha Freedom Party (except among whites, whose anti-IFP feelings were never widespread in the first place), and the growth of ill will toward PAGAD.

The findings from this portion of the survey are encouraging in two important respects. First, group animosities have dispersed somewhat, at least in terms of specific groups (if not in terms of the broader political interests and viewpoints represented by the groups). Not even within a race do many groups attract a majority of respondents naming them as among their most disliked political enemies. Second, the highly dangerous conflict between most black South Africans and the IFP has significantly abated. To some degree, group animosities have been transferred from the major competitors for political power in South Africa (like the IFP) to more marginal and fringe groups like PAGAD. This is perhaps an encouraging finding.

On the other hand, the growth of animosity toward Afrikaners among Africans is a significant and ominous finding. It appears from these data that Africans are no closer to reconciliation with their former Afrikaner masters now than they were in the early days of the transition. Nor are whites any more sympathetic toward the ANC. Thus, a picture of substantial race-based political animosity emerges from these data. From this perspective, it seems that reconciliation is now less likely than in the past.

Perhaps the most important finding of this analysis is that political antipathy is strongly shaped by race. In this survey, knowing whom a South African dislikes can be fairly easily predicted from his or her race. Polarization is especially strong when it comes to the ANC and Afrikaners. Whites dislike the ANC a great deal, and blacks dislike Afrikaners a great deal. Attitudes are largely independent of race toward only two significant groups—the IFP and PAGAD. The *level* of group animosity is fairly high and *not* dependent on race: all racial groups express a comparable degree of antipathy toward the groups we consider. Moreover, in comparison to a comparable survey conducted five years earlier, political antipathy has become even more racially polarized. These findings do not bode well for my consideration of threat perceptions and political intolerance.

Contemporary Threat Perceptions

Dislike for political opponents is no doubt common in even the most stable democratic political systems, so we must move beyond the simple examination of intergroup antipathy to consider whether political enemies are not only disliked but perceived as threatening as well. One of the most well established relationships in research on the origins of political tolerance is that those who perceive their political enemies as more threatening are more likely not to tolerate them. This venerable hypothesis has been confirmed in research in many different countries, including our earlier research in South Africa (for example, Gibson and Gouws 2003).

I have measured perceptions of the threat posed by the group named as most disliked by the respondent using a series of adjective pairs describing attributes of the group. For instance, the respondents were asked to judge the group on a seven-point scale ranging from "committed to democracy" to "not committed to democracy." Table 6.5 reports South Africans' perceptions of their hated political enemies. Since the same questions were asked in our 1996 survey, I report those findings as well. The results are displayed for the most disliked group named by the respondent and for another group from the list of most disliked groups (the "other highly disliked group").[9]

The least-liked measurement technology was indeed successful in selecting a group that each of the respondents disliked a great deal. For instance, in 2001, 60.7 percent of the respondents evaluated their most disliked group at the most extreme score on the continuum indicating the dangerousness of the group to South African society. Other threat perceptions are not quite so intemperate, although clearly the groups identified by the respondents are in general quite threatening.

However, these groups are *not* judged to be very powerful or efficacious. For instance, only 10.8 percent of the respondents rate the group as extremely powerful, and even fewer (7.5 percent) estimate that the group is likely to gain significant power in the future. South Africans certainly believe that they would be adversely affected were the group to get power (for example, almost half say their personal freedom would be reduced), but it appears

Table 6.5 The Perceived Threat of Highly Disliked Groups, 1996 and 2001

Perception	At Most Extreme Score	Mean[a]	Standard Deviation	Number of Cases
Most disliked group				
Dangerous to society				
1996	68.2%	6.2	1.5	2,503
2001	60.7	6.1	1.5	3,695
Unpredictable				
1996	57.1	5.8	1.8	2,502
2001	43.5	5.4	1.9	3,695
Dangerous to the normal lives of people				
1996	54.2	5.7	1.9	2,503
2001	43.7	5.5	1.8	3,696
Likely to gain a lot of power in South Africa				
1996	6.1	2.5	1.9	2,504
2001	7.5	2.9	1.9	3,696
Likely to affect how well my family and I live				
1996	32.1	4.6	2.2	2,502
2001	27.1	4.6	2.1	3,696
Angry toward the group				
1996	53.3	5.4	2.1	2,498
2001	44.2	5.3	2.0	3,692
Unwilling to follow the rules of democracy				
1996	62.6	6.1	1.5	2,499
2001	50.0	5.9	1.5	3,692
Powerful				
1996	13.0	3.2	2.2	2,499
2001	10.8	3.4	2.1	3,692
If got power, everything would change				
1996	n.a.	n.a.	n.a.	n.a.
2001	46.4	5.3	2.1	3,691
If got power, my freedom would be reduced				
1996	n.a.	n.a.	n.a.	n.a.
2001	44.6	5.6	1.7	3,688
If got power, my personal security would be reduced				
1996	n.a.	n.a.	n.a.	n.a.
2001	45.0	5.6	1.7	3,692

Table 6.5 (Continued)

Perception	At Most Extreme Score	Mean[a]	Standard Deviation	Number of Cases
Another highly disliked group				
Dangerous to society				
1996	43.4	5.1	2.1	2,492
2001	36.4	5.2	1.9	3,601
Unpredictable				
1996	43.4	5.3	1.9	2,491
2001	33.2	5.0	1.9	3,600
Dangerous to the normal lives of people				
1996	34.2	4.8	2.1	2,493
2001	27.4	4.8	2.0	3,601
Likely to gain a lot of power in South Africa				
1996	4.7	2.6	1.8	2,491
2001	6.1	3.0	1.9	3,601
Likely to affect how well my family and I live				
1996	21.7	4.0	2.2	2,498
2001	18.0	4.3	2.0	3,598
Angry toward the group				
1996	36.1	4.8	2.2	2,498
2001	25.6	4.5	2.1	3,599
Unwilling to follow the rules of democracy				
1996	44.1	5.3	1.9	2,493
2001	31.3	5.2	1.8	3,599
Powerful				
1996	10.5	3.0	2.1	2,492
2001	7.7	3.4	1.9	3,601

Source: Author's compilation from the 2001 Truth and Reconciliation Survey.
Note: n.a. = not asked.
[a]High scores in every instance indicate greater degrees of perceived threat.

that few accept that the group they dislike the most will achieve political power.[10]

Since the same questions using the least-liked technology were asked in our 1996 survey, it is possible to compare the levels of threat perceived in 2001 with threat perceptions five years earlier. Two caveats are important. First, this is not a panel survey, so the comparison can be made only of aggregate responses, not of individual South Africans, and second, the distribution of the specific groups asked about varies between the two surveys. In both instances, the respondents were asked their opinions of groups they dislike the most, which is a useful basis for comparing threat perceptions, but the particular mixture of groups is not necessarily the same in the two surveys.

Perceptions of group threat seem to have declined rather substantially between 1996 and 2001. For instance, in 1996, 54.2 percent of the respondents gave the most extreme negative rating when asked whether the group was dangerous to the normal lives of people. This figure declined in 2001 to 43.7 percent. Similar declines characterize most of the attributes on which the groups were rated (as well as the ratings of the other highly disliked group). It seems from these data that the intensity of intergroup antipathy may have moderated a bit as South Africa's democracy has matured. This is an important finding.

When I conducted a factor analysis of the items measuring threat perceptions of the most disliked group, three factors emerged (see table 6.6).[11] The first factor is dominated by the following perceptions (with pattern loadings shown in parentheses): that the least-liked group is dangerous to the normal lives of people (.74); that it is dangerous to society (.58); that the respondent is angry toward the group (.54); that the group will affect how well the respondent lives (.46); and to a marginal degree, that the group is unwilling to follow the rules of democracy (.34). Thus, this factor is largely made of *sociotropic threat perceptions*—perceptions of the threat of the group to the larger South African society. The second factor consists of the two items measuring the power of the group: the perception that the group is powerful (.70) and the perception that it is likely to gain power in South Africa (.68). That perceptions of power make up their own factor is consistent with earlier findings from South Africa (Gibson and Gouws 2003). The final factor represents *egocentric threat perceptions*, with the following variables defining the factor: perceptions that the group would reduce the respondent's personal freedom (.83); perceptions that the group would affect the respondent's personal security; and to a marginal

Table 6.6 The Structure of Perceptions of Threat from Least Liked Group

Perception	Sociotropic Threat	Group Power	Egocentric Threat
Dangerous to the normal lives of people	.74		
Dangerous to society	.58		
Angry toward the group	.54		
Likely to affect how well my family and I live	.46		
Unwilling to follow the rules of democracy	.34		
Powerful		.70	
Likely to gain a lot of power in South Africa		.68	
If got power, would reduce my freedom			.83
If got power, would reduce my security			.63
If got power, everything would change			.38
Unpredictable			

Source: Author's compilation from the 2001 Truth and Reconciliation Survey.
Note: The table entries are pattern loadings. All loadings greater than or equal to .30 are shown in the table. The adjective pair "predictable" versus "unpredictable" loads significantly on none of the factors. The eigenvalues of the first four factors are: 2.85, 1.66, 1.21, and .98, respectively.

extent, perceptions that if the group got power, everything would change (.38).[12]

The intercorrelations of these factors are quite revealing. Based on the factor scores, perceptions of group power (and power potential) are only weakly related to perceptions of sociotropic threat ($r = -.12$) and only moderately to egocentric threat ($r = -.22$). However, not only are these correlations modest, but the direction of these relationship is *not* as expected: those who perceive greater group power are *less* threatened, on both aspects of threat. These relationships thus reflect the rather odd nature of perceptions of group power in South Africa.[13]

Perceptions of sociotropic and egocentric threat are strongly related ($r = .62$). Those who perceive more of one type of threat are likely to perceive more of the other threat. Though the relationship is strong, it is not so overwhelming as to render the distinction between types of threat meaningless, and in light of the fact that a separate factor emerged for the egocentric threat items, these two types of threat should be understood as related but distinct. By treating threat perceptions as tridimensional, we will be able to determine with more precision exactly which aspects of threat are most relevant for political intolerance.

There are significant and substantial racial differences with respect to each of these threat perceptions. In terms of both sociotropic and egocentric threats, Africans are substantially more threatened than other South Africans. Colored South Africans are the least threatened. But in terms of perceptions of group power, whites are the most likely to view their least liked group as powerful; Africans are the least likely to hold such views. This difference obviously stems from different groups being selected as least liked by blacks (who typically name the AWB) and by whites (who typically name the ANC). Racial differences are strongest on sociotropic threat perceptions (η = .28) and weakest on egocentric perceptions (η = .17). For example, the percentages of respondents within each racial group who rate their political enemy at the highest point on the scale representing "danger to the normal lives of people" are 48.8 percent, 29.3 percent, 30.9 percent, and 37.1 percent, for blacks, whites, Colored people, and those of Asian origin, respectively. Conversely, the percentages who assert that, if the group got power, it would reduce the freedom of the respondent are 47.6 percent, 38.5 percent, 38.5 percent, and 35.1 percent for the four groups respectively. Thus, South Africans of different races view sociotropic threats quite differently—while at the same time egocentric threats are judged relatively similarly—with Africans feeling particularly vulnerable.

One-third of the respondents actually know a member of their most disliked group, although there is tremendous variability in the degree to which people selecting different groups as most disliked claim to know a representative of the group. For instance, fewer than 10 percent of the respondents who name Communists, supporters of a one-party state, and PAGAD actually know a person of this political persuasion or affiliation. In contrast, over half of those who name the ANC or the IFP as the most disliked group know a member of the party. In terms of the three types of threat perceptions, in no instance is there a substantively significant difference between those who know and those who do not know a member of the most disliked group.

Political Intolerance

We measured political intolerance by asking the respondents whether their hated political foes should be allowed to engage in certain types of political activity. The following questions were asked with regard to the group in South African politics the respondent disliked the most and another highly disliked group:

> Members of the [disliked group] should be prohibited from standing as a candidate for an elected position.
>
> Members of the [disliked group] should be allowed to hold street demonstrations in your community.
>
> The [disliked group] should be officially banned in your community.

Thus, as the first question, many respondents were asked to agree or disagree with the following assertion: "Members of PAGAD should be prohibited from standing as a candidate for an elected position."

These specific activities were selected because they are all actions that must be allowed in a democracy.[14] In each instance, the action involves competition for political power, and obviously such rights would not be denied to mainstream political parties or to the respondent's own political party or group. Political tolerance requires that unpopular groups be "put up with," by which I mean that they must be given the same opportunities to compete for political power as are given to any other political group in society. I do not contend that every sort of activity must be allowed—democracies can clearly ban terrorism—but any right or privilege that would be claimed by the groups in power must be extended to those who would challenge those groups.

Table 6.7 reports the replies to these tolerance questions in both 1996 and 2001. Though the least-liked measurement strategy does not ensure the nominal equivalence of groups, the responses in both surveys are in reference to the political group the respondent disliked the most and to another highly disliked group (using exactly the same methodology). In the table, I report the means and standard deviations from the continuous variables; the percentages are based on collapsing strong and not so strong responses on the Likert response set.

Political tolerance is in relatively short supply in South Africa. For instance, nearly three-fourths of the respondents would not allow a demonstration by members of the political group they dislike the most. Tolerance for allowing that group to field candidates for office and to exist as a political group is somewhat higher, but still substantial majorities would not allow their most hated political enemies ordinary opportunities to compete for political power. Though South Africans are somewhat less intolerant of the other highly disliked group, fully two-thirds would not allow a demonstration by that group either. These responses indicate that intolerance is at least twice as prevalent as is tolerance.

In terms of change between the two surveys, the overwhelming impression given by the data in table 6.7 is one of stasis. The mean scores from the two surveys are virtually identical, and the percentages willing to tolerate their least liked groups certainly did not significantly increase between 1996 and 2001. Indeed, the similarity in the figures produced by the two surveys is quite remarkable, even as it is discouraging from the point of view of reconciliation.

The evidence that tolerance has not increased in the country despite the diminution of political violence and threat perceptions is a most unwelcome finding. The relationship between threat and tolerance will be investigated more carefully later in this chapter, but the implication from the findings reported here is that tolerance and threat became less strongly connected between 1996 and 2001.

Table 6.7 Levels of South African Political Intolerance, 1996 and 2001

	Intolerant	Uncertain	Tolerant	Mean[a]	Standard Deviation	Number of Cases
Most disliked group						
Allow candidates						
1996	61.8%	10.7%	27.4%	2.4	1.4	2,512
2001	69.0	9.6	21.4	2.2	1.3	3,689
Allow demonstrations						
1996	74.3	10.5	15.2	1.9	1.2	2,512
2001	76.9	8.1	15.0	1.9	1.2	3,686
Not banned						
1996	65.3	12.1	22.6	2.2	1.3	2,510
2001	63.1	12.6	24.2	2.3	1.3	3,686
Tolerance index						
1996	—	—	—	2.2	1.0	2,515
2001	—	—	—	2.1	1.0	3,693
Another highly disliked group						
Allow candidates						
1996	53.7	11.7	34.6	2.6	1.4	2,509
2001	58.6	11.6	29.8	2.4	1.3	3,600
Allow demonstrations						
1996	66.8	11.2	22.0	2.3	1.2	2,508
2001	66.7	9.8	23.5	2.4	1.2	3,600
Not banned						
1996	54.0	13.7	32.3	2.6	1.4	2,507
2001	53.1	15.9	31.0	2.6	1.3	3,600
Tolerance index						
1996	—	—	—	2.5	1.1	2,508
2001	—	—	—	2.5	1.0	3,600

Source: Author's compilation from the 2001 Truth and Reconciliation Survey.
Note: The percentages total to 100 percent across these three columns, except for rounding errors.
[a]High scores indicate greater political tolerance.

Perceptions of the Intolerance of Others

We also asked the respondents about their perceptions of the intolerance of other South Africans. The question asked for an estimate of the proportion of people who agree with the respondent's own view of whether candidates representing the most disliked group should be banned from running for office. As is typically the case with questions of this type, most South Africans (70.0 percent) perceive others to be in agreement with them. Racial differences, however, are quite substantial, with 74.0 percent of Africans perceiving agreement but only 50.8 percent of whites believing their view to be in the majority. Moreover, there is a very strong relationship between intolerance and perceptions of agreement, with 81.7 percent of those who are intolerant but only 46.5 percent of those who are tolerant asserting that most South Africans agree with their views on this matter.[15] Thus, intolerant South Africans are much more likely than tolerant South Africans to view their position as conventional and widely shared by others; and, unfortunately, they are correct in that perception. To the extent that one believes oneself to be surrounded by like-minded people, one's attitudes are emboldened and empowered, and intolerance in South Africa therefore holds considerable pernicious potential.

Racial Differences in Levels of Intolerance

Racial differences in levels of intolerance can be found in these data, though the disparity is not tremendous. For instance, for the most disliked group, the differences in mean levels of tolerance are statistically significant, but not large ($\eta = .19$). For the other highly disliked group, the differences are even smaller ($\eta = .11$). In general, Africans are the most intolerant, followed by Colored people and those of Asian origin, with whites being significantly more tolerant than other South Africans. Figure 6.1 reports the intergroup differences, based on whether the respondent is willing to tolerate *any* of the three activities by the most disliked group. While nearly two-thirds of Africans would deny all three types of actions to their most disliked group, the figure for whites just barely exceeds one-half. Colored and Asian respondents are not as

Figure 6.1 Interracial Differences in Intolerance of the Most Disliked Group

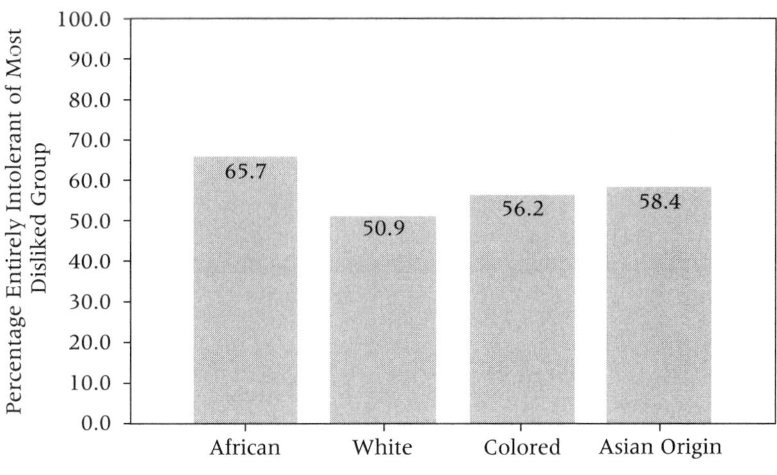

Source: Author's compilation from the 2001 Truth and Reconciliation Survey.

intolerant as blacks but are more intolerant than whites. Generally, however, this is a conservative test of intolerance (for example, "don't know" responses are implicitly treated as not intolerant), so the levels of intolerance among all four racial groups must be judged to be remarkably high.[16]

I should note as well that substantial differences exist within these racial groups according to language and ethnicity. For instance, among Africans, the least intolerant are those who speak Xhosa (55.8 percent are completely intolerant of their most disliked group), while the most intolerant are Shangaan-speakers (78.9 percent intolerant). Even the difference between Xhosa- and Zulu-speakers is nearly twenty percentage points.[17] Among whites, the difference between Afrikaans- and English-speakers is statistically significant but not great, although the linguistic difference among Colored people is slightly more substantial: 59.2 percent of Afrikaans-speakers versus 44.6 percent of English-speakers are completely intolerant of their most disliked group. We must be mindful in the following analysis that intolerance varies by both race and ethnicity and language.

The Threat-Tolerance Connection

Perhaps the most interesting finding from this portion of the survey concerns how the three threat dimensions are related to political intolerance. Perhaps unexpectedly, intolerance is most closely related to sociotropic threat perceptions ($\beta = -.31$), is only quite weakly related to egocentric threat perceptions ($\beta = -.11$), and is basically independent of perceptions of group power ($\beta = .06$). *The form of threat that has the greatest influence on intolerance is threat to the group, not threat to the individual.*[18] Moreover, the perceived power of the group has little if anything to do with the degree to which it is tolerated by South Africans.

The finding that sociotropic threat perceptions have the greatest consequences for intolerance reveals something about the nature of intolerance. Intolerance is a social, not an individual, attitude. It refers to what people think their political system ought to do about political nonconformists. As such, the finding fits with the general conclusion from earlier research that interpersonal intolerance is independent of political intolerance (see, for example, Sullivan, Piereson, and Marcus 1982). Intolerance increases not necessarily when people feel that their own security is at risk but rather when they perceive a threat to the larger system of which they are a part.

This finding is consistent with the more general conclusion that sociotropic factors are typically more influential in politics than egocentric factors. For instance, Bryan Caplan (2002, 417) concludes that, "while people may be selfish in private life, when they enter the political sphere it is ideas, not interests, that dominate." His analysis produces evidence that "is highly consistent with political scientists' findings on the surprisingly weak impact of self-interest on beliefs about social questions." In my research, intolerance flows from threats to the community, to its ideologies, and to its ways of life, not necessarily from perceptions that the individual's material self-interest is immediately at stake (see also Feldman 2003).

I must note that these findings are not entirely consistent across all four racial groups, although in every instance sociotropic threat perceptions are the strongest predictors of intolerance. Among Africans, and perhaps those of Asian origin as well, egocentric threat perceptions contribute to some degree to intolerance (for example, $\beta = -.16$ among Africans; $\beta = -.11$ among those of Asian origin). Another slight anomaly is that among those of Asian origin, perceptions of greater group power are associated with *more* tolerance ($\beta = .20$), and a similar but much weaker relationship exists among whites ($\beta = .10$). Still, the basic conclusion that sociotropic threat perceptions dominate political intolerance strongly characterizes each of these groups. Intolerance stems from perceived threats to the community and its ideology, not from threats to the individual member of the community.[19]

Truth Acceptance and Political Tolerance

To what degree are truth acceptance and political tolerance connected? We might expect that accepting the TRC's truth contributes to tolerance, because the message the commission promoted was overwhelmingly one urging tolerance. On the other hand, the lessons of the TRC may also have contributed to greater intolerance, since the TRC's revelations about human rights abuses may have increased the amount of threat perceived by South Africans from their political enemies. On balance, however, the TRC was so strongly associated with tolerance that I expect a positive relationship between truth acceptance and political tolerance.

To test this hypothesis, I created a simple index of tolerance based on the responses to the questions concerning the most disliked and the other highly disliked group. The correlations for each of the four groups between this index and the measure of acceptance of the TRC's truth are:

African	Truth acceptance—.06*** → Tolerance
White	Truth acceptance—.24*** → Tolerance
Colored	Truth acceptance—.13*** → Tolerance
Asian origin	Truth acceptance—−.02 → Tolerance

Among most South Africans, truth acceptance and tolerance tend to at least some degree to go together. The relationship is particularly strong among whites, but particularly weak (indeed, virtually trivial, even though highly statistically significant) among Africans. Among those of Asian origin, no such relationship exists.

Perhaps one reason why truth acceptance is not more strongly related to tolerance is that truth acceptance is generally related to greater perceptions of group threat. For instance, these data provide some evidence that those who are more accepting of the TRC's collective memory are more likely, not less, to perceive their most disliked group as directly threatening to their own welfare. On the other hand, those who accept more of the TRC's truth are *less* likely to perceive their most disliked political enemy as powerful, and the correlations between truth acceptance and perceptions of sociotropic threat vary widely across the four groups. The effect of truth on the various threat perceptions is not consistent, however, and the possibility of a strong negative correlation with tolerance is thus undermined.

Among most South Africans, then, truth acceptance does not seem to play a dominant role in shaping political tolerance.

Social Identities, Threat Perceptions, and Intolerance

As noted earlier in this chapter, significant and substantial differences exist in levels of intolerance among those of different races, ethnicities, and languages. Perhaps some of these differences are in fact a function not strictly of race but of variability in group identities among these various subgroups. For instance, while 66.5 percent of the Zulu-speaking respondents assert that it is important to support their group's views, this figure balloons to 83.5 percent among Shangaan-speakers. Similarly large differences exist between Afrikaans- and English-speaking whites (72.8 percent versus 55.4 percent), although no such difference can be found among Colored people of different home languages. I observe comparable variability in beliefs about the political relevance of groups: some view groups as highly relevant to South African politics, but others are not so convinced. Thus, it is probably a mistake to think of racial differences in terms of simple and uniform distinctions; the meaning of identity within South Africa's various racial and ethnic communities seems to vary substantially.

Our own earlier research in South Africa (Gibson and Gouws 2003, 93) has demonstrated that important determinants of intolerance can be found in social identity theory. We discovered that some, but not all, aspects of South African social identities breed political intolerance. Specifically, we concluded: "It is not identity per se but the collateral attitudes that sometimes arise from identities that are consequential for democratic values." The primary collateral attitudes are beliefs about the value of group solidarity and the perceived psychic benefits of one's group membership. Those who believe more strongly in the need for group solidarity and those who derive more psychic benefits from their group associations are more likely to be threatened by their political enemies, and this heightened sense of threat directly translates into greater political intolerance (for similar South African findings, see Duckitt and Mphuthing 1998). Simply claiming a South African identity has no consequences for group antipathy, threat perceptions, or intolerance. It is thus useful and important to consider whether social identities continue to frame threat perceptions and intolerance in contemporary South Africa.

In an entirely different context, Paul Sniderman and Thomas Piazza (2002, 162) report comparable findings. They discover that strong group identities among African Americans in Chicago are *not* associated with intolerance: "We can find no connection of any consequence between black Americans' readiness to be prejudiced against Jews and their feeling a sense of solidarity with fellow blacks, desire to build up black pride and self-respect, or aspiration to increase black Americans' measure of economic autonomy." They do, however, observe a modest relationship between "Afrocentrism" (a collateral attitude) and black anti-Semitism. Their understanding of the causal process involved is similar to that of Gibson and Gouws (2003): "Our principal finding . . . is that other forms of racial identification only appear to be related to anti-Semitism because they are related to Afrocentrism" (162).

The theory connecting social identities and intolerance is straightforward. Following Gibson and Gouws (2003), I expect strong positive in-group identities to give rise to both strong negative out-group feelings and beliefs about the value of maintaining group solidarity. In this case, I hypothesize that *those who judge their group identity as more important and those who derive more psychic benefits from their identities are more likely to be able to identify a group with which they negatively identify. They should also be more likely to assert the value of maintaining strong group solidarity.* These hypotheses can be tested with the data in table 6.8, which provides the intercorrelations among the various measures of group identity.[20]

The data provide no evidence whatsoever that strong in-group attachments produce strong negative reactions to out-groups. In every instance, the correlations between the two measures of identity strength (strength of primary identity and psychic benefits of identity) and the ability to name an out-group (any anti-identity) are insignificant and trivial, and indeed the strongest observed correlation (−.11, among those of Asian origin) is wrongly signed. Stronger in-group attachments *do not* predict that South Africans will be able to identify a group with which they negatively identify.

On the other hand, strong identities are indeed related to strong commitments to group solidarity. For instance, among white South Africans, those who derive greater psychic benefits from their group identities are much more likely to endorse strong group solidarity ($r = .31$). The relationships are similarly strong for Colored people and those of Asian origin, although they are weaker but still highly statistically significant among Africans. For instance, while 40 percent of those who rate their group identity as not important at all assert that it is important to support their group's point of view, fully 76 percent of those who rate their group identity as very important hold that belief (data not shown).

Table 6.8 also confirms that the mere existence of a national identity (claims South African identity) is not closely connected to the importance that the respondent ascribes to being a South African. Nor does nominal national identity have any consistent connections to the other aspects of group affiliations. For instance, among whites and Colored people, claiming a South African identity is associated with a higher likelihood of identifying a negative identity, but not strongly, and no such relationship exists among Africans or those of Asian origin.

The rated importance of being South African (in contrast to nominal national identity) is far more closely and consistently related to the other dimensions of social identities. For instance, as noted earlier, those who more strongly proclaim their South African identity are also likely to rate their group identification as important and to derive psychic benefits from their group identification. These findings hold for all four racial groups. Within none of the racial groups is there a relationship between the importance of a national identity and the existence of an anti-identity. Finally, those who ascribe greater importance to being a South African are more likely to judge group solidarity to be important and, except for those of Asian origin, are more likely to see group memberships as politically relevant in South Africa. Thus, national identities are centrally located within the constellation of identity attitudes. Most important, national identity is not an antidote to group identity but instead seems to be complementary to group associations.

In sum, not all of the hypotheses of social identity theory are supported by these data. In particular, firm group and national identities are not antithetical; instead, they tend strongly to go together. Moreover, identity by itself does not seem to directly produce antipathy toward out-groups. Identities are associated with certain attitudes about the significance of groups, but not inevitably. These results concerning the interconnection of various aspects of group identities imply that clear and simple relationships between the identity variables and political tolerance will not be found in these data.

Connecting Identities with Threat Perceptions and Political Intolerance

Figure 6.2 presents the hypothesized pathway through which I expect that group identities lead to political intolerance. None of these relationships is inevitable; each causal arrow (→) represents only a tendency for the two variables to be linked. In words, this theory claims:

Table 6.8 Intercorrelations of Social Identity Measures

	1.	2.	3.	4.	5.	6.	7.
African South Africans							
1. Claims South African identity	1.00						
2. Strength of primary identity	.06**	1.00					
3. Psychic benefits of identity	.03	.33***	1.00				
4. Any anti-identity	−.01	−.00	.02	1.00			
5. Group solidarity	−.01	.13***	.10***	.11***	1.00		
6. Political relevance of groups	−.05*	.06**	.01	.08***	.69***	1.00	
7. Importance of national identity	.10***	.28***	.19***	.00	.24***	.15***	1.00
White South Africans							
1. Claims South African identity	1.00						
2. Strength of primary identity	−.06	1.00					
3. Psychic benefits of identity	−.12***	.28***	1.00				
4. Any anti-identity	.12***	−.07	.00	1.00			
5. Group solidarity	.04	.34***	.31***	.04	1.00		
6. Political relevance of groups	.09**	.17***	.13***	.04	.70***	1.00	
7. Importance of national identity	.01	.22***	.23***	.03	.28***	.22***	1.00

Colored South Africans							
1. Claims South African identity	1.00						
2. Strength of primary identity	.10*	1.00					
3. Psychic benefits of identity	−.06	.25***	1.00				
4. Any anti-identity	.16***	.06	.05	1.00			
5. Group solidarity	.05	.26***	.27***	−.03	1.00		
6. Political relevance of groups	.05	.11*	.17***	−.03	.67***	1.00	
7. Importance of national identity	.09*	.14***	.17***	.06	.16***	.11**	1.00
South Africans of Asian origin							
1. Claims South African identity	1.00						
2. Strength of primary identity	.17**	1.00					
3. Psychic benefits of identity	.03	.40***	1.00				
4. Any anti-identity	−.03	−.07	−.11	1.00			
5. Group solidarity	.03	.29***	.25***	−.02	1.00		
6. Political relevance of groups	−.03	.09	.12	−.04	.59***	1.00	
7. Importance of national identity	.03	.35***	.42***	.06	.23***	.02	1.00

Source: Author's compilation from the 2001 Truth and Reconciliation Survey.
Note: Entries are bivariate correlation coefficients.
***$p < .001$; **$p < .01$; *$p < .05$

- Group memberships typically lead to psychological associations with groups. Individuals affiliate with many groups; group identifications vary in the degree to which they are strong and central to the individual.
- Strong group identifications often generate psychic benefits for individuals, such as feelings of self-worth and security.
- Those who derive psychological benefits from group membership tend to develop beliefs about the macrolevel importance of their membership. In particular, they come to see groups as shaping their interests in the larger political and social system in which individuals are embedded.
- Believing in the social and political relevance of one's group is often associated with belief in the necessity of maintaining group solidarity. To the extent that groups are relevant, care must be taken to maintain the integrity of the group and its borders.
- Belief in the need for group solidarity tends to reinforce perceptions of group difference (differentiation). Sympathy toward one's own group is associated with and may generate antipathy toward relevant group competitors (out-groups).
- Groups that are disliked are often seen as threatening.
- Groups that are threatening are often not tolerated.
- Political intolerance is a major source of political repression and intergroup conflict.

Each of these hypotheses can be tested with the data at hand.

Hypothesis 1: Identification Strength and Benefits Figure 6.2 reports the bivariate correlations between the two variables for each of the four racial groups.[21]

Strength of Identification → Psychic Benefits of Identification

.33—African***

.28—White***

Figure 6.2 Theoretical Linkages Between Group Identities and Political Intolerance

Source: Author's compilation from the 2001 Truth and Reconciliation Survey.

.25—Colored***

.40—Asian origin***

Note: ***p ≤ .001

Obviously, this hypothesis is strongly and uniformly supported. Those who ascribe greater significance to their group identities are substantially more likely to derive psychological benefits from those identities (such as thinking better of themselves).

Hypothesis 2: Beliefs About Groups

Psychic Benefits of Identification → Beliefs About Group Solidarity

.10—African***

.31—White***

.27—Colored***

.25—Asian origin***

Note: ***p ≤ .001

Here we find that those who derive more benefits from their group identification are more likely to assert the value of maintaining group solidarity. The relationships are significant for all groups, although the weakness of the correlation among Africans should be noted.

Hypothesis 3: Linkage to Group Antipathy and Threat Perceptions A crucial hypothesis from social identity theory is that beliefs about identities lead to perceptions of political foes as threatening, especially in terms of sociotropic group threat. As the following data make plain, this hypothesis is only weakly and partially supported by the data. Very little relationship exists among whites and Colored people; among Africans, some relationship exists; and among those of Asian origin, the relationship is slightly stronger. There is certainly nothing in these data indicating that group identities constitute a strong threat to democracy by breeding perceptions that one's political enemies are threatening.

Beliefs About Group Solidarity → Sociotropic Threat Perceptions

.10—African***

.06—White*

.07—Colored

.16—Asian origin***

Note: ***p ≤ .001; *p ≤ .05

Perhaps a portion of the weak relationship I observe here is due to the skewness in threat perceptions. After all, the group asked about is the group named by the respondent as most disliked, and therefore the individual threat perception variables are obviously skewed (an inevitable consequence of using the least-liked measurement technology). Thus, perhaps a fairer test of the hypothesis would address the broader issue of group antipathy, not just threats perceived from extreme political enemies. Therefore, I reconsider this relationship, focusing on the measure of the extent of group antipathy (used earlier in this chapter).

Beliefs About Group Solidarity → Group Antipathy

.02—African

.19—White***

.03—Colored

.16—Asian origin*

Note: ***$p \leq .001$; *$p \leq .05$

These data indicate some degree of relationship among whites and those of Asian origin, but none at all among Africans and Colored people. Thus, among most South Africans, beliefs about the value of in-group solidarity do not readily translate into out-group antipathy. These findings represent an important challenge to social identity theory.

Hypothesis 4: Threat Perceptions and Intolerance Though I have already addressed this hypothesis in this chapter, for completeness I now reproduce the correlations. Threat perceptions do indeed lead to political intolerance, and the relationships are strong and consistent.

Sociotropic Threat Perceptions → Political Tolerance

−.33—African***

−.29—White***

−.28—Colored***

−.33—Asian origin***

Note: ***$p \leq .001$

This analysis has carefully examined the crucial linkages in the theory connecting group identities to intolerance, focusing on the individual coefficients that link each variable in the hypothesized process. It is useful and necessary as well to consider the impact of identities on intolerance within the context of a more comprehensive multivariate equation.

Multivariate Analysis

Table 6.9 reports the results of regressing intolerance on the various dimensions of threat perceptions and the various indicators of group identity. Because truth acceptance is significantly related to tolerance in the bivariate case among whites and Colored people, I have added that index to the equation as well.

It should surprise no one to find that threat perceptions have a strong direct impact on tolerance, even when the other variables are incorporated into the analysis. As I earlier noted, the most efficacious component of threat perceptions is sociotropic threat, and this is true for blacks, whites, Colored people, and South Africans of Asian origin. The effect of the perceived power of the group is not consistent, but the positive signs on these coefficients indicate that groups viewed as more powerful are, among some, more likely to be tolerated.

The most interesting findings reported in this table have to do with the identity variables. Among Africans and whites, *none of the identity variables are meaningfully related to tolerance.* Virtually the same conclusion can be drawn about South Africans of Asian origin, with the slight possible exception that those who believe more in the value of group solidarity tend to be less tolerant (although this coefficient does not achieve statistical significance). Only for Colored people is there a relationship of any strength and substantive import (the $\beta = -.17$ for group solidarity). Generally, the conclusion must be that political tolerance is largely independent of how strongly South Africans identify with their groups and the attitudes that are closely associated with such identifications. This finding is entirely incompatible with social identity theory.

The degree of acceptance of the TRC's truth is to a limited degree related to political tolerance. Among whites the relationship is substantial, even in the multivariate context, and among Colored people some slight relationship exists. Among Africans, the coefficient is statistically significant but trivial (although still larger than most of the identity measures). Among those of Asian origin, truth acceptance and tolerance are unrelated. As with the earlier analysis of interracial reconciliation, it is perhaps important to note that truth acceptance does not contribute to *intolerance*, even if its influence on tolerance is limited.

A central hypothesis of the theory of social identities is that those who identify more strongly with their groups are more likely to be more threatened by their political enemies. Table 6.10 tests this hypothesis by reporting the correlations between seven dimensions of identities and three dimensions of threat perceptions.

Note first that the signs on all coefficients in the table are expected to be positive: stronger identities should enhance threat perceptions. The only possible exception would be the correlations with national identities, although as we have just seen, national identities do not seem to stand in opposition to group identities. The coefficients I deem to support the hypotheses are highlighted in table 6.10.[22]

Part of the reason why the group identity variables are unrelated to political tolerance is that they bear little relationship to threat perceptions. In no instance is the strength of the primary group identity related to any of the dimensions of threat perceptions. With only a single, weak exception does a significant relationship exist between the psychic benefits of identity and any of the perceptions of group threat. Moreover, among Africans and whites, very few of the coefficients exceed the minimum threshold of substantive significance. Identities among Colored people and those of Asian origin seem to be somewhat more significant for their perceptions of group threat. However, few consistent relationships exist across the three dimensions of threat perceptions. Some troubling puzzles also appear in the table—for instance, psychic benefits are positively correlated with sociotropic threat, while the benefit variable is *negatively* correlated with egocentric threat perceptions. The coefficients in this table point to one general conclusion: group identities per se do not contribute very much to

Table 6.9 Multivariate Determinants of Political Tolerance Among Four Racial Groups

	African			White		
	b	Standard Error	β	b	Standard Error	β
Sociotropic threat	−.25	.02	−.28***	−.26	.03	−.31***
Group power	.02	.01	.03	.08	.02	.14***
Egocentric threat	−.12	.02	−.17***	−.02	.02	−.03
Strength of primary identity	−.02	.04	−.01	−.03	.05	−.02
Psychic benefits of identity	−.03	.03	−.03	−.09	.04	−.07*
Importance of national identity	−.04	.03	−.03	−.03	.04	−.02
Group solidarity	−.02	.04	−.01	−.07	.05	−.06
Political relevance of groups	−.08	.04	−.07*	−.06	.06	−.04
Truth acceptance	.09	.03	.07**	.25	.04	.18***
Intercept	4.08	.24		3.05	.32	
Standard deviation—dependent variable	1.01			.99		
Standard error of estimate	.93			.91		
R-squared			.15***			.16***
Number of cases	1,976			935		

Table 6.9 (Continued)

	Colored			Asian Origin		
	b	Standard Error	β	b	Standard Error	β
Sociotropic threat	−.20	.04	−.26***	−.23	.05	−.29***
Group power	.04	.03	.08	.12	.04	.21***
Egocentric threat	−.06	.03	−.10*	−.09	.04	−.13*
Strength of primary identity	.11	.08	.06	−.04	.11	−.02
Psychic benefits of identity	−.03	.06	−.03	−.04	.09	−.03
Importance of national identity	.02	.06	.01	−.01	.08	−.00
Group solidarity	−.20	.08	−.17**	−.14	.11	−.10
Political relevance of groups	.14	.08	.11	−.01	.10	−.01
Truth acceptance	.14	.07	.10*	.06	.09	.04
Intercept	2.57	.50		3.43	.63	
Standard deviation—dependent variable	.95			.95		
Standard error of estimate	.90			.88		
R-squared			.11***			.18***
Number of cases	460			245		

Source: Author's compilation from the 2001 Truth and Reconciliation Survey.
***$p < .001$; **$p < .01$; *$p < .05$

Table 6.10 Intercorrelations of Social Identity and Threat Perceptions for Four Racial Groups

	Sociotropic Threat	Group Power	Egocentric Threat
Black South Africans			
South African identity	.02	−.03	.09***
Strength of primary identity	−.04*	−.05**	.04*
Psychic benefits of identity	.08***	.06**	.03
Any anti-identity	.02	−.01	.04
Group solidarity	.10***	.10***	.05**
Political relevance of groups	.02	.08***	−.04
Importance of national identity	.05**	−.01	.06**
White South Africans			
South African identity	.04	.00	.06*
Strength of primary identity	−.05	.09**	.01
Psychic benefits of identity	.02	.07*	−.09**
Any anti-identity	.10***	.03	.05
Group solidarity	.06*	.09**	−.03
Political relevance of groups	.04	.09**	−.09**
Importance of national identity	−.10***	.02	−.06*
Colored South Africans			
South African identity	.01	.04	.21***
Strength of primary identity	.05	.08*	.01
Psychic benefits of identity	.11**	.05	−.13**
Any anti-identity	.24***	.06	.13**
Group solidarity	.07	.12**	−.06
Political relevance of groups	.02	.17***	−.20***
Importance of national identity	.07	−.01	.07
South Africans of Asian origin			
South African identity	−.01	.05	.13*
Strength of primary identity	−.05	−.13*	−.01
Psychic benefits of identity	−.06	.05	−.07
Any anti-identity	.04	−.11*	.12*
Group solidarity	.16**	.09	−.04
Political relevance of groups	.10	.20***	−.11*
Importance of national identity	−.12*	−.06	.01

Source: Author's compilation from the 2001 Truth and Reconciliation Survey.
Note: Entries are bivariate correlation coefficients.
***$p \leq .001$; **$p \leq .01$; *$p \leq .05$

threat perceptions. Strong group identification, by itself, has few consequences for how South Africans view their political foes.[23]

Concluding Comments

The survey has discovered that political tolerance is not very widespread in South Africa. Moreover, some evidence suggests that levels of tolerance have not risen over the past five or so years. South Africans are apparently not well schooled in the theory of democratic tolerance. Perhaps this finding is not unexpected: for decades (or more) South Africans learned from their government that the appropriate response to those of differing political ideologies was to ban them or to try to exterminate them. It would be unreasonable to expect that people would easily put that lesson aside and embrace political tolerance immediately upon the ascension of the ANC to power.

The finding that tolerance has not increased is all the more puzzling since, as we might have predicted, levels of perceived threat from political enemies apparently declined as organized political violence essentially ended in South Africa during the closing years of the twentieth century. The decline in threat was not matched by an increase in tolerance, a finding suggesting that tolerance materializes only when threat recedes to a certain threshold. That threshold in South Africa seems to be very low.

It appears from these data that political tolerance is less widespread than interracial reconciliation. Direct comparison of the two attitudes is a bit problematic, since tolerance refers to hated political enemies and interracial reconciliation refers to people of the opposite race as a whole, but South Africans seem more committed to multiracialism than they are to putting up with threatening political ideologies. Thus, it is a bit ironic that I refer to tolerance as a "minimalist" form of reconciliation. In empirical terms, tolerance may be "maximalist" in the sense that it is the most difficult type of reconciliation to achieve.

The findings further suggest that tolerance might be achieved only at advanced stages of reconciliation. One theory—the theory on which I have implicitly relied—asserts that tolerance precedes any sort of interpersonal reconciliation. When political groups are tolerated, people come to see that the views that others advocate are not so dangerous and unreasonable and perhaps that those expressing those views should not be shunned. From this viewpoint, reconciliation might unfold as follows: state-enforced political tolerance contributes to greater political tolerance among ordinary citizens. Tolerance then begets interpersonal acceptance and reconciliation.

It seems, however, that in South Africa the process proceeds otherwise. It may well be that interpersonal reconciliation is a necessary condition to tolerance rather than vice versa. Only after people accept those who are different are they willing to allow political advocacy by those who are different. Whether my understanding of the causal flow is correct or not, South Africa enjoys today more interracial reconciliation than it does inter-ideology reconciliation (political tolerance).

The driving force in creating political intolerance is perceptions of threat. I have already suggested that threat may profit from a threshold effect and that intolerance is generated at fairly low levels of perceived threat (and therefore that a slight diminution of threat does not produce more tolerance). But threat perceptions are even more complicated than this. I have shown that perceptions of group threat are multidimensional and, to my surprise, that perceptions of the power or efficacy of the group have little to do with the conversion of threat into intolerance. Indeed, the driving force in producing intolerance is the perception that the opponent is threatening to one's group (sociotropic threat), not necessarily that the enemy is threatening to one's own security (egocentric threat). This is an important finding, because it reinforces the distinction between interpersonal relations and intergroup relations. One can be friends with "one of them" even when tolerating their alien ideology is unacceptable. This understanding is also compatible with the finding that a decline in political violence has not raised tolerance levels. Even if an ANC member is no longer fearful that the IFP will attack him in KwaZulu Natal, he is not any more likely to put up with the IFP. Threats to a group's "way of life" are the most relevant when it comes to political tolerance.

Understanding threats in this way naturally implicates social identity theory, in the sense that those more strongly attached to their group would be expected to be more threatened and hence more intolerant. Here, the data are especially unkind to the social identity hypotheses. I find little or no relationship between any of the elements of group identities (including national identities) and either threat perceptions or intolerance. We would expect that if identities were ever important in contributing to intolerance, it would be in a context like South Africa. The lack of connection between the identity variables and intolerance thus presents a major challenge for some versions of identity theory, one that requires a great deal of reconceptualization and investigation of the conditions under which identities become pernicious.

Though tolerance may be a "minimalist" view of reconciliation, it seems to be one of the most illusive aspects of a reconciled South Africa. How can a multicultural, ideologically divided society succeed at democratic governance without political tolerance? Unfortunately, no clear answer to that question emerges from this research.

Chapter 7

Judging the Fairness of Amnesty

> We have a nation of victims, and if we are unable to provide complete justice on an individual basis—and we need to try and achieve maximum justice within the framework of reconciliation—it is possible for us . . . to ensure that there is historical and collective justice for the people of our country. If we achieve that, if we achieve social justice and move in that direction, then those who today feel aggrieved that individual justice has not been done will at least be able to say that our society has achieved what the victims fought for during their lifetimes. And that therefore at that level, one will be able to say that justice has been done.
>
> —Abdullah M. Omar, foreword to *Confronting Past Injustices*, edited by Medard R. Rwelamira and Gerhard Werle (1996, xii)

Reconciliation is certainly about coming to terms with the past. I have stressed in earlier chapters the individual's own response to the past—as in the willingness, for instance, of individual South Africans to accept the collective memory created by the Truth and Reconciliation Commission. Social and political reactions are important as well, as in the way the state deals with misdeeds done prior to or as part of the transition. How the state addresses the past, and how citizens evaluate the efforts of the state, are of crucial importance to attempts at democratization.

One institutional mechanism for dealing with the past in South Africa has been the TRC, and in particular the process of granting amnesty to those who engaged in gross human rights violations prior to the transition from apartheid. Especially when the struggle for political change produces no unequivocal winner, negotiation characterizes the transition, and one of the key points under negotiation is often accountability for the crimes of the past. Countries throughout the world have established processes through which amnesty may be given to the combatants in the transitional struggle in exchange for truth, reconciliation, and acquiescence to the new political order.

But amnesty does not come without a price. One important cost is that expectations of retribution are unsatisfied. To the extent that granting amnesty to those who committed gross human rights violations contributes to unrequited expectations for justice, a *justice deficit* may be created for the new regime, with the possibility that the new state and its institutions will be deprived of life-giving legitimacy. If amnesty undermines regime legitimacy, then that is indeed a very high price to pay.

Nowhere is this problem of amnesty and justice more acute than in South Africa. During the transition, the leadership of the African National Congress made a Faustian bargain in order to secure majority rule in a democratic South Africa.[1] The ANC traded amnesty for peace; the leaders of the apartheid government accepted freedom from prosecution for human rights abuses in exchange for power sharing. At one level, the bargain succeeded—the ANC acquired power through peaceful and legitimate elections, and few if any white South Africans have been punished for the misdeeds of the apartheid system.[2] Yet the desire of many if not most South Africans for justice—including some sort of reconciliation with the past—continues to play a significant role in contemporary South African politics. And withering criticisms have been laid against the leaders of the New South Africa for failure to achieve some measure of retributive justice as part of the transition process.

My purpose in this chapter is to investigate the importance of justice expectations for the South African transition. Focusing on public reactions to the amnesty decisions of the TRC, I begin from the premise that granting amnesty to those who have admitted gross human rights violations is an inherently unfair policy, in the sense that evil deeds seem to be excused, if not rewarded. Amnesty makes retributive justice impossible. This research then asks specifically whether other forms of justice can compensate for this apparent unfairness, rendering amnesty less difficult for South Africans to stomach.

The compensatory justice contemplated by those who created the truth and reconciliation process is primarily distributive—those who came before the TRC and told their stories of abuse were promised at least some material compensation for their injuries. But other forms of justice may be important as well. For instance, many argue that the opportunity for the victims and their families to discuss their injuries publicly (a form of procedural justice) has done much to defuse anger over the granting of amnesty to perpetrators. No one knows, however, whether alternative forms of justice—including nondistributive forms—can ameliorate the apparent affront of failing to get vengeance against those who have admitted to engaging in gross human rights violations.

Thus, my purpose here is to examine the judgments that ordinary South Africans make about amnesty, testing hypotheses about whether four types of justice perceptions—distributive, procedural, retributive, and restorative—influence assessments of the fairness of amnesty to those who were victimized by the amnesty applicants. These hypotheses are grounded in the extant literature on the psychology of justice. I test these hypotheses through an experiment embedded within my representative national survey. As a consequence, this analysis has unusually strong claims to both internal and external validity (causality and generalizability). By assessing the efficacy of different forms of justice motives in South Africa, this chapter seeks to contribute to a more general understanding of the role of justice considerations in the political judgments of ordinary South Africans.

It should be clear at the outset that I do not contend that attitudes toward granting amnesty to gross human rights violators represent an independent dimension of reconciliation, nor that a reconciled South African must hold any particular view toward the fairness of amnesty. But I do assert that it is important to consider whether amnesty necessarily delegitimizes the new political and legal system. It may be that, as a package of justice considerations, the amnesty-granting process can be judged to be not entirely unfair, and therefore the future may not be damned by this means of addressing the past. Granting amnesty to gross human rights violators may be unfair, but perhaps other aspects of justice can make up the justice deficit created by granting amnesty. That is the overriding hypothesis of this chapter.

Amnesty and Reconciliation in South Africa

Addressing human rights violations under the apartheid regime has been a painful experience for South Africa.[3] The amnesty hearings have revealed atrocities almost beyond belief (see, for example, de Kock 1998; Pauw 1997), reopening many old wounds. Many South Africans have been appalled that such vicious perpetrators have received amnesty for their actions (see Gibson and Gouws 1999).

Many have bitterly criticized South Africa for its decision to allow those who committed gross human rights violations to go free. The critiques take various forms and include dismay at the speed of the amnesty-granting process in comparison to the snail's pace of the process of providing compensation to victims. The failure of South Africans to receive retribution is often cited as among the great failures of the truth and reconciliation process. This is not just a matter of principle: some believe that amnesty undermines the essential legitimacy of the new South African state. For instance, Richard Wilson (2001, 228) asserts: "The most damaging outcome of truth commissions is a result of their equating of human rights with reconciliation and amnesty. This delegitimizes them enormously in relation to popular understandings of justice and can lead to greater criminal activity in society." Wilson is especially critical of the religious veneer often associated with the truth and reconciliation process:

> It is misguided to delegitimize human rights at the national level by detaching them from a retributive understanding of justice and attaching them to a religious notion of reconciliation-forgiveness, a regrettable amnesty law and an elite project of nation-building. Democratizing regimes should not seek legitimacy through nation-building, efforts to forge a moral unity and communitarian discourses, but on the basis of accountability and justice defined as proportional retribution and procedural fairness. The role of human

> rights and the rule of law in all this is to create the bedrock of accountability upon which democratic legitimacy is built. (230)

For Wilson and others, the legacy of the truth and reconciliation process in South Africa is the decoupling of criminality and punishment and the threat it presents to the legitimacy of the new political and legal institutions in the country.

Theories of Justice and Reactions to Amnesty

What are the consequences of the state's failure to punish admitted miscreants?[4] To answer this question, we need to assess how a mix of justice considerations might compensate for the apparent unfairness of amnesty. The research literature suggests that four types of justice may be relevant to how ordinary South Africans perceive and evaluate amnesty as provided for in the truth and reconciliation process. The most obvious of these has to do with compensation for the victims and their families, or distributive justice.

Distributive Justice

Those who designed the amnesty process placed a great deal of emphasis on compensating the victims of apartheid for their losses.[5] For instance, the TRC *Final Report* asserts: "In the context of the South African Truth and Reconciliation Commission, *reparation is essential to counterbalance amnesty*. The granting of amnesty denies victims the rights to institute civil claims against perpetrators. The government should accept responsibility for reparation" (Truth and Reconciliation Commission 1998, vol. 5, p. 170, emphasis added). From the beginning of the process, most expected that monetary reparations would be paid by the government (see, for example, Daniel 2000, 4). Though it has provided limited interim reparations,[6] by 2001 criticism of the government for failure to provide compensation became increasingly widespread and even virulent.[7] The most obvious justice hypothesis is therefore that compensation can perhaps correct for amnesty: *if those who were victimized receive some form of reparations, then people judge the truth and reconciliation process to have been fair.*

Restorative Justice

Though the most obvious hypothesis of this research concerns distributive justice, I also hypothesize that *expectations of restorative justice are important for judgments of the truth and reconciliation process.* Some argue that restorative justice is especially significant in the African context:[8]

> In traditional African thought, the emphasis is on restoring evildoers to the community rather than on punishing them. The term *ubuntu*, which derives from the Xhosa expression *Umuntu ngumuntu ngabanye bantu* (People are people through other people), conveys the view that an environment of right relationships is one in which people are able to recognize that their humanity is inextricably bound up in others' humanity. *Ubuntu* emphasizes the priority of "restorative" as opposed to "retributive" justice. (Graybill 1998, 47, emphasis in the original)

Or as Desmond Tutu has described ubuntu:

> Ubuntu says I am human only because you are human. If I undermine your humanity I dehumanize myself. You must do what you can to maintain this great harmony, which is perpetually undermined by resentment, anger, desire for vengeance. That's why African jurisprudence is restorative rather than retributive. (Gevisser 1996, quoted in Graybill 1998, 47, emphasis in the original; see also Tutu 1999, 54–55)

When South Africans talk about restorative justice, they often refer to processes such as restoring the "dignity" of the victims (see, for example, Villa-Vicencio 2000, 202; see also Truth and Reconciliation Commission 1998, vol. 1, p. 125).[9]

One important form of restoration involves an apology.[10] An apology can be influential, since "an apology is a gesture through which an individual splits himself into two parts, the part that is guilty of an offense and the part that dissociates itself from the delict and affirms a belief in the offended rule" (Goffman 1971, 113). A considerable literature in political psychology investigates the effectiveness of apologies in mitigating blame (for example,

Darby and Schlenker 1989; Ohbuchi, Kameda, and Agarie 1989; Weiner et al. 1991; see also Vidmar 2001, 52–54). Generally, that literature concludes that apologies can contribute to forgiveness and reconciliation under some circumstances (see, for example, Scher and Darley 1997). Apologies seem to mitigate blame and may well make the failure to get retributive justice palatable (see, for example, Minow 1998, 114).

Those who designed the truth and reconciliation process in South Africa chose not to require an apology from amnesty applicants, largely owing to skepticism about the sincerity of such expressions of regret rather than doubts about whether sincere apologies would be useful and effective. Thus, it is reasonable to hypothesize that apologies *recognized as sincere* ameliorate the negative effects of amnesty. I expect that *when sincere apologies are given, South Africans judge amnesty as more fair to the victims and their families.*

Procedural Justice

Also important is the expectation of procedural justice, especially through processes by which victims are given "voice" (Tyler and Mitchell 1994).[11] A great deal of emphasis can be found in South Africa on the importance of the TRC hearings at which victims and their families were able to tell their stories (see, for example, Orr 2000). As Justice Ismail Mahomed wrote in the Constitutional Court decision legitimizing the truth and reconciliation process: "The Act seeks to . . . [encourage] survivors and the dependents of the tortured and the wounded, the maimed and the dead to unburden their grief publicly, to receive the recognition of a new nation that they were wronged and crucially, to help them to discover what did in truth happen to their loved ones, where and under what circumstances it did happen, and who was responsible" (*Azanian Peoples Organization [AZAPO] and others v. President of the Republic of South Africa and others* CCT 17/96 [July 25, 1996]). In general, the literature on procedural justice suggests that *procedural outcomes—even apart from distributive outcomes—contribute a great deal to perceptions of fairness* (see, for example, Lind and Tyler 1988; Tyler 1990; Tyler et al. 1997; Tyler and Lind 2001). That is one of the hypotheses of this research.

Retributive Justice

Recently, increasing attention has been given to the importance of retributive justice for political and legal systems (see, for example, Tyler and Boeckmann 1997; Vidmar 2001). "Retribution is a passionate reaction to the violation of a rule, norm, or law that evokes a desire for punishment of the violator" (Sanders and Hamilton 2001, 6). Sometimes referred to as "disinterested punishment" (see, for example, Scheler 1961; Ranulf 1964), retribution concerns the desire of individuals who are dissociated from the victim or the act and its consequences to seek the punishment of offenders.

The starting point for my analysis is the assumption that amnesty subverts retributive justice. Nonetheless, many have argued that having to make a public confession of one's dastardly deeds is itself punishment (see, for example, Tutu 1999, 51–54). For instance, Justice Richard Goldstone has asserted (2000, x) that "the perpetrators suffered a very real punishment—the public confession of the worst atrocities with the permanent stigma and prejudice that it carries with it." Moreover, many perpetrators experienced other penalties, ranging from having to pay large fees to their attorneys to being condemned by their friends and family. Thus, I hypothesize that *when the perpetrator is portrayed as having experienced some degree of punishment, South Africans judge amnesty to be more fair to the victims and their families.*

Thus, the overarching hypothesis of this research is that it may be possible to compensate for the inherent injustice of amnesty. If South Africans perceive that the victims and their families are given other forms of justice—procedural, retributive, restorative, and distributive—then amnesty may become a more acceptable part of the transitional process.

Justice Priorities

Ideally, I would be able to predict the priorities that individual South Africans attach to each of these forms of justice. Unfortunately, there has been little theorizing about when one form of justice will become more salient than others. From the point of view of contemporary politics in South Africa, it seems likely that distributive justice concerns will have the most substantial impact on attitudes toward amnesty, since the original theory of amnesty was that it would be counterbalanced by compensation. I also predict that retributive justice will have the least influence, since being relieved of any civil or criminal penalties for one's gross human rights violations most likely overshadows any subsidiary penalties imposed on perpetrators. Unfortunately, I see no way to anticipate the relative influence of restorative and procedural justice on amnesty judgments.

General Views of Amnesty in South Africa

Before turning to the results of the experimental vignette, it is useful to consider how South Africans view the amnesty process in general. Fortunately, several questions during the interview addressed this issue. We first asked: "The TRC has granted amnesties to those who have come forward and admitted committing atrocities during the struggle over apartheid. Do you approve of amnesty being given to those who admitted committing atrocities during the struggle over apartheid?" In general, South Africans are *not* opposed to amnesty, with a majority (57.3 percent) approving of amnesty to at least some degree. Racial differences are statistically significant ($\eta = .30$), with black South Africans being far more likely to approve of amnesty (71.6 percent) than those of any other race (less than a majority of whites, Colored people, and those of Asian origin). It is perhaps a bit surprising that amnesty is so widely supported among Africans, since the most common reports about amnesty in the truth and reconciliation process generally concerned agents of the apartheid state being allowed to go free after confessing to having committed gross human rights violations against members of the liberation forces.

Approval of amnesty, however, does not necessarily mean that one views it as fair. We asked whether amnesty is fair to three groups: those who died during the struggle over apartheid, the victims, and "ordinary people like you." Judgments of fairness vary significantly depending on the frame of reference. A large majority of South Africans (72.7 percent) believe that amnesty is unfair to those who died in the struggle, and most (65.2 percent) believe that it is unfair to the victims. Further, a majority (52.6 percent) of South Africans view amnesty as unfair to ordinary people, with only 33.5 percent viewing it as fair to this group. On this question of fairness to ordinary people, racial differences barely achieve a low level of statistical significance, and the strength of association between race and opinions is slight indeed ($\eta = .05$).[12] Thus, generally speaking, amnesty may be acceptable to most South Africans, but its unfairness renders it a necessary evil.

Why would South Africans approve of amnesty even if they judge it unfair? A full analysis of the responses to these questions is beyond the scope of this chapter, but it seems likely that many accept amnesty because they view it as contributing to the peaceful transition to majority rule in South Africa. For instance, when asked whether they agree or disagree with the statement "The TRC was essential to avoid civil war in South Africa during the transition from white rule to majority rule," the percentages of those agreeing (either "somewhat" or "strongly") are 65 percent black, 18 percent white, 36 percent Colored, and 47 percent Asian origin. Thus, amnesty is thought by many to have been necessary to a peaceful transition to majority rule in South Africa.

In light of the analysis that follows, it is also important to note that judgments of fairness to the victims and fairness to ordinary South Africans are very strongly correlated ($r = .56$; $\phi = .89$). Only 18.7 percent of the respondents reached opposite conclusions about the fairness of amnesty to the victims and to ordinary people. None of the other correlations across fairness judgments is as strong. These findings support the view that *judgments of fairness to the victims are essentially the same thing as judgments of fairness to the larger South African society.*

I also analyze judgments of the fairness of amnesty to the families of the victims. These judgments are important because they concern the aspects of amnesty most likely to be offensive to most South Africans. The failure of the victims' families to receive any sort of retributive justice—since the perpetrator was allowed to go free after admitting her or his gross human rights violations—is perhaps the most salient and egregious aspect of the unfairness of amnesty. When South Africans talk about perpetrators "getting away with murder," what they mean is that amnesty represents a fundamental unfairness to the victims, and hence to the larger society. Because the victims fail to receive justice, society itself fails to receive justice. Moreover, as I have already noted, it is not fruitful to distinguish empirically between perceptions of overall fairness and fairness to the victims and their families. Thus, the interesting question addressed in this chapter has to do with how ordinary South Africans evaluate the fairness of amnesty in terms of its impact on the aggrieved.[13]

Of course, these general views are devoid of context. To understand the influence of different types of justice on amnesty attitudes, a different methodology—an experimental methodology—is necessary.

Analysis

The Experiment

We included in our survey what we called the Justice and Amnesty Experiment. This experimental vignette employed four manipulations in what is technically referred to as a two-by-two-by-two-by-two fully crossed factorial design.[14] That is, four (dichotomous) characteristics were manipulated, resulting in sixteen versions of the vignette. This portion of the interview began with a short story about "Phillip" and his effort to gain amnesty for crimes he committed under apartheid.[15] Phillip was identified (through the least-liked technology developed by Sullivan, Piereson, and Marcus 1982; see chapter 6) as a member of a political group that the respondent disliked a great deal. This ensures that each subject was reacting to an amnesty application from an objectionable ideology. Each respondent heard only a single story, and people were randomly assigned to vignette versions. The manipulations were orthogonal to each other, and the four resulting dummy variables are therefore uncorrelated. Embedding an experiment within a nationally representative survey yields the substantial advantages of both internal and external validity—that is, external generalizability and internal confidence in causal inferences.[16]

The Structure of the Experimental Vignette

All vignette versions began with the following: "Phillip was a member of [the respondent's least-liked group]. Phillip sought amnesty for setting off a bomb that killed several innocent people." We then manipulated four types of justice in the vignettes.[17]

1. Procedural Justice. Victims can be given procedural justice by giving them an opportunity to tell their story. Research has shown that giving people "voice" is the most important aspect of fair procedure (Tyler and Mitchell 1994; Tyler et al. 1997), and during the TRC hearings there was much discussion of the cathartic effect of being able to tell one's story publicly. Thus, the procedural justice manipulation is:

1A. At Phillip's amnesty hearing, the families of the victims got to tell how the bombing has affected their lives.

1B. At Phillip's amnesty hearing, the families of the victims were denied a chance to tell how the bombing has affected their lives, even though they had insisted that they wanted to tell their story.[18]

2. Retributive Justice. Though the amnesty law rules out formal retribution, some have argued that simply having to admit publicly one's crimes is a form of punishment.[19] This is especially likely if the perpetrator's admission is associated with some level of shame at what she or he did. We tried to capture the punishment that a perpetrator might have experienced with the following:

2A. Phillip then told his version of the bombing. In reaction to Phillip's disclosures, Phillip's family said that they were deeply ashamed of what he had done, and his wife subsequently divorced him.

2B. Phillip then told his version of the bombing. In reaction to Phillip's disclosures, Phillip's family said that they understood why he did what he did, and that they stood by him.

Throughout the truth and reconciliation process, there were several well-publicized incidents in which perpetrators were publicly condemned by their families.

3. Restorative Justice. The idea here is that the victims should get something from the process that restores them to their status prior to the atrocity. Of course, nothing can really compensate people for the losses they endured under apartheid. But the truth and reconciliation process is based, at least in part, on the assumption that the dignity of the victims can be restored through the process. Dignity is an amorphous concept, but it may have something to do with apologies. The issuing and receiving of apologies establishes clearly that a wrong has been committed and creates a relationship of equality—however tenuous—between the victim and the perpetrator. Thus, we included the following manipulation:

3A. Phillip apologized for his actions, and his apology was accepted by the families of the victims.

3B. Phillip apologized for his actions, but his apology was rejected as insincere by the families of the victims.

So as to rule out the possibility that all apologies are thought to be insincere, the vignette clearly states that the families themselves legitimized the apology by accepting it.

4. Distributive Justice. Compensation is the clearest form of distributive justice, so we manipulated the outcome for the family of the victim (even in light of the general finding that people rate punishing offenders as more important than compensating victims; see, for example, Hogan and Emler 1981).

4A. Phillip was granted amnesty. Afterward, the families of the victims were given financial compensation by the government for the loss of their loved ones.

4B. Phillip was granted amnesty. Afterward, the families of the victims were not given any financial compensation, because the government said it had no funding for compensating victims. The government did, however, express its sympathy for the families.

Thus, the general hypothesis is that the outcome will be judged most fair and amnesty will most likely be accepted when the families of the victims are given:

Procedural justice: an opportunity to tell their story

Restorative justice: an apology

Retributive justice: perpetrator shame and punishment

Distributive justice: compensation

The vignette version I hypothesize to generate the *highest* fairness judgments is one in which all four types of justice are realized:

> Phillip was a member of [the respondent's least-liked group]. Phillip sought amnesty for setting off a bomb that killed several innocent people [1A]. At his amnesty hearing, the families of the victims were allowed to tell how the bombing had affected their lives [2A]. Phillip then told his version of the bombing. In reaction to Phillip's disclosures, Phillip's family said that they were deeply ashamed of what he had done, and his wife subsequently divorced him [3A]. Phillip apologized for his actions, and his apology was accepted by the families of the victims [4A]. Phillip was granted amnesty. Afterward, the families of the victims were given financial compensation by the government for the loss of their loved ones.

The vignette depicting the absence of all four types of justice reads:

> Phillip was a member of [the respondent's least-liked group]. Phillip sought amnesty for setting off a bomb that killed several innocent people [1B]. At his amnesty hearing, the families of the victims were denied a chance to tell how the bombing had affected their lives, even though they had insisted that they wanted to tell their story [2B]. Phillip then told his version of the bombing. In reaction to Phillip's disclosures, Phillip's family said that they understood why he did what he did and that they stood by him [3B]. Phillip apologized for his actions, but his apology was rejected as insincere

> by the families of the victims [4B]. Phillip was granted amnesty. Afterward, the families of the victims were not given any financial compensation, because the government said it had no funding for compensating victims. The government did, however, express its sympathy for the families.

Manipulation Checks

Whether each manipulation was actually perceived by the respondents can be assessed through "manipulation check" questions that parallel each of the experimental factors. We asked the respondents how certain they were about their perceptions of various aspects of the stories. For instance, the procedural justice check question was: "Do you think that the families of the victims were given a chance to tell how the bombing has affected their lives?" The response set varied from "certain they were" to "certain they were not." I have reflected the original responses so that higher scores always indicate great certainty. Table 7.1 reports the results of these manipulation checks.

The data in this table provide *very strong* evidence that the manipulations in this experiment "succeeded" in the sense that they were accurately perceived. Indeed, compared to other research based on this methodology (for example, Gibson and Gouws 1999), the experimental manipulations were extremely and uniformly successful.[20] For example, 71.4 percent of those who were told that the family was allowed to tell its story correctly perceived this manipulation, while 74.4 percent of those who were told that the family was denied the chance to tell its story accurately answered the manipulation check. (The percentages depicting accurate perceptions are shaded in table 7.1.) Perhaps because the truth and reconciliation process has been so salient in South Africa, these vignettes seem to have caught the attention of our respondents.

Fairness Judgments: The Dependent Variables

The dependent variable in this analysis is judgments of fairness. We asked: "First, considering all aspects of the story, how fair do you think the outcome is to the families of the victims?"[21] The question continued: "If 10 means that you believe the outcome is

Table 7.1 Perceptions of the Experimental Manipulations (Manipulation Checks)

Independent Variables	Not Perceived	Perceived	Mean	Standard Deviation	Number of Cases
Manipulation: Procedural justice[a]					
Family got voice	26.0%	71.4%	3.70	1.42	1,883
No voice	74.4	22.4	2.06	1.38	1,835
Manipulation: Retributive justice[b]					
Phillip was punished	31.5	63.9	3.48	1.45	1,864
Not punished	73.8	21.1	2.03	1.34	1,855
Manipulation: Restorative justice[c]					
Family received apology	34.5	63.5	3.43	1.50	1,879
No apology	78.8	18.7	1.89	1.27	1,842
Manipulation: Distributive justice[d]					
Family got compensation	23.3	73.5	3.81	1.43	1,855
No compensation	84.2	13.2	1.66	1.19	1,862

Source: Author's compilation from the 2001 Truth and Reconciliation Survey.

Note: These two percentages total to 100 percent, except for "don't know" responses. The dependent variable for each manipulation check is a five-point scale, with higher scores indicating greater degrees of certainty that the action happened.

The questions used to check the manipulations were:

"Do you think that the families of the victims were given a chance to tell how the bombing has affected their lives?" Certain they were, probably were, probably were not, certain they were not. (Don't know)

"Do you think that Phillip's apology was accepted by the families of the victims?" Certain it was, probably was, probably was not, certain it was not. (Don't know)

"Do you think that Phillip was punished by the actions of his own family?" Certain he was, probably was, probably was not, certain he was not. (Don't know)

"Do you think that the families of the victims received compensation for what happened to them?" Certain they did, probably did, probably did not, certain they did not. (Don't know)

[a]Difference of means test: $p < .000$; $\eta = .51$.
[b]Difference of means test: $p < .000$; $\eta = .46$.
[c]Difference of means test: $p < .000$; $\eta = .48$.
[d]Difference of means test: $p < .000$; $\eta = .63$.

completely fair to the families of the victims and 1 means the outcome is completely unfair to them, which number from 10 to 1 best describes how you feel? For example, you might answer with a 4 if you think the outcome is only somewhat unfair, or a 7 if you think the outcome is somewhat fair to the families of the victims." Table 7.2 reports these assessments for each of the versions of the vignette.

The mean fairness scores in table 7.2 reveal that the first vignette—the story in which the family received all four types of justice—is judged to have produced the fairest outcome, while the last vignette—in which the family got no justice—is perceived as the least fair. This is a very encouraging finding. Generally, the mean fairness scores vary considerably: using a dichotomous measure of the dependent variable, the percentages judging the outcome to be fair range from 6.7 percent (version 16) to 45.7 percent (version 1). From the point of view of the politics of amnesty, this is substantial variation indeed.

Generally speaking, the outcome in this vignette (Phillip's amnesty) is not judged to be very fair to the families of the victims.[22] Across all vignette versions, only 24.3 percent of the respondents find the outcome fair, and only a minority of these consider the outcome to be quite fair (8.7 percent of all respondents). Indeed, fully 51.2 percent of the respondents judge the outcome as quite *unfair* to the families of the victims, with another 22.9 percent assessing it as somewhat unfair.[23] Though the combination of the four types of justice significantly influences the fairness judgment, when the families are portrayed as receiving all four types of justice, 45.7 percent judge the outcome as fair, while 52.7 percent still believe it was unfair to at least some degree. Thus, in the analysis that follows, the bulk of the variability being considered concerns how *unfair* the outcome is judged to be. This finding of course confirms the original intuition undergirding this project—that amnesty, even under the best of circumstances, is not thought of as fair by most South Africans.

The Effect of the Experimental Manipulations

Table 7.3 reports the effect of each of the experimental manipulations on judgments of fairness to the families. I include several sta-

Table 7.2 The Variability in Fairness Judgments Across Versions of the Vignette

Version	Manipulations: Type of Justice				Judgments of Fairness[a]		
	Procedural	Retributive	Restorative	Distributive	Mean	Standard Deviation	Number of Cases
1	Voice	Punishment	Apology	Compensation	5.19	3.16	245
2	Voice	Punishment	Apology	No compensation	3.14	2.67	242
3	Voice	Punishment	No apology	Compensation	4.52	3.04	220
4	Voice	Punishment	No apology	No compensation	2.97	2.45	238
5	Voice	No punishment	Apology	Compensation	5.11	3.14	231
6	Voice	No punishment	Apology	No compensation	3.29	2.82	237
7	Voice	No punishment	No apology	Compensation	4.21	3.00	235
8	Voice	No punishment	No apology	No compensation	2.65	2.42	236
9	No voice	Punishment	Apology	Compensation	4.15	2.92	235
10	No voice	Punishment	Apology	No compensation	2.60	2.24	224
11	No voice	Punishment	No apology	Compensation	4.03	2.87	230
12	No voice	Punishment	No apology	No compensation	2.45	2.16	230
13	No voice	No punishment	Apology	Compensation	4.70	3.21	231
14	No voice	No punishment	Apology	No compensation	2.58	2.28	232
15	No voice	No punishment	No apology	Compensation	3.84	2.99	227
16	No voice	No punishment	No apology	No compensation	2.24	2.00	224
Total					3.61	2.90	3,716

Source: Author's compilation from the 2001 Truth and Reconciliation Survey.
Note: Difference of means across versions: $\eta = .33$; $F = 30.14$; $p < .001$.
[a]Higher mean scores indicate perceptions of greater fairness.

Table 7.3 The Effect of Justice Manipulations on Judgments of Fairness to the Victims

	Unfair	Fair	Mean	Standard Deviation	Number of Cases
Manipulation: Procedural justice[a]					
Family got voice	70.1	28.4	3.88	2.99	1,883
No voice	78.2	20.2	3.30	2.77	1,833
Manipulation: Retributive justice[b]					
Phillip was punished	74.2	24.1	3.64	2.86	1,863
Not punished	74.0	24.6	3.58	2.93	1,853
Manipulation: Restorative justice[c]					
Family received apology	70.1	28.5	3.85	3.00	1,877
No apology	78.2	20.2	3.36	2.76	1,839
Manipulation: Distributive justice[d]					
Family got compensation	63.1	34.9	4.47	3.07	1,853
No compensation	85.1	13.9	2.75	2.42	1,862

Source: Author's compilation from the 2001 Truth and Reconciliation Survey.
Note: The percentages are based on dichotomizing the continuous variable and placing "uncertain" or "don't know" responses between "unfair" and "fair." The percentages in the table do not total to 100 percent, since some small proportion of the respondents were unable to arrive at a view of whether the families of the victims were fairly treated in the vignette.
[a]Difference of means test: $p < .001$; $\eta = .10$.
[b]Difference of means test: $p > .05$; $\eta = .01$.
[c]Difference of means test: $p < .001$; $\eta = .09$.
[d]Difference of means test: $p < .001$; $\eta = .30$.

tistics: the percentage who view the outcome as to any degree unfair, the comparable percentage of those who judge the families to have been fairly treated, and the mean and standard deviation of the continuous fairness judgment.

Perhaps not surprisingly, the single strongest predictor of perceived fairness is the distributive justice manipulation (see the eta coefficients in the notes to the table). The mean scores on the fairness index differ substantially (and of course statistically significantly as well). When the government promises compensation, over one-third of the respondents think that the families were fairly treated, as compared to only 13.9 percent when compensation is denied. This is a substantial statistical and substantive effect.

Two other manipulations influence fairness assessments as well. When the families were given the opportunity to "tell their stories" (voice), they are judged to have received significantly more fairness than when they were denied the opportunity to speak. The restorative justice manipulation also influences judgments of fairness: when the family accepted the apology, the outcome is judged to be more fair than when no legitimate apology was forthcoming, with a statistically significant difference of 8.3 percentage points in (dichotomized) justice judgments and a highly significant difference in the continuous measures of perceived fairness. This finding is all the more noteworthy since the research literature would not expect apologies (even sincere ones) to be very effective under the conditions of the truth and reconciliation process: the apology was for a serious offense (a gross human rights violation), there was little doubt about the culpability of the perpetrator, and no formal punishment was given to the amnesty applicant.

Finally, the retributive justice manipulation had no influence at all: 24.1 percent of those hearing that Phillip was punished think the outcome was fair, compared to 24.6 percent of those who hear that Phillip was *not* punished. Perhaps because so many view Phillip as profiting from the amnesty process, whatever incidental punishment he may have received is inconsequential to most respondents.[24]

Both the positive and negative findings from the experiment are substantively important. That the distributive justice manipulation is the most influential variable is significant in light of the continuing controversy in South Africa over the reparations issue. But it is also noteworthy that the influence of compensation is not enormous and that *even when compensation is posited, most South Africans view the treatment received by the families of the victims as unfair*. Indeed, only slightly more than one-third of the respondents think that the outcome was fair even when compensation was given by the government. There is clearly more to fairness in South Africa than monetary restitution.

Why does distributive justice not have more influence? This finding may have something to do with the unresolved nature of the compensation issue at the time of the survey. Perhaps if people think that compensation will be more sizable and more likely, then the effect of this manipulation will be larger in terms of convincing people that amnesty was fair to the families of the victims.

The influence of procedural justice also warrants emphasis. The simple act of giving people the opportunity to describe their plight publicly is more than one-third as influential on fairness judgments as monetary compensation. Procedural justice is less influential than distributive justice, but it is nonetheless important to remember that simple and relatively inexpensive processes can often contribute substantially to perceptions of fairness. Similarly, a sincere apology from the perpetrator has an important influence on perceptions that the families of the victims were treated fairly. Indeed, the effects of procedural and restorative justice together are roughly two-thirds the size of the effect of distributive justice. Clearly, compensation is not the only palliative for the injustice of amnesty.

Multivariate Analysis

It remains to consider how the conclusions are affected by the inclusion of the perceptual variables in the equation predicting fairness assessments. Table 7.4 reports the results of two regression analyses of perceptions of fairness. Model 1 considers only the four dichotomous manipulations as predictors; model 2 adds the four perceptions of the experimental stimuli (the manipulation check variables) to the equation. The results from model 1 are identical to those discussed earlier, so no further comment is warranted. Model 2 provides the data of most interest.[25]

The first thing to note from the analysis reported in table 7.4 is that the direct effects of the experimental manipulations are strongly mediated by the perceptual variables, as they should be. For instance, the coefficients for the procedural and restorative justice manipulations achieve statistical significance in the first equation but not in the second. Only the distributive justice manipulation has a direct effect in the multivariate equation. This means that even controlling for perceptions of whether the families would get some form of compensation, something about the compensation story has a net influence on perceived fairness. This finding is particularly surprising in that this manipulation is the most accurately perceived of the four (as shown by the η coefficients re-

Table 7.4 The Effect of the Experimental Manipulations and Perceptions of the Manipulations on Judgments of Fairness

	Model 1				Model 2			
Independent Variables	b	Standard Error	β	r	b	Standard Error	β	r
Manipulations								
Procedural justice	.56	.09	.10***	.10	−.06	.10	−.01	.10
Retributive justice	.06	.09	.01	.01	−.16	.10	−.03	.01
Restorative justice	.48	.09	.08***	.09	−.07	.10	−.01	.09
Distributive justice	1.73	.09	.30***	.30	.91	.11	.16***	.30
Perceptions of manipulations								
Procedural justice					.30	.03	.17***	.25
Retributive justice					.12	.03	.07***	.13
Restorative justice					.31	.03	.17***	.27
Distributive justice					.32	.03	.19***	.36
Intercept	2.19	.10			.41	.13		
R-squared			.11***				.21***	
Standard deviation—dependent variable	2.90				2.90			
Standard error of estimate	2.74				2.58			

Source: Author's compilation from the 2001 Truth and Reconciliation Survey.
Note: N = 3,710.
***p < .001; **p < .01; *p < .05

ported in table 7.1), and therefore its effect should be funneled through perceptions. To the extent that each of the other manipulations influences the dependent variable, the pathway of influence is through perceptions.

The explanation of this first finding may well lie in the supplementary meaning that the respondents received from the compensation manipulation. In addition to providing information about the compensation given to the families of the victims (information that was quite accurately perceived), additional certification of the legitimacy of the families' claim may have been implicitly provided by the fact that the government agreed to give the families compensation. And indeed, those who were told that the family received compensation are more likely to assert as well that the families received restorative and procedural justice (but not retributive justice; data not shown). But even beyond these particular forms of justice, getting payment for one's pain enhances perceptions of the fairness of the outcome of the amnesty hearing.

Three of the perceptual variables—procedural, restorative, and distributive justice—have roughly equal influence in shaping fairness judgments (see both the standardized and unstandardized regression coefficients in table 7.4). It is noteworthy that the statistical advantage that objective distributive justice has is reduced to parity when the perceptual variables are considered. Those who *perceive* a legitimate apology are almost as likely to judge the outcome as fair as those who perceive that the families were compensated. Moreover, the cumulative effect of these three forms of justice is quite substantial: the mean fairness rating for the 418 South Africans who strongly perceive no justice on all three of the relevant justice variables is 1.8 (with 97.4 percent judging the outcome as unfair), while the mean for the 170 respondents asserting strongly that the families received all three forms of justice is 6.1 (with 40.2 percent judging the outcome as unfair and 59.8 percent perceiving it as fair). This is enormous variation indeed.

The lack of a dominating influence of distributive justice is a significant finding here. Whether the families are perceived to have gotten compensation is important, but it is little more important than whether the families were given voice through the truth and reconciliation process and whether the families received a credible apology from the perpetrator. South Africans are not much influenced by retribution (at least as represented in the vignette), but they think about fairness in the truth and reconciliation process in terms of far more than simple distributive justice.

Racial Differences in Judgments of Fairness to the Families of the Victims

The analysis to this point pertains to all South Africans. But race continues to divide the country, perhaps particularly on matters of amnesty and reconciliation, so it is therefore necessary to consider whether these results characterize all four racial groups in the country.

I begin this analysis with a saturated interactive model. That is, I supplement model 2 with (a) a set of three dummy variables representing whites, Colored people, and South Africans of Asian origin, (b) a set of interactions between the race dummy variables and the formal manipulations in the experiment, and (c) a set of interactions between the race variables and the indicators of perceptions of the experiment. This analysis reveals that the addition of each of the sets of variables is highly statistically significant, confirming the hypothesis that at least some differences exist in how the experiment affects various racial groups. Consequently, a more refined analysis of racial differences is required.

The central question of interest is whether other (minority) racial groups in South Africa differ from the African majority. Therefore, I conducted three separate regression analyses, in each instance comparing a group with the views of blacks. These results are reported in table 7.5. For instance, the first equation compares whites with blacks, with the null hypotheses for the dummy and interactive variables predicting no racial differences in the coefficients.[26]

The findings for the black versus Colored regression are unequivocal: neither the dummy variable nor the interactions achieve statistical significance. When it comes to judgments of fairness, black and Colored South Africans differ little.

South Africans of Asian origin do differ from Africans, however,

Table 7.5 Racial Differences in Reactions to the Amnesty Experiment

	Equation Comparing Blacks With:		
Independent Variables	Whites	Coloreds	Asian Origin
Manipulations			
Procedural justice	n.s.	n.s.	n.s.
Retributive justice	n.s.	n.s.	n.s.
Restorative justice	n.s.	n.s.	n.s.
Distributive justice	.000	.000	.000
Perceptions of manipulations			
Procedural justice	.000	.000	.000
Retributive justice	.037	.038	.034
Restorative justice	.000	.000	.000
Distributive justice	.000	.000	.000
Race dummy variable	.000	n.s.	.033
Race—manipulation interactions			
Procedural justice	n.s.	n.s.	n.s.
Retributive justice	n.s.	n.s.	n.s.
Restorative justice	.029	n.s.	n.s.
Distributive justice	n.s.	n.s.	n.s.
Race—perceptions interactions			
Procedural justice	n.s.	n.s.	.068
Retributive justice	.058	n.s.	n.s.
Restorative justice	n.s.	n.s.	.039
Distributive justice	.002	n.s.	n.s.
Equation statistics			
Intercept (standard error)	.21 (.18)	.21 (.18)	.21 (.17)
R-squared	.20***	.23***	.24***
Standard deviation—dependent variable	2.86	2.92	2.87
Standard error of estimate	2.56	2.57	2.52
Number of cases	2,979	2,476	2,245

Source: Author's compilation from the 2001 Truth and Reconciliation Survey.
Note: Cell entries are the significance of the test of the null hypothesis that the regression coefficient is indistinguishable from zero. H_0: b = 0. All probabilities greater than .10 are shown. When coefficients are statistically significant, the actual coefficients are reported in the text.
n.s. = not statistically significant at $p < .10$.
***$p < .001$

in a few important respects. First, the intercept varies significantly (represented by the dummy variable), with those of Asian origin being more likely to judge the outcome as fair to the families of the victims (b = 1.06, standard error = .50). Second, there is a slight tendency for those of Asian origin to be less influenced by their perceptions of the apology (b = −.27, standard error = .13) and perhaps also less influenced by their perceptions of procedural justice (b = −.24, standard error = .13); each of these perceptions has little effect on the fairness judgments of Asians but some influence on the judgments of Africans.[27] None of the other differences achieve statistical significance—overall, Asian South Africans and black South Africans reacted to the experiment fairly similarly.

The largest and most significant racial differences are between blacks and whites. Each of the sets of race-based interactive variables contributes to a significant increase in explained variance. Whites tend in general to view the outcome as more fair (b = 1.16, standard error = .29), to be less influenced by their perceptions of compensation (b = −.25, standard error = .08), to be less affected by the apology manipulation (b = −.52, standard error = .24), and perhaps to be more affected by their judgments of how severely Phillip was punished by his family (b = .15, standard error = .08). This last finding, though only marginally significant, is the only instance in which the punishment variable has any influence on fairness judgments, and it may reflect a tendency among white South Africans to empathize with the white seekers of amnesty. None of the other interactive coefficients achieves statistical significance.

In general, racial differences in reactions to amnesty in South Africa are not as pronounced as such differences are in many other areas of political life. Although two of the three dummy variable coefficients achieve statistical significance (whites and South Africans of Asian origin), only three of twenty-four interactive coefficients are significant at .05, and only two additional coefficients are significant at $.05 < p < .10$. It is noteworthy that black South Africans are somewhat more likely than other South Africans to judge the fairness of amnesty in terms other than strictly distributive outcomes. Nonetheless, it is worth reiterating that the dominant view in all racial communities is that the outcome of the vignette—Phillip getting amnesty—was unfair.

This last point requires an important qualification. As I noted earlier, the character given amnesty in the vignette is a member of a group that the respondent dislikes a great deal. Presumably, not many South Africans object to amnesty being given to members of the groups with which they are affiliated or of which they approve. Amnesty is controversial in South Africa because the people who are going free are those who did dastardly things to one's compatriots—and this is true for blacks, for whites, for Colored people, and for those of Asian origin. Because almost everyone feels aggrieved by the unfairness of amnesty, racial differences in fairness assessments are neutralized.[28]

Concluding Comments

This statistical analysis supports conclusions about three important topics: assessments of amnesty by ordinary South Africans; the political psychology of justice judgments; and the politics of amnesty in contemporary South Africa.

Most South Africans oppose granting amnesty to those who committed gross human rights violations during the struggle over apartheid. However necessary amnesty may have been to the transitional process, the failure to achieve any sort of retributive justice is deeply unpopular. Even when all four forms of justice investigated here are present, only half of the South African population approves of amnesty. The other half seems unable to reconcile with granting amnesty to those who committed gross human rights violations during the struggle over apartheid.[29]

But justice does matter. Whether people are willing to tolerate amnesty depends in part on whether other forms of justice are present. That judgments of the fairness of amnesty change by nearly forty percentage points—from the condition under which no justice is received to that in which all four types of justice are received—is highly significant for the politics of amnesty. To some important degree, alternative forms of justice can make up for the inherent unfairness of amnesty, at least for a sizable portion of the South African population.

And justice is about more than compensation. Of course reparations matter, and in the objective portions of this experiment (the formal manipulations), compensation to the families of the victims has the strongest influence on perceptions of fairness in the granting of amnesty. But other, far less costly types of justice are influential as well. Sincere apologies matter, as do opportunities for victims to tell their stories. Those contemplating truth and reconciliation processes elsewhere should take note of the importance of these two nonmonetary factors in generating popular acceptance of amnesty.

In this sense, strict economic instrumentalism is not the only motivating factor in judging amnesty. Social scientists are slowly beginning to understand that even rational actors attempt to maximize many types of benefits, including symbolic, nonmaterial benefits (see Chong and Marshall 1999). That people's political judgments are influenced by more than how much the victims get—that it is crucial *whether what they get is considered fair*—can no longer be questioned. Theories of political behavior must pay far more attention to the role of justice considerations in politics.

I have made little progress here toward understanding the dynamics of when different forms of justice expectations will become salient and dominant. My analysis is able to order different aspects of justice according to their salience within the South African context, and the empirical results generally satisfy those expectations. Unfortunately, we have little understanding about how various aspects of justice are mobilized, adjudicated, and applied in general. In this experiment (as in most experiments), the vignettes were structured so that the four types of justice were orthogonal to (independent of) each other. Such is surely not often the case in actual disputes over justice. Indeed, real controversies perhaps make inseparable some of the dimensions of justice; without at least some distributive justice, for instance, it may be that no restorative justice is possible.[30] Experimental research can dissect and disassemble the various components of a problem, which is invaluable for ascertaining causal structures and processes. But figuring out how all of these justice considerations fit back together in real controversies over the fairness of political decisions and outcomes is a task much in need of additional theoretical and empirical attention.

In terms of theories of justice, this chapter demonstrates the utility of moving beyond the conventional emphasis on distributive and/or procedural justice. Justice is a multifaceted concept, and research ought to be sensitive to the importance of its different aspects or components. And of course we can ascertain which type of justice is relevant to a particular dispute only if all types are simultaneously measured and tested in the analysis. Future research should also make an effort to test theories of justice more directly against material or instrumental theories.

Though I have made some progress here, we certainly need to understand more about the role of public apologies in political controversies. In my research, I purposefully neutralized the issue of the sincerity of the apology, but of course suspicions of insincerity dog most apologies in real political controversies. One value of experimental vignettes is their ability to incorporate contextual factors into the analysis. Understanding how context shapes the influence of apologies is an important area for future inquiry.

I should reiterate the obvious point that the analysis reported in this chapter refers to the views of ordinary South Africans, not specifically those who were victimized under apartheid. The processes I have identified here may well work quite differently with victims. Victims may be more focused on compensation, for instance, than on other aspects of fairness. I do not argue that the findings from a study of observers of the truth and reconciliation process necessarily characterize the participants in the process. Nor do I assert that the views of victims are unimportant. But from the larger perspective of South African society making peace with its past and moving forward toward some sort of reconciliation, the views of the entire population of South Africans are of the greatest importance and political significance.

These findings have clear implications for the current South African government. First, the original assumption of the truth and reconciliation legislation was that the inherent unfairness of amnesty could be assuaged through compensation. That assumption has empirical validity. If the government wants to influence South Africans to judge the amnesty process as acceptable, it ought to provide adequate compensation to those who established themselves as victims of gross human rights violations during the apartheid era. Indeed, at this stage in the process few mechanisms are available to the government to enhance the perceived fairness of amnesty, so perhaps the only option available to it to affect perceptions is to properly compensate the victims.

At one level the TRC seems to have been fairly successful in South Africa, and certainly the procedures employed by the TRC have influenced judgments of fairness. It seems unlikely that more formal processes of dealing with those who admit gross human rights abuses (trials, for instance) would be as successful at giving voice to the victims and their families and making apologies meaningful. Truth and reconciliation hearings seem to be an instance in which informal justice has some significant advantages over formal justice mechanisms (see, for example, Tyler and Lind 2001, 84–85). Whatever the liabilities of less formal justice mechanisms—and there are many—the goal of rendering amnesty decisions more acceptable seems to be well served by processes like those employed by South Africa's TRC.

Finally, for South African leaders to ignore the demand for justice emanating from the mass public would be a serious mistake. The new South African regime is unlikely to be able to satisfy economic expectations in the foreseeable future. But people want more from politics than economic success. They want fairness as well. The failure to satisfy expectations of justice can quite readily undermine the legitimacy of the regime—and ultimately that of the democratic transition itself.

As noted, I do not argue that those who are reconciled necessarily must hold any particular view of the amnesty process. Amnesty addresses the past; reconciliation looks toward the future. But the evidence of this chapter is that granting amnesty to gross human rights violators did not necessarily undermine the moral authority of the new regime. Amnesty denied certain forms of justice, to be sure, but the process itself contributed to other types of justice. Granting amnesty to perpetrators was not an unequivocal failure of justice; instead, the process created some injustice, but some justice as well. Thus, the consequences of not punishing those who admitted gross human rights violations are probably less dire than many expected.

Many of the arguments surrounding amnesty have to do with the legitimacy of South Africa's institutions. The next chapter addresses institutional legitimacy—the final subdimension of reconciliation—in more rigorous and comprehensive terms.

Chapter 8

The Legitimacy of the Political Institutions of the New South Africa

> If we understand legitimacy as the moral authority to make binding public policy, there are surely few powers more important to the efficacy, stability, and maintenance of political and legal institutions in democratic nations. Thus, the process by which institutions acquire or lose legitimacy is a critical subject for policy-makers in this changing world and an essential area of inquiry for students of law and society.
>
> —Gregory Caldeira, "Legitimacy, Compliance, and the Roots of Justice" (1994, 1)

In a new political system, few resources are more coveted than political legitimacy. Legitimacy is the endorphin of the democratic body politic; it is the substance that oils the machinery of democracy, reducing the friction that inevitably arises when people are not able to get everything they want from politics. Legitimacy is loyalty; it is a reservoir of goodwill that allows the institutions of government to go against what people may want at the moment without suffering debilitating consequences. Without legitimacy, the institutions of South Africa's new democracy will be fragile and tentative indeed.[1]

The purpose of this chapter is to consider a fourth aspect of reconciliation: the willingness of South Africans to extend legitimacy to their Constitutional Court and national Parliament. Unless South Africans accept these crucial political institutions as legitimate, it is difficult to imagine that any sort of political reconciliation can be consolidated in South Africa. Thus, this chapter presents an empirical analysis of the degree to which the Constitutional Court and Parliament enjoy the *loyalty* of their constituents. I also address the hypothesis that institutional legitimacy contributes to the willingness of citizens to accept policy decisions with which they disagree. If South Africa's political institutions do not have the leeway to make controversial and unpopular decisions as necessary—decisions that will be respected and accepted by the people—then democracy may fall prey to excessive majoritarianism and repudiation of the rule of law. Before turning to the data, however, a panoply of theoretical and conceptual issues must be explicitly addressed, beginning with further consideration of the question of what exactly legitimacy has to do with reconciliation.

Connecting Institutional Legitimacy and Reconciliation

In none of the legislation concerning the truth and reconciliation process in South Africa is there an explicit discussion of the extension of legitimacy to political institutions as a form of reconciliation. Nonetheless, the TRC's *Final Report* does refer often to "legitimacy," and it uses the term in roughly the same way that I employ it here.[2] For instance, the report discusses the illegitimacy of the apartheid state, as well as the necessity of establishing legitimacy in the New South Africa for a culture respectful of human rights.

Moreover, some scholars have pursued the proposition that reconciliation involves the creation of legitimacy for South Africa's new institutions. According to Richard Wilson (1995, 41): "Truth commissions have become one of the main mechanisms by which transitional regimes seek to create legitimacy for state institutions still tainted by the legacy of authoritarian rule." In his book *The Politics of Truth and Reconciliation in South Africa* (2001), he develops this idea at some length, ultimately concluding that the truth and reconciliation process did *not* do a very good job of establishing the legitimacy of the new regime and the principles on which it was founded. According to Wilson, the major shortcoming of the truth and reconciliation process was its failure to provide retributive justice for the abuses committed under apartheid, with the consequence that disrespect for human rights and lack of legitimacy for law and legal institutions were fostered. For instance, he asserts: "Human rights talk has become the language of pragmatic political compromise rather than the language of principle and accountability" (2001, 228). Further, "it is misguided to delegitimize human rights at the national level by detaching them from a retributive understanding of justice and attaching them to a religious notion of reconciliation-forgiveness" (230).[3] Others in South Africa (for example, Sarkin 1998; Corder 1995) share Wilson's deep concern about the legitimacy of the country's political and legal institutions, even if they do not necessarily agree on the etiology of institutional illegitimacy in South Africa.

"Legitimacy" is a term widely used by scholars and practitioners, even though the concept is not always given exacting theoretical and operational content. In the section that follows, I explicate legitimacy theory in some detail and the various concepts and hypotheses embedded in the theory. For the moment I do not worry too much about the precise meaning of legitimacy but instead try to connect my concern with the legitimacy of South Africa's institutions with my overarching emphasis on reconciliation.

Granting Legitimacy as a Form of Reconciliation

Earlier chapters in this book have investigated different forms of reconciliation. For instance, chapter 4 addresses reconciliation between individuals of different races. Chapter 5 considers reconciliation in terms of willingness to embrace a human rights culture in South Africa, based specifically on the objectives of the truth and reconciliation process as enumerated in the language creating the TRC. Chapter 6 examines interpersonal political tolerance by focusing on the willingness of South Africans to allow their political adversaries full rights of democratic citizenship. Thus, reconciliation between *people*, reconciliation with basic constitutional *principles*, and reconciliation among *groups* have all been investigated.

It is important as well to investigate the *institutions* that serve as the backbone of South Africa's new democracy. As noted earlier, liberal democracy is both a set of formal institutions and a set of cultural values. For instance, South Africans must come to tolerate each other and to be willing to countenance the expression of displeasing political ideas. But they must also come to support institutions that have the authoritative means of enforcing political tolerance as effective public policy. Just as the truth and reconciliation process sought to encourage respect for human rights in South Africa, it also implicitly sought support for the institutions charged with the protection of those human rights.[4] If South Africans fail to extend legitimacy to the institutions of majority rule and to the protection of minority rights, it would be difficult indeed to consider them reconciled with the newly implemented democratic system. To extend these institutions legitimacy is to accept South Africa's new system of democratic rule at a very elemental level and to reconcile with the new political dispensation in the country.

Legitimacy is always important for the effective functioning of political institutions. But in periods of transition, legitimacy is especially significant, both because the new institutions typically face a substantial legitimacy deficit and because foundational political and legal issues are often put before these institutions for resolution. The problem is exacerbated in transitional regimes because under such circumstances institutions can rarely make decisions that are pleasing to all. Thus, legitimacy is a crucial institutional asset at all times, but especially during periods of political transition.

To this point, I have been a bit vague about the specific institutions that must be granted legitimacy by the South African people. Perhaps I need not have been, since my theory is simple. I focus on two political institutions: the South African Parliament and the South African Constitutional Court.[5] I investigate these two institutions because they have the closest connection to democratic theory.[6] Parliament is obviously a crucial instrument of majority rule, as the numerous struggles over parliamentary representation under apartheid so clearly illustrate.[7] In some respects, the Parliament is the institution most clearly charged with representing the will of the people. Should citizens not extend legitimacy to South Africa's Parliament, democracy would be imperiled, and it would be difficult indeed to speak of any sort of political reconciliation in the country.

The Constitutional Court is the institution most clearly associated with the "minority rights" portion of the democratic equation, in the sense that the Court is charged with regulating the actions of the majority to ensure that they comport with constitutional requirements. With its "counter-majoritarian powers" (the ability to overturn acts of Parliament), the Court can (and should, according to liberal democratic theory) play a crucial role in protecting minorities (alleged criminals, for instance) and political nonconformists from the wrath of the majority. Such actions, however, are unlikely to curry favor with the majority. And of course, because the Constitutional Court lacks the crucial legitimacy-conferring electoral connection (the justices of the Court are appointed to the bench, with no direct connection to their constituents), the institution is deprived of a natural source of democratic legitimacy. Thus, I hypothesize that the Court probably suffers from a fairly substantial legitimacy deficit.

The consolidation of democratic change in South Africa requires that the ultimate institutions of majority rule and respect for minority rights—the Parliament and the Constitutional Court—be granted legitimacy by their constituents, the South African people. A South African who is politically reconciled is one who extends legitimacy to the democratic institutions of the New South Africa, including Parliament and the Constitutional Court. Before turning to an empirical analysis of legitimacy, however, a considerably more rigorous explication of legitimacy theory is necessary.

A Theory of Institutional Legitimacy

Considerable agreement exists among political scientists on most of the major contours of legitimacy theory. For instance, most agree that legitimacy is a normative concept that has something to do with the *right* (moral and legal) to make decisions. "Authority" is sometimes used as a synonym for legitimacy. Legitimate institutions are those with a widely accepted mandate to render judgments for a political community; those without legitimacy often find their authority contested.[8]

Many scholars believe that legitimacy is closely connected to decisionmaking processes (for example, Tyler 2001). Fair procedures are an important source of the legitimacy of institutions. As Lawrence Friedman (1998, 256) notes: "Basically, when people say that laws are 'legitimate,' they mean that there is something rightful about the way the laws came about. . . . The legitimacy of law rests on the way it comes to be: if that is legitimate, then so are the results, at least most of the time." For Tyler (2001, 422), "even-handedness, factuality, and the lack of bias or favoritism (neutrality)" are crucial for legitimacy (see also Hibbing and Theiss-Morse 1995). This is particularly important for democratic political institutions because liberal democracy so strongly focuses on procedures, in terms of both the ways by which people acquire authority (such as elections) and the decisionmaking procedures that institutions employ while making public policy.

Legitimacy becomes particularly relevant when people disagree about public policy. When a court, for instance, makes a decision that is pleasing to all, discussions of legitimacy are rarely relevant or necessary and therefore do not emerge. Satisfied constituents typically do not question the legitimacy of pleasing public policies. When conflict over policy exists, however, then some may ask whether the institution has the authority, the "right," to make the decision. Legitimate institutions are those one recognizes as appropriate decisionmaking bodies *even when* one disagrees with the outputs of the institution. Thus, legitimacy takes on its primary relevance in the presence of an *objection precondition.* As Friedman (1977, 141) rightly noted long ago: "We do not need a theory of legitimacy to explain why people obey a person with a gun, or adhere to an order that brings them personal honor or gain; or obey their religions or their moral codes." Questions of legitimacy arise mainly when people are not getting what they want from their political institutions.[9]

Empirically oriented scholars have long been dissatisfied with the amorphous nature of the concept of legitimacy.[10] Under the influence of David Easton (1965, 1975), researchers have instead been attracted to the notion of institutional[11] "support" and often make a distinction between "diffuse" and "specific" support. Though a few important scholars (for example, Mishler and Rose 1994) doubt that the two types of support can be differentiated empirically, most recognize a difference, at least at the theoretical level, between approval of policy outputs in the short term and more fundamental loyalty to an institution over the long term. This analysis embraces this distinction.

Diffuse support refers to "a reservoir of favorable attitudes or good will that helps members to accept or tolerate outputs to which they are opposed or the effects of which they see as damaging to their wants" (Easton 1965, 273). Diffuse support is therefore institutional *loyalty*; it is support that is *not* contingent upon satisfaction with the immediate outputs of the institution. David Easton's apt phrase—a "reservoir of goodwill"—captures the idea that people have confidence in institutions to make desirable public policy in the long run. "Loyalty" suggests that failure to make policy that is pleasing in the short term does not necessarily undermine basic commitments to support the institution. Institutions without a reservoir of goodwill may be limited in their ability to go against the preferences of a determined majority.[12] And as Easton notes, legitimacy is most relevant when people are not getting what they want from an institution's policy outputs.

Specific support is satisfaction with the contemporary outputs of the institution. Following the objection precondition idea, when specific support is low (that is, when people are dissatisfied), diffuse support becomes particularly important. Over the long term the two types of support should be related (and may converge), although disagreement about the meaning of any given cross-sectional correlation is quite possible (see Gibson, Caldeira, and Baird 1998, 344, esp. n. 3). At any given point in time, an institution's supporters may be loyal toward the institution and satisfied with its performance, or they may be loyal but not at all happy with institutional policy outputs. Thus, the meaning of a cross-sectional correlation between diffuse and specific support is very difficult to ascertain.

Though there are many ways to think about the views of ordinary citizens toward the major political institutions of a polity, I contend that the most important attitudes have to do with loyalty. Institutions such as parliaments, and especially courts, need the leeway to be able to go against public opinion (as for instance in protecting unpopular political minorities). Thus, a crucial attribute of political institutions is the degree to which they enjoy the loyalty of their constituents.

The Consequences of Institutional Legitimacy

At this point in the theory, an important disagreement over definitions characterizes the literature. Some scholars *equate* legitimacy with compliance; others treat legitimacy as one of many possible *causes* of compliance. I take the latter tack, conceptualizing the decision to obey or not obey a law as *conceptually* independent of whether an institution is judged to have the authority to make a decision. To do otherwise renders tautological the relationship between perceived legitimacy and compliance and precludes consideration of the determinants of compliance that are not grounded in legitimacy.[13]

For instance, John Yoo (2001, 225) uses the following definition: "We can think of institutional 'legitimacy' as the belief in the binding nature of an institution's decisions, even when one disagrees with them." By "binding" he means an obligation to obey. I contend that people obey laws for many reasons and that the degree to which legitimacy and compliance are related must be treated as an empirical question, as it is in this chapter.

Indeed, one of the most interesting unresolved questions in this literature has to do with the "legitimacy-conferring" powers of courts (see, for example, Clawson, Kegler, and Waltenburg 2001). First clearly articulated by Robert Dahl (1957), this theory asserts that a court ruling can induce people to accept the decision of another institution because the court has ratified and sanctified the decision. Because courts rarely challenge the ruling coalition (Dahl 1957), the judiciary essentially places its imprimatur on policies, thereby encouraging citizens to accept outcomes with which they disagree. Jeffrey Mondak and others (for example, Choper 1980) refer to this as the "political capital" of courts and note that institutions must husband this capital and spend it wisely if they are to be effective. As Mondak (1992, 461) notes, "sponsoring a policy is a type of gamble; the possibility of negative reaction endangers the institution's lifeblood, institutional legitimacy."

This is exactly the theory that scholars are relying on when they assert that the U.S. Supreme Court wounded itself by its decision in *Bush v. Gore* in the disputed 2000 U.S. presidential election.[14] In that decision, the Supreme Court, even though badly divided, effectively ended the election controversy. The Court ruling eroded Al Gore's support, making it difficult if not impossible to continue his challenge to the election outcome. Whether acceptance of the Court's decision was a function of the legitimacy ascribed to the institution cannot be determined without rigorous statistical analysis, but on its face, the 2000 election dispute seems to have provided powerful evidence in support of legitimacy theory.[15]

Thus, how much legitimacy an institution attracts from its constituents is an issue of considerable theoretical and practical importance. Consequently, the remainder of this chapter addresses the nature of the attitudes of ordinary South Africans toward their Constitutional Court and Parliament.

Expectations Regarding Racial Differences in Institutional Loyalties

Do South Africans of all races extend legitimacy to the primary political institutions of their new democratic system? In one sense, this question seems trivial. Why would not black South Africans grant legitimacy to the political institutions that are now directly accountable to them, the black majority? After all, it is in the interests of Africans to support the institutions that represent them, the institutions for which they struggled for so long. Instrumental considerations alone seem to dictate that the new majority would support South Africa's political institutions.

However, the African majority may not feel the same about the Court and the Parliament. Democracy is a compromised institutional structure. By that I mean that democracy is a system in which multiple interests can gain access to political power. The best points of access for majorities are the presidency and the parliament. By definition, the majority wins in majoritarian arenas. One who supports the ANC should be quite content with the institution of the Parliament (even if displeased with any given policy action by the legislature), since that institution is designed to reflect majority interests and preferences. One might not always be satisfied with one's party or representatives, but the institution itself is structured so as to be accountable to those in the majority and is thereby worthy of institutional loyalty.

Not all democratic institutions, however, are so accountable to the majority. Courts in particular are established to provide a means for minorities—those whose interests and preferences are shared by less than half of the population—to pursue at least some of their interests. To win in majoritarian contexts requires assembling a majority. To win in minoritarian institutions like courts requires only the resources necessary to file a lawsuit.[16] Courts are often established specifically as a means of checking majoritarianism, especially when granted the power to say what the constitution means (as in South Africa). The majority is not free to do anything it wishes or to adopt any policy that seems desirable at the moment. Instead, courts provide an avenue for a minority to try to prevent the majority from achieving its goals, and therefore judicial institutions should be especially favored by those who perceive themselves as part of a minority.

I have tried to be careful with the word "minority" by using it to refer only to those whose interests and preferences are not shared by half or more of the people in a political system. When I refer to "minorities," I certainly do not necessarily intend to imply underprivileged minorities. The minority capable of taking advantage of minoritarian institutions is often (if not typically) a privileged minority (see, for example, Dahl 1957). In a sense (but only in a sense), institutions are insensitive to the substantive interests of those who seek advantage through the institutions. Courts therefore may be a means through which those with power under the old apartheid system (now a minority) attempt to maintain their positions of power and privilege.

Consequently, a most difficult task for South Africa lies in building the legitimacy of the judiciary under the new system. The courts in the New South Africa are only remotely accountable to the majority. These courts also have access to a fabulously liberal constitution that is at odds with majority opinion in many important respects (the easiest example is the prohibition against the use of the death penalty, which most South Africans support). Moreover, the doctrine of parliamentary supremacy that reigned under apartheid has been abrogated by the new constitution. Now Parliament, the instrument of the majority, is subservient to the constitution and to those whose job it is to say what the constitution means—the judges. Thus, even if Africans should logically support the new parliament, whether they should extend legitimacy to South Africa's new courts—especially the Constitutional Court—is less obvious.

A similar, but opposite logic, should characterize the views of white South Africans (and those of Asian origin as well, and perhaps even Colored people). It is unlikely that many white South Africans will directly profit from majoritarian political institutions in the near future.[17] Thus, whites can be expected to be particularly supportive of institutions like courts because they are more likely to advance the interests of minorities. For whites, the Parliament is problematical since that institution is unlikely to be responsive to the demands of the small white minority. This problem is exacerbated by the fact that whites have little hope of ever becoming a majority; they are consigned to minority status (so long as race-based politics prevails, as it is likely to do so). Thus, the problem for South Africa's new system is to find a way to induce white South Africans to extend legitimacy to all political institutions, including those biased toward representing the interests of the majority.

My basic argument here is that if South African democracy is to prosper, then South Africans must extend legitimacy even to those institutions that do not necessarily advance their short-term interests. The problem of legitimacy is the problem of decoupling instrumentalism from institutional support (see Tyler 2001). Citizens must be willing to extend support to an institution even when it is not advancing their immediate interests. For an institution to be legitimate, support must *not* be contingent upon the satisfaction of policy demands and preferences.

Given this formulation, it should be easy now to see why I treat "loyalty" as a synonym for legitimacy. One who is loyal toward an institution is one who supports that institution *even when* its policies are displeasing. Loyalty means little without some displeasure. Loyalty does not describe one's reactions to a friend who gives one a valuable gift. Instead, loyalty applies when a friend does something displeasing. Loyalty means supporting a friend *even when* the friend's behavior is less than satisfactory (or when there is some other cost for doing so). Being loyal to an institution means recognizing the legitimate authority of the institution to act and decide even with the recognition that the actions and policies may not be entirely to one's liking.

The first empirical question addressed in this chapter is whether South Africans extend legitimacy to their Constitutional Court and Parliament. As indicated, I expect support for the Parliament to be more widespread than support for the Constitutional Court, given the electoral connection the Parliament has to its constituents. And based on a simple theory of self-interests (individual and group), I also hypothesize that the African majority will extend more support to the Parliament than to the Constitutional Court, while whites will express greater allegiance to the Court than to the Parliament.

Public Attitudes Toward South African Political Institutions

Just how do South Africans feel about their Constitutional Court and Parliament? Before this question can be considered, one important methodological issue must be addressed.

The Attentive Publics for the Court and the Parliament

Not all South Africans hold a great deal of information about the political institutions that govern them. As a means of screening out those without much awareness, we asked the respondents to indicate the degree to which they are knowledgeable about the Constitutional Court and the South African Parliament. I of course treat these responses with a grain of salt inasmuch as mass publics everywhere in the world have only a limited store of information about the institutions that govern them. But I think it is important not to ask people questions about an institution about which they have never even heard.

Not surprisingly, virtually all South Africans claim to know something about their Parliament, with only 1.1 percent of the sample proclaiming no awareness of that institution. However, when it comes to the Constitutional Court, ignorance is considerably more widespread, with 16.9 percent saying that they had never heard of the Court prior to the interview.[18]

For the analysis that follows, I have screened the data, discarding those respondents who have no awareness of the institution. This excludes very few South Africans for our questions about the Parliament but about 629 of the respondents (17 percent of the sample) for our questions about the Constitutional Court. Following earlier research, I refer to these subsamples as the "attentive public" for the institution.[19]

South Africans' Loyalty Toward Their Constitutional Court and Parliament

My thinking about institutional loyalty follows a considerable body of research on conceptualizing and measuring mass perceptions of high courts (see Caldeira and Gibson 1992, 1995; Gibson, Caldeira, and Baird 1998; Gibson and Caldeira 1995, 1998, 2003).[20] That research conceptualizes loyalty as opposition to making fundamental structural and functional changes in the institution (see Boynton and Loewenberg 1973) and is grounded in the history of attacks by politicians against courts in the United States (see Caldeira 1987) and elsewhere (for example, the manipulation of courts' jurisdiction—for many contemporary examples, see Schwartz 2000).[21] As we have described it elsewhere (Caldeira and Gibson 1992, 638), those who have no loyalty toward the U.S. Supreme Court are willing "to accept, make, or countenance major changes in the fundamental attributes of how the high bench functions or fits into the U.S. constitutional system" (see also Loewenberg 1971). Loyalty is also characterized by a generalized trust that the institution will perform acceptably in the future. To the extent that people support fundamental structural changes in an institution and distrust that institution, they are extending to it little legitimacy. Conceptually, loyalty thus ranges from complete unwillingness to support the continued existence of the institution to staunch institutional fealty.

Table 8.1 reports the responses to our questions about loyalty toward the Court and the Parliament. The table is structured so that the third column reports the percentage of respondents who give a supportive answer to the statement, irrespective of whether the answer is "agree" or "disagree." For instance, 27.1 percent of South Africans (the Court's "attentive public")[22] disagree with the statement: "If the South African Constitutional Court started making a lot of decisions that most people disagree with, it might be better to do away with Court altogether." I deem a disagree response to represent loyalty toward the institution, and therefore the level of support for the Court is 27.1 percent. Note that for the last item in the table—having to do with the Court's jurisdiction—no comparable question was included for the Parliament.

Generally speaking, the Parliament receives a bit more support from South Africans than does the Constitutional Court. The difference is most extreme on the first item: 27.1 percent of the sample are willing to stick by the Court even if it makes unpopular decisions, while 37.9 percent give a loyal response with regard to the Parliament. This is a substantial (and statistically significant) disparity. However, on the next two propositions the differences are entirely trivial, with a majority in each instance expressing some loyalty toward both institutions. For example, 60.0 percent assert that generally the Court can be trusted; 60.6 percent express trust in the Parliament. Considering only the three items asked about both institutions, on average, 1.4 of the Court items evoked a supportive response, compared to 1.5 items for the Parliament. This is indeed a trivial difference.

It is always difficult to judge whether survey percentages are "high" or "low," since expectations have everything to do with how statistics are evaluated. That only 19.4 percent of the respondents endorse all three Parliament items and only 15.9 percent endorse all three Court items may be taken as indicative of fairly low

Table 8.1 Indicators of Loyalty Toward the South African Constitutional Court and Parliament, Attentive Publics

	Not Supportive of the Institution	Uncertain	Supportive of the Institution	Mean	Standard Deviation	Number of Cases
Do away with the Court	49.7%	23.2%	27.1%	2.65	1.19	3,094
Do away with the Parliament	42.9	19.1	37.9	2.91	1.29	3,683
Court can be trusted	12.1	27.9	60.0	3.65	.97	3,092
Parliament can be trusted	14.0	25.4	60.6	3.67	1.02	3,684
Court favors some groups	15.7	31.7	52.6	3.52	1.09	3,092
Parliament favors some groups	20.2	26.6	53.3	3.48	1.15	3,682
Reduce Court jurisdiction	36.7	36.2	27.1	2.86	1.07	3,091

Source: Author's compilation from the 2001 Truth and Reconciliation Survey.

Note: The percentages are calculated on the basis of collapsing the five-point Likert response set (for example, "agree strongly" and "agree" responses are combined). The means and standard deviations are calculated on the uncollapsed distributions.

The difference of means on the first item ("do away with") is statistically significant at $p < .001$. Neither of the other two cross-institutional differences of means is statistically significant ($p > .05$).

The propositions are:

"If the [the institution] started making a lot of decisions that most people disagree with, it might be better to do away with [the institution] altogether."

"The [institution] can usually be trusted to make decisions that are right for the country as a whole."

"The [institution] treats all groups who come before it—black, white, Colored, and Asian—the same."

"The right of the South African Constitutional Court to decide certain types of controversial issues should be done away with."

levels of support. Since 20.3 percent endorse none of the Parliament items and 25.3 percent endorse none of the Court items, perhaps the most reasonable conclusion is that these institutions enjoy a low to moderate level of support from their constituents.

It is unusual to find equivalent levels of support for a high court and a parliament (see Gibson and Caldeira 1998). In most established political systems (and especially in the United States), courts draw far more loyalty from ordinary citizens than do parliaments.[23] Parliaments are often tainted with all the unsavory business of democratic politics—compromise, partisanship, log-rolling, and so on—that people find displeasing (see, for example, Hibbing and Theiss-Morse 1995). Courts, on the other hand, usually shroud their proceedings in secrecy, presenting a public image of solemnity, dignity, and reasoned and impartial decisionmaking. Nothing could be more different from the way in which parliaments are typically portrayed (for example, as having notorious and unruly question periods). That the South African Constitutional Court attracts no more loyalty than the Parliament suggests that the Court has been unable to differentiate itself, that the image of the institution as doing something quite different from the other branches of government, and in a different way, has not yet penetrated the consciousness of the South African mass public.[24] Failure to establish itself as a strictly legal institution has impeded the growth of the legitimacy of the Constitutional Court.

Of course, it might be appropriate to treat the "*inattentive* public" as failing to extend loyalty to the institution. Because the Constitutional Court is considerably less well known than the Parliament, inclusion of the inattentive public subsample in the analysis would diminish substantially my estimate of the extent of support for the Constitutional Court. Thus, it is reasonable to conclude that, in the population as a whole, support for the Parliament is more widespread than support for the Court.

Changing Attitudes Toward the Constitutional Court

For the Constitutional Court, a different basis for interpreting these figures is available. I can first compare these data to the responses to identical questions asked in our comparable 1997 survey.[25] This

Table 8.2 Indicators of Loyalty Toward the South African Constitutional Court, Attentive Publics, 1997 and 2001

	Not Supportive of the Institution	Uncertain	Supportive of the Institution	Mean	Standard Deviation	Number of Cases
Do away with the Court						
2001	49.7%	23.2%	27.1%	2.7	1.2	3,094
1997	39.5	32.6	27.9	2.9	1.1	1,083
Court can be trusted						
2001	12.1	27.9	60.0	3.7	1.0	3,092
1997	9.9	34.7	55.4	3.6	.9	1,083
Reduce Court jurisdiction						
2001	36.7	36.2	27.1	2.9	1.1	3,091
1997	29.5	42.3	28.2	3.0	1.0	1,081

Source: Author's compilation from the 2001 Truth and Reconciliation Survey.
Note: The percentages are calculated on the basis of collapsing the five-point Likert response set (for example, "agree strongly" and "agree" responses are combined). The means and standard deviations are calculated on the uncollapsed distributions.

The propositions are:

"If the South African Constitutional Court started making a lot of decisions that most people disagree with, it might be better to do away with the Court altogether."

"The South African Constitutional Court can usually be trusted to make decisions that are right for the country as a whole."

"The right of the South African Constitutional Court to decide certain types of controversial issues should be done away with."

comparison is shown in table 8.2 for the items included in both surveys.

The most readily supported conclusion from these data is that *support for the Court seemed to change little between 1997 and 2001*. The mean scores are in every instance very similar, as are the percentages of respondents giving a supportive answer. However, we can also see that the percentage of respondents giving nonsupportive answers is higher in 2001 on each question than in 1997. Indeed, in 2001 the proportion of respondents *unwilling* to stand by the Court even if it makes unpopular decisions *increased* by about ten percentage points. At the same time, the percentage of respondents asserting that the Court can be trusted increased by about five percentage points, so contrary trends are evident. This is largely a function of the decline in the percentage of respondents with no opinion about the Court, which is surely due to the growing salience of the institution.[26] Though these are not panel data—and so some speculation is required—these findings imply that some of those who had no opinion about the institution in the past have since become more positively oriented toward the Court, but that others have become more negative, and that perhaps the size of the latter group is larger than the former. Generally, it is difficult to find in these data any evidence that loyalty toward the Court has increased in the last few years. Instead, the minimalist conclusion to be drawn from this analysis is that the Court did *not* broaden its support in the four years between the two surveys.

Cross-National Comparisons

One other basis of comparison is available. Since we have conducted similar surveys in many countries in the last few years, I can compare the South African results with findings from other polities. Table 8.3 reports data on the summary indicator of support for the South African Constitutional Court in 1997 and 2001 as well as for high courts in about twenty other countries.

These data support several conclusions. First, in comparative perspective, the salience of the Constitutional Court is only slightly lower than average (see column 1). Though virtually all Americans have heard of their Supreme Court, the size of the attentive public

Table 8.3 Average Diffuse Support for National High Courts Among Attentive Publics

	Unaware of Court	Mean	Standard Deviation	Number of Cases
Spain (1993)	10.3%	46.3	22.3	258
Bulgaria	13.4	48.8	18.4	860
Germany (East)	1.0	49.4	22.4	301
Belgium	9.2	52.2	22.0	211
South Africa (1997)	15.1	53.8	17.4	1,083
Spain (1995)	10.7	53.9	17.2	658
South Africa (2001)	16.9	54.2	16.9	3,095
Ireland	1.6	54.5	18.3	291
France (1995)	9.2	55.0	19.6	660
France (1993)	7.6	55.2	20.8	278
Russia	50.8	56.6	14.4	360
Canada	1.0	56.7	19.6	594
Hungary	9.0	57.1	20.5	654
Italy	9.0	57.8	23.3	271
Great Britain	1.7	58.0	20.2	295
Luxembourg	25.0	58.8	21.5	145
Portugal	17.7	61.6	22.0	235
United States	.6	62.2	19.7	804
Poland	11.7	62.5	20.5	696
Greece	6.1	65.0	23.0	281
Germany (West)	1.5	65.4	20.4	194
Denmark	1.3	66.6	20.3	295
Netherlands	6.0	69.9	22.4	282

Source: Author's compilation from the 2001 Truth and Reconciliation Survey.
Note: The 100-point summated index is created from responses to the items reported in table 8.1. The countries are ranked according to the degree of support for the national high court (lowest to highest). Most of the data from countries other than South Africa are taken from Gibson, Caldeira, and Baird (1998) and are drawn from surveys conducted in 1993 or 1995. For some countries, survey data are available for more than one year. In these instances, the year of the survey is indicated in the table.

in South Africa is about the same as that of Portugal. Second, as I have already noted, support for the Court changed very little between the surveys in 1997 and 2001.

Third, in comparison to other courts, the Constitutional Court does not enjoy a very wide or deep "reservoir of goodwill"—only a handful of institutions have lower support scores than the South African Court. Finally, though the South African Court is a young institution, it does not fare particularly well even in comparison to high courts in transitional polities like Poland and Hungary. (The South African Court does, however, attract more support than the much-embattled Bulgarian high court.)

All of the data I have considered point to the same conclusion: the Constitutional Court has achieved only low to moderate legitimacy within the South African mass public. The Court has no more support than the Parliament (though courts in established democracies typically are more favored than legislatures), there has been no increase in support in the last few years, and in cross-national comparisons the South African Court does not stack up particularly well. From the point of view of reconciliation and institutional legitimacy, these findings are discouraging.

Racial Differences in Attitudes Toward the Parliament and the Court

Of course, it is always difficult to speak of a single, unified South African mass public; when it comes to politics, racial differences in attitudes are typically profound. Consequently, it is necessary to reconsider the issue of institutional loyalty, this time from the point of view of how South Africans of different races judge these two institutions.

Table 8.4 reports a summary measure of attitudes toward the Constitutional Court and the Parliament. The index is simply the number of loyal responses, based on the three propositions asked about each institution.[27] I report as well the percentage of respondents who gave at least two supportive responses to our queries—an indicator of relatively high support for the institution.

The intuition that racial differences exist in attitudes toward the Court and Parliament is borne out by the data, although perhaps the findings are not entirely as expected. Africans are significantly more likely to express support for *both* institutions than whites, Colored people, and South Africans of Asian origin. The difference between Africans and whites is particularly stark, with roughly half of the black respondents expressing a high degree of loyalty toward

Table 8.4 Racial Differences in Loyalty Toward the South African Constitutional Court and Parliament, Attentive Publics

	High Support[a]	Mean[b]	Standard Deviation	Number of Cases
African				
Constitutional Court	54.2%	1.50	.99	1,646
Parliament	59.9	1.66	.98	1,981
White				
Constitutional Court	35.3	1.11	1.08	931
Parliament	30.0	1.12	1.01	983
Colored				
Constitutional Court	38.9	1.16	1.08	378
Parliament	40.9	1.24	1.11	479
Asian origin				
Constitutional Court	48.6	1.41	1.04	222
Parliament	49.6	1.46	1.03	240

Source: Author's compilation from the 2001 Truth and Reconciliation Survey.
[a]"High support" is defined as two or three supportive responses to the three items.
[b]Racial differences in attitudes toward the Court and the Parliament are statistically significant at $p < .001$. For the Constitutional Court, $\eta = .18$; for the Parliament, $\eta = .23$.

these institutions but only about one-third of the whites holding loyal attitudes. The Colored respondents are also characterized by relatively low loyalty toward the Court and Parliament, while those of Asian origin tend to be closer to Africans in their attitudes. Generally, race makes an important difference in how these institutions are judged.

It is noteworthy as well that in terms of relative support, the Constitutional Court and the Parliament are judged similarly within all four racial groups. The Parliament perhaps has a slight edge among Africans (for the cross-institutional difference of means, $p < .001$, $\eta = .08$), and perhaps the Court draws slightly more support from whites (though the difference is not statistically significant), but generally the difference in attitudes toward these two institutions is inconsequential within each racial group. The simpleminded view that minority South Africans tend to be especially supportive of minoritarian political institutions like courts while majority South Africans support majoritarian institutions like parliaments must be rejected.

That white South Africans extend so little support to the Constitutional Court is perplexing. We might have guessed that whites would view the Court as the institution most capable of advancing their interests, since the Court is a decidedly minoritarian institution. Instead, whites seem to judge the Court in the same way they judge the Parliament: they express little loyalty to either institution. The fears, widely expressed during the constitution-making process in the early to mid-1990s, that the Court would become an institution for protecting white privileges seem not to have been realized, at least from the point of view of most white South Africans.[28]

One of the interesting aspects of these data is that attitudes toward the Court are generally not very distinctive. Table 8.5 reports the cross-institutional correlations for three institutional assessments. For instance, the first correlation (based, by the way, on the entire sample, not just the attentive public) indicates the relationship between awareness of the Parliament and of the Constitutional Court. The data reveal quite strong cross-institutional similarities. For instance, among all South Africans, those who are aware of the Parliament tend strongly to also be aware of the Court; those who approve of the Parliament's policymaking also approve of the Court's, and those who express loyalty to the Parliament also express loyalty toward the Court.

Still, some racial differences in these coefficients exist. In terms of institutional loyalty, for instance, most Africans in particular fail to distinguish a great deal between their support for the Court and for the Parliament, perhaps in part because these institutions are cut from the same cloth as the New South Africa. The cross-institutional correlations of the loyalty indices are somewhat weaker among whites, Colored people, and those of Asian origin, but they are still formidable relationships. In general, these data seem to indicate that the Constitutional Court has not emerged as a distinctive legal institution in the minds of most South Africans. How they feel about one institution predicts well how they feel about the other.

Table 8.5 Cross-Institutional Similarities in Institutional Assessments by the Four Racial Groups

Perceptions of Constitutional Court and Parliament	African	White	Colored	Asian Origin
Awareness	.47	.47	.57	.42
Specific support	.44	.34	.51	.47
Institutional loyalty	.59	.44	.45	.40

Source: Author's compilation from the 2001 Truth and Reconciliation Survey.
Note: Entries are Pearson correlation coefficients indicating the relationship between responses toward the Parliament and toward the Constitutional Court.

If the Constitutional Court is not viewed as a distinctively legal institution, then to what degree does institutional loyalty differ from simple approval of the immediate policy outputs of the institutions? That is, it is possible that specific support and diffuse support are indistinguishable because insufficient time has elapsed for loyalty to emerge as a stable attribute of the beliefs and evaluations of individual South Africans. Perhaps at this point in South Africa's nascent democracy, how one judges a political institution is based on little more than whether one views that institution as producing desirable public policy.

This raises the important question of how people form impressions of institutions, especially in transitional political systems. Little prior research on this question exists, so not much is known about the processes involved. However, in earlier research (Gibson, Caldeira, and Baird 1998), my colleagues and I have drawn several important conclusions from our cross-national study of the legitimacy of national high courts that have some bearing on this question. We argue that courts first acquire specific support by gaining visibility. Visibility leads to satisfaction in part because judges are adept at framing their decisions with reference to the law. Courts claim credit for pleasing decisions but disperse responsibility for displeasing decisions, blaming "the law" for any odious outcomes. They refer to this as a "positivity bias," by which they mean that courts profit from pleasing decisions and are not harmed by displeasing decisions. Judges are able to "frame issues in a light favorable to the maintenance of institutional legitimacy, thereby blunting the effect of unpopular decisions" (356). We therefore suggest that legitimacy is built through the cumulation over time of satisfied minorities.[29] Thus, our findings on how awareness, satisfaction with contemporary outputs, and institutional loyalty are connected may be of considerable significance for South Africa.

Figure 8.1 reports the connections between awareness, specific support, and institutional loyalty for both institutions and for each of the four racial groups. The first conclusion supported by the table is that increased awareness of these South African institutions does indeed seem to increase satisfaction with their performance, as is generally true in other countries. Strong correlations exist between these two variables for all except white attitudes toward the Parliament. Furthermore, for all four groups, the correlations between awareness and satisfaction are stronger for assessments of the Constitutional Court than for assessments of the Parliament, perhaps indicating that what people learn about the legislature does not always please them. In general, a strong positivity bias does seem to exist, in the sense that satisfaction directly and strongly results from knowledge of the institution. To know more about these institutions is to be more pleased by their decisions.

Those with greater awareness of the activities of courts tend to support them more, in part because awareness is strongly associated with approval of the performance of the institution. From one perspective, this finding is odd. Knowledge of an institution often increases as a result of political controversies, since controversies are typically judged to be more newsworthy than decisions to which no one objects. Citizens in general then find out about courts within the context of decisions that are contested. Yet a strong relationship exists between awareness and satisfaction.

One explanation for this puzzle is that awareness exposes citizens to judicial procedures, not just outcomes. As one becomes aware of the activities of a court, one observes solemn and dignified procedures, reasoned arguments, claims of principle and nonpartisanship, and deference to the institution. When citizens report that they are satisfied with the performance of an institution, perhaps they are reporting their satisfaction more with procedure than with policy outcomes. Few other explanations can account for such a strong—and consistently strong—relationship between

Figure 8.1 Bivariate Connections Between Institutional Awareness, Performance Satisfaction, and Loyalty Among the Four Racial Groups

Constitutional Court | Parliament

African

Satisfaction
.48
.33
Awareness
Loyalty
.24

Satisfaction
.34
.35
Awareness
Loyalty
.27

White

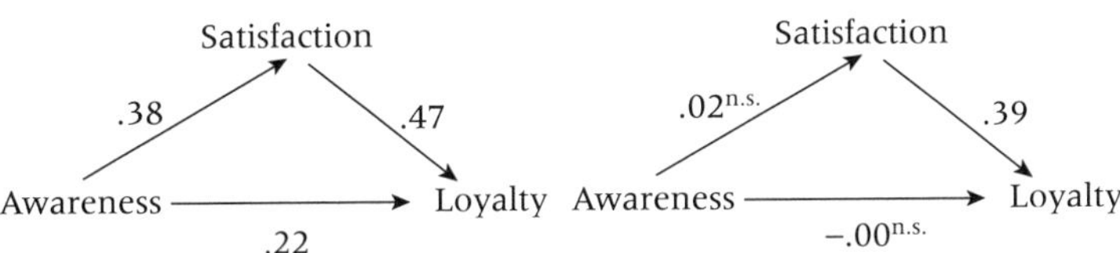

Colored

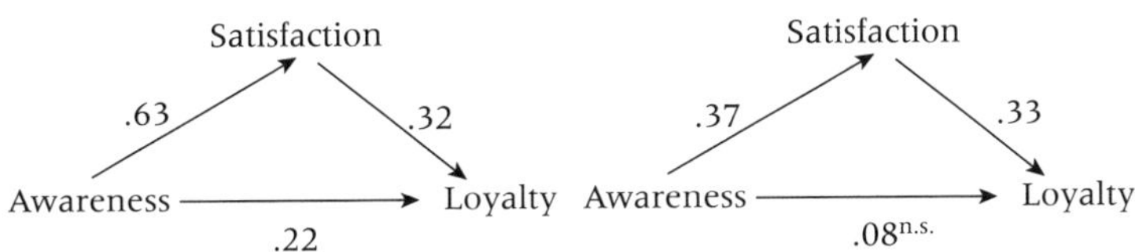

Asian Origin

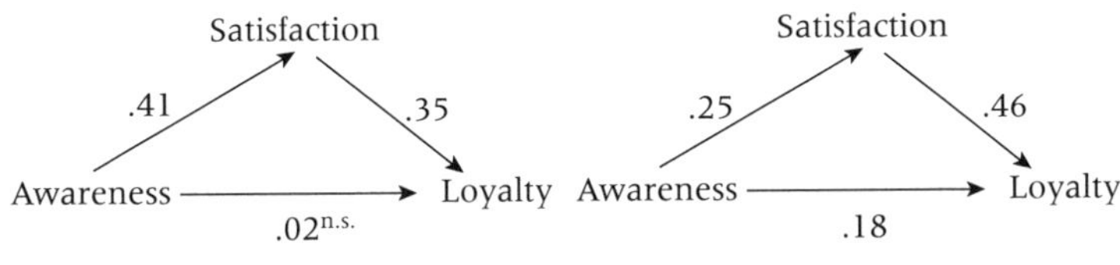

Source: Author's compilation from the 2001 Truth and Reconciliation Survey.
Note: n.s. = not statistically significant at $p \geq .10$. All other coefficients are significant at $p < .001$.

knowledge of what courts are doing and satisfaction with their decisions.

The finding that exposure to courts tends to be associated with approval of their performance has now been confirmed in a wide variety of contexts (for example, Gibson, Caldeira, and Baird 1998; Scheb and Lyons 2000). As my colleagues and I (Gibson, Caldeira, and Spence 2002, 553) have argued in relation to the U.S. Supreme Court and the disputed presidential election of 2000:

> These results may reflect the bias of "positivity frames" when it comes to the Court (and perhaps judicial institutions in general), in the sense that exposure to courts—including exposure associated with controversial circumstances—enhances rather than detracts from judicial legitimacy, even among those who are disgusted with the Court's ruling. When courts become salient, people become exposed to the symbolic trappings of judicial power—"the marble temple, the high bench, the purple curtain, the black robes" (Scheb and Lyons 2000, 929). When the news media covered the Court's deliberations surrounding the election, it generally did so with the greatest deference and respect. The contrast in images of the "partisan bickering" in Florida and the solemn judicial process in Washington could not be more stark. No matter how one judges the outcome in *Bush v. Gore*, exposure to the legitimizing symbols of law and courts is perhaps the dominant process at play. Thus, the effect of displeasure with a particular court decision may be muted by contact with these legitimizing symbols. To know courts is indeed to love them, in the sense that to know about courts is to be exposed to these legitimizing symbols.

Thus, we suggest that a positivity bias results from exposure to the highly effective legitimizing symbols in which courts typically drape themselves. The same seems to be true of South Africa.

Figure 8.1 also reports the relationships between approval of the performance of the institution (specific support) and institutional loyalty (diffuse support), separately for the two institutions. The coefficients indicate that institutional loyalty is in every instance substantially related to levels of satisfaction. Those pleased with the performance of the Court are generally more likely to express diffuse support for it. All of these relationships are reasonably strong.

Loyalty is very much a function of satisfaction with the performance of the institution.

Several conclusions emerge from this analysis. First, I should repeat the caveat that cross-sectional correlations between satisfaction and loyalty are always difficult to interpret, since they depict a static relationship in what is a dynamic process. Second, these coefficients differ little from those produced by a multivariate analysis in which both satisfaction and knowledge are used to predict loyalty. In that analysis, the direct effect of knowledge on loyalty is slight. Third, in comparison to findings from other countries, these relationships are not unusual (see Gibson, Caldeira, and Baird 1998).

I have found that satisfaction and loyalty are themselves closely related. In the South African case, perhaps they are too closely related. We can speculate that the strength of this relationship is in part a function of the short time during which these institutions have been operating. Developing loyalty toward an institution is a slow, incremental process. We suspect that, over time, the relationship between satisfaction and loyalty would grow steadily weaker as loyalty becomes inured to dissatisfaction. At this point in time, neither the South African Constitutional Court nor the Parliament has accumulated this level of loyalty.

But the most important conclusion is that these data seem to indicate that loyalty has not emerged as a firm and independent attitude of most South Africans. That the relationships are so similar across the two institutions suggests that loyalty is still dependent to some considerable degree on satisfaction with the outputs of the institution. Given the length of time these institutions have been in operation, this is perhaps not surprising. However, for diffuse support to provide a reservoir of goodwill for an institution, it must ultimately become divorced from short-term satisfaction with outputs.

Acquiescence to Court Decisions

My contention is that reconciliation requires that all South Africans accept the country's new political institutions as legitimate.

This is a matter of principle and theory: for people to live together in a common political system, it is essential that there be at least some degree of consensus that the institutions of the system have the necessary authority to make binding policy decisions for the people as a whole.

There is also a more concrete reason for being concerned about legitimacy. As I have noted, legitimacy is necessary for a political system because legitimate institutions are assumed to be more successful at bringing about compliance with their decisions. This is especially important in a polity characterized by deep ideological divisions (whether based on class, race, history, or other factors), since some means of inducing those who lose at politics to accept the unfavorable outcomes must be found. Institutional legitimacy may be part of the solution to the problem of noncompliance with law.

As I have discussed, it is useful to distinguish between acquiescing to an outcome and extending legitimacy to the institution making the decision, since people may accept a decision for reasons other than institutional legitimacy. For instance, it may be their habit to do so (see, for example, Hyde 1983), the costs of acting may be too high in comparison to any likely benefits (see, for example, Spriggs 1996, 1997), or it may be that people have no opportunities to give behavioral expression to their resistance. To this point, I have considered legitimacy alone. It is useful to examine as well whether legitimacy has any consequences for acquiescing to unpopular institutional decisions. Because the survey addressed only acquiescence to a Constitutional Court ruling, I cannot consider the Parliament in this portion of the analysis.[30]

So as to consider the legitimacy-acquiescence hypothesis empirically, I included in the survey an "acquiescence" experiment, which we called the Justice and Amnesty Experiment. This experiment was built around a short story told to the respondents (a "vignette") about a fellow ("Phillip") seeking amnesty for setting off a bomb that killed several innocent people (for details, see chapter 7). Within the vignette, several circumstances were experimentally varied. For instance, half of the respondents (randomly assigned) were told that Phillip issued an apology that was accepted by the families of the victims; the other half were told that Phillip apologized for his actions, but that the families of the victims rejected the apology as insincere. These manipulations were part of my investigation of the factors that contribute to overcoming the inherent unfairness of granting amnesty to those who admitted gross human rights violations (for the findings, see chapter 7). The details of the experiment itself need not concern this particular analysis of legitimacy and acquiescence.

After hearing the story, the respondents were asked whether Phillip should or should not have been granted amnesty. Most thought not (63.2 percent), some were uncertain (6.4 percent), and a minority of respondents were willing to see Phillip receive amnesty (30.4 percent).

Those who believed that Phillip should be granted amnesty were then told: "Now we would like you to imagine that the Constitutional Court decided that Phillip should *not* be granted amnesty. Using this same scale from 10 to 1, would you accept the Constitutional Court's decision not to give Phillip amnesty, or would you try to get the Court's decision reversed?" Those who had asserted that amnesty should not be given to Phillip were told: "Now we would like you to imagine that the Constitutional Court decided that Phillip *should* be granted amnesty. Using this same scale from 10 to 1, would you accept the Constitutional Court's decision to give Phillip amnesty, or would you try to get the Court's decision reversed?"[31] Thus, in every instance the respondents were asked to consider a decision by the Constitutional Court that was contrary to their expressed preferences on the matter of amnesty.

This experiment attempted to replicate the conditions under which legitimacy in fact matters: when people disagree with the policy decisions of an institution. People require little incentive to accept decisions with which they agree; why would they do otherwise? Indeed, it does not even make much sense to ask people about whether they would accept a decision when they already agree with it. Legitimacy becomes relevant only when the policy decisions of an institution are displeasing to a citizen.[32]

Table 8.6 reports willingness to accept a contrary court decision according to the respondent's initial view on granting amnesty.

Table 8.6 Racial Differences in Willingness to Accept a Contrary Constitutional Court Decision on Amnesty

Amnesty Attitude: Accept Court Decision	African	White	Colored	Asian Origin
Strong grant				
Mean[a]	6.59	5.61	6.42	5.14
Standard deviation	3.27	3.67	3.45	3.11
Number of cases	266	73	67	14
Accept the Court decision	64.7%	48.6%	58.2%	50.0%
Probably grant				
Mean[a]	6.38	6.59	6.21	6.72
Standard deviation	2.47	2.30	2.73	2.29
Number of cases	417	186	67	34
Accept the Court decision	62.4%	67.7%	49.3%	70.6%
Probably not grant				
Mean[a]	4.27	5.42	4.30	4.65
Standard deviation	2.43	2.53	2.42	2.51
Number of cases	452	217	94	39
Accept the Court decision	21.9%	44.0%	22.3%	23.1%
Strong not grant				
Mean[a]	2.79	3.33	3.48	2.86
Standard deviation	2.42	2.70	2.75	2.64
Number of cases	734	444	208	154
Accept the Court decision	12.1%	18.9%	15.9%	17.5%
η, across amnesty attitudes (within race)	.53	.45	.40	.48

Source: Author's compilation from the 2001 Truth and Reconciliation Survey.
[a]Higher scores indicate greater willingness to accept the decision.

Average scores for the continuous acceptance variable are reported, as are the percentages of respondents willing to any degree to accept the decision (scores of 6 or higher on the ten-point acceptance continuum). Thus, 64.7 percent of the African respondents who strongly favor granting amnesty to Phillip would accept a decision by the Constitutional Court to deny Phillip amnesty.

The data in this table support many interesting conclusions. First, for all racial groups, there is a substantial asymmetry in acceptance depending on the initial viewpoint of the respondent. Those who would grant amnesty are far more willing to accept a decision to withhold it than those who would deny amnesty are willing to accept a decision to award amnesty. Consider the African respondents. Substantial majorities of those who favor granting amnesty would accept a contrary Court decision. For example, even among those who strongly believe that Phillip should receive amnesty, 64.7 percent would acquiesce to a Constitutional Court decision to deny his application. However, among those who oppose amnesty, only a small minority would accept a contrary decision (12.1 percent among those who strongly oppose granting amnesty). This pattern holds for South Africans of every race.[33] Perhaps a Court decision to deny amnesty is not as objectionable as a decision to grant amnesty, although this asymmetry exists even among those without strong opinions on the issue of amnesty.

A second important conclusion supported by the data in this table is that, while some racial differences exist, they are not consistent across different types of amnesty attitudes and are therefore difficult to interpret. For instance, among those who strongly believe that amnesty should be granted, black South Africans tend to be more willing to accept the decision than others (64.7 percent versus, for example, 48.6 percent for whites). But among those who more moderately support granting amnesty, Africans are no more or less likely to accept a contrary decision (62.4 percent versus, for example, 67.7 percent for whites). Among those who believe strongly that amnesty should not be granted, racial differences are statistically significant but very small (η = .11). The patterns here are so inconsistent that it seems likely that variables other than race are the driving force at work in these data.

Nor does attitudinal intensity explain much of the variance in this table. We might expect that those holding strong attitudes would be *less* likely to acquiesce to the Court decision, but this is not uniformly the case, especially among those who would grant Phillip amnesty. Among whites, the hypothesis is strongly supported, but not among Colored people, and only partially among Africans. For instance, among Colored people who strongly prefer granting Phillip amnesty, 58.2 percent would accept the Court's decision, compared to 49.3 percent of Colored people without strong views. Some of these findings are probably influenced by the relatively small number of cases, and generally those holding strong views are somewhat less likely to accept a contrary Court decision, but the relationships are neither strong nor consistent.[34]

These findings may nonetheless have something to do with the degree to which the Court decision is judged to be objectionable. Recall the structure of the experiment leading up to the acquiescence question: the vignette posits that a member of a political group hated by the respondent is applying for amnesty. Consequently, those who believe amnesty ought to be granted are reacting to an admitted gross human rights abuse by a fellow who represents an entirely repugnant ideology, so it is perhaps not surprising that those who believe that Phillip should be granted amnesty would be unwilling to work to challenge a Court decision to deny it to him. It is hard enough in the first place to accept that amnesty ought to be granted. To be expected to mobilize to challenge a decision to deny amnesty to one who admits to gross human rights violations is, it appears, asking too much of most South Africans.

Those who would deny Phillip amnesty are faced with a more difficult Court decision, so it seems reasonable that they would be less likely to accept it. Challenging the decision may therefore be a function of the strength and consistency of their initial attitudes. Unlike those who would grant amnesty to a gross human rights violator, these South Africans experience no internal dissonance. They do not like what Phillip stands for, and his deed (to which he admits) is reprehensible, so they believe he should be punished and would deny him amnesty; only a small fraction would be willing to accept a Court decision to the contrary. The internal psychological dissonance experienced by those who would grant amnesty surely has something to do with their greater willingness to accept a contrary Court decision.

A Simulation of Reactions to a Court Decision

With the aid of a few assumptions, it is possible to simulate the effect of a Constitutional Court decision on South African public opinion. According to the initial preferences of our respondents, before the Court issued an opinion 61 percent opposed amnesty being given to Phillip, 7 percent were uncertain, and the remaining 32 percent favored granting him amnesty. With two simple assumptions, I can derive estimates of the total effect of a Court ruling:

1. Those who are uncertain before a Court ruling remain uncertain after the Court weighs in on the matter, and therefore they would not challenge a decision that they do not oppose.
2. Those who are faced with a Court decision *of which they approve* maintain their initial attitude on the question of whether Phillip should be granted amnesty, and therefore they would not challenge a decision that they do not oppose.

Neither of these assumptions is contentious; they simply assert that attitudes do not change if people get what they prefer from institutions or if they do not care about the issue, and that therefore people accept decisions with which they agree.

To estimate the effects of a Court ruling, I rely on the acquiescence replies when the respondents are told that the Court made an objectionable decision. If the Court were to decide in favor of granting amnesty, the 32 percent of the sample who agree with the outcome would not change their opinions; the 7 percent who were initially uncertain would surely accept the Court's decision, since they do not care about the issue; and as it turns out, 18 percent of those who oppose amnesty would acquiesce to the decision of the Court. Putting these various portions of the sample back together (and assuming that those who became uncertain of their views as a result of the ruling would not actively challenge the Court decision), a pro-amnesty ruling would lead to 52 percent of the South African population accepting the outcome and 48 percent remaining unwilling to accept the Court decision. Thus, the intervention of the Court boosts the portion of the public willing to tolerate amnesty from 39 percent to 52 percent.

A Court decision opposing amnesty would lift the percentage who are likely to accept the decision from 68 percent to a whopping 89 percent (since fully 63 percent of those who favor amnesty would accept a contrary Court decision). Were the Constitutional Court to rule against amnesty, virtually no opposition to the Court's ruling would persist.

Thus, public opinion on amnesty for gross human rights violators would be significantly swayed by the intervention of the Constitutional Court. Because of the large asymmetry between proponents and opponents of amnesty in their willingness to countenance a Court decision, the Court's effectiveness is itself asymmetrical. Still, were the Court to rule in favor of amnesty, a (slim) majority of South Africans would be willing to accept the outcome. Perhaps for many different reasons, the Court has at least a moderate ability to induce compliance with its controversial decisions.

Of course, not all acquiescence to the Court is due to the perception that the Court is a legitimate institution. Some may accept a contrary decision out of a sense of futility, some may desist from opposition out of a sense of personal inefficacy, and some may not care enough about the issue to pursue it. Within the theoretical framework advanced here, it is important to distinguish conceptually between legitimacy and acquiescence and to assess empirically the degree to which acquiescence is dependent on legitimacy. Assessing the legitimacy-acquiescence hypothesis is the purpose of the next section of this chapter.

The Legitimacy-Acquiescence Connection

To what degree is acquiescence attributable to the legitimacy of the Constitutional Court? Table 8.7 reports the bivariate connection between loyalty toward the Court and willingness to acquiesce to an unwanted decision by the Court. In each instance, I expect a positive correlation: those who extend more legitimacy to the Court are hypothesized to be more likely to acquiesce.

Only two of the coefficients in the table achieve statistical significance. The hypothesis is supported among those Africans and whites who initially favored denying amnesty to Phillip. For Colored people and those of Asian origin who also favored denying amnesty, legitimacy has nothing to do with whether they would accept a Court decision to grant amnesty.

Table 8.7 Bivariate Correlations Between Institutional Legitimacy and Acquiescence, by Race

	Initial Position	
	Deny Amnesty (Number of Cases)	Grant Amnesty (Number of Cases)
African	.13*** (966)	.01 (586)
White	.08* (623)	.05 (248)
Colored	−.07 (228)	.06 (122)
Asian origin	.02 (175)	.21 (44)

Source: Author's compilation from the 2001 Truth and Reconciliation Survey.
***p < .001; **p < .01; *p < .05

Among those who favored granting amnesty, only among South Africans of Asian origin does the legitimacy of the Court have much to do with acquiescence. The coefficient does not achieve statistical significance, owing to the small number of cases, but the relationship is sizable. An insignificant similar tendency exists among Colored people and whites, but no relationship exists among Africans. Generally, the coefficients in this table provide no consistent evidence that the Court profits in citizen acquiescence from its institutional legitimacy.[35]

These findings are consistent with those of our earlier research (Gibson and Caldeira 2003, 23) based on a similar survey conducted in South Africa in 1997. We concluded: "Acquiescence does not necessarily require legitimacy. . . . Many are willing to accept a Court decision irrespective of how much legitimacy they ascribe to the institution." Exactly the same conclusion characterizes this current survey.

Concluding Comments

The analysis in this chapter has not produced results that are particularly encouraging from the point of view of institutional reconciliation. To the extent that political reconciliation requires that all South Africans express a basic loyalty to the primary institutions of democracy, then reconciliation has a long way to go. South Africans do not strongly and uniformly recognize the legitimacy of their Parliament and Constitutional Court.

Perhaps it is not surprising that these two institutions have not yet attracted the loyalty of most South Africans. After all, South African democracy was not even a decade old at the time of the survey. These findings make particular sense if loyalty is treated as something like a "running tally"—a cumulation over time of likes and dislikes. Early in the tenure of an institution, people do not have stable views of it. Each impression, positive or negative, therefore has a disproportionate effect on institutional loyalty. That legitimacy would be heavily dependent at this stage of South Africa's democratic development on perceptions of the performance of an institution is therefore not shocking. In this sense, both the Parliament and the Constitutional Court are serving a probationary period. People have not come to reject these institutions as illegitimate. But neither have they embraced them as entirely worthy of respect and acquiescence.

The Constitutional Court took some highly controversial actions shortly after it was created.[36] According to Spitz and Chaskalson (2000), the Court was obliged to make quite salient disputatious decisions by the failure of those negotiating South Africa's transition to majority rule to resolve many fundamental issues. Spitz and Chaskalson refer to these as the "compromises and fudges" that provided the Court on the day of its inception with a panoply of crucial, unresolved political issues. They rightly note that this thrust a policymaking role on the Court immediately. The Court's active and explicit policymaking apparently led some to question whether it is really "right that a court would be adjudicating on such issues as the validity of the death penalty, abortion, culturally exclusive schooling, and the balance between central and provincial government" (Spitz and Chaskalson 2000, 418). Casting the Court in such a role inevitably generated challenges to its institutional legitimacy: "As soon as a court adjudicates on something as fundamental as the death penalty, it is difficult—especially for those who oppose its decisions—to avoid levelling the accusation that the court is a politicised forum. Such an accusation may not be healthy for the court in question or for the body politic as a whole" (418). My survey data seem to provide some evidence in support of the views of Spitz and Chaskalson.

Perhaps some institution at the beginning of a regime must sacrifice a portion of its legitimacy for the common good of the transition. Hard decisions must be made, courts are great places to get decisions out of the explicitly partisan arena, and perhaps it is better for a court to lose some of its legitimacy than for a more fundamental and salient political institution, like the parliament, to be deemed less legitimate. Since courts typically find it more difficult than legislatures to avoid making decisions, controversial decisions often find their way to the judicial doorstep. It is therefore not surprising that South Africa's Constitutional Court is not yet viewed as a distinctly legal, as opposed to political, institution.

One of the most important findings of this chapter is that support for the Parliament and the Constitutional Court are closely intertwined. It is not surprising that many view these two institutions similarly, since they are crucial linchpins in the new democratic structure. But the failure of the Constitutional Court to acquire a distinctive legal identity is worrisome. Courts profit most when they are seen as unique, as "above" ordinary politics. The Constitutional Court seems to have had little success at conveying this message to the South African mass public, and its legitimacy has therefore suffered.

That white South Africans are not inordinately supportive of the Constitutional Court is an important finding. The simple view that minorities are attracted to minoritarian institutions turns out to be too simplistic. Instead, whites find little solace in either the Parliament or the Court, and few seem to believe that the South African judiciary is an effective institution for blocking majority preferences. The feared favoritism toward whites within the judiciary seems not to have materialized, at least not in the perceptions of whites themselves.

The findings on acquiescence are also of some importance. To begin, acquiescence is far more widespread than would be predicted on the basis of legitimacy alone. People accept institutional outputs for many reasons; legitimacy is only one of those reasons. This finding should give pause to those who would *equate* legitimacy and acquiescence.

And of course it should be noted that the acquiescence experiment represents a difficult and perhaps extreme case. On most issues addressed by courts and parliaments, people care little about the outcome and accept the policy outputs of those institutions. My experiment addresses an instance in which court policy is directly contrary to the expressed preferences of the individual and in which there is no slippage due to people being unaware of or confused about the specific nature of institutional policy. The experiment thus mimics the reality of controversial judicial decisions, even if it does not address the routine business of judicial institutions. There can be little doubt that the routine business of the South African Court is routinely greeted with acceptance and acquiescence (or even ignorance).

An institution's reservoir of goodwill must be drawn upon, however, when it is called upon to make displeasing decisions. For instance, this survey has shown that a decision by the Court protecting the political rights of a widely disliked political minority (like the AWB or the IFP) would not be welcomed by most South Africans. Indeed, most South Africans would endorse depriving such groups of many basic human rights. Could the Court make a pro–human rights ruling stick? Would South Africans accept such a decision, or would they instead mobilize in an attack on the institution? The survey data do not indicate that the Court would be without any allies, but those who would penalize the institution for unpopular rulings considerably outnumber those who would stand by the Court even when they disagree with its opinion.

Southern Africa has recently witnessed just what a court can suffer when it has insufficient legitimacy to serve as a buffer against a strong and determined political authority. In Zimbabwe, Robert Mugabe has been successful at rendering subservient the once-independent high court. Judicial independence is a fragile commodity, and there are many devices through which the independence of courts can be circumscribed. Legitimacy is perhaps an institution's most effective resource for fending off attacks on its authority.

Without a reservoir of goodwill, an institution is tied to the apron strings of public opinion, and making hard judicial choices becomes even harder. If the South African Constitutional Court is to be able to fulfill its role as a protector of the integrity of the democratic political system, greater effort must be expended to enhance its institutional legitimacy.

Chapter 9

Lessons for South Africa's Future and for the World

This book provides evidence on three important sets of questions. The first addresses the issue of whether the truth and reconciliation process in South Africa succeeded in any meaningful way. The second set of questions concerns more theoretical issues, including the processes of interpersonal and intergroup relations. And the final group of questions revolves around the likelihood that South Africa's democratic transition will be successfully consolidated. In this final chapter, I address each of these in turn.

The Success of the Truth and Reconciliation Process in South Africa

Few would quibble with the assertion that I have attempted a most difficult task in this book in trying to draw conclusions about whether reconciliation has come to South Africa and whether the truth process has contributed to any such reconciliation. Reconciliation is a big question that perhaps can be addressed only through longitudinal analysis extending over a decade or more. Thus, I readily concede that my approach to truth and reconciliation examines only a narrow slice of the transitional pie and that the conclusions that can be drawn from this analysis are consequently limited.

Nonetheless, the enormity and difficulty of the question should not be allowed to stifle attempts at assessing whether truth has contributed to reconciliation. Instead of putting the question on hold for ten or twenty years, social science can provide at least some insights into the contemporary connections between truth and reconciliation. Those who wonder whether the truth process contributed to South Africa's transition can either flip a coin (heads—yes, tails—no) or rely on admittedly imperfect findings such as those adduced in this book. Thus, while trying to avoid becoming too speculative, I attempt here to move slightly beyond the survey data (which tell us about individual South Africans in 2001) to address the nature of and prospects for reconciliation in South Africa.

At some level, the truth and reconciliation process clearly succeeded in South Africa. In the early 1990s many feared a civil war would engulf the country, and political violence was widespread. Even the relatively more optimistic feared massive white flight and destabilization. And with the ANC holding nearly enough power to change the constitution unilaterally and at will, some prognosticators dreaded the prospect of South Africa going the way of the many failed democracies of Africa.

None of these things happened. It thus appears certain that something altered the course of the South African transition.

If reconciliation means nothing more than accepting the Truth and Reconciliation Commission's truth about the past, then at least some degree of reconciliation has indeed taken place in South Africa. Although my analysis certainly introduces caveats, the fact that large majorities of blacks, Colored people, and those of Asian origin accept that apartheid was a crime against humanity is a profoundly important finding. Apartheid was not a noble experiment, and few in South Africa believe that it was. Whether these beliefs are due to the TRC cannot be clearly established with the data at hand, but I believe, and the data suggest, that the TRC's revelations played some role in producing a common understanding among all South Africans of the country's apartheid past.

This aspect of South Africa's collective memory is certainly important, but perhaps not as important as the belief that both sides in the struggle over apartheid did horrible things. I have argued that this is the most significant and consequential message of the truth and reconciliation process. Accepting the viewpoint that both sides did terrible things is perhaps the first tentative step on the road toward reconciliation. As has been asserted, it is difficult indeed to reconcile with infinite evil, especially if one is perched on a mountain of unlimited rectitude. But to try to reach an accommodation with those who are quite but not entirely bad is a much less difficult task, especially once one realizes that one's own side is responsible for evil deeds as well. It is the moderating truth of the truth and reconciliation process that I believe has contributed to reconciliation: not all truth, but truth that tends to challenge dogmatic assertions about the virtues of the parties engaged in the struggle over apartheid.

The central contention of this book is that the truth and reconciliation process itself contributed to reconciliation in South Africa. This is a strong claim, one that many skeptics are not prepared to accept, so it is perhaps worthwhile to present a brief reconsideration of the empirical evidence on levels of reconciliation in contemporary South Africa.

Overall Levels of Reconciliation in Contemporary South Africa

I conceptualize a reconciled South African as one who trusts and is respectful of those of different races, who is tolerant of her or his political enemies, who is committed to protecting human rights through the rule of law, and who extends legitimacy to the political institutions of the new South Africa. How many such people are there in South Africa? How reconciled is contemporary South Africa?

Summary score cards are always misleading to at least some degree, but at the same time, people often demand such summaries when addressing complex questions such as these. Table 9.1 attempts to sum up the empirical results on the four types of reconciliation investigated in this book. So as to provide at least a smidgen of rigor for these global assessments, I also report for each group the percentages for each subdimension that scored as at least somewhat reconciled.[1]

In terms of the individual components of reconciliation, none of the racial groups is very reconciled at all when it comes to political tolerance; all are at least somewhat reconciled when it comes to institutional legitimacy. Levels of reconciliation in terms of interracial attitudes and support for a human rights culture lie in between those for legitimacy and tolerance.

Table 9.1 Summary Levels of Reconciliation Among the Four South African Racial Groups, 2001

Dimension of Reconciliation[a]	African	White	Colored	Asian Origin
Interracial reconciliation	Not very	Somewhat	Somewhat	Somewhat
Support for a human rights culture	Not very	Somewhat	Somewhat	Somewhat
Political tolerance	Not very	Not very	Not very	Not very
Institutional legitimacy	Somewhat	Somewhat	Somewhat	Somewhat
	Somewhat or Highly Reconciled			
Interracial reconciliation	37.2%	57.4%	71.7%	59.2%
Support for a human rights culture	44.9	77.0	62.4	54.3
Political tolerance	21.4	34.5	26.2	25.3
Institutional legitimacy	81.2	62.3	77.5	66.5

Source: Author's compilation from the 2001 Truth and Reconciliation Survey.
[a]The possible scores on each dimension of reconciliation are: highly reconciled, somewhat reconciled, not very reconciled, and hardly reconciled at all.

Based on a summary of these summary scores, one might draw the following conclusions about the level of reconciliation prevalent among South Africa's various racial groups: Africans—not very reconciled; whites—somewhat reconciled; Colored South Africans—somewhat reconciled; and South Africans of Asian origin—somewhat reconciled. That is, using a mean score summarizing *all four subdimensions* of reconciliation (data not shown), Colored South Africans are the most reconciled, followed by whites, then South Africans of Asian origin, and finally Africans. After categorizing that mean, I find the following percentages of each group are at least somewhat reconciled: 33 percent of Africans, 56 percent of whites, 59 percent of Colored people, and 48 percent of those of Asian origin (see figure 9.1). Thus, whites, Colored people, and those of Asian origin hold similar, moderately reconciled views, but Africans are significantly less reconciled. In terms of the various ethnic and linguistic groups, the most reconciled are English-speaking Colored people (75 percent), followed by English-speaking whites (64 percent). The least reconciled South Africans are North Sotho–speaking blacks (17 percent). Thus, enormous variability exists in levels of reconciliation across the various groups.

In South Africa as a whole, which of course comprises mainly Africans, the data reveal that about 44 percent of the population is at least somewhat reconciled (data not shown). What overall conclusions about reconciliation can be drawn from this figure?

No comparable data exist to indicate levels of reconciliation during the rule of apartheid. It seems entirely reasonable to assume, however, that reconciliation as defined in this research (racial and political tolerance, support for human rights, and willingness to extend legitimacy to political institutions) was considerably lower than 44 percent. That nearly one-half of the South African population expresses some degree of reconciliation within less than a decade after the formal demise of apartheid represents, from my perspective, an unexpectedly high level of reconciliation. Reconciliation seems to have made inroads into a sizable portion of the South African population.

Still, it would be hard to characterize South Africa as a widely or deeply reconciled society. Progress has been made since the transi-

Figure 9.1 Racial Differences Among South Africans in Overall Levels of Reconciliation

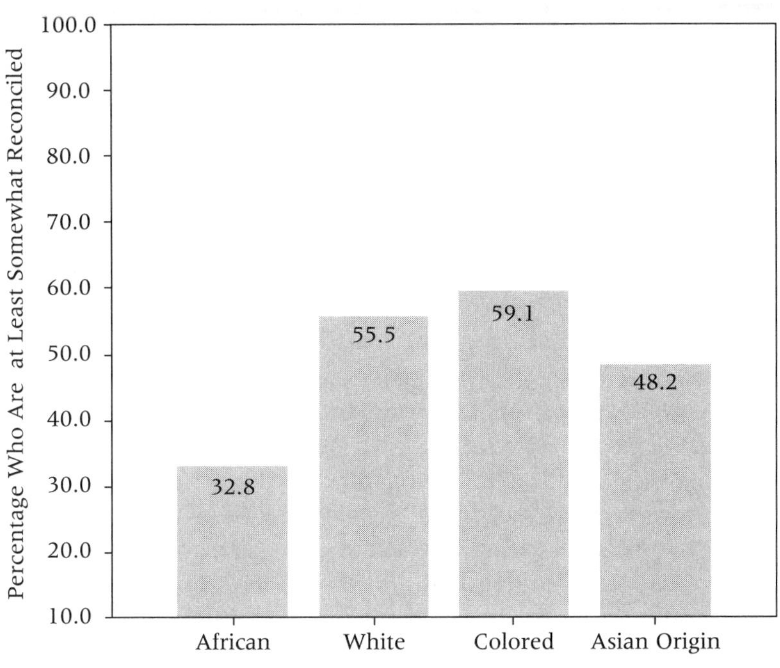

Source: Author's compilation from the 2001 Truth and Reconciliation Survey.

tion, but a long road must be traversed before reconciliation predominates in all sectors of the South African population.

Did Truth Contribute to Reconciliation?

I need not repeat the many caveats associated with drawing conclusions about the causal relationship between truth and reconciliation. I shall, however, risk drawing a clear conclusion about the success of South Africa's truth and reconciliation process.

Many people associated with the truth and reconciliation process believe in the TRC's moderate view of responsibility for the abuses conducted during the struggle over apartheid, but few are as clearly associated with it as Desmond Tutu. Perhaps then the effectiveness of South Africa's truth and reconciliation process should be laid at the feet of Archbishop Tutu.

Another explanation for the successful transition is certainly Nelson Mandela. The most admired man in the world, Mandela's message of nonracialism and reconciliation dominated the early days of the transition. Few doubt that had a different message been broadcast by the ANC leadership, a different outcome could easily have resulted.

Still, it is difficult to imagine that the influence of leaders like Mandela and Tutu is the sole ingredient contributing to reconciliation in South Africa. Throughout this book, I have argued that a variety of other factors have been influential as well.

The data demonstrate that truth and reconciliation do indeed go together and are compatible with the view that the collective memory produced by the truth and reconciliation process has contributed to the levels of reconciliation achieved in South Africa. I reach this conclusion because I find only slight racial differences across groups in understandings about the country's apartheid past, and because for blacks, whites (especially), Colored people, and (to a limited degree) those of Asian origin, *those who are more accepting of the TRC's version of the truth are more likely to be reconciled.* Using the index summarizing all four subdimensions of reconciliation, the correlations between truth acceptance and reconciliation are:

Africans Truth acceptance—.23 → Reconciliation

Whites Truth acceptance—.53 → Reconciliation

Colored People Truth acceptance—.34 → Reconciliation

Asian Origin Truth acceptance—.09 → Reconciliation

I resist pursuing a more complicated analysis of this relationship, since the reconciliation index is so highly aggregated (and therefore represents many different types of attitudes toward reconciliation). There can be little doubt from these data, however, that truth acceptance and reconciliation, particularly for whites, are to some degree positively intertwined.

Nevertheless, the issue of causality remains. It may well be that those already predisposed to reconciliation are more likely to accept the findings of the TRC and that consequently the causal flow is not as I have designated it here. With cross-sectional data, the question of causality can never be definitively answered. This book's statistical analysis of the causal flow (for example, two-stage least squares) supports the view that truth caused reconciliation, not vice versa, but causal inferences can never be more than inferences in which we have more or less confidence. Nonetheless, and at a minimum, these data entitle me to conclude that *accepting the TRC's truth certainly did not contribute to "irreconciliation"* (that is, no negative relationship exists), as so many feared, and that the bulk of the available statistical evidence is compatible with the view that truth did indeed contribute to producing more reconciled South Africans.

The Generalizability of the Findings

I do not argue on the basis of this analysis that truth inevitably leads to reconciliation. The most puissant characteristic of the collective memory created by South Africa's TRC was the commission's willingness to attribute blame to all parties in the struggle over apartheid. Because all sides did horrible things during the struggle, all sides are compromised to some degree, and legitimacy adheres to the complaints of one's enemies about abuses. All South Africans were victimized by apartheid. Whites cannot believe today that their apartheid state committed no atrocities against blacks. Blacks cannot believe today that the liberation forces did not unfairly injure both black and white South Africans. Once one concedes that the other side has legitimate grievances, it becomes easier to accept their claims and ultimately to affirm the new political dispensation in South Africa.

A different truth process might well have led to an entirely different outcome. A truth process that points to unilateral blame is not one likely to produce reconciliation. Discussing truth and reconciliation attempts in other countries, Pumla Gobodo-Madikizela (2003, 171) asserts:

> Their tendency to focus only on perpetrators on one side of a political conflict may, however, disrupt whatever fragile unity might be forged by two sides previously at war with each other. This could then fuel the anger of one side, which may feel that the law is biased against it as the "oppressor" group, when in fact there is often a record of human rights crimes committed by the oppressed group as well. The issue is not a simple one, for in recognizing that both sides produced victims, one may seem to be applying the same moral standards to the actions of the oppressor and those of the group that was fighting to end its oppression. But in societies trying to break the cycle of hatred and revenge, it is important first to acknowledge, as did the TRC, that human rights abuses were committed by both sides, and then to find an effective way of moving society forward.

Obviously, the truth that can be produced by a truth and reconciliation process is constrained to some degree by reality; not just any collective memory can be fabricated out of any given set of historical circumstances. But truth commissions can seek to act impartially, allocating blame wherever it may lie, or truth commissions can engage in a form of "victors' justice" in which the victors are held to lower human rights standards than the vanquished. The South African TRC sought the path of impartiality (dubbed "poisonous evenhandedness" by its critics), choosing to cast the net of blame widely. It is unclear that the circumstances that gave the TRC such authority and motivated the leaders of the TRC to set reconciliation as their consummate goal can be easily reproduced elsewhere.[2]

To the extent that truth processes involve granting amnesty, they begin with a debilitating "justice deficit." This deficit is created by exonerating guilty people, a particularly bitter pill for victors to swallow. In the South African case, this problem was exacerbated by revelations during the truth and reconciliation process that the apartheid state had engaged in far more barbarous and far-flung (and illegal) human rights abuses than even most blacks had imagined. For many who thought they had won the war, losing the peace was a bitter experience.

This research suggests that another effective but idiosyncratic element of South Africa's truth and reconciliation process was its emphasis on nonretributive forms of justice. Even despite granting amnesty to gross human rights violators, the truth and reconciliation process in South Africa generated justice that appeared to satisfy many—the "justice deficit" was overcome. The justice was in part distributive (too small a part, in the view of many) but was also procedural and restorative. Allowing people to come forward and tell their stories—and allowing South Africans to hear these stories, in all their gory, human detail—had a tremendous effect on how people reacted to the truth and reconciliation process. And undoubtedly some perpetrators expressed heartfelt remorse and apologized for their actions in terms that were widely understood to be sincere. The truth and reconciliation process contemplated that distributive justice (compensation) might ameliorate the pain of failing to receive retributive justice. But few who designed and participated in the process anticipated that procedural and restorative justice could have such salutary consequences. Other truth processes have most likely foundered on their inability to generate compensatory forms of justice capable of mollifying citizens and getting them to accept the injustices forced on them by the transitional process.

South Africa's truth process had, I believe, other characteristics that contributed to its success. Because the process was open, humanized, and procedurally fair, the TRC was able to penetrate the consciousness of virtually all segments of the South African populace with its message. Through numerous hearings in every part of the country, including the hinterland, the truth and reconciliation process made known, in excruciating detail, the suffering of thousands of individual South Africans. The atrocities committed during the struggle over apartheid were not abstractions but deeply human losses that resonated with South Africans of every color.

Furthermore, it seems likely that the *lack of* legalistic proceedings made the hearings more accessible to ordinary people. Although litigation sometimes forced the TRC process to adopt fair proceedings, it would have been difficult to observe that process and conclude that victims, witnesses, and perpetrators were treated unfairly (even if there were some complaints about the relative amount of attention given to abuses by the various sides in the struggle). The TRC probably succeeded in part because its processes were transparent and fair and understandable to ordinary people.

Finally, the roles of Tutu and Mandela were no doubt instrumental in getting people to accept the TRC's collective memory and therefore to get on with reconciliation. Tutu's message of forgiveness, though irritating to many, set a compelling frame of reference for moving beyond the atrocities uncovered. Mandela's constant and insistent calls for reconciliation, coupled with his willingness to accept the findings of the TRC (even when the ANC did not), were surely persuasive for many South Africans. The two giants of the anti-apartheid struggle defused and delegitimized much of the potential criticism of the truth and reconciliation process.

The TRC did not engage in a "witch hunt," as some extreme segments of the white Afrikaans-speaking population alleged. Because it did not, its findings and conclusions were not widely rejected, and so most South Africans had little justification for repudiating the collective memory out of hand. Whether this process can be replicated in other parts of the globe is unclear—and certainly unanswered by this research.

Theoretical Contributions of This Research

This research has not clearly articulated a theory of reconciliation. Such a theory is generally not likely to emerge, because reconciliation is a syndrome of attitudes, not a discrete value. Like treatments for the common cold, no single therapy is likely to produce more reconciled South Africans. I therefore cannot claim an overarching theory of cultural transition and change based on reconciliation.

Nonetheless, the analysis reported in this book has contributed to several bodies of theory. I count the first theoretical offering of this research as my general conceptual and operational approach to understanding reconciliation. The concept has earlier been used in a variety of ways, and often without clear conceptual content. This research articulates and expands the concept, incorporating several extant bodies of theory (such as tolerance). Even those who disagree with this approach will find it exceedingly easy to know exactly what I mean by the term "reconciliation."

But the more important contribution of my approach to reconciliation is in the operationalizations of the concept. I treat reconciliation as multidimensional and give each subdimension clear conceptual and operational content. Without this rigorous and systematic approach to measuring reconciliation, my research would have failed completely. Though some may prefer alternative views of the concept, few would question whether the subdimensions I incorporate are of great relevance to South African reconciliation. Measurement is often not given its due in political science; if nothing else, this research provides replicable (valid and reliable), quantitative indicators of reconciliation.

In a similar fashion, this project has contributed to theories of collective memory. Aside from the work of Howard Schuman and his colleagues, collective memory is not typically a concept given rigorous and clear meaning. Here, I am aided greatly by the explicit attempt of South Africa's TRC to create a collective memory. Thus, my approach has been to measure the degree to which individual South Africans participate in the truth as proclaimed by the commission (not the truth as I might see it). Truth acceptance is treated here not as an element of reconciliation but rather as a predictor of reconciliation; nevertheless, the finding that the various racial groups in South Africa do not differ greatly in their understanding of the country's apartheid past is a finding of considerable importance. Perhaps future researchers will be more self-conscious about specifying exactly what they mean when they speak of collective understandings of history.

Much of this research has addressed the legacy of apartheid in South Africa. Rather than assuming that people (and peoples) had similar experiences under apartheid and therefore hold comparable attitudes, I have asked the respondents how they fared under the system and how they look back on it. My findings have often been startling: black South Africans do not uniformly condemn apartheid, either in its principles or in its practices. Apartheid treated individuals—not just groups—differently, so it is not surprising that experiences and judgments of that system differ. Understanding just how complicated apartheid was—and is—is an important theoretical and empirical contribution of this research.

Beyond rigorous and comprehensive measurement, this research contributes to several different bodies of theory. Most important and obvious perhaps is contact theory. One significant cause of irreconciliation in South Africa is racial isolation. Indeed, that black South Africans have so little contact with whites is an important finding of my research. The significance of the discovery is underscored by the fact that interracial contact contributes substantially to interracial reconciliation among all races. In a sense, this finding is not revolutionary, since it has been demonstrated in earlier research. But confirming contact theory in a multiracial and repressive political system like South Africa is important documentation of the generalizability of that venerable theory.

Many elements of theories of political tolerance have also been confirmed. For instance, intolerance flows directly—indeed, perhaps "naturally"—from perceptions that other political groups are threatening. Though this relationship is strong, a peculiar finding is that levels of perceived threat have declined in the last few years in South Africa but tolerance has not increased. Clearly, there is more to intolerance than threat alone.

Perhaps one of the most important findings of this portion of my research has to do with identifying different subdimensions of threat perceptions and documenting that intolerance is more likely to be a consequence of perceived threats *to the group* than of threats *to the individual*. Moreover, though I predicted that the perceived power (or power potential) of the group is an important component of threat perceptions, the data do not support the expectation. Thus, my research makes obvious that threat is a multidimensional concept and that different aspects of threat have different consequences for political tolerance and reconciliation. This is a more variegated understanding of threat perceptions than has appeared in past research on political intolerance.

When it comes to social identity theory, perhaps my contributions are more in terms of unearthing new unanswered questions than in confirming hypotheses drawn from extant theory. The data have shown that South Africans do indeed identify with groups and that they derive important psychological value from such identifications. Those more strongly attached to groups are more likely to hold attitudes about the need for group maintenance (for example, through solidarity) than those with weak attachments. All of these findings then are compatible with social identity theory.

The major conundrum for that theory has to do with the hypothesis that in-group identification leads to rejection of out-groups. The data provide no support whatsoever for this expectation: for instance, those who strongly identify with their group are no more or less threatened by their political enemies and therefore are neither more nor less tolerant of them. Indeed, the data suggest that South Africans hold multiple identities simultaneously and that identity is thus not a limited and scarce form of capital. Future research must examine carefully the conditions under which in-group sympathy is associated with out-group antipathy: the relationship is far from natural, automatic, and inevitable.

Legitimacy theory has not performed especially well in the South African context, though perhaps for entirely understandable reasons. South Africa's Constitutional Court and Parliament do not have wide stores of institutional legitimacy, and perhaps because these are young institutions, what legitimacy they have does not readily translate into acquiescence. I have argued that legitimacy attitudes are not efficacious in South Africa, by which I mean that they have not acquired the affective mass that makes them so important in established democracies. Because institutional legitimacy has been so lacking in the past, under apartheid, whether people accept an institutional decision with which they disagree depends very little on the legitimacy of the policymaking institutions. These conclusions are contrary to findings from more established democracies and therefore strongly suggest the need for additional research on how institutional legitimacy is built or acquired in transitional regimes.

In terms of theories of human rights, this research has produced several innovations. When most scholars think about human rights, they think about institutions, such as laws, constitutions, and courts. I certainly share this concern, as with my examination of the legitimacy of South Africa's Constitutional Court. But the sanctity of human rights cannot be "guaranteed" by institutions alone. Instead, human rights can be secured only when ordinary people come to judge the violation of human rights as illegitimate and unacceptable. A crucial element of a democratic political system is according legitimacy to the rule of law, an essential building block of a political culture respectful of human rights.

Of course, few would accept that the state, or fellow citizens, should be allowed to violate the rights of citizens indiscriminately. Perhaps nearly all South Africans reject the lawless means by which the apartheid state sought to maintain its position of political power. But that does not mean that human rights are necessarily secure in contemporary South African culture.

Instead, the issues of human rights violations in South Africa in the twenty-first century have little to do with apartheid. Many fear instead that crime and terrorism are the vehicles through which South Africans will come to support the suspension of basic rights such as governance by the rule of law. My findings suggest otherwise; at present, fear of crime does *not* drive attitudes toward the rule of law. This finding should encourage supporters of a human rights culture in South Africa, although a great deal more research must be conducted on the question of how citizens come to value human rights and the circumstances under which they are willing to trade such rights for other valued goods. Perhaps this research is a significant start in thinking about support for human rights as an attribute of the political culture of a country.

A panoply of theoretical questions remain unanswered by this research. Certainly, the causal linkage between truth and reconciliation needs further exploration. The most effective and powerful research design would be a longitudinal one, but much can be learned about the processes linking these two variables through experimental research (perhaps patterned after that utilized in this survey). I have placed a considerable amount of emphasis on the moderating effect of the truth as produced by the TRC, but I have adduced no dispositive evidence that this is the precise process leading to reconciliation. Perhaps creative experimentation can provide further purchase on the causal mechanisms involved.

Indeed, many of the processes addressed here are much in need of dynamic analysis. For instance, how do citizens convert their satisfaction with the performance of an institution into more obdurate loyalty toward that institution (legitimacy)? Understanding this process can advance only with longitudinal analysis.

Perhaps the single most significant set of unanswered questions emerging from this research is associated with social identity theory. There is widespread agreement in the social sciences that Tajfel got most of the elements of the theory correct, and there can be little doubt that his contributions to our understanding of identities are enormous. But puzzles remain. In this instance, group identities do not undermine national identities. On the contrary, there seems to be a generalized propensity of individuals to identify with groups, such that those who identify more with their "tribe" *also* identify more with their nation-state. Identities are not locked in zero-sum competition with each other. And as some social identity theorists have recognized, in-group identities do not inevitably give rise to out-group antipathies. Much is perhaps understood about how individuals come to identify with groups, but little is understood about how (and the conditions under which) these identities contribute to the definition of political foes, and especially to the willingness to support repression (or worse) against those foes. That findings from South Africa, a cradle of multiculturalism, would contribute to confusing social identity theory is perhaps not surprising. More research must be conducted in the hotbeds of multiculturalism found throughout the world if we are to unravel the many puzzles associated with social identity theory.

A final point to reemphasize is that social science can make important contributions to understanding the dynamics of reconciliation in South Africa. Some might be critical of the empirical meaning I have given to reconciliation in this book, but even if my approach is not the most useful, other rigorous, empirical strategies are possible and necessary. Establishing causality is the most difficult task for all of the sciences, so it is not surprising that some of my conclusions about causality are tentative and constrained. But the questions facing South Africa are too important to turn over to pundits and soothsayers, just as they are too important for social scientists to ignore.

Reconciliation and the Consolidation of the Democratic Transition in South Africa

In the end, this research has actually proven little about processes of democratization. I posit that reconciliation contributes to the consolidation of democratic change, but I certainly have not established that connection empirically. No cross-sectional study can provide such proof. Nor have I the hubris to suggest or imply that the future of South African democracy can be foretold simply from the results of a survey of the attitudes and views of ordinary citizens. Whether democratic reform is consolidated depends on an assortment of other knotty and complicated factors.

Indeed, I must acknowledge that the individual-level reconciliation I analyze in this book ignores macrolevel processes. For instance, the intolerance of citizens may be neutralized by strong (and legitimate) political institutions capable of serving as guardians of democracy. Agreements among political elites may foreclose opportunities for interracial coalitions, irrespective of the desires of ordinary citizens. South African democracy depends on more than the degree to which each South African is reconciled, even if such microreconciliation is an important determinant of the likelihood of consolidating South Africa's democratic transition.

How much reconciliation is necessary for the consolidation of democratic reform in South Africa? This question is difficult, if not impossible, to answer with any degree of certitude. I can, however, sketch the outlines of a theory specifying how reconciliation both helps and hinders the practice of democratic politics.

The conventional wisdom is that democracies require that people form political allegiances based on *interests,* not identities. To the extent that group boundaries are rigidly established and group members perceive themselves as having little in common with people of other groups, multigroup, interest-based coalitions are difficult to assemble. It is for this reason that I have often considered in this book whether various attitudes, perceptions, and values held by South Africans are based in race. From this perspective, irreconciliation clearly undermines the formation of like-minded coalitions, which are essential to democracy.

Reconciliation contributes to democracy by breaking down the walls built around racial groups, making interracial cooperation possible. To the extent that South Africans view those of other races with suspicion, it is unlikely that such cooperation will emerge. Perhaps one hopeful scenario is that tolerance of different groups will lead to a recognition of a certain degree of commonality of interests, which in turn will contribute to the respect and understanding that facilitates political coalitions. It is surely too soon to predict that truly multiracial political movements will form in South Africa—and ironically, the most likely such candidate today is the nascent coalition of Afrikaans-speaking whites and Colored people—but without some degree of interracial accommodation, I confidently predict that the South African experiment in democratic change will founder.

I must acknowledge at least one pathway through which reconciliation might *undermine* the consolidation of democratic change rather than contribute to it. Democracies thrive on conflict; they are at their best when citizens and groups disagree with one another, when pluralism prevails. To the extent that reconciliation generates pressures toward consensus, pressures that delegitimize difference and differing points of view, reconciliation does not serve democracy. In a liberal democracy people do not have to agree with one another; they do not even have to respect the views of others. Instead, they must agree to disagree and accept a set of institutional and cultural norms that allow all competitors to enter the marketplace of ideas. If reconciliation means treating strong political differences and animosities as somehow illegitimate, then reconciliation will not have served South Africa's democratic transition.[3]

In the end, South Africa is an African nation, a breed of states not notable for their success at democratic governance. The threats to successful democratization are numerous and formidable (as in the pressing need for economic equality and wealth redistribution). But if South Africans can come to accept those of other races—or at least to put up with their political foes—within the context of a culture in which support for human rights is widespread and political institutions are empowered with the legitimacy necessary to protect those human rights, then perhaps the past can at last be overcome and democracy will prevail in the land once dominated by apartheid.

Appendix A: The Design of the Survey

The research reported in this book is based on a survey of a representative sample of the South African population conducted at the close of 2000 and the beginning of 2001. The survey was managed by Decision Surveys International (DSI) in Johannesburg under the direction of Carroll Moore and Mokhele Makhothi. The purpose of this appendix is to provide some details on the technical aspects of the survey.

The fieldwork for the project began in November 2000, and "mop-up" interviews were completed by February 2001. The sample is representative of the entire South African population (eighteen years old and older), and a total of 3,727 interviews were completed.

The sampling was divided into two parts: a primary sample, including South Africans of all races, and a boost sample of white South Africans. In the main sample, 3,139 interviews were completed. The boost sample was composed only of white South Africans, with a control for language (English versus Afrikaans). A total of 588 additional whites were interviewed.

The overall response rate for the survey was approximately 87 percent (after treating "break-offs" as unsuccessful interviews). The main reason for failing to complete the interview was inability to contact the respondent; refusal to be interviewed accounted for approximately 27 percent of the failed interviews. From the response rate alone, the representativeness of the sample seems assured.

Such a high rate of response can be attributed to the general willingness of the South African population to be interviewed, the large number of callbacks we employed, and the use of an incentive for participating in the interview.[1]

Weighting and Poststratification

Because the various racial and linguistic groups were not selected in proportion to their size in the South African population, it is necessary to weight the data according to the inverse of the probability of selection. In addition, we have applied poststratification weights to the final data to make the sample more representative of the South African population.

After correcting for unequal probabilities of selection, we poststratified the data according to three variables: size of place of residence, respondent's age, and respondent's race. Size of place of residence is a trichotomy: metro areas; other urban areas (cities, large towns, and small towns); and rural areas (villages, farms, and kraals). Age categories were defined as eighteen to twenty-four years old, thirty-five to forty-four years old, forty-five to fifty-four years old, fifty-five to sixty-four years old, and sixty-five years old and older. The four major racial groups in South Africa were used. After trimming the weight and adjusting the weights to the actual number of completed interviews (3,727), the poststratification weight variable ranges from .29 to 2.02.[2]

The Survey Instrument

The questionnaire we used in this survey was designed in part on the basis of focus groups we conducted in mid-2000. The purpose of the focus groups was to observe how ordinary people think and speak about truth and reconciliation in South Africa (on the methodology of focus groups, see Delli Carpini and Williams 1994). We sought to capture their language, understand the degree of salience of different aspects of the process, and test in an extremely preliminary way ideas about what constitutes a "reconciled" South African.

During June 2000, six focus groups were held, two each in Cape Town, Durban, and Johannesburg. Focus-group participants, who of course could not constitute a representative sample of any population, were recruited by DSI staff and paid to participate in the discussions. The focus groups were held at the DSI offices. The focus-group participants were recruited so as to make each group racially homogeneous. The criteria used to recruit individuals were:

1. *Race*: We decided that the most frank discussions of the truth and reconciliation process would be held among South Africans of the same race.

2. *Gender*: All focus groups were mixed-gender except one. We empaneled an all-female African group so as to be able to focus on the specific experiences of women under apartheid. Most of those who directly experienced human rights violations under apartheid were men; the injuries to women were of a more limited nature. We sought to get the respondents to discuss this topic.

3. *Religiosity*: Because we felt we already had reasonable insight into how religious people address processes of reconciliation, we overrepresented relatively less religious South Africans in the focus groups.

All of the moderators were female. With one exception, the moderators of the focus groups matched the race of the participants. The exception was a white moderator used with the Indian South Africans in Durban.

The focus groups lasted approximately two hours. They were filmed and observed through a one-way mirror. The focus groups were recorded on video and audio tape, and the conversations were transcribed. In a postdeliberation questionnaire, the respondents judged both the group and their own participation as honest and open. We treat the focus groups as a pretest of some of the ideas that the survey was designed to address.

After we finished analyzing the focus groups, we produced a full draft of the questionnaire. The questionnaire was first prepared in English and then translated into Afrikaans, Zulu, Xhosa, North Sotho, South Sotho, Tswana, and Tsonga. The methodology of creating a multilingual questionnaire follows closely that recommended by Richard Brislin (1970). After producing an English-language version of the questionnaire, trained translators (employed by the survey firm) translated the questionnaire, and then another translator translated the translated questionnaire back into English. The "input" and the "output" English were then reconciled in a large and lengthy meeting involving all of the translators, back-translators, and survey firm staff (and me). At these meetings a version of the questionnaire was prepared for the pretesting.

A formal pretest of the questionnaire was conducted, based on 59 interviews. On the basis of statistical analysis of the pretest data, the questionnaire was further revised. Virtually all revisions involved deleting items from the pretest instrument.

The Respondents and the Interviewers

Interviews were completed with 3,727 individuals, including 2,004 Africans, 991 whites, 487 Colored people, and 245 South Africans of Asian origin. The average length of interview was 84 minutes. (The median was 80 minutes, with a standard deviation of 22.2 minutes and a range from 30 to 235 minutes.) Interviews were conducted in the language of choice of the respondent, with interviews fielded in eight languages. A large plurality of the interviews were conducted in English (44.5 percent).

Most of the interviewers were females, and interviewers of every race were employed in the project. The vast majority of respondents were interviewed by an interviewer of their own race. The percentage of same-race interviews for each of the racial groups was 99.8 percent for Africans, 98.7 percent for whites, 71.5 percent for Colored people, and 73.9 percent for those of Asian origin. Only four black respondents were interviewed by a white interviewer; no whites were interviewed by blacks. Roughly half of the Colored respondents not interviewed by a Colored interviewer were interviewed by a white interviewer, and the other half by a black interviewer. None of the respondents of Asian origin were interviewed by a white interviewer. Thus, the overwhelming pattern in the interviews was to have same-race interviewers, and where we deviated from that pattern, only 75 interviews involved a white interviewer interviewing a nonwhite respondent.

Given that two-thirds of our interviewers were female, same-gender interviews were not as common. For female respondents,

68.0 percent of the interviews were by females; for males, the percentage was roughly the same (67.2 percent).

Interviewers

A total of 149 interviewers were employed in this project. The average number of interviews completed was 25, with a standard deviation of 19 and a median of 20. The number of interviews ranged from 1 to 81. Two-thirds (67.6 percent) of the interviewers were females, and 74.3 percent were black South Africans.

Interviewer Judgments of the Interviewees

According to the interviewers, cooperation with the interview was widespread: 69.3 percent of the respondents were rated as "friendly and interested" in the interview, and another 22.5 percent were said to be "cooperative, but not particularly interested." As with all surveys in countries with high proportions of illiterate respondents, the respondents had some difficulty with our questions. When asked to rate the respondents in terms of how well they understood the questions, 69.2 percent were judged to have understood them well, 25.0 percent not very well, and 5.6 percent poorly. Only 64.6 percent of the subjects were able to read our showcards without any apparent difficulty. We should note, however, that understanding of the vignette was more common (72.3 percent understood it well).

Summary

Generally, the design of this survey is as rigorous and systematic as any survey ever conducted in South Africa. Nearly all relevant segments of the South African population are included in the sample, and representative subsamples of at least 250 respondents of most major racial, ethnic, and linguistic groups are included. Great care was taken in preparing the survey instrument and ensuring comparability in the questions across the different languages included in the survey. The evidence suggests that most respondents were cooperative and willing to answer our questions openly and honestly.

However, our survey certainly taxed a portion of the sample, in part owing to illiteracy. As a result, a certain amount of random error (and perhaps some systematic error) is reflected in our variables. To the extent that the error is randomly distributed, its effect is to attenuate correlation coefficients. Since the amount of random error surely varies by race, we must adjust our standards for judging the magnitude of the coefficients we consider, especially among the African majority.

Appendix B: The Questionnaire

PROJECT TOLERANCE III	DSI 14/2000	Q.No.1-6	

ENG/AFR

SAMPLE DETAILS			
Main	Boost	Male	Female
7-1	2	8-1	2

Folder no. 9-12

DETAILS OF CALLS	1ST CALL	2ND CALL	3RD CALL	4TH CALL	NO OF CALLS ....
DAY OF WEEK					
Monday	13-1	16-1	19-1	22-1	RECALL BEST DAY
Tuesday	2	2	2	2	
Wednesday	3	3	3	3	
Thursday	4	4	4	4	
Friday	5	5	5	5	
Saturday	6	6	6	6	....
Sunday	7	7	7	7	
TIME OF DAY					
Morning (9am-1pm)	14-1	17-1	20-1	23-1	BEST TIME
Afternoon (1pm-5pm)	2	2	2	2	
Evening (5pm-6pm)	3	3	3	3	....
Evening (6pm & later)	4	4	4	4	
SUCCESSFUL					
Yes	15-1	18-1	21-1	24-1	
No	2	2	2	2	

25

- How many males/females, aged 18 years and over, live in this household?
  Hoeveel mans/vrouens, 18 jaar en ouer, woon in hierdie huishouding?

COLUMN A NUMBER IN HOME	INTERVIEW THE PERSON ENCIRCLED OPPOSITE THE NUMBER IN HOME UNDER COLUMN "A"				
	Oldest	2nd oldest	3rd oldest	4th oldest	5th oldest
1	1	-	-	-	-
2	1	2	-	-	-
3	1	2	3	-	-
4	1	2	3	4	-
5	1	2	3	4	5

IF NON-COMPLETE:

House empty	26-1
No one at home after 4 calls	2
Selected respondent not available	3
Wrong age	4
Refused	5
Refused to continue – give reasons	6
Completed	7

NAME:

ADDRESS:

TEL (H)

(W)

MAGISTERIAL DIST. 27-30

DATE: 31-34

INTERVIEWER:

INTERVIEWER No.: 35-37

CHECKED:

BACKCHECKED:

W/O:

VIGNETTE VERSION PHILLIP

38-39	01	02	03	04	05	06	07	08	09	10	11	12	13	14	15	16

ENG/AFR

PROJECT TOLERANCE III - ii - **DSI 14/2000**

SEX		AGE						RACE			
Male	Female	18-24	25-34	35-44	45-54	55-64	65+	B	W	C	I
42-1	2	43-1	2	3	4	5	6	44-1	2	3	4

PROVINCE								
Gauteng	Northern	Mpumalanga	North West	Free State	N Cape	KZN	E Cape	W Cape
45-1	2	3	4	5	6	7	8	9

METRO AREAS										
Jhb	Pta	Reef	Vaal ▲	Soweto	Dbn	Pmb	CT	PE	EL	Bloem
46-1	2	3	4	5	6	7	47-1	2	3	4

OFFICE ONLY:

COMMUNITY SIZE						
Metro	City	Large Town	Small Town	Village	Farm	Kraal
48-1	2	3	4	5	6	7

TIME INTERVIEW STARTED 49-50 [|] HR 51-52 [|] MIN

TIME INTERVIEW FINISHED 53-54 [|] HR 55-56 [|] MIN

TOTAL MINUTES 57-59 [| |]

80 - ①

ENG/AFR

PROJECT TOLERANCE III	DSI 14/2000	CARD 2	Q.No.1-6	

INTERVIEWER: SHOW CARD 1

Q.1a) How often do you watch or listen to news programmes on television or on the radio?
• *Hoe gereeld kyk of luister u na nuusprogramme op televisie of op die radio?*

Never • *Nooit*	7-0
Less than once a week • *Minder as een keer 'n week*	1
Once a week • *Een keer 'n week*	2
Several times a week • *'n Aantal kere per week*	3
Every day • *Elke dag*	4
DON'T KNOW	8
REFUSED/NO ANSWER	9

INTERVIEWER: SHOW CARD 1

Q.1b) And what about newspapers? How often do you read them?
• *En wat van koerante? Hoe dikwels lees u hulle?*

Never • *Nooit*	8-0
Less than once a week • *Minder as een keer 'n week*	1
Once a week • *Een keer 'n week*	2
Several times a week • *'n Aantal kere per week*	3
Every day • *Elke dag*	4
DON'T KNOW	8
REFUSED/NO ANSWER	9

Q.2 When you get together with your friends, would you say you discuss political matters frequently, occasionally or never?
• *Wanneer u met u vriende verkeer, sou u sê dat u politieke kwessies dikwels, af en toe of nooit bespreek nie?*

Frequently • *Dikwels*	9-1
Occasionally • *Af en toe*	2
Never • *Nooit*	3
DON'T KNOW	8
REFUSED/NO ANSWER	9

ENG/AFR

PROJECT TOLERANCE III	**- 2 -**	**CARD 2 DSI 14/2000**

Q.3 How do you think the general economic situation in South Africa has changed over the last 12 months? Would you say it has ..... ? **(READ OUT)**

• *Hoe dink u het die algemene ekonomiese situasie in Suid-Afrika oor die laaste twaalf maande verander? Sou u sê dit het ..... ?*

Got a lot worse • *Baie erger geraak*	10-1
Got a little worse • *'n Bietjie erger geraak*	2
Stayed the same • *Dieselfde gebly*	3
Got a little better • *'n Bietjie verbeter*	4
Got a lot better • *Baie verbeter*	5
DON'T KNOW	8
REFUSED/NO ANSWER	9

Q.4 How do you think the economic situation in South Africa will change in the next 12 months? Will it ..... ? **(READ OUT)**

• *Hoe dink u sal die ekonomiese situasie in Suid-Afrika oor die volgende 12 maande verander? Sal dit ..... ?*

Get a lot worse • *Baie erger raak*	11-1
Get a little worse • *'n Bietjie erger raak*	2
Stay the same • *Dieselfde bly*	3
Get a little better • *'n Bietjie verbeter*	4
Get a lot better • *Baie verbeter*	5
DON'T KNOW	8
REFUSED/NO ANSWER	9

Q.5 Compared with 12 months ago, would you say your family's living standards are .... ? **(READ OUT)**

• *In vergelyking met 12 maande gelede, sou u sê u familie se lewenstandaarde is ..... ?*

Much worse • *Baie erger*	12-1
A little worse • *'n Bietjie erger*	2
Nothing has changed • *Niks het verander nie*	3
A little better • *'n Bietjie beter*	4
Much better • *Baie beter*	5
DON'T KNOW	8
REFUSED/NO ANSWER	9

PROJECT TOLERANCE III	- 3 -	CARD 2 DSI 14/2000

Q.6 And what about the next 12 months? How do you think your family's living standard will be compared to now? Would you say you and your family's living standard will ..... ?

• *En wat van die volgende twaalf maande? Hoe dink u sal u familie se lewenstandaarde wees, in vergelyking met nou? Sou u sê u en u familie se lewenstandaarde sal ..... ?*

READ OUT

Be much worse • *Baie slegter wees*	13-1
Be a little worse • *'n Bietjie slegter wees*	2
Nothing will change • *Niks sal verander nie*	3
Be a little better • *'n Bietjie beter wees*	4
Be much better • *Baie beter wees*	5
DON'T KNOW	8
REFUSED/NO ANSWER	9

Q.7 Please tell me how well each of the following statements describes you? Would you say it describes you, extremely well, pretty well, but not completely, doesn't describe me very well, or doesn't describe me at all?

• *Sê asseblief vir my hoe goed elk van die volgende stellings u beskryf? Sou u sê dit beskryf u uiters goed, redelik goed, maar nie heeltemal nie, beskryf my nie baie goed nie, of beskryf my glad nie?*

	INTERVIEWER: SHOW CARD 2	DESCRIBES ME EXTREMELY WELL	PRETTY WELL, BUT NOT COMPLETELY	DOESN'T DESCRIBE ME VERY WELL	DOESN'T DESCRIBE ME AT ALL	DON'T KNOW	REFUSED/ NO ANSWER
1	It is usually easy for me to like people who have different values from me • *Dit is gewoonlik maklik vir my om van mense te hou wat verskillende waardes as ek het*	14-1	2	3	4	8	9
2	I feel that what happens in my life is mostly determined by powerful people • *Ek voel dat wat in my lewe gebeur word meestal deur magtige mense bepaal*	15-1	2	3	4	8	9
3	Listening to opposing viewpoints is usually a waste of time • *Om na teenstellende sienswyses te luister is gewoonlik 'n mors van tyd*	16-1	2	3	4	8	9
4	I generally don't like people who have different ideas from me • *Ek hou oor die algemeen nie van mense wat ander idees as ek het nie*	17-1	2	3	4	8	9
5	It is not always wise for me to plan too far ahead because many things turn out to be a matter of good or bad fortune • *Dit is nie altyd wys vir my om te vêr vooruit te beplan nie, want baie dinge hang af van goeie of slegte geluk*	18-1	2	3	4	8	9
6	I can usually accept other people as they are, even when they are very different from me • *Ek kan gewoonlik ander mense aanvaar soos wat hulle is, selfs al is hulle baie anders as ek*	19-1	2	3	4	8	9
7	I can pretty much determine what will happen in my life • *Ek kan min of meer bepaal wat in my lewe gaan gebeur*	20-1	2	3	4	8	9
8	When I get what I want, it's usually because I worked hard for it • *Wanneer ek kry wat ek wil hê, is dit gewoonlik omdat ek hard daarvoor gewerk het*	21-1	2	3	4	8	9

ENG/AFR

PROJECT TOLERANCE III — -4- — CARD 2 DSI 14/2000

Q.8 How much do you agree or disagree with the following statements? Would you say you agree strongly, agree, are uncertain, disagree or disagree strongly?

- *Hoeveel stem u saam of verskil u van die volgende stellings? Sou u sê u stem sterk saam, stem saam, is onseker, verskil of verskil sterk?*

	INTERVIEWER: SHOW CARD 3	AGREE STRONGLY	AGREE	UNCERTAIN	DISAGREE	DISAGREE STRONGLY	DON'T KNOW	REFUSED
1	Political reform in this country is moving too rapidly • *Politieke hervorming in hierdie land beweeg te vinnig*	22-1	2	3	4	5	8	9
2	In order to fight crime, police should be granted greater power, even if it means searching houses without permission • *Om misdaad te beveg, moet meer mag aan die polisie toegestaan word, selfs al beteken dit dat huise sonder toestemming deursoek mag word*	23-1	2	3	4	5	8	9
3	The government should never be allowed to interfere with people's privacy • *Die regering mag nooit toegelaat word om met mense se privaatheid in te meng nie*	24-1	2	3	4	5	8	9
4	Sometimes it might be better to ignore the law and solve problems immediately rather than wait for a legal solution • *Somtyds is dit beter om die wet te ignoreer en probleme onmiddelik op te los eerder as om te wag vir 'n regsbeslissing*	25-1	2	3	4	5	8	9
5	There are better ways to choose our political leaders than elections amongst candidates from several parties • *Daar is beter maniere om ons politieke leiers te kies as deur verkiesings tussen kandidate van verskeie partye*	26-1	2	3	4	5	8	9
6	If the leaders we elect cannot improve the situation in the country, then it is better not to have competitive elections in the future • *Indien die leiers wat ons kies nie die situasie in die land kan verbeter nie, dan is dit beter om kompiterende verkiesings in die toekoms te laat vaar*	27-1	2	3	4	5	8	9
7	Those supporting multi-party elections are doing harm to the country • *Diegene wat veelparty verkiesings ondersteun benadeel die land*	28-1	2	3	4	5	8	9
8	It's alright to get around the law as long as you don't actually break it • *Dis aanvaarbaar om die wet te omseil solank 'n mens dit net nie werklik breek nie*	29-1	2	3	4	5	8	9
9	In times of emergency, the government ought to be able to suspend the law to solve pressing social problems • *In tye van nood, behoort die regering in staat te wees om wette op te skort om dringende sosiale probleme op te los*	30-1	2	3	4	5	8	9
10	People shouldn't accept everything the authorities say without questioning it • *Mense behoort nie alles wat die gesaghebbendes sê te aanvaar sonder om dit te bevraagteken nie*	31-1	2	3	4	5	8	9
11	All this country really needs is a single political party to rule the country • *Al wat hierdie land werklik nodig het, is 'n enkele politieke party om die land te regeer*	32-1	2	3	4	5	8	9
12	People should not try to change how society works but just accept the way it is • *Mense moet nie probeer om die wyse waarop die samelewing werk te verander nie, maar moet dit net aanvaar soos wat dit is*	33-1	2	3	4	5	8	9
13	Racially integrated schools should not be required by law because they make many people angry • *Rasgeïntegreerde skole behoort nie deur die wet vereis te word nie, want hulle maak baie mense kwaad*	34-1	2	3	4	5	8	9
14	A country made up of many ethnic groups should be ruled by only one political party to prevent too much ethnic conflict from occurring • *'n Land wat uit baie etniese groepe bestaan behoort deur slegs een politieke party regeer te word om te voorkom dat daar te baie etniese konflik plaasvind*	35-1	2	3	4	5	8	9

ENG/AFR

PROJECT TOLERANCE III - 5 - **CARD 2 DSI 14/2000**

Q.8 CONT/... How much do you agree or disagree with the following statements? Would you say you agree strongly, agree, are uncertain, disagree or disagree strongly?

- *Hoeveel stem u saam of verskil u van die volgende stellings? Sou u sê u stem sterk saam, stem saam, is onseker, verskil of verskil sterk?*

		AGREE STRONGLY	AGREE	UNCERTAIN	DISAGREE	DISAGREE STRONGLY	DON'T KNOW	REFUSED
15	Democracy in South Africa is too fragile to allow many political parties to compete with each other • *Demokrasie in Suid-Afrika is te swak om toe te laat dat baie politieke partye met mekaar meeding*	36-1	2	3	4	5	8	9
16	The party that gets the support of the majority of the people ought not to have to share political power with the political minority • *Die party wat die steun van die meerderheid mense verkry behoort nie politieke mag met die politieke minderheid te deel nie*	37-1	2	3	4	5	8	9
17	It is not necessary to obey the laws of a government that I did not vote for • *Dit is nie nodig om die wette na te kom van 'n regering waarvoor ek nie gestem het nie*	38-1	2	3	4	5	8	9
18	The government should provide free medical care for people with HIV/AIDS • *Die regering moet gratis mediese behandeling bied vir mense met HIV/VIGS*	39-1	2	3	4	5	8	9
19	The constitution is just like any other law; if the majority of the people want to change it, it should be changed • *Die grondwet is net soos enige ander wet; as die meerderheid mense dit wil verander, moet dit verander word*	40-1	2	3	4	5	8	9
20	A special tax should be imposed on big business to help fund housing for the homeless • *'n Spesiale belasting moet op groot besighede opgelê word om te help om behuising vir die haweloses te finansier*	41-1	2	3	4	5	8	9
21	If the majority of the people want something, the constitution should not be used to keep them from getting what they want • *As die meerderheid mense iets wil hê, moet die grondwet nie gebruik word om dit vir hulle te weier nie*	42-1	2	3	4	5	8	9

43-44

Q.9 Next I will read through a list of rights and freedoms. Please tell me how important these rights are to you personally on a scale from 1 (not very important) to 5 (very important).

- *Volgende gaan ek deur 'n lys van regte en vryhede lees. Sê asseblief vir my hoe belangrik hierdie regte vir u persoonlik is op 'n skaal van 1 (nie baie belangrik nie) tot 5 (baie belangrik).*

INTERVIEWER: SHOW CARD 4

		VERY IMPORTANT *BAIE BELANGRIK*	IMPORTANT *BELANGRIK*	SOMEWHAT IMPORTANT *IETWAT BELANGRIK*	SLIGHTLY IMPORTANT *'N BIETJIE BELANGRIK*	NOT VERY IMPORTANT *NIE BAIE BELANGRIK NIE*	DON'T KNOW	REFUSED/ NO ANSWER
		5	4	3	2	1		
1	The freedom to express your political views • *Die vryheid om uitdrukking te gee aan u politieke sienswyses*	45-5	4	3	2	1	8	9
2	The freedom to join and participate in social and political groups and unions • *Die vryheid om aan te sluit en deel te neem aan sosiale en politieke groepe en unies*	46-5	4	3	2	1	8	9
3	The right to be treated equally under the law • *Die reg om gelyk voor die reg behandel te word*	47-5	4	3	2	1	8	9
4	The right to a job • *Die reg tot 'n werk*	48-5	4	3	2	1	8	9
5	The right to own land • *Die reg om grond te besit*	49-5	2	3	2	1	8	9
6	The right to a clean and safe environment, free from pollution • *Die reg tot 'n skoon en veilige omgewing vry van besoedeling*	50-5	4	3	2	1	8	9
7	The right to education in my own language • *Die reg tot onderrig in my eie taal*	51-5	4	3	2	1	8	9
8	The right to strike • *Die reg om te staak*	52-5	4	3	2	1	8	9
9	The right to adequate housing • *Die reg tot voldoende behuising*	53-5	4	3	2	1	8	9
10	The right to own a gun • *Die reg om 'n vuurwapen te besit*	54-5	4	3	2	1	8	9

ENG/AFR

PROJECT TOLERANCE III	- 6 -	CARD 2 DSI 14/2000

Q.10 How much do you agree or disagree with the following statements? Would you say you agree strongly, agree, are uncertain, disagree or disagree strongly?

• *Hoeveel stem u saam of verskil u van die volgende stellings? Sou u sê u stem sterk saam, stem saam, is onseker, verskil of verskil sterk?*

INTERVIEWER: SHOW CARD 5

		AGREE STRONGLY	AGREE	UNCERTAIN	DISAGREE	DISAGREE STRONGLY	DON'T KNOW	REFUSED
1	People should go along with whatever is best for the group, even when they disagree • *Mense behoort akkoord te gaan met wat ookal die beste is vir die groep, selfs al stem hulle nie saam nie*	55-1	2	3	4	5	8	9
2	People today are too quick to blame others for their failures and shortcomings, rather than taking responsibility for themselves • *Mense is vandag te vinnig om ander te blameer vir hul mislukkings en tekortkominge, eerder as om verantwoordelikheid vir hul eie optrede te neem*	56-1	2	3	4	5	8	9
3	It is more important to do the kind of work society needs than to do the kind of work I like • *Dit is belangriker om die soort werk te doen wat die samelewing nodig het as om die soort werk te doen waarvan ek hou*	57-1	2	3	4	5	8	9
4	One problem with South African society today is that few people take responsibility for their own actions • *Een probleem met die Suid-Afrikaanse samelewing vandag is dat min mense verantwoordelikheid vir hul eie aksies neem*	58-1	2	3	4	5	8	9
5	People have to look after themselves; the community shouldn't be responsible for the actions of each citizen • *Mense moet na hulself kyk; die gemeenskap behoort nie verantwoordelik te wees vir die dade van elke burger nie*	59-1	2	3	4	5	8	9
6	It is very good that people today have greater freedom to protest against things they do not like • *Dit is baie goed dat mense vandag groter vryheid het om te protesteer teen dinge waarvan hulle nie hou nie*	60-1	2	3	4	5	8	9
7	People in South Africa today place too much blame on the past as an excuse for their failures and shortcomings • *Mense in Suid-Afrika plaas vandag te veel blaam op die verlede as 'n verskoning vir hul mislukkings en tekortkominge*	61-1	2	3	4	5	8	9
8	The most important thing to teach children is obedience to their parents • *Die heel belangrikste ding om kinders te leer is gehoorsaamheid aan hul ouers*	62-1	2	3	4	5	8	9

63

Q.11 Some people say individuals should take more responsibility for providing for themselves. Others say the state should take more responsibility to ensure that everyone is provided for. Others have views somewhere in between. How would you place your views on this scale?

• *Sommige mense sê dat individue meer verantwoordelikheid behoort te neem om vir hulself te sorg. Ander sê die staat behoort meer verantwoordelikheid te neem om te verseker dat elkeen versorg is. Ander se sienswyses is êrens tussen-in. Hoe sou u u sienswyses op hierdie skaal plaas?*

INTERVIEWER: SHOW CARD 6

1	2	3	4	5	6	7	8	9	10	Don't know	Refused
Individuals should take more responsibility for providing for themselves *Individue behoort meer verantwoordelikheid te neem om vir hulself te sorg*						The state should take more responsibility to ensure that everyone is provided for *Die staat behoort meer verantwoordelikheid te neem om te verseker dat elkeen versorg is*				98	99

64-65

ENG/AFR

PROJECT TOLERANCE III	- 7 -	CARD 2 DSI 14/2000

Q.12a) People see themselves in many different ways. Using this list, which of these best describes you? Please take a moment to look at all of the terms on the list. **(ONE ONLY)**

• *Mense dink aan hulself op baie verskillende maniere. Deur hierdie lys te gebruik, watter van hierdie beskryf u die beste? Kyk asseblief vir 'n oomblik na al die terme op hierdie lys.*

INTERVIEWER: SHOW CARD 7

African	66-1
Afrikaner	2
Asian	3
Black	4
Boer	5
Brown	6
Christian	7
Coloured	8
English	9
European	67-1
Hindu	2
Indian	3
Jewish	4
Malaysian	5
Moslem	6
North Sotho/Sepedi	7
Seswati/Swazi	8
South Sotho/Sesotho	9
South African	68-1
Tsonga/Shangaan	2
Tswana	3
Venda	4
White	5
Xhosa	6
Zulu	7
Ndebele	8
Other (specify)	

69 [ ]

Q.12b) How important is this identity to you? Would you say it is very important; somewhat important; not very important; or not important at all for you to think of yourself as ..... ? **(READ ANSWER GIVEN IN Q.18a)**

• *Hoe belangrik is hierdie identiteit vir u? Sou u sê dit is baie belangrik, ietwat belangrik, nie baie belangrik nie, of glad nie vir u belangrik om uself te sien as ..... ?*

Very important • *Baie belangrik*	70-1
Somewhat important • *Ietwat belangrik*	2
Not very important • *Nie baie belangrik nie*	3
Not important at all • *Glad nie belangrik nie*	4
DON'T KNOW	8
REFUSED/NO ANSWER	9

ENG/AFR

PROJECT TOLERANCE III	- 8 -	CARD 2 DSI 14/2000

Q.13 Still looking at the card, do you think of yourself in any of the other terms as well? **(WRITE IN)**
• *Kyk nog steeds na die kaart, dink u aan uself in enige van die ander terme ook?*

____

____

____

____

______________________________ 71-72

Q.14 Still looking at the card, which would you say most strongly does NOT describe you? **(WRITE IN)**
• *Kyk nog steeds na die kaart, watter sou u sê beskryf u glad NIE?*

____

____

____

____

______________________________ 73-74

Q.15 People have different sorts of feelings as a result of being a member of a group. Which of the following characteristics describes how you feel about being a .... [GROUP]? **(ANSWER GIVEN IN Q.12a) (READ OUT)**
• *Mense het verskillende soorte gevoelens as gevolg van hul lidmaatskap tot 'n groep. Watter van die volgende eienskappe beskryf hoe u voel om 'n lid te wees van die .... [GROEP]?*

a)

It makes me feel very secure to be a ..... • *Dit laat my baie veilig voel om 'n .... te wees*	75-1
It makes me feel fairly secure to be a ..... • *Dit laat my redelik veilig voel om 'n ..... te wees*	2
How secure I feel does not depend on being a ..... • *Hoe veilig ek voel hang nie af of ek 'n ..... is nie*	3
DON'T KNOW	8
REFUSED/NO ANSWER	9

b)

It makes me feel very important to be a ..... • *Dit laat my baie belangrik voel om 'n ..... te wees*	76-1
It makes me feel fairly important to be a ..... • *Dit laat my redelik belangrik voel om 'n ..... te wees*	2
How important I feel does not depend on being a ..... • *Hoe belangrik ek voel hang nie af of ek 'n ..... is nie*	3
DON'T KNOW	8
REFUSED/NO ANSWER	9

c)

It makes me think much better of myself as a ..... • *Dit laat my baie beter van myself dink as 'n .....*	77-1
It makes me think a little better of myself as a ..... • *Dit laat my redelik beter van myself dink as 'n .....*	2
How I feel about myself does not depend on being a ..... • *Hoe ek omtrent myself voel hang nie af of ek 'n .... is nie*	3
DON'T KNOW	8
REFUSED/NO ANSWER	9

79 - 80 - 02

ENG/AFR

Q.16 How much do you agree or disagree with the following statements? Would you say you agree strongly, agree, are uncertain, disagree or disagree strongly?

• *Hoeveel stem u saam of verskil u van die volgende stellings? Sou u sê u stem sterk saam, stem saam, is onseker, verskil of verskil sterk?*

INTERVIEWER: SHOW CARD 8

		AGREE STRONGLY	AGREE	UNCERTAIN	DISAGREE	DISAGREE STRONGLY	DON'T KNOW	REFUSED
1	The way South Africa is right now, if one group gets more power it is usually because another group is getting less power • *Soos dit nou in Suid-Afrika is, as een groep meer mag kry is dit gewoonlik omdat 'n ander groep minder mag kry*	7-1	2	3	4	5	8	9
2	The trouble with politics in South Africa is that it is always based on what group you are a member of • *Die probleem met politiek in Suid-Afrika is dat dit altyd gebaseer is op jou lidmaatskap van 'n groep*	8-1	2	3	4	5	8	9
3	If people don't realise we are all South Africans and stop thinking of themselves as Xhosa or Afrikans or Zulu or whatever, South Africa will have a very difficult political future • *As mense nie besef dat ons almal Suid-Afrikaners is nie en nie ophou om aan hulleself as Xhosa of Afrikans of Zulu of wat ookal te dink nie, sal Suid-Afrika 'n baie moeilike politieke toekoms hê*	9-1	2	3	4	5	8	9

Q.17 Now I would like to ask you a few more questions about how you feel about being a ...... **(ANSWER GIVEN IN Q.12a)** Would you say you agree strongly, agree, are uncertain, disagree or disagree strongly?

• *Nou wil ek u graag nog 'n paar vrae vra oor hoe u daaroor voel om 'n ..... te wees? Sou u sê u stem sterk saam, stem saam, is onseker, verskil of verskil sterk?*

INTERVIEWER: SHOW CARD 8

		AGREE STRONGLY	AGREE	UNCERTAIN	DISAGREE	DISAGREE STRONGLY	DON'T KNOW	REFUSED
1	Of all the groups in South Africa ..... are the best • *Uit al die groepe in Suid-Afrika is .... die beste*	10-1	2	3	4	5	8	9
2	Even though I might sometimes disagree with the standpoint/viewpoint taken by other .... it is extremely important to support the ..... point of view • *Selfs al sou ek partykeer verskil van die standpunt/ sienswyse deur ander ..... ingeneem is, is dit uiters belangrik om die .... se sienswyse te ondersteun*	11-1	2	3	4	5	8	9
3	What happens to .... in South Africa will affect my life a great deal • *Wat met .... in Suid-Afrika gebeur sal my lewe grootliks beïnvloed*	12-1	2	3	4	5	8	9
4	When it comes to politics, it is important for all .... to stand together • *Wanneer dit by politiek kom, is dit belangrik vir alle ... om saam te staan*	13-1	2	3	4	5	8	9
5	Unless you are a member of a group like .... it is very difficult to get much out of South African politics • *Tensy u 'n lid van 'n groep soos .... is, is dit baie moeilik om veel uit Suid-Afrikaanse politiek te kry*	14-1	2	3	4	5	8	9
6	The well-being of .... has more to do with politics than it does with our own hard work • *Die welstand van ... het meer met politiek te doen as met ons eie harde werk*	15-1	2	3	4	5	8	9

Q.18 How much do you agree or disagree with the following statements? Would you say you agree strongly, agree, are uncertain, disagree or disagree strongly?

- *Hoeveel stem u saam of verskil u van die volgende stellings? Sou u sê u stem sterk saam, stem saam, is onseker, verskil of verskil sterk?*

INTERVIEWER: SHOW CARD 8

		AGREE STRONGLY	AGREE	UNCERTAIN	DISAGREE	DISAGREE STRONGLY	DON'T KNOW	REFUSED
1	People should have the right to set up their own communities, and not allow those of a different race to live in their communities • *Mense behoort die reg te hê om hul eie gemeenskappe te skep en nie toe te laat dat diegene van 'n ander ras in hul gemeenskappe woon nie*	16-1	2	3	4	5	8	9
2	The Truth Commission will only end badly – therefore South Africans should look to the future and forget the past • *Die Waarheidskommissie sal net sleg afloop – daarom behoort Suid-Afrikaners na die toekoms te kyk en die verlede te vergeet*	17-1	2	3	4	5	8	9
3	There can be no reconciliation in South Africa unless people – both black and white – have confessed to their apartheid crimes • *Daar kan geen versoening in Suid-Afrika wees tensy mense – beide swart en wit – hulle apartheidsmisdade bely het nie*	18-1	2	3	4	5	8	9
4	Newspapers should publish the views of all political parties, not just the party they support • *Koerante moet die siening van alle politieke partye publiseer, nie net die party wat hulle ondersteun nie*	19-1	2	3	4	5	8	9
5	Newspapers, radio and television should be responsible for presenting all points of view, even those that some people could consider racist • *Koerante, radio en televisie behoort verantwoordelik te wees om alle sienswyses te verteenwoordig, selfs dié wat party mense as rasisties kan beskou*	20-1	2	3	4	5	8	9
6	Voting in South African elections should be limited to those who own property • *Stemreg in Suid-Afrikaanse verkiesings moet beperk word tot diegene wat eiendom besit*	21-1	2	3	4	5	8	9
7	The mass media should be protected by law more than they are now from control by the government • *Die massamedia behoort meer deur die wet beskerm te word teen beheer van die regering, as wat nou die geval is*	22-1	2	3	4	5	8	9
8	It is better to live in an orderly society than to allow people so much freedom that they can become disruptive • *Dit is beter om in 'n ordelike samelewing te woon as om mense soveel vryheid toe te laat dat hulle ontwrigtend kan raak*	23-1	2	3	4	5	8	9
9	Free speech is just not worth it if it means that we have to put up with the danger to society of radical political views • *Vrye spraak is net nie die moeite werd as dit beteken dat ons die gevaar wat radikale politieke sienswyses vir die samelewing inhou moet verdra nie*	24-1	2	3	4	5	8	9
10	A politician's skin colour doesn't matter; they are all untrustworthy • *'n Politikus se velkleur maak nie saak nie, hulle is almal onbetroubaar*	25-1	2	3	4	5	8	9
11	Society shouldn't have to put up with political views that are fundamentally different from the views of the majority of the people • *Dit behoort nie vir die samelewing nodig te wees om politieke sienswyses te verdra wat fundamenteel verskillend is van die sienswyses van die meerderheid van die mense*	26-1	2	3	4	5	8	9

PROJECT TOLERANCE III	- 11 -	CARD 3 DSI 14/2000

Q.18 CONT/... How much do you agree or disagree with the following statements? Would you say you agree strongly, agree, are uncertain, disagree or disagree strongly?

• *Hoeveel stem u saam of verskil u van die volgende stellings? Sou u sê u stem sterk saam, stem saam, is onseker, verskil of verskil sterk?*

INTERVIEWER: SHOW CARD 8

		AGREE STRONGLY	AGREE	UNCERTAIN	DISAGREE	DISAGREE STRONGLY	DON'T KNOW	REFUSED
12	It is better for society to let some guilty people go free than to risk convicting an innocent person • *Dit is beter vir die samelewing om sommige skuldige mense vry te laat as om toe te laat dat 'n onskuldige persoon skuldig bevind word*	27-1	2	3	4	5	8	9
13	Because demonstrations frequently become disorderly and disruptive, radical and extremist groups shouldn't be allowed to demonstrate • *Omdat betogings dikwels wanordelik en ontwrigtend raak, behoort radikale en ekstremistiese groepe nie toegelaat te word om te betoog nie*	28-1	2	3	4	5	8	9
14	If police obtain evidence illegally, it should not be permitted in court, even if it would help convict a guilty person • *As die polisie bewyse onwettig verkry, moet dit nie in die hof toegelaat word nie, selfs al help dit om 'n skuldige persoon skuldig te vind*	29-1	2	3	4	5	8	9
15	Rate payers should be taxed to build daycare centres for people living in poverty stricken areas • *Huiseienaars moet belas word om dagsorgsentrums vir mense wat in arm areas bly te bou*	30-1	2	3	4	5	8	9
16	In order to reduce poverty in South Africa, it is necessary that taxes be increased • *Om armoede in Suid-Afrika te verminder, is dit noodsaaklik om belasting te verhoog*	31-1	2	3	4	5	8	9
17	It makes me proud to be called a South African • *Dit maak my trots om 'n Suid-Afrikaner genoem te word*	32-1	2	3	4	5	8	9
18	Being a South African is a very important part of how I see myself • *Om 'n Suid-Afrikaner te wees is 'n baie belangrike deel van hoe ek myself sien*	33-1	2	3	4	5	8	9

Q.19 Are you very interested; interested; not very interested; or not at all interested in politics?

• *Is u baie geïnteresseerd, geïnteresseerd, nie baie geïnteresseerd nie of glad nie geïnteresseerd in politiek nie?*

Very interested • *Baie geïnteresseerd*	34-1
Interested • *Geïnteresseerd*	2
Not very interested • *Nie baie geïnteresseerd nie*	3
Not at all interested • *Glad nie geïnteresseerd nie*	4
DON'T KNOW	8
REFUSED/NO ANSWER	9

ENG/AFR

Q.20 We are interested in your thoughts about how things might have changed since the election of 1994 and the end of apartheid in South Africa. Would you say the following have improved a great deal, improved somewhat, worsened somewhat, or worsened a great deal?

• *Ons stel belang in u gedagtes oor hoe dinge dalk mag verander het sedert die verkiesing van 1994 en die einde van apartheid in Suid-Afrika. Sou u sê die volgende het baie verbeter, ietwat verbeter, ietwat versleg of baie versleg?*

INTERVIEWER: SHOW CARD 9

		IMPROVED A GREAT DEAL	IMPROVED SOMEWHAT	WORSENED SOMEWHAT	WORSENED A GREAT DEAL	DON'T KNOW	REFUSED
A	Ability to earn a living • *In staat wees om 'n lewe te maak*	35-1	2	3	4	8	9
B	Race relations • *Rasseverhoudings*	36-1	2	3	4	8	9
C	Personal freedom • *Persoonlike vryheid*	37-1	2	3	4	8	9
D	Equality • *Gelykheid*	38-1	2	3	4	8	9
E	Hope for the future • *Hoop vir die toekoms*	39-1	2	3	4	8	9

Q.21 – Q.25 INTERVIEWER INSTRUCTION:

	RING GROUP ASKED ABOUT
IF RESPONDENT IS BLACK ASK ABOUT WHITES	40-1
IF RESPONDENT IS WHITE/COLOURED/INDIAN ASK ABOUT BLACKS	40-2

Q.21 Now we would like to ask about the type of contacts you have with **[GROUP]**. In your work, on a typical working day, how much contact do you have with **[GROUP]**?

• *Nou wil ons vra oor die tipe kontakte wat u het met* ***[GROEP]****. In u werk, op 'n tipiese werksdag, hoeveel kontak het u met* ***[GROEP]****?*

READ OUT

A great deal • *Baie*	41-1
Some • *Bietjie*	2
Not very much • *Nie baie nie*	3
Hardly any contact • *Amper niks kontak nie*	4
No contact at all • *Geen kontak*	5
DON'T KNOW	8
REFUSED	9

Q.22 Outside your work, how much contact do you have with **[GROUP]**?

• *Buite u werk, hoeveel kontak het u met* ***[GROEP]****?*

READ OUT

A great deal • *Baie*	42-1
Some • *Bietjie*	2
Not very much • *Nie baie nie*	3
Hardly any contact • *Amper niks kontak nie*	4
No contact at all • *Geen kontak*	5
DON'T KNOW	8
REFUSED	9

Q.23 How often have you eaten a meal with **[GROUP]**?

• *Hoe gereeld eet u saam met* ***[GROEP]****?*

READ OUT

Quite often • *Heel gereeld*	43-1
Not very often • *Nie baie gereeld nie*	2
Never • *Nooit*	3
DON'T KNOW	8
REFUSED	9

Q.24 How many [GROUP] people would you call "true" friends?
• *Hoeveel [GROEP] mense sou u "ware" vriende noem?*

READ OUT

Quite a number of [GROUP] people • *'n Groot hoeveelheid [GROEP] mense*	44-1
Only a small number of [GROUP] people • *Net 'n klein hoeveelheid [GROEP] mense*	2
Hardly any [GROUP] people • *Amper niks [GROEP] mense*	3
None • *Geen*	4
DON'T KNOW	8
REFUSED	9

Q.25 Now we would like to ask your opinion about [GROUP]. Would you say you agree strongly, agree, are uncertain, disagree or disagree strongly with the following statements.
• *Nou wil ons u opinie vra oor [GROEP]. Sou u sê u stem sterk saam, stem saam, is onseker, verskil of verskil sterk?*

	INTERVIEWER: SHOW CARD 10	AGREE STRONGLY	AGREE	UNCERTAIN	DISAGREE	DISAGREE STRONGLY	DON'T KNOW	REFUSED
1	I find it difficult to understand the customs and ways of ..... • *Ek vind dit moeilik om die tradisies en gewoontes van .... te verstaan*	45-1	2	3	4	5	8	9
2	It is hard to imagine ever being friends with a ..... • *Dis moeilik om voor te stel om ooit vriende te wees met 'n ......*	46-1	2	3	4	5	8	9
3	More than most groups, ... are likely to engage in crime • *Meer as die meeste groepe, is .... gewoonlik betrokke in misdaad*	47-1	2	3	4	5	8	9
4	..... are untrustworthy • *..... is onbetroubaar*	48-1	2	3	4	5	8	9
5	..... are selfish, and only look after the interests of their group • *..... is selfsugtig, en sien slegs om na die belange van hul eie groep*	49-1	2	3	4	5	8	9
6	I feel uncomfortable when I am around a group of ..... • *Ek voel ongemaklik wanneer ek tussen 'n groep .... is*	50-1	2	3	4	5	8	9
7	Most ..... are <u>not</u> racist • *Meeste ..... is <u>nie</u> rasisties nie*	51-1	2	3	4	5	8	9
8	I often don't believe what .... say to me • *Ek glo dikwels nie wat ..... vir my sê nie*	52-1	2	3	4	5	8	9
9	South Africa would be a better place if there were no .... in the country • *Suid-Afrika sou 'n beter plek wees indien daar geen ..... in die land is nie*	53-1	2	3	4	5	8	9
10	I could never imagine being part of a political party made up mainly of ..... • *Ek kan myself nooit voorstel om deel te wees van 'n politieke party wat meestal uit .... bestaan nie*	54-1	2	3	4	5	8	9

PROJECT TOLERANCE III	- 14 -	CARD 3 DSI 14/2000

Q.26 One hears people describe South Africa's history in many different ways. We are interested in your opinions on the following statements about South Africa's past. Would you say that the following statements are certainly true, probably true, probably not true, or certainly not true.

• *Ons hoor hoe mense Suid-Afrikaanse geskiedenis op baie verskillende maniere beskryf. Ons stel belang in u opinies oor die volgende stellings oor Suid-Afrika se verlede. Sou u sê die volgende stellings is verseker waar, moontlik waar, moontlik nie waar nie of verseker nie waar nie?*

	INTERVIEWER: SHOW CARD 11	CERTAINLY TRUE	PROBABLY TRUE	PROBABLY NOT TRUE	CERTAINLY NOT TRUE	DON'T KNOW	REFUSED
1	When it comes to South Africa's past, we must learn from the mistakes that were made in order to avoid making the same mistakes again • *Wanneer dit kom by Suid-Afrika se verlede, moet ons leer uit die foute wat gemaak is om te voorkom dat dieselfde foute nie weer gemaak word nie*	55-1	2	3	4	8	9
2	It's better not to open old wounds by talking about what happened in the past • *Dit is beter om nie ou wonde oop te krap deur te praat oor wat in die verlede gebeur het nie*	56-1	2	3	4	8	9
3	I do not want my children to learn about the horrific atrocities that were committed in the past • *Ek wil nie hê my kinders moet leer van die afgryslike wreedhede wat in die verlede gepleeg is nie*	57-1	2	3	4	8	9
4	There were certainly some abuses under the old apartheid system, but the ideas behind apartheid were basically good ones • *Daar was verseker sommige misbruike onder die ou apartheid sisteem, maar die idees agter apartheid was basies goed*	58-1	2	3	4	8	9
5	In the past, whites profited greatly from apartheid, and most continue to profit today from the legacy of apartheid • *In die verlede, het blankes baie voordeel getrek uit apartheid, en die meeste gaan vandag aan om voordeel te trek uit die erfenis van apartheid*	59-1	2	3	4	8	9
6	Whites' fear of communism was real and motivated many of their actions in defense of the apartheid state • *Blankes se vrees vir kommunisme was eg en het baie van hulle aksies ter verdediging van die apartheid toestand gemotiveer*	60-1	2	3	4	8	9
7	The struggle to preserve apartheid was just • *Die stryd om apartheid te beskerm was regverdig*	61-1	2	3	4	8	9
8	Most white South Africans had no idea that the state was committing horrific atrocities against those struggling against apartheid • *Meeste blanke Suid-Afrikaners het nie geweet dat die staat afgryslike wreedhede teen dié wat teen apartheid 'n stryd gevoer het, gepleeg het nie*	62-1	2	3	4	8	9
9	Apartheid was a crime against humanity • *Apartheid was 'n misdaad teen die menslikheid*	63-1	2	3	4	8	9

64-78 BLANK

79 - 80 - 03

ENG/AFR

PROJECT TOLERANCE III	- 15 -	CARD 4 DSI 14/2000

Q.27 And now I'd like to ask you about your attitudes towards some groups of people. I am going to read you a list of some groups that are currently active in social and political life.

• *En nou wil ek u graag uitvra omtrent u houding teenoor sommige groepe mense. Ek gaan aan u 'n lys voorlees van sommige groepe wat huidiglik aktief is in die sosiale en- politieke lewe.*

Here is a card showing a scale from 1 to 11. The number "1" indicates that you dislike the group very much; the number "11" indicates that you like the group very much. The number "6" means that you neither like nor dislike the group. The numbers 2 to 5 reflect varying amounts of dislike; and the numbers 7 to 10 reflect varying amounts of like towards the group.
The first group I'd like to ask you about is Afrikaners. If you have an opinion about Afrikaners please indicate which figure most closely describes your attitude towards them. If you have no opinion, please be sure to tell me. What is your opinion of .....?

• *Hier is 'n kaart wat 'n skaal van 1 tot 11 vertoon. Die nommer "1" dui aan dat u baie min van die groep hou; die syfer "11" dui aan dat u baie van die groep hou. Die syfer "6" beteken dat u nie 'n voorkeur of afkeer van die groep het nie. Die syfers 2 tot 5 dui op variërende hoeveelhede van afkeer en die syfers 7 tot 10 dui op variërende hoeveelhede van teenoor die groep.*
Die eerste groep waaroor ek u wil uitvra is Afrikaners. Indien u 'n mening omtrent Afrikaners het, dui asseblief aan watter syfer u houding teenoor hulle die naaste beskryf. Indien u nie 'n mening het nie, sê my asseblief. Wat is u mening omtrent .....?

INTERVIEWER: SHOW CARD 12 READ OUT		Dislike very much *Hou baie min van*		Dislike *Hou nie van*					Like *Hou van*			Like very much *Hou baie van*	DON'T KNOW	REFUSED	
Afrikaners • *Afrikaners*	7-8	1	2	3	4	5	6	7	8	9	10	11	98	99	33-34
Supporters of the ANC • *Ondersteuners van die ANC*	9-10	1	2	3	4	5	6	7	8	9	10	11	98	99	35-36
Supporters of the AWB • *Ondersteuners van die AWB*	11-12	1	2	3	4	5	6	7	8	9	10	11	98	99	37-38
Supporters of the South African Communist Party • *Ondersteuners van die Suid-Afrikaanse Kommunistiese Party*	13-14	1	2	3	4	5	6	7	8	9	10	11	98	99	39-40
Supporters of the Pan Africanist Congress • *Ondersteuners van die PAC*	15-16	1	2	3	4	5	6	7	8	9	10	11	98	99	41-42
Supporters of the New National Party • *Ondersteuners van die Nuwe NP*	17-18	1	2	3	4	5	6	7	8	9	10	11	98	99	43-44
Supporters of the Democratic Party • *Ondersteuners van die DP*	19-20	1	2	3	4	5	6	7	8	9	10	11	98	99	45-46
Supporters of the Inkatha Freedom Party • *Ondersteuners van die IVP*	21-22	1	2	3	4	5	6	7	8	9	10	11	98	99	47-48
People who say we should have a one party state • *Mense wat sê dat ons 'n een-party staat behoort te hê*	23-24	1	2	3	4	5	6	7	8	9	10	11	98	99	49-50
Supporters of People Against Gangsterism and Drugs (PAGAD) • *Ondersteuners van PAGAD*	25-26	1	2	3	4	5	6	7	8	9	10	11	98	99	51-52
Supporters of the Mishlenti Society • *Ondersteuners van die Mishlenti Vereniging*	27-28	1	2	3	4	5	6	7	8	9	10	11	98	99	53-54
Supporters of trade unions • *Ondersteuners van die Vakbonde*	29-30	1	2	3	4	5	6	7	8	9	10	11	98	99	55-56
Muslims • *Moslems*	31-32	1	2	3	4	5	6	7	8	9	10	11	98	99	57-58

*** GROUP ....**

INTERVIEWER START WITH GROUP MARKED 01 AND WORK DOWN THE LIST THEN TO THE TOP AGAIN UNTIL ALL GROUPS ARE ANSWERED

ENG/AFR

Q.28a) Is there any <u>other</u> group active in the life of our country that you dislike enough to rate at a "3" or a "2" or a "1" on this scale?
• *Is daar enige <u>ander</u> groep wat aktief is in die lewe van ons land waarvan u min genoeg hou om as 'n "3" or 'n "2" of 'n "1" op hierdie skaal te evalueer?*

Yes/*Ja*	59-1	→ GO TO Q.28b)
No/*Nee*	2	→ GO TO Q.30a)
DON'T KNOW	8	
REFUSED	9	

<u>IF YES IN Q.28a)</u>:
Q.28b) What is the name of the group? **(INTERVIEWER: WRITE IN)**
• *Wat is die naam van die groep?*

60-62

Q.29 Would you rate **(THE GROUP NAMED IN Q.28b)** as a "3", "2" or "1" on the scale that's on the card?
• *Sal u (GROEP IN V.28b GENOEM) as 'n "3", "2" of "1" evalueer op die skaal wat op die kaart is?*

1	2	3	DON'T KNOW	REFUSED
63-1	2	3	8	9

INTERVIEWER: WRITE THE NAME OF THE GROUP THE RESPONDENT NAMED IN Q.28b) ON LOOSE SHOW CARD 13 BEFORE HANDING IT TO THE RESPONDENT

INTERVIEWER: SHOW CARD 13

<u>ASK ALL</u>:
Q.30a) This card presents a list of groups we have already spoken about. Which of the following groups do you dislike the most?
• *Hierdie kaart vertoon 'n lys groepe waaroor ons reeds gepraat het. Van watter van die volgende groepe hou u die minste?*

INTERVIEWER: WRITE THE NAME OF THE GROUP

i) The group that you dislike the most.
• *Die groep waarvan u die heel minste hou.*

GPA 64-65

ii) The next most disliked group.
• *Die groep waarvan u tweede minste hou.*

GPB 66-67

iii) And your third most disliked group.
• *En die groep waarvan u derde minste hou.*

GPC 68-69

iv) Finally, which is your fourth most disliked group?
• *Laastens, die groep waarvan u vierde minste hou?*

GPD 70-71

→ GO TO Q.31

NO GROUP DISLIKED 72-1 **ASK Q.30b)**

79 - 80 - 04

ENG/AFR

Q.30b) Do you dislike either of the following groups of people?
• *Het u 'n afkeer aan enige van die volgende groepe mense?*

	YES	NO	DON'T KNOW	REFUSED
Those who would re-impose apartheid in the country • *Diegene wat weer apartheid in die land wil instel*	7-1	2	8	9
Those who would force all whites to leave South Africa • *Diegene wat alle blankes wil forseer om Suid-Afrika te verlaat*	8-1	2	8	9

IF YES TO BOTH GROUPS, ASK:
Which of the two groups of people do you dislike the most?
• *Van watter van die twee groepe mense hou u die heel minste?*

Re-impose apartheid • *Stel apartheid weer in*	9-1
Force all whites to leave South Africa • *Forseer alle blankes om Suid-Afrika te verlaat*	2

ASK ALL:

INTERVIEWER: ASK ABOUT GPA **IN Q.30a), IF NO** GPA **ASK ABOUT GROUP RATED LOWEST IN Q.27**

10-11

WRITE DOWN NAME OF GROUP: ____________ GPA

Q.31a) Now let's consider the .... **(GROUP IN Q.30a) GPA)** a bit more. To what extent do you agree strongly, agree, are uncertain, disagree or disagree strongly with the following statements about ..... ?
• *Kom ons oorweeg die .... (GROEP IN V.30a) GPA) 'n bietjie meer. Tot watter mate stem u sterk saam, stem saam, is onseker, verskil of verskil sterk?*

INTERVIEWER: SHOW CARD 14

		Q.31a (i)							Q.31a(ii)
		AGREE STRONGLY	AGREE	UNCERTAIN	DISAGREE	DISAGREE STRONGLY	DON'T KNOW	REFUSED	% THAT AGREE
1	Q.31a (i) Members of the .... (GPA) should be prohibited from standing as candidates for elected positions • *Lede van die (GPA) behoort verbied te word om as kandidaat vir 'n verkose posisie te staan*	12-1	2	3	4	5	8	9	
	Q.31a (ii) And about what percentage of the people in South Africa do you think agree with you on this issue • *En omtrent watter persentasie van die mense in Suid-Afrika dink u stem saam met u oor hierdie aangeleentheid*								13-15
2	Members of the ..... (GPA) should be allowed to hold street demonstrations in your community • *Lede van die (GPA) behoort toegelaat te word om straatbetogings in u gemeenskap te hou*	16-1	2	3	4	5	8	9	
3	..... (GPA) should be officially banned in your community • *..... (GPA) behoort amptelilk in u gemeenskap verban te word*	17-1	2	3	4	5	8	9	

IF DON'T KNOW PERCENTAGE IN Q.31a(ii), GO TO Q.31b)

IF RESPONDENT ANSWERS "DON'T KNOW" TO PERCENTAGE QUESTION IN Q.31a), ASK Q.31b):
Q.31b) Do you think most South Africans agree with your view or disagree with your view on this issue?
• *Dink u die meestse Suid-Afrikaners stem saam met of verskil van u sienswyse oor hierdie aangeleentheid?*

INTERVIEWER: SHOW CARD 15

		MOST AGREE	MOST DISAGREE	CAN'T SAY WHICH	DON'T KNOW	REFUSED
1	Members of the .... (GPA) should be prohibited from standing as a candidate for an elected position • *Lede van die ... (GPA) behoort verbied te word om as 'n kandidaat vir 'n verkose posisie te staan*	18-1	2	3	8	9

ENG/AFR

ASK ALL:

INTERVIEWER: NOW ASK ABOUT GROUP GPD **IN Q.30a, IF NO GROUP LISTED, ASK ABOUT** GPC .... GPB

LOOKING AT YOUR SHEET, WRITE DOWN THE NAME OF THE GROUP ______ GP 19-20

Q.32 Now let's consider the .... **(GPD/GPC/GPB)** a bit more. To what extent do you agree strongly, agree, are uncertain, disagree or disagree strongly with the following statements about ..... ?

• *Kom ons oorweeg nou die (GPD, GPC/GPB) 'n bietjie meer. Tot watter mate stem u sterk saam, stem u saam, is u onsker, verskil u of versil u sterk met die volgende stellings oor .... ?*

INTERVIEWER: SHOW CARD 16

		AGREE STRONGLY	AGREE	UNCERTAIN	DISAGREE	DISAGREE STRONGLY	DON'T KNOW	REFUSED
1	Members of the ( ) should be prohibited from standing as candidates for elected positions • *Lede van die ( ) behoort verbied te word om as 'n kandidaat vir 'n verkose posisie te staan*	21-1	2	3	4	5	8	9
2	Members of the ( ) should be allowed to hold street demonstrations in your community • *Lede van die ( ) behoort toegelaat te word om straatbetogings in u gemeenskap te hou*	22-1	2	3	4	5	8	9
3	( ) should be officially banned in your community • *( ) behoort amptelik in u gemeenskap verbied te word*	23-1	2	3	4	5	8	9

NO LEAST DISLIKED GROUP NAMED 24-1

ENG/AFR

PROJECT TOLERANCE III	- 19 -	CARD 5 DSI 14/2000

Now I would like to read you a short story and ask your opinions about it.

• *Nou wil ek vir u 'n kort storie lees en u opinie oor dit vra.*

And now here are some questions about what happened in the story.

• *En nou is hier 'n aantal vrae oor wat in die storie gebeur het.*

CIRCLE HERE IF THE RESPONDENT ASKS THAT THE STORY BE RE-READ

25-1

Q.33 First considering all aspects of the story, how fair do you think the outcome is to the families of the victims? If 10 means that you believe the outcome is completely fair to families of the victims and 1 means the outcome is completely unfair to them, which number from 10 to 1 best describes how you feel? For example, you might answer with a 4 if you think the outcome is only somewhat unfair, or a 7 if you think the outcome is somewhat fair to the families of the victims.

• *Eerstens, agnemende van al die aspekte van die storie, hoe reverdig dink u is die uitkoms teenoor die families van die slagoffers? As 10 beteken dat u dink die uitkoms is heeltemal regverdig teenoor die families van die slagoffers en 1 beteken die uitkoms is heeltemal onregverdig teenoor hulle, watter nommer tussen 10 en 1 sal die beste beskryf hoe u voel? Byvoorbeeld, mag u moontlik met 4 antwoord as u dink die uitkoms is ietwat onregverdig, of 'n 7 as u dink die uitkoms is ietwat regverdig teenoor die families van die slagoffers.*

INTERVIEWER: SHOW CARD 17

Completely fair *Heeltemal regverdig*									Completely unfair *Heeltemal onregverdig*	DK	REFUSED	
10	9	8	7	6	5	4	3	2	1	98	99	26-27

CIRCLE HERE IF THE RESPONDENT ASKS THAT THE STORY BE RE-READ

28-1

Q.34 Using the same scale, how fair do you think the outcome is to Phillip?

• *Deur gebruik te maak van dieselfde skaal, hoe regverdig is die uitkoms teenoor Phillip?*

INTERVIEWER: SHOW CARD 17

Completely fair *Heeltemal regverdig*									Completely unfair *Heeltemal onregverdig*	DK	REFUSED	
10	9	8	7	6	5	4	3	2	1	98	99	29-30

CIRCLE HERE IF THE RESPONDENT ASKS THAT THE STORY BE RE-READ

31-1

ENG/AFR

INTERVIEWER: DO NOT RE-READ STORY

Thinking back on the story.
• *Dink nou terug na die story.*

Q.35 Do you think that the families of the victims were given a chance to tell how the bombing has affected their lives? **(READ OUT)**
• *Dink u die families van die slagoffers is 'n geleentheid gegee om te sê hoe die bomontploffing hul lewens beinvloed het?*

Certain they were • *Hulle was verseker*	32-1
Probably were • *Hulle was moontlik*	2
Probably were not • *Hulle was moontlik nie*	3
Certain they were not • *Hulle was verseker nie*	4
DON'T KNOW	8
REFUSED	9

Q.36 Do you think that the families of the victims say they found out what happened to their loved ones? **(READ OUT)**
• *Dink u die families van die slagoffers sê dat hulle uitgevind het wat met hulle geliefdes gebeur het?*

Certain they were • *Hulle was verseker*	33-1
Probably were • *Hulle was moontlik*	2
Probably were not • *Hulle was moontlik nie*	3
Certain they were not • *Hulle was verseker nie*	4
DON'T KNOW	8
REFUSED	9

Q.37 Do you think that Phillip's apology was accepted by the families of the victims? **(READ OUT)**
• *Dink u dat Phillip se verskoning was aanvaar deur die families van die slagoffers?*

Certain it was • *Hulle was verseker*	34-1
Probably was • *Hulle was moontlik*	2
Probably was not • *Hulle was moontlik nie*	3
Certain it was not • *Hulle was verseker nie*	4
DON'T KNOW	8
REFUSED	9

Q.38 Do you think that Phillip was punished by the actions of his own family? **(READ OUT)**
• *Dink u dat Phillip gestraf is deur die aksies van sy eie familie?*

Certain he was • *Hulle was verseker*	35-1
Probably was • *Hulle was moontlik*	2
Probably was not • *Hulle was moontlik nie*	3
Certain he was not • *Hulle was verseker nie*	4
DON'T KNOW	8
REFUSED	9

Q.39 Do you think that the families of the victims received compensation for what happened to them? **(READ OUT)**
• *Dink u dat die families van die slagoffers kompensasie ontvang het vir wat met hulle gebeur het?*

Certain they did • *Hulle was verseker*	36-1
Probably did • *Hulle was moontlik*	2
Probably did not • *Hulle was moontlik nie*	3
Certain they did not • *Hulle was verseker nie*	4
DON'T KNOW	8
REFUSED	9

Q.40a) Would you forgive Phillip for what happened in the story?
• *Sou u Phillip vergewe vir wat in die storie gebeur het?*

Yes • *Ja*	37-1	→ **GO TO Q.40b)**
No • *Nee*	2	→ **GO TO Q.41**
DON'T KNOW	8	
REFUSED	9	

<u>IF YES IN Q.40a), ASK</u>:
Q.40b) How much would you forgive Phillip? **(READ OUT)**
• *Hoeveel sou u Phillip vergewe?*

I would definitely forgive him completely • *Ek sal hom definitief heeltemal vergewe*	38-1
I would probably forgive him • *Ek sal hom moontlik vergewe*	2
I would not forgive him • *Ek sal hom nie vergewe nie*	3
DON'T KNOW	8
REFUSED	9

Q.41 Now, what about the amnesty? Do you think Phillip should have been granted amnesty for his actions? **(READ OUT)**
• *Nou, wat van amnestie? Dink u amnestie moes aan Phillip verleen word vir sy aksies?*

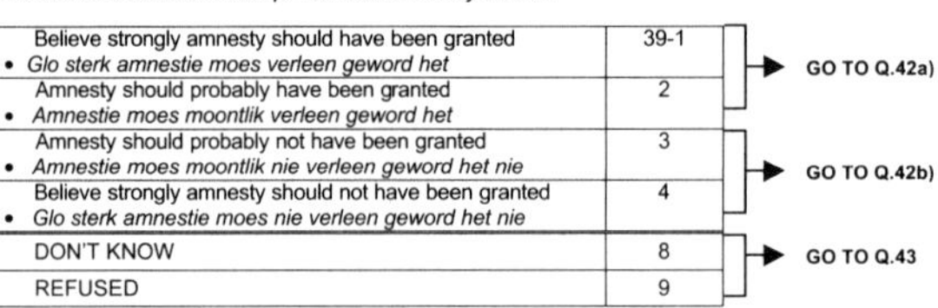

Believe strongly amnesty should have been granted • *Glo sterk amnestie moes verleen geword het*	39-1	→ **GO TO Q.42a)**
Amnesty should probably have been granted • *Amnestie moes moontlik verleen geword het*	2	
Amnesty should probably not have been granted • *Amnestie moes moontlik nie verleen geword het nie*	3	→ **GO TO Q.42b)**
Believe strongly amnesty should not have been granted • *Glo sterk amnestie moes nie verleen geword het nie*	4	
DON'T KNOW	8	→ **GO TO Q.43**
REFUSED	9	

ENG/AFR

INTERVIEWER:

IF ANSWERED [BELIEVE STRONGLY AMNESTY SHOULD HAVE BEEN GRANTED] OR [AMNESTY SHOULD PROBABLY HAVE BEEN GRANTED] IN Q.41, ASK Q.42a):

IF ANSWERED 3 [AMNESTY SHOULD PROBABLY NOT HAVE BEEN GRANTED] OR [BELIEVE STRONGLY AMNESTY SHOULD NOT HAVE BEEN GRANTED] IN Q.41, ASK Q.42b):

Q.42a) Now we would like you to imagine that the Constitutional Court decided that Phillip should NOT be granted amnesty. Using this same scale from 10 to 1, would you accept the Constitutional Court's decision to not give Phillip amnesty or would you try to get the Court's decision reversed?

• *Nou wil ons hê dat u uself moet veronderstel dat die Grondwetlike Hof besluit het om nie amnestie aan Phillip toe te staan nie. Deur gebruik te maak van dieselfde skaal van 10 tot 1, sal u die Konstitutionele Hof se beslissing aanvaar om nie aan Phillip amnestie toe te staan nie, of sal u probeer om die Hof se beslissing om te keer?*

INTERVIEWER: SHOW CARD 18

Accept the court's decision *Aanvaar die hof se beslissing*									Try to get the court's decision reversed *Probeer om die hof se beslissing om te keer*	DK	REFUSED	
10	9	8	7	6	5	4	3	2	1	98	99	40-41

OR

Q.42b) Now we would like you to imagine that the Constitutional Court decided that Phillip SHOULD BE granted amnesty. Using this same scale from 10 to 1, would you accept the Constitutional Court's decision to give Phillip amnesty or would you try to get the court's decision reversed?

• *Nou wil ons hê dat u moet voorstel dat die Grondwetlike Hof besluit het dat amnestie aan Phillip toegestaan MOET WORD. Deur gebruik te maak van dieselfde skaal van 10 tot 1, sou u die Grondwetlike Hof se beslissing aanvaar om aan Phillip amnestie te verleen, of sal u probeer om die hof se beslissing om te draai?*

INTERVIEWER: SHOW CARD 18

Accept the court's decision *Aanvaar die hof se beslissing*									Try to get the court's decision reversed *Probeer om die hof se beslissing om te keer*	DK	REFUSED	
10	9	8	7	6	5	4	3	2	1	98	99	42-43

ASK ALL:

Q.43 Would it really matter very much to you, one way or another, if Phillip got amnesty?

• *Sou u regtig omgee, een kant toe of ander kant toe, of Phillip amnestie verkry?*

READ OUT

Would matter a great deal to me • *Sal baie vir my saak maak*	44-1
Would matter some to me • *Sal ietwat vir my saak maak*	2
Would not matter much to me • *Sal nie baie vir my saak maak nie*	3
Wouldn't matter to me at all • *Sal glad nie vir my saak maak nie*	4
DON'T KNOW	8
REFUSED	9

PROJECT TOLERANCE III	**- 23 -**	**CARD 5 DSI 14/2000**

Q.44 How much do you agree or disagree with the following statements? Would you say you agree strongly, agree, are uncertain, disagree or disagree strongly?

• *Tot watter mate stem u saam met of verskil u van die volgende stellings? Sou u sê u stem sterk saam, stem saam, is onseker, verskil of verskil sterk?*

	INTERVIEWER: SHOW CARD 19	AGREE STRONGLY	AGREE	UNCERTAIN	DISAGREE	DISAGREE STRONGLY	DON'T KNOW	REFUSED
1	There are two kinds of people in this world: those who are for the truth and those who are against it • *Daar is twee soorte mense in hierdie wêreld: dié wat vir die waarheid is en dié wat daarteen is*	45-1	2	3	4	5	8	9
2	The people who run the country are not really concerned with what happens to people like me • *Mense wat aan bewind van die land is, is nie regtig besorg oor wat met mense soos ek gebeur nie*	46-1	2	3	4	5	8	9
3	Affirmative action is necessary to make up for the harm done to people in our apartheid past • *Regstellende aksie is noodsaaklik om op te maak vir die skade wat aan mense in ons apartheid verlede aangerig is*	47-1	2	3	4	5	8	9
4	A group which tolerates too many differences of opinion among its own members cannot exist for long • *'n Groep wat te veel verskille van opinie tussen sy eie lede verdra, kan nie lank bestaan nie*	48-1	2	3	4	5	8	9
5	If public officials are not interested in hearing what people like me think, there is really no way to make them listen • *As regeringsamptenare nie belangstel om te hoor wat mense soos ek dink nie, is daar regtig geen manier om hulle te mààk luister nie*	49-1	2	3	4	5	8	9
6	To compromise with our political opponents is dangerous because it usually leads to the betrayal of our own side • *Dit is gevaarlik om kompromieë met ons politieke teenstanders aan te gaan, want dit lei gewoonlik tot verraad van ons eie kant*	50-1	2	3	4	5	8	9
7	In our country, all political power is concentrated in the hands of a small group of people and it is impossible for the rest of us to influence what the government does • *In ons land, is al die politieke mag gekonsentreer in die hande van 'n klein groepie mense en dit is onmoontlik vir die res van ons om wat die regering doen, te beïnvloed*	51-1	2	3	4	5	8	9
8	Most of those who are profiting from Affirmative Action don't really deserve it • *Meeste van diegene wat deur regstellende aksie bevoordeel word verdien dit nie regtig nie*	52-1	2	3	4	5	8	9
9	The government pays too much attention to the needs of rich South Africans, and too little attention to the needs of the poor • *Die regering gee te veel aandag aan die behoeftes van ryk Suid-Afrikaners, en te min aandag aan die behoeftes van die armes*	53-1	2	3	4	5	8	9

ENG/AFR

INTERVIEWER: THE NEXT QUESTION IS AGAIN RELATED TO THE GROUP THE RESPONDENT DISLIKES THE MOST (Q.30a)

PLEASE WRITE DOWN THE NAME OF THE GROUP: .... GPA [ ] CODE

54-55 [ ][ ]

Q.45a) Here is a list of words that can be used to describe various political groups. Taking them one at a time, please tell me how you feel about the least liked group. The first pair of words is "not dangerous to society" versus "dangerous to society". If you consider (GPA) to be not dangerous at all, tell me the number 1. If you see (GPA) as very dangerous, tell me the number 7. The numbers 2 through 6 represent increasing degrees of danger. How dangerous to society do you think (GPA) is?

• *Hier is 'n lys woorde wat gebruik kan word om verskeie politieke groepe te beskryf. Deur een op 'n slag te neem, sê asseblief vir my hoe u oor (GPA) voel. Die eerste paar woorde is "nie gevaarlik vir die samelewing" teenoor "gevaarlik vir die samelewing". As u (GPA) as glad nie gevaarlik beskou nie, noem vir my die syfer 1. As u (GPA) as baie gevaarlik beskou, noem vir my die syfer 7. Die syfers 2 tot 6 verteenwoordig toenemende grade van gevaar. Hoe gevaarlik dink u is (GPA) vir die samelewing?*

INTERVIEWER: SHOW CARD 20

56

Not dangerous to society *Nie gevaarlik vir samelewing*								Dangerous to society *Gevaarlik vir samelewing*	Uncertain/ don't know	Refused/no answer
Not dangerous	1	2	3	4	5	6	7	Dangerous	8	9

Q.45b) **INTERVIEWER: SHOW CARD 21**

57

To what degree do you think ..... are *Tot watter mate dink u is ....*									Uncertain/ don't know	Refused/no answer
Predictable *Voorspelbaar*	1	2	3	4	5	6	7	Unpredictable *Onvoorspel-baar*	8	9

Q.45c) **INTERVIEWER: SHOW CARD 22**

58

To what degree do you think ..... present: *Tot watter mate dink u ..... hou .*									Uncertain/ don't know	Refused/no answer
Danger to the normal lives of people *Gevaar in vir die normale lewens van mense*	1	2	3	4	5	6	7	No danger to the normal lives of people *Nie gevaar in vir die normale lewens van mense nie*	8	9

Q.45d) **INTERVIEWER: SHOW CARD 23**

59

To what degree do you think ..... are likely to *Tot watter mate dink u is dit waarskynlik dat .....*									Uncertain/ don't know	Refused/no answer
Gain a lot of power in South Africa *Baie mag in Suid-Afrika sal inwin*	1	2	3	4	5	6	7	Unlikely to gain a lot of power in South Africa *Onwaarskynlik baie mag in Suid-Afrika sal inwin*	8	9

Q.45e) **INTERVIEWER: SHOW CARD 24**

60

To what degree do you think ..... are *Tot watter mate dink u is ....*									Uncertain/ don't know	Refused/no answer
Likely to affect how well my family and I live *Dit waarskynlik dat .... hoe goed ek en my familie leef sal affekteer*	1	2	3	4	5	6	7	Unlikely to affect how well my family and I live *Dit waarskynlik dat ... hoe goed ek en my familie leef sal affekteer*	8	9

Q.45f) **INTERVIEWER: SHOW CARD 25**

61

To what degree are you ..... *Tot watter mate is u ....*									Uncertain/ don't know	Refused/no answer
Angry towards the group (GPA) *Kwaad vir die groep (GPA)*	1	2	3	4	5	6	7	Indifferent towards the group (GPA) *Onpartydig teenoor die groep (GPA)*	8	9

PROJECT TOLERANCE III	- 25 -	CARD 5	DSI 14/2000

Q.45g) **INTERVIEWER: SHOW CARD 26**

62

To what degree do you think ..... are: *Tot watter mate dink u is .....*									Uncertain/ don't know	Refused/no answer
Willing to follow the rules of democracy *Gewillig om reëls van demokrasie te volg*	1	2	3	4	5	6	7	Not willing to follow the rules of democracy *Onwillig om reëls van demokrasie te volg*	8	9

Q.45h) **INTERVIEWER: SHOW CARD 27**

63

To what degree do you think ..... are: *Tot watter mate dink u is .....*									Uncertain/ don't know	Refused/no answer
Powerful *Magtig*	1	2	3	4	5	6	7	Not powerful *Nie magtig nie*	8	9

Q.46a) Let's suppose, for a minute, that the (GPA) came to power in South Africa. Using the scale where 1 means that nothing would change, and 7 means that everything would change completely, please estimate how much you think the political situation in the country would change.

• *Laat ons vir 'n minuut veronderstel dat die (GPA) aan bewind kan in Suid-Afrika. Deur gebruik te maak van die skaal waar 1 beteken niks sal verander nie, en 7 beteken dat alles heeltemal sal verander, skat asseblief hoeveel u dink die politieke situasie in die land sal verander.*

INTERVIEWER: SHOW CARD 28

64

Nothing would change *Niks sal verander nie*							Everything would change *Alles sal verander*	Uncertain/ don't know	Refused/no answer
1	2	3	4	5	6	7		8	9

Q.46b) And how much would the (GPA) affect you personally if it comes to power? Considering your own political freedom, to what extent would this group, if it gained power, affect your personal political freedom?

• *En hoeveel sal die (GPA) u persoonlik affekteer as dit aan bewind kom? Neem in ag u eie politieke vryheid, tot watter mate sou hierdie groep, as dit aan bewind kom, u persoonlike politieke vryheid affekteer?*

INTERVIEWER: SHOW CARD 29

65

Would not affect my personal political freedom at all *Sal glad nie my persoonlike politieke vryheid affekteer nie*							Would greatly reduce my personal political freedom *Sal my persoonlike politieke vryheid baie affekteer*	Uncertain/ don't know	Refused/no answer
1	2	3	4	5	6	7		8	9

Q.46c) Considering your own personal security, to what extent would the (GPA), if it gained power, affect your personal security?

• *Neem in ag u eie persoonlike sekuriteit, tot watter mate sou die (GPA), as dit aan bewind kom, u persoonlike sekuriteit affekteer?*

INTERVIEWER: SHOW CARD 30

66

Would not affect my personal security at all *Sal glad nie my persoonlike sekuriteit affekteer nie*							Would greatly affect my personal security *Sal my persoonlike sekuriteit baie affekteer*	Uncertain/ don't know	Refused/no answer
1	2	3	4	5	6	7		8	9

Q.47 Do you personally know at least one member of the (GPA)?

• *Ken u ten minste een lid van die (GPA)?*

Yes •	67-1
No •	2
DON'T KNOW	8
REFUSED	9

79 - 80 - 05

ENG/AFR

PROJECT TOLERANCE III - 26 - CARD 6 DSI 14/2000

INTERVIEWER: ASK ABOUT THE GROUP NAMES GPD OR GPC OR GPB

WRITE DOWN THE NAME OF THE GROUP: ________ GPD GPC GPB

7-8

9

INTERVIEWER: SHOW CARD 31

Q.48a) And to what degree do you think .... GPD OR GPC OR GPB is ..... ?
• *En tot watter mate dink u is .... (GPD) OF (GPC) OF (GPB) .... ?*

10

Not dangerous to society *Nie gevaarlik vir die samelewing nie*							Dangerous to society *Gevaarlik vir die samelewing*	Uncertain/ don't know	Refused/no answer
Not dangerous 1	2	3	4	5	6	7	Dangerous	8	9

Q.48b) **INTERVIEWER: SHOW CARD 32**

11

To what degree do you think ..... are *Tot watter mate dink u is .....*									Uncertain/ don't know	Refused/no answer
Predictable *Voorspelbaar*	1	2	3	4	5	6	7	Unpredictable *Onvoorspel-baar*	8	9

Q.48c) **INTERVIEWER: SHOW CARD 33**

12

To what degree do you think ..... present a: *Tot watter mate dink u .... hou*									Uncertain/ don't know	Refused/no answer
Danger to the normal lives of people *Gevaar in vir die normale lewens van mense*	1	2	3	4	5	6	7	No danger to the normal lives of people *Gevaar in vir die normale lewens van mense nie*	8	9

Q.48d) **INTERVIEWER: SHOW CARD 34**

13

To what degree do you think ..... are likely to *Tot watter mate dink u is dit ..... dat .....*									Uncertain/ don't know	Refused/no answer
Gain a lot of power in South Africa *Waarskynlik baie mag in Suid-Afrika sal inwin*	1	2	3	4	5	6	7	Unlikely to gain a lot of power in South Africa *Onwaarskynlik baie mag in Suid-Afrika sal inwin*	8	9

Q.48e) **INTERVIEWER: SHOW CARD 35**

14

To what degree do you think ..... are *Tot watter mate dink u is ....*									Uncertain/ don't know	Refused/no answer
Likely to affect how well my family and I live *Dit waarskynlik dat ... hoe goed ek en my familie leef sal affekteer*	1	2	3	4	5	6	7	Unlikely to affect how well my family and I live *Dit onwaarskynlik dat ... hoe goed ek en my familie leef sal affekteer*	8	9

ENG/AFR

Q.48f) **INTERVIEWER: SHOW CARD 36**

15

To what degree are you ..... *Tot watter mate is u ....*									Uncertain/ don't know	Refused/no answer
Angry towards the group ( ) *Kwaad vir die groep (...)*	1	2	3	4	5	6	7	Indifferent towards the group ( ) *Onpartydig teenoor die groep ( )*	8	9

Q.48g) **INTERVIEWER: SHOW CARD 37**

16

To what degree do you think ..... are: *Tot watter mate dink u is ....*									Uncertain/ don't know	Refused/no answer
Willing to follow the rules of democracy *Gewillig om reëls van demokrasie te volg*	1	2	3	4	5	6	7	Not willing to follow the rules of democracy *Onwillig om reëls van demokrasie te volg*	8	9

Q.48h) **INTERVIEWER: SHOW CARD 38**

17

To what degree do you think ..... are: *Tot watter mate dink u is .....*									Uncertain/ don't know	Refused/no answer
Powerful *Magtig*	1	2	3	4	5	6	7	Not powerful *Nie magtig nie*	8	9

Q.49 How much do you know about the activities of the Truth and Reconciliation Commission (TRC)? **(READ OUT)**
• *Hoeveel weet u van die aktiwiteite van die Waarheids- en Versoeningskommissie (WVK)?*

A great deal • *Baie*	18-1
Some, but not a great deal • *'n Bietjie, maar nie baie nie*	2
Not very much • *Nie baie nie*	3
Nothing at all • *Niks nie*	4
DON'T KNOW	8
REFUSED	9

PROJECT TOLERANCE III	- 28 -	CARD 6	DSI 14/2000

Q.50 In general, how do you feel about the activities of the TRC? Would you say you ..... ?
• *Oor die algemeen, hoe voel u oor die aktiwiteite van die WVK? Sou u sê u ..... ?*

READ OUT

Strongly approve of what the TRC has done • *Sterk goedkeur oor wat die WVK gedoen het*	19-1
Somewhat approve • *Ietwat goedkeur*	2
Somewhat disapprove • *Ietwat afkeur*	3
Strongly disapprove of what the TRC has done • *Sterk afkeur oor wat die WVK gedoen het*	4
DON'T KNOW	8
REFUSED	9

Q.51 The TRC is often said to have several important jobs. We would like your opinion about how well the TRC has done each of these jobs. Would you say that the TRC has done an excellent job, pretty good job, pretty bad job or poor job?
• *Daar word dikwels gesê dat die WVK verskeie belangrike werke het. Ons wil u opinie hê oor hoe goed die WVK elk van hierdie werke gedoen het? Sou u sê die WVK het 'n puik werk gedoen, nogal goeie werk gedoen, nogal sleg werk gedoen, of 'n slegte werk gedoen?*

	INTERVIEWER: SHOW CARD 39	EXCELLENT JOB	PRETTY GOOD JOB	PRETTY BAD JOB	POOR JOB	DON'T KNOW	REFUSED
1	Letting the families of people know what happened to their loved ones • *Die families van mense laat weet wat met hul geliefdes gebeur het*	20-1	2	3	4	8	9
2	Providing a true and unbiased account of South Africa's history • *Voorsien 'n ware en onpartydige verklaring van Suid-Afrika se geskiedenis*	21-1	2	3	4	8	9
3	Awarding compensation to those who suffered abuses under the apartheid regime • *Voorsien vergoeding vir diegene wat mishandel is onder die apartheid bewind*	22-1	2	3	4	8	9
4	Ensuring that human rights abuses will not happen again in South Africa's future • *Verseker dat die misbruik van menlike reg nie weer in Suid-Afrika se toekoms sal gebeur nie*	23-1	2	3	4	8	9
5	Making sure that those guilty of atrocities are punished • *Maak seker dat daardie wat skuldig is aan misbruike gestraf word*	24-1	2	3	4	8	9

Q.52 Now do you agree strongly, agree, are uncertain, disagree or disagree strongly that: The TRC was essential to avoid civil war in South Africa during the transition from white rule to majority rule.
• *Stem u nou sterk saam, stem u saam, is u onseker, verskil u, of verskil u sterk dat: Die WVK was noodsaaklik om burger-oorlog in Suid-Afrika te voorkom tydens die oorgang van blanke bewind tot meerderheids bewind.*

INTERVIEWER: SHOW CARD 40

Agree Strongly	Agree	Uncertain	Disagree	Disagree Strongly	Don't Know	Refused
25-1	2	3	4	5	8	9

ENG/AFR

PROJECT TOLERANCE III	- 29 -	CARD 6 DSI 14/2000

Q.53 The TRC granted amnesties to some of those who came forward and admitted committing atrocities during the struggle over apartheid. Do you approve of amnesty being given to those who admitted committing atrocities during the struggle over apartheid? **(READ OUT)**

• *Die WVK het amnestie verleen aan sommige van diegene wat vorendag gekom het en erken het dat hulle gruweldade gepleeg het tydens die stryd teen apartheid. Keur u dit goed dat mense wat hul misdade erken tydens die stryd teen apartheid amnestie verleen word?*

Strongly approve • *Keur dit sterk goed*	26-1
Approve somewhat • *Keur dit ietwat goed*	2
Disapprove somewhat • *Keur dit iewat af*	3
Disapprove a great deal • *Keur dit sterk af*	4
DON'T KNOW	8
REFUSED	9

Q.54a) In general, how fair do you think it is to the victims that these people were given amnesty? **(READ OUT)**

• *Oor die algemeen, hoe regverdig dink u is dit vir die slagoffers dat hierdie mense amestie verleen is?*

Extremely fair • *Uiters regverdig*	27-1
Fair • *Regverdig*	2
Not very fair • *Nie baie regverdig nie*	3
Not fair at all • *Glad nie regverdig nie*	4
DON'T KNOW	8
REFUSED	9

Q.54b) And what about those seeking amnesty? How fair was it to them? **(READ OUT)**

• *En wat van diegene wat amnestie versoek? Hoe regverdig was dit vir hulle?*

Extremely fair • *Uiters regverdig*	28-1
Fair • *Regverdig*	2
Not very fair • *Nie baie regverdig nie*	3
Not fair at all • *Glad nie regverdig nie*	4
DON'T KNOW	8
REFUSED	9

Q.54c) And to ordinary people like you? How fair was it? **(READ OUT)**

• *En vir gewone mense soos u? Hoe regverdig was dit?*

Extremely fair • *Uiters regverdig*	29-1
Fair • *Regverdig*	2
Not very fair • *Nie baie regverdig nie*	3
Not fair at all • *Glad nie regverdig nie*	4
DON'T KNOW	8
REFUSED	9

Q.54d) And to those who died during the struggle over apartheid? How fair was it to them? **(READ OUT)**

• *En vir diegene wat gesterf het tydens die stryd oor apartheid? Hoe regverdig was dit vir hulle?*

Extremely fair • *Uiters regverdig*	30-1
Fair • *Regverdig*	2
Not very fair • *Nie baie regverdig nie*	3
Not fair at all • *Glad nie regverdig nie*	4
DON'T KNOW	8
REFUSED	9

ENG/AFR

We are interested in your view of those who received amnesty from the TRC. As you know, those who sought amnesty had to come forward and talk about the horrible things they did in the past. In exchange for telling the truth, they were granted amnesty.

- *Ons stel belang in u siening oor diegene wat amnestie verleen is deur die WVK. Soos u weet, moes diegene wat amnestie verlang het vorendag kom en praat oor die afgryslike dinge wat hulle in die verlede gedoen het. In ruil vir die waarheid, is amnestie aan hulle verleen.*

Q.55a) Do you think those who were granted amnesty were punished by the fact that they had to publicly confess to doing horrible things? *Dink u diegene waaraan amnestie verleen is, is gestraf deur die feit dat hulle in die openbaar moes erken dat hulle afgryslike dinge gedoen het?*

(NOTE: IF CANNOT ANSWER ABOUT ALL, ASK ABOUT MOST)

IF RESPONDENT REFERS TO MOST INSTEAD OF ALL, CIRCLE HERE 31-1

SHOW CARD 41

READ OUT

Were punished harshly • *Is hard gestraf*	32-1
Were punished, but not too harshly • *Is gestraf, maar nie te hard nie*	2
Were punished only a little • *Is net 'n bietjie gestraf*	3
Were not punished at all • *Is glad nie gestraf nie*	4
DON'T KNOW	8
REFUSED	9

Q.55b) Do you think those who were granted amnesty are being punished today, by their own consciences? **(NOTE: IF CANNOT ANSWER ABOUT ALL, ASK ABOUT MOST)**

- *Dink u diegene waaraan amnestie verleen is, word vandag gestraf, deur hul eie gewete?*

SHOW CARD 41

READ OUT

Were punished harshly • *Is hard gestraf*	33-1
Were punished, but not too harshly • *Is gestraf, maar nie te hard nie*	2
Were punished only a little • *Is net 'n bietjie gestraf*	3
Were not punished at all • *Is glad nie gestraf nie*	4
DON'T KNOW	8
REFUSED	9

Q.56 Would you strongly support, support, oppose, or strongly oppose doing the following to those who were granted amnesty?

- *Sou u dit sterk ondersteun, ondersteun, teenstaan, of sterk teenstaan dat die volgende gedoen word aan diegene waaraan amnestie verleen is?*

	INTERVIEWER: SHOW CARD 42	STRONGLY SUPPORT	SUPPORT	OPPOSE	STRONGLY OPPOSE	DON'T KNOW	REFUSED
1	Prohibiting them from being employed by the state • *Belet die staat om hulle in diens te neem*	34-1	2	3	4	8	9
2	Forcing them to pay some money to those whom they victimised • *Dwing hulle om geld te betaal aan diegene wat hulle geviktimiseer het*	35-1	2	3	4	8	9
3	Forcing them to say that they are sorry for what they have done • *Dwing hulle om te sê hulle is jammer oor wat hulle gedoen het*	36-1	2	3	4	8	9
4	Expelling them from South Africa • *Verban hulle uit Suid-Afrika uit*	37-1	2	3	4	8	9

Q.57 There have been some proposals to give compensation to those whom the TRC finds to be victims of human rights violations. Have you heard any talk about giving compensation to victims?

- *Daar was sommige voorstelle om vergoeding te gee aan diegene wat deur die WVK erken is as slagoffers van menseregteskendings. Het u enige uitsprake gehoor om vergoeding wat aan slagoffers gegee gaan word?*

Have heard • *Het gehoor*	38-1
Have not heard • *Het nie gehoor nie*	2
DON'T KNOW	8
REFUSED	9

PROJECT TOLERANCE III - 31 - CARD 6 DSI 14/2000

Q.58 One idea is that the victims would receive compensation directly from the current government. Would you strongly support, support, oppose, or strongly oppose the current government providing the following kinds of compensation?

• *Een voorstel is dat slagoffers direk vergoeding sal kry van die huidige regering. Sou u dit sterk ondersteun, ondersteun, teenstaan of sterk teenstaan dat die regering die volgende fondse vir vergoeding verleen?*

INTERVIEWER: SHOW CARD 42

		STRONGLY SUPPORT	SUPPORT	OPPOSE	STRONGLY OPPOSE	DON'T KNOW	REFUSED
1	Public apologies to the victims • *Openbare apologie aan die slagoffers*	39-1	2	3	4	8	9
2	Special priority for jobs, housing and education • *Spesiale prioriteit vir werke, behuising en opvoeding*	40-1	2	3	4	8	9
3	Direct financial contributions to the victims and/or their families • *Direkte finansiele bydraes aan die slagoffers en/of hulle families*	41-1	2	3	4	8	9

Q.59 Some have proposed that the costs of these types of compensation should be paid by institutions other than the government. Would you strongly support, support, oppose, or strongly oppose requiring the following to pay some of the costs of compensating the victims?

• *Sommiges het voorgestel dat die kostes van hierdie tipes van vergoeding betaal moet word deur ander instansies eerder as die regering. Sou u dit sterk ondersteun, ondersteun, teenstaan of sterk teenstaan dat daar van die volgende instansie verwag sal word om van die kostes van die vergoeding van die slagoffers te betaal?*

INTERVIEWER: SHOW CARD 42

		STRONGLY SUPPORT	SUPPORT	OPPOSE	STRONGLY OPPOSE	DON'T KNOW	REFUSED
1	Large businesses in South Africa • *Groot besighede in Suid-Afrika*	42-1	2	3	4	8	9
2	The Afrikans churches/kerke • *Die Afrikaanse churches/kerke*	43-1	2	3	4	8	9
3	White South Africans • *Blanke Suid-Afrikaners*	44-1	2	3	4	8	9
4	Individual companies – like mining companies – that directly profited from apartheid • *Individuele maatskappye – soos mynmaatskappye – wat direk uit apartheid wins getrek het*	45-1	2	3	4	8	9
5	South African farmers • *Suid-Afrikaanse boere*	46-1	2	3	4	8	9
6	The perpetrators themselves • *Die skuldiges self*	47-1	2	3	4	8	9
7	Black South Africans who are currently benefiting from Affirmative Action • *Swart Suid-Afrikaners wat tans voordeel trek uit Regstellende Aksie*	48-1	2	3	4	8	9
8	New taxes on all South Africans • *Nuwe belasting vir alle Suid-Afrikaners*	49-1	2	3	4	8	9
9	Special taxes on wealthy South Africans • *Spesiale belasting vir ryk Suid-Afrikaners*	50-1	2	3	4	8	9

Q.60 There are currently many disputes in South Africa over the ownership of land. We are interested in your opinions about this matter. Do you agree strongly, agree, are uncertain, disagree or disagree strongly with the following statements?

• *Daar is huidiglik baie onenigheid in Suid-Afrika oor die eiendomsreg van grond. Ons stel belang in u opinie oor hierdie kwessie? Sou u sê u stem sterk saam, stem saam, is onseker, verskil of verskil sterk?*

INTERVIEWER: SHOW CARD 43

		AGREE STRONGLY	AGREE	UNCERTAIN	DISAGREE	DISAGREE STRONGLY	DON'T KNOW	REFUSED
1	Most land in South Africa was taken unfairly by white settlers, and they therefore have no right to the land today • *Die meeste grond in Suid-Afrika was onregverdig in besit geneem deur blanke setlaars, en daarom het hulle vandag geen reg tot grond nie*	51-1	2	3	4	5	8	9
2	Since it is impossible to tell who really owns land in South Africa, we should just accept that current owners have the right to keep their land • *Siende dat dit onmoontlik is om te sê wie regtig grond besit in Suid-Afrika, moet ons net aanvaar dat die huidige eienaars die reg het om hul grond te behou*	52-1	2	3	4	5	8	9
3	Something like <u>amnesty</u> ought to be given to the current owners of land so that it doesn't matter how they acquired their land and so that they can keep their property • *Iets soos <u>amnestie</u> behoort aan die huidige eienaars van grond verteen te word sodat dit nie saak maak hoe hulle hul grond verkry het nie en sodat hulle hul eiendom kan behou*	53-1	2	3	4	5	8	9
4	Land must be returned to blacks in South Africa, no matter what the consequences are for the current owners and for political stability in the country • *Grond moet teruggegee word aan swartes in Suid-Afrika, maak nie saak wat die gevolge vir die huidige eienaars is nie, en vir politieke stabiliteit in die land*	54-1	2	3	4	5	8	9

ENG/AFR

PROJECT TOLERANCE III - 32 - CARD 6 DSI 14/2000

Q.61 On the whole, do you agree that most people can be trusted or that you can't be too careful in dealing with people?
• *In die geheel, stem u saam dat die meeste mense vertrou kan word of dat u nie te versigtig kan wees wanneer u met mense te doen het nie?*

INTERVIEWER: SHOW CARD 44

Strongly agree that most people can be trusted • *Stem sterk saam dat die meeste mense vertrou kan word*	55-1
Agree that most people can be trusted • *Stem saam dat die meeste mense vertrou kan word*	2
Uncertain • *Onseker*	3
Agree that you can't be too careful in dealing with people • *Stem saam dat mens nie versigtig genoeg kan wees in omgang met mense nie*	4
Strongly agree that you can't be too careful • *Stem sterk saam dat 'n mens nie versigtig genoeg kan wees nie*	5
DON'T KNOW	8
REFUSED/NO ANSWER	9

Q.62 And what about the people you know – can they be trusted, or do you have to be very careful when dealing with people whom you know?
• *En wat van mense wat u ken, kan hulle vertrou word, of moet u baie versigtig wees, wanneer u met mense wat u ken, te doen kry?*

INTERVIEWER: SHOW CARD 45

Strongly agree that majority can be trusted • *Stem sterk saam dat die meerderheid vetrou kan word*	56-1
Agree that majority can be trusted • *Stem saam dat die meerderheid vertrou kan word*	2
Uncertain • *Onseker*	3
Agree that is necessary to be careful • *Stem saam dat dit nodig is om versigtig te wees*	4
Strongly agree that is necessary to be careful • *Stem sterk saam dat dit nodig is om versigtig te wees*	5
DON'T KNOW	8
REFUSED/NO ANSWER	9

Q.63 Please look at this card and tell me, for each item listed, how much confidence you have in them. Is it a great deal, quite a lot, not very much or none at all?
• *Kyk asseblief na hierdie kaart, en sê vir my, vir elkeen wat gelys is, hoeveel vertroue het u in elk van hulle. Dit is baie, nogal baie, nie baie nie of glad niks nie?*

	INTERVIEWER: SHOW CARD 46	A GREAT DEAL	QUITE A LOT	NOT VERY MUCH	NONE AT ALL	UNCERTAIN/ DON'T KNOW	REFUSED/ NO ANSWER
1	Thabo Mbeki	57-1	2	3	4	8	9
2	The legal system • *Die regstelsel*	58-1	2	3	4	8	9
3	The mass media • *Die massa media*	59-1	2	3	4	8	9
4	The police • *Die polisie*	60-1	2	3	4	8	9
5	Parliament • *Die parlement*	61-1	2	3	4	8	9
6	Local courts • *Plaaslike howe*	62-1	2	3	4	8	9
7	The South African political system • *Die Suid-Afrikaanse politieke stelsel*	63-1	2	3	4	8	9
8	The Constitutional Court • *Die Grondwetlike Hof*	64-1	2	3	4	8	9
9	The Truth and Reconciliation Commission • *Die Waarheids- en Versoeningskomissie*	65-1	2	3	4	8	9
10	Traditional leaders • *Tradisionele leiers*	66-1	2	3	4	8	9

ENG/AFR

PROJECT TOLERANCE III	- 33 -	CARD 6/7 DSI 14/2000

Q.64 There has been some talk recently about crime in South Africa. In terms of how it affects you personally, would you say that in the last year the level of crime has got worse, has not changed, or has got better?
• *Daar was onlangs sprake gewees van misdaad in Suid-Afrika. In terme van hoe dit u persoonlik raak, sou u sê dat in die laaste jaar het die vlak van misdaad versleg, dieselfde gebly, of verbeter?*

Got better • *Verbeter*	67-1	ASK Q.66a)
Has not changed • *Nie verander nie*	2	ASK Q.66a)
Got worse • *Versleg*	3	ASK Q.65
DON'T KNOW	8	ASK Q.66a)
REFUSED	9	ASK Q.66a)

Q.65 Would you say that crime has got a great deal worse, moderately worse, or only a little worse in comparison to last year?
• *Sou u sê dat misdaad het baie vererger, matiglik vererger, of net 'n bietjie vererger in vergelyking met verlede jaar?*

Got a great deal worse • *Baie erger geraak*	68-1
Got moderately worse • *Het redelik erger geraak*	2
Only a little worse • *Net 'n bietjie erger*	3
DON'T KNOW	8
REFUSED	9

ASK ALL:
Q.66a) Over the last year have you or your family been the victims of a crime?
• *Was u of u familie die afgelope jaar slagoffers van misdaad?*

Yes • *Ja*	69-1	ASK Q.66b) AND Q.67a)
No • *Nee*	2	ASK Q.68
REFUSED TO ANSWER	9	ASK Q.68

79 - 80 - 06

IF YES, ASK:
Q.66b) What type/kind of crime was it? **(MULTIMENTIONS POSSIBLE)**
• *Wat se tipe/soort misdaad was dit?*

Vehicle (car/van/truck) stolen • *Vervoermiddel (motor/paneelwa) gesteel*	7-1
Car hijacking • *Motor gekaap*	8-1
Home burglarised • *Huisinbraak*	9-1
Property stolen • *Eiendom gesteel*	10-1
Sexual harassment or sexual abuse or rape • *Seksuele teistering of seksuele mishandeling of verkragting*	11-1
Physically attacked by someone (shot, stabbed, beaten, etc.) • *Fisies aangeval deur iemand (geskiet, gesteek, geslaan, ens.)*	12-1
Other – pickpocket, car radio theft • *Ander – sakkeroller, motor radio gesteel*	13-1
Other (specify)	

14-15 [ ][ ]

16-17 [ ][ ]

18-19 [ ][ ]

ENG/AFR

Q.67a) Did you or anyone report the incident to the police?
• *Het u of enige iemand hierdie insident by die polisie gerapporteer?*

Yes • *Ja*	20-1	→ ASK Q.67b)
No • *Nee*	2	→ GO TO Q.68
REFUSED TO ANSWER	9	

IF YES:
Q.67b) Would you say that you were very satisfied, somewhat satisfied, not very satisfied, very dissatisfied with the way the police dealt with your report?
• *Sou u sê dat u baie tevrede was, ietwat tevrede was, nie baie tevrede was, baie ontevrede met die manier hoe die polisie u klag hanteer het?*

Very satisfied • *Baie tevrede*	21-1
Somewhat satisfied • *Ietwat tevrede*	2
Not very satisfied • *Nie baie tevrede nie*	3
Very dissatisfied • *Baie ontevrede*	4
DON'T KNOW	8
REFUSED	9

ASK ALL:
Q.68 How much do you agree, or disagree with each statement? Would you say that you agree strongly, agree, are uncertain, disagree or disagree strongly with each of these statements?
• *Hoeveel stem u saam of stem u nie saam met elke stelling? Sou u sê u stem sterk saam, stem saam, is onseker, verskil of verskil sterk met elk van hierdie stellings?*

INTERVIEWER: SHOW CARD 47

		AGREE STRONGLY	AGREE	UNCERTAIN	DISAGREE	DISAGREE STRONGLY	DON'T KNOW	REFUSED
1	I feel that I have a pretty good understanding of the important political issues facing our country • *Ek voel dat ek 'n redelike goeie begrip het van die belangrike politieke aangeleenthede wat ons land in die gesig staar*	22-1	2	3	4	5	8	9
2	Under the right circumstances, most people are capable of committing the most horrific crimes • *Onder die regte omstandighede, is die meeste mense instaat om die mees gruwelike misdade te pleeg*	23-1	2	3	4	5	8	9
3	I feel well prepared for participating in political life • *Ek voel goed voorbereid om aan die politieke lewe deel te neem*	24-1	2	3	4	5	8	9
4	Both those struggling for and those struggling against the old apartheid system did unforgivable things to people • *Beide diegene wat vir en diegene wat teen die ou apartheidstelsel 'n stryd geveer het, het onvergeeflik dade aan ander mense gedoen*	25-1	2	3	4	5	8	9
5	The abuses under apartheid were largely committed by a few evil individuals, not by the state institutions themselves • *Die skendings onder apartheid was grootliks deur 'n paar bose individue gepleeg, nie deur die staatsinstellings self nie*	26-1	2	3	4	5	8	9
6	Sometimes politics seems so complicated that a person like me can't really understand what's going on • *Partykeer lyk die politiek so ingewikkeld dat 'n persoon soos ek nie regtig kan verstaan wat aan die gang is nie*	27-1	2	3	4	5	8	9

ENG/AFR

Q.69 We are interested in your views about who was responsible for creating and maintaining the old apartheid state and its institutions. How much should the following groups be blamed for the creation of and maintenance of the apartheid state in South Africa?

• *Ons stel belang in u sienings oor wie verantwoordelik was vir die skepping en handhawing van die ou apartheidstaat en sy instellings. Hoeveel moet die volgende groepe blameer word vir die skepping en handhawing van die ou apartheidstaat in Suid-Afrika?*

INTERVIEWER: SHOW CARD 48

		BLAMED A GREAT DEAL	BLAMED SOMEWHAT	NOT BLAMED VERY MUCH	LITTLE, IF ANY BLAME	DON'T KNOW	REFUSED/ NO ANSWER
1	The National Party • *Die Nasionale Party*	28-1	2	3	4	8	9
2	White Afrikaners • *Blanke Afrikaners*	29-1	2	3	4	8	9
3	White English • *Blanke Engelse*	30-1	2	3	4	8	9
4	The Afrikans churches • *Die Afrikaanse kerke*	31-1	2	3	4	8	9
5	The white business community • *Die blanke besigheidsgemeenskap*	32-1	2	3	4	8	9
6	Askaris (traitors) • *Askaris (verraaiers)*	33-1	2	3	4	8	9
7	Coloured people • *Kleurlinge*	34-1	2	3	4	8	9
8	South Africans of Asian origin • *Suid-Afrikaners van Asiatiese oorsprong*	35-1	2	3	4	8	9
9	Communists • *Kommuniste*	36-1	2	3	4	8	9

Q.70a) Now I'd like to ask you a few questions about the South African Constitutional Court. Would you say you are very aware, somewhat aware, not very aware or have you never heard of the South African Constitutional Court?

• *Nou wil ek u 'n paar vrae vra oor die Suid-Afrikaanse Grondwetlike Hof. Sou u sê u is baie bewus, ietwat bewus, nie baie bewus nie, of het u nog nooit van die Suid Afrikaanse Grondwetlike Hof gehoor nie?*

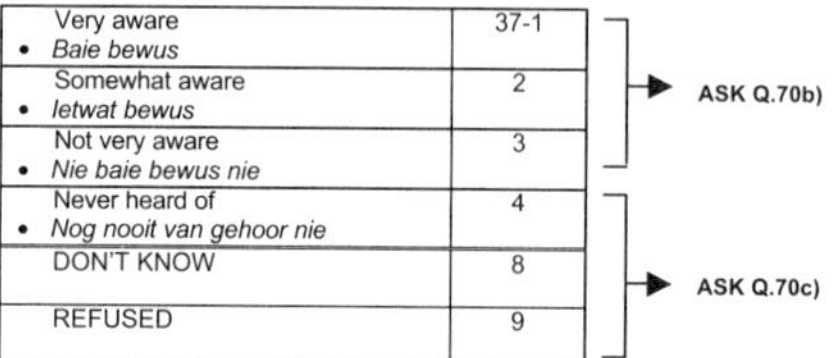

Very aware • *Baie bewus*	37-1	→ ASK Q.70b)
Somewhat aware • *Ietwat bewus*	2	
Not very aware • *Nie baie bewus nie*	3	
Never heard of • *Nog nooit van gehoor nie*	4	→ ASK Q.70c)
DON'T KNOW	8	
REFUSED	9	

Q.70b) From what you have heard or read, would you say you are very satisfied, somewhat satisfied, not very satisfied or not satisfied at all with the way the South African Constitutional Court has been working?

• *Van wat u gehoor of gelees het, sou u sê u is baie tevrede, ietwat tevrede, nie baie tevrede nie, of glad nie tevrede nie met die manier hoe die Suid-Afrikaanse Grondwetlike Hof werk?*

Very satisfied • *Baie tevrede*	38-1	→ ASK Q.71a)
Somewhat satisfied • *Ietwat tevrede*	2	
Not very satisfied • *Nie baie tevrede nie*	3	
Not satisfied at all • *Glad nie tevrede nie*	4	
DON'T KNOW	8	
REFUSED	9	

Q.70c) Would you say you are very satisfied, somewhat satisfied, not very satisfied or not satisfied at all with the way the South African Constitutional Court has been working?

• *Sou u sê u is baie tevrede, ietwat tevrede, nie baie tevrede nie of glad nie tevrede nie met die manier hoe die Suid-Afrikaanse Grondwetlike Hof werk nie?*

Very satisfied • *Baie tevrede*	39-1
Somewhat satisfied • *Ietwat tevrede*	2
Not very satisfied • *Nie baie tevrede nie*	3
Not satisfied at all • *Glad nie tevrede nie*	4
DON'T KNOW	8
REFUSED	9

ASK ALL:

Q.71a) And what about the Parliament – would you say you are very aware, somewhat aware, not very aware or have you never heard of the South African Parliament?

• *En wat van die parlement – sou u sê u is baie bewus, ietwat bewus, nie baie bewus nie of het u nog nooit van die Suid-Afrikaanse Parlement gehoor nie?*

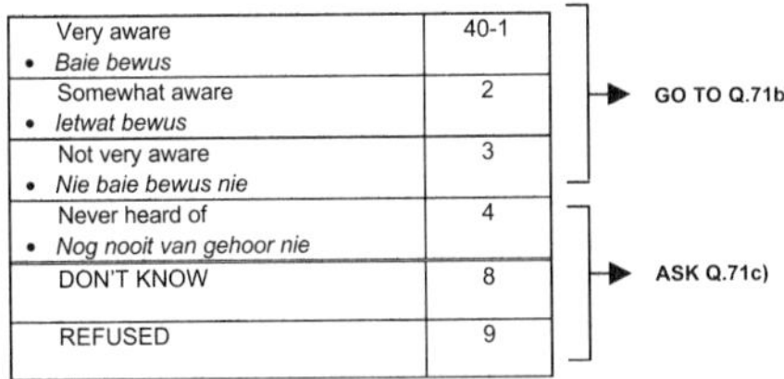

Very aware • *Baie bewus*	40-1	→ GO TO Q.71b)
Somewhat aware • *Ietwat bewus*	2	
Not very aware • *Nie baie bewus nie*	3	
Never heard of • *Nog nooit van gehoor nie*	4	→ ASK Q.71c)
DON'T KNOW	8	
REFUSED	9	

Q.71b) From what you have heard or read, would you say you are very satisfied, somewhat satisfied, not very satisfied or not satisfied at all with the way the South African Parliament has been working?

• *Van wat u gehoor of gelees het, sou u sê u is baie tevrede, ietwat tevrede, nie baie tevrede nie, of glad nie tevrede nie met die manier hoe die Suid-Afrikaanse Parlement werk?*

Very satisfied • *Baie tevrede*	41-1	→ GO TO Q.72
Somewhat satisfied • *Ietwat tevrede*	2	
Not very satisfied • *Nie baie tevrede nie*	3	
Not satisfied at all • *Glad nie tevrede nie*	4	
DON'T KNOW	8	
REFUSED	9	

Q.71c) Would you say you are very satisfied, somewhat satisfied, not very satisfied or not satisfied at all with the way the South African Parliament has been working?

• *Sal u sê u is baie tevrede, ietwat tevrede, nie baie tevrede nie, of glad nie tevrede nie met die manier hoe die Suid-Afrikaanse Parlement werk?*

Very satisfied • *Baie tevrede*	42-1
Somewhat satisfied • *Ietwat tevrede*	2
Not very satisfied • *Nie baie tevrede nie*	3
Not satisfied at all • *Glad nie tevrede nie*	4
DON'T KNOW	8
REFUSED	9

ASK ALL:

Q.72 If there were an election in the next few days, how likely would you be to go out and vote? **(READ OUT)**

• *As daar binne die volgende paar dae 'n verkiesing sou wees, hoe waarskynlik is dit dat u sal gaan stem?*

Very likely • *Baie waarskynlik*	43-1
Quite likely • *Redelik waarskynlik*	2
Not very likely • *Nie baie waarskynlik nie*	3
Not at all likely • *Glad nie waarskynlik nie*	4
DON'T KNOW	8
REFUSED	9

PROJECT TOLERANCE III	**- 37 -**	**CARD 7 DSI 14/2000**

Q.73 If there were an election in the next few days, which party would you vote for? **(DO <u>NOT</u> READ OUT)**

• *As daar binne die volgende paar dae 'n verkiesing sou wees, vir watter party sou u stem?*

Afrikaner Volksunie	44-1
Afrikaner Volksfront	2
African National Congress (ANC)	3
Afrikaner Weerstandsbeweging (AWB)	4
Azanian People's Organisation (AZAPO)	5
Bophuthatswana Progressive People's Party (BPPP)	6
Christian Democratic Movement	7
Christian Democratic Party (CDP)	8
Conservative Party (CP)	9
Democratic Party (DP)	45-1
Dikwantwetla Party	2
Inkatha Freedom Party (IFP)	3
Intando Yesizwe Party	4
Inyandza National Movement	5
Labour Party (LP)	6
National People's Party (NPP)	7
Pan Africanist Congress (PAC)	8
Solidarity	9
South African Communist Party (SACP)	46-1
Transvaal Indian Congress (TIC)	2
United Democratic Movement (UDM)	3
United People's Front	4
Ximoko Progressive Party	5
Alliance (ANC/SACP/COSATU ALLIANCE ONLY)	6
M.K. (UMKHONTO WE SIZWE)	7
Other (specify)	
DON'T KNOW	47-8
WON'T VOTE	7
NONE	0
REFUSED	9

ENG/AFR

Q.74a) Before Nelson Mandela was elected in 1994, did you ever vote in favour of or support the National Party?
• *Voordat Nelson Mandela in 1994 verkies is, het u ooit vir die Nasionale Party gestem of die party ondersteun?*

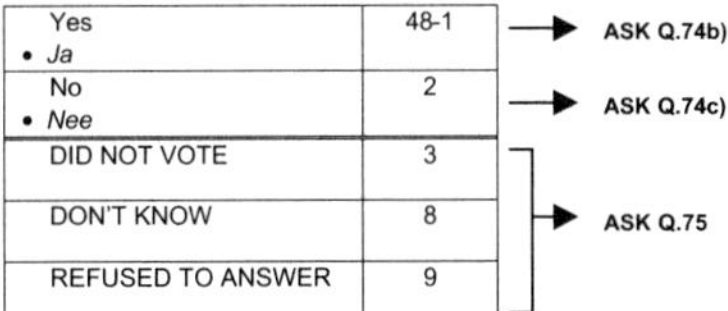

Yes • *Ja*	48-1	ASK Q.74b)
No • *Nee*	2	ASK Q.74c)
DID NOT VOTE	3	ASK Q.75
DON'T KNOW	8	ASK Q.75
REFUSED TO ANSWER	9	ASK Q.75

<u>**IF YES**</u>:
Q.74b) Was your support for the National Party due to its position on apartheid?
• *Was u ondersteuning vir die Nastionale Party as gevolg van sy standpunt oor apartheid?*

Yes • *Ja*	49-1	ASK Q.75
No • *Nee*	2	ASK Q.75
DON'T REMEMBER	8	ASK Q.75

<u>**IF NO**</u>:
Q.74c) Was your lack of support for the National Party due to its position on apartheid?
• *Was u gebrek aan ondersteuning vir die Nasionale Party as gevolg van sy posisie oor apartheid?*

Yes • *Ja*	50-1
No • *Nee*	2
DON'T REMEMBER	8

<u>**ASK ALL**</u>:
Q.75 Please tell me how important each of the following problems is to you personally – very important, important, not very important, or not important at all?
• *Sê asseblief vir my hoe belangrik is elk van die volgende probleme vir u persoonlik – baie belangrik, belangrik, nie baie belangrik nie, of glad nie belangrik nie?*

	INTERVIEWER: SHOW CARD 49	VERY IMPORTANT	IMPORTANT	NOT VERY IMPORTANT	NOT IMPORTANT AT ALL	DON'T KNOW	REFUSED
1	Pollution • *Besoedeling*	51-1	2	3	4	8	9
2	Drugs • *Dwelms*	52-1	2	3	4	8	9
3	Poverty • *Armoede*	53-1	2	3	4	8	9
4	Unemployment • *Werkloosheid*	54-1	2	3	4	8	9
5	Level of crime • *Vlak van misdaad*	55-1	2	3	4	8	9
6	Racism and discrimination • *Rassisme en diskriminasie*	56-1	2	3	4	8	9
7	HIV/AIDS • *HIV/VIGS*	57-1	2	3	4	8	9
8	Corruption • *Korrupsie*	58-1	2	3	4	8	9
9	Affirmative Action • *Regstellende Aksie*	59-1	2	3	4	8	9
10	Illiteracy • *Ongeletterdheid*	60-1	2	3	4	8	9
11	Finding out the truth about the past • *Om die waarheid oor die verlede uit te vind*	61-1	2	3	4	8	9
12	Racial reconciliation • *Rasseversoening*	62-1	2	3	4	8	9
13	Problems of land ownership and redistribution • *Probleme met grondbesit en herverdeling*	63-1	2	3	4	8	9

PROJECT TOLERANCE III	- 39 -	CARD 7	DSI 14/2000

Q.76 Do you agree or disagree with the following statements? Would you say that you agree strongly, agree, are uncertain, disagree, disagree strongly will each of the following statements?

• *Stem u saam of nie met die volgende stellings? Sou u sê u stem sterk saam, stem saam, is onseker, verskil of verskil sterk met elk van die volgende stellings?*

INTERVIEWER: SHOW CARD 50

		AGREE STRONGLY	AGREE	UNCERTAIN	DISAGREE	DISAGREE STRONGLY	DON'T KNOW	REFUSED
1	The way things are, I have no future in South Africa • *Soos dinge nou is, het ek geen toekoms in Suid-Afrika nie*	64-1	2	3	4	5	8	9
2	Our government is corrupt – it only does things for itself and not for the people • *Ons regering is korrup – hulle doen net dinge vir hulleself en nie vir die bevolking nie*	65-1	2	3	4	5	8	9
3	The government only helps the upper class and not the poor • *Die regering help net die hoër klas en nie die armes nie*	66-1	2	3	4	5	8	9

Q.77 How much change do you believe there has been in South Africa since 1994? **(READ OUT)**

• *Hoeveel verandering glo u was daar in Suid-Afrika vanaf 1994?*

The country has changed a great deal • *Die land het baie verander*	67-1
The country has changed somewhat • *Die land het ietwat verander*	2
The country has not changed very much • *Die land het nie baie verander nie*	3
The country has not changed at all • *Die land het glad nie verander nie*	4
DON'T KNOW	8
REFUSED	9

Q.78 How hopeful are you about your future? **(READ OUT)**

• *Hoe hoopvol is u oor u toekoms?*

1	Extremely hopeful • *Uiters hoopvol*	68-1
2	Somewhat hopeful • *Ietwat hoopvol*	2
3	Not very hopeful • *Nie baie hoopvol nie*	3
4	Not hopeful at all • *Glad nie hoopvol nie*	4
5	DON'T KNOW	8
6	REFUSED	9

Q.79 In what year were you born?
• *In watter jaar is u gebore?*

Year • *Jaar*		69-72
UNCERTAIN/DON'T KNOW	9998	
REFUSED/NO ANSWER	9999	

Q.80 What is your highest educational qualification?
• *Wat is u hoogste opvoedkundige kwalifikasie?*

No formal school • *Geen formele skool*	73-1	
Sub A or B/Grade 1 or 2 • *Sub A of B/Graad 1 of 2*	2	
Standard 1 up to 5/Grade 3 up to Grade 7 • *Standerd 1 tot 5/Graad 3 tot 7*	3	
Standard 6 up to 10/Grade 8 up to Grade 12 • *Standerd 6 tot 10/Graad 8 tot 12*	4	
Standard 1 up to 9/Grade 3 up to Grade 11 plus diploma • *Standerd 1 tot 9/Graad 3 tot 11 plus diploma*	5	→ **ASK Q.81 AND Q.82**
Matric/Std 10/Grade 12 plus diploma • *Matriek/Std 10/Graad 12 plus diploma*	6	→ **ASK Q.81 AND Q.82**
B or Honours Degree • *B of Honneursgraad*	7	
Master's Degree • *Meestersgraad*	8	
Doctor's Degree • *Doktersgraad*	9	
Other professional (specify)		

74

IF DIPLOMA, ASK:

Q.81 Specify highest school standard passed.
• *Spesifiseer hoogste skoolstanderd geslaag.*

Std 1/Grade 3 • *Std 1/Graad 3*	75-1
Std 2/Grade 4 • *Std 2/Graad 4*	2
Std 3/Grade 5 • *Std 3/Graad 5*	3
Std 4/Grade 6 • *Std 4/Graad 6*	4
Std 5/Grade 7 • *Std 5/Graad 7*	5
Std 6/Grade 8 • *Std 6/Graad 8*	6
Std 7/Grade 9 • *Std 7/Graad 9*	7
Std 8/Grade 10 • *Std 8/Graad 10*	8
Std 9/Grade 11 • *Std 9/Graad 11*	9
Std 10/Grade 12 • *Std 10/Graad 12*	0

79 - 80 - 07

PROJECT TOLERANCE III	- 41-	CARD 8 DSI 14/2000

IF DIPLOMA, ASK:

Q.82 Specify kind of diploma.
• *Spesifiseer soort diploma.*

Technicon diploma • *Tegnikon diploma*	7-1
Technical college diploma • *Tegniese kollege diploma*	8-1
Business college diploma • *Besigheidskollege diploma*	9-1
Teaching/nursing diploma • *Onderwys/verpleging diploma*	10-1
Trade e.g. hairdressing diploma • *Ambagsdiploma (bv. haarkappery)*	11-1
Others •	

12-13		
14-15		
16-17		

ASK ALL:

Q.83 What language do you speak mostly at home?
• *Watter taal praat u meestal tuis?*

Afrikaans	18-1
English	2
Portuguese	3
Xhosa	4
Zulu	5
Venda	6
South Sotho/Sesotho	7
Setswana/Tswana	8
North Sotho/Sepedi	9
Seswati	19-1
Shangaan	2
Ndebele	3
Other European	4
Other black	5
Indian language	6

ENG/AFR

Q.84 If you consider yourself as belonging to a particular religion or church could you please tell me what religion or church you belong to?
• *As u uself sien as deel van 'n besondere godsdiens of kerk, kan u asseblief vir my sê aan watter godsdiens of kerk u behoort?*

Anglican/Church of England	20-1
Baptist	2
Church of Nazareth	3
Dutch Reformed	4
Christian Scientist	5
Lutheran	6
Jehovah's Witness/7th Day Adventist	7
Methodist	8
Presbyterian	9
Roman Catholic	21-1
Jewish	2
Zion Christian Church	3
Charismatic – Rhema/ Apostolic/Pentecostal/Evangelical	4
African Independent Church	5
Moslem/Islam	6
Hindu	7
Buddhist	8
Bahai	9
Traditional/Animist	22-1
United Congregational	2
Mission Churches	3
Other (please specify)	
None	0
REFUSED	9

23 [ ]

Q.85 How often do you now attend or go to a place of worship or attend major religious festivals?
• *Hoe dikwels woon u nou dienste by of gaan u na 'n plek van aanbidding?*

INTERVIEWER: SHOW CARD 51

More than once a week • *Meer as eenkeer per week*	24-1
Once a week • *Eenkeer per week*	2
2 to 3 times a month • *2 tot 3 keer per maand*	3
Once a month • *Eenkeer per maand*	4
Often but less than once a month • *Dikwels maar minder as eenkeer per maand*	5
2-3 times a year • *2-3 keer per jaar*	6
Hardly ever/seldom • *Amper nooit/selde*	7
Never • *Nooit*	8

PROJECT TOLERANCE III	- 43 -	CARD 8	DSI 14/2000

Q.86 When you yourself hold a strong opinion, do you ever find yourself persuading your friends, relatives or fellow workers to share your views? **(READ OUT)**

- *Wanneer u 'n sterk mening huldig, vind u ooit dat u u vriende, familiebetrekkinge of mede-werkers oorreed om u sienswyse te deel?*

Often • *Dikwels*	25-1
From time to time • *Af en toe*	2
Rarely • *Selde*	3
Never • *Nooit*	4
UNCERTAIN/DON'T KNOW	8
REFUSED/NO ANSWER	9

Q.87a) How would you evaluate the following statements about the South African Constitutional Court? Would you say that you agree strongly, agree, are uncertain, disagree, disagree strongly with each of the following statements?

- *Hoe sou u die volgende stellings oor die Suid-Afrikaanse Grontwetlike Hof evalueer? Sou u sê u stem sterk saam, stem saam, is onseker, verskil of verskil sterk met die volgende stellings?*

	INTERVIEWER: SHOW CARD 52	AGREE STRONGLY	AGREE	UNCERTAIN	DISAGREE	DISAGREE STRONGLY	DON'T KNOW	REFUSED
1	If the South African Constitutional Court started making a lot of decisions that most people disagree with, it might be better to do away with the court altogether • *Indien die Suid-Afrikaanse Grondwetlike Hof begin om baie besluite te neem waarmee die meeste mense nie saamstem nie, sal dit dalk beter wees om heeltemal weg te doen met die hof*	26-1	2	3	4	5	8	9
2	The right of the South African Constitutional Court to decide certain types of controversial issues should be done away with (eliminated) • *Die reg van die Suid-Afrikaanse Grondwetlike Hof om te besluit oor sekere tipes kontroversiële kwessies moet uit die reg gelaat word*	27-1	2	3	4	5	8	9
3	The South African Constitutional Court can usually be trusted to make decisions that are right for the country as a whole • *Die Suid-Afrikaanse Grondwetlike Hof kan gewoonlik vertrou word om besluite te maak wat reg is vir die land in geheel*	28-1	2	3	4	5	8	9
4	The South African Constitutional Court treats all people who bring their cases to it – black, white, coloured, and Asian – the same • *Die Suid-Afrikaanse Grondwetlike Hof behandel almal wat voor dit kom – swart, wit, kleurling en Asiër – dieselfde*	29-1	2	3	4	5	8	9

Q.87b) Would you say that all, most or few of the judges on the Constitutional Court are white?

- *Sou u sê al die regters, meeste van die regters, of slegs 'n paar van die regters van die Grondwetlike Hof is blank?*

All • *Almal*	30-1
Most • *Meeste*	2
Few • *'n Paar*	3
DON'T KNOW	8
REFUSED	9

ENG/AFR

Q.88 What is your present marital status?
• *Wat is u huidige huwelikstatus?*

Never married/single • *Nooit getroud nie/enkel*	31-1
Married • *Getroud*	2
Living as married • *Woon saam asof getroud*	3
Divorced • *Geskei*	4
Separated • *Vervreem*	5
Widowed • *Weduwee/wewenaar*	6
REFUSED	9

Q.89 What is your current employment status? **(DO NOT READ OUT)**
• *Wat is u huidige werkstatus?*

Unemployed (not looking for work) • *Werkloos (soek nie na werk nie)*	32-1
Unemployed (looking for work) • *Werkloos (soek na werk)*	2
Housewife (not looking for work) • *Huisvrou (soek nie na werk nie)*	3
Housewife (looking for work) • *Huisvrou (soek na werk)*	4
Student/scholar • *Student/Skolier*	5
Pensioner • *Pensioenaris*	6
Army/Armed forces • *Weermag/Troepe*	7
Work in informal sector (looking for permanent work) • *Werk in 'n informele sektor (soek na permanente werk)*	8
Work in informal sector (not looking for permanent work) • *Werk in 'n informele sektor (soek nie na permanente werk nie)*	9
Self-employed (part-time) • *In eie diens (deeltyds)*	33-1
Self-employed (full-time) • *In eie diens (voltyds)*	2
Employed (part-time) • *Werksaam (deeltyds)*	3
Employed (seasonally) • *Werksaam (seisoenaal)*	4
Employed (full-time) • *Werksaam (voltyds)*	5
Disabled not looking for permanent work • *Ongeskik, soek nie na permanente werk nie*	6
Other (specify) • *Ander (spesifiseer)*	
DON'T KNOW	8
REFUSED	9

34 ☐

Q.90 How much does the thought worry you that, during the next 12 months, you or some member of your family might become unemployed? **(READ OUT)**
• *Hoeveel bekommer die gedagte u dat u of 'n familielid binne die volgende 12 maande werkloos mag wees?*

Not at all worried • *Glad nie bekommerd nie*	35-1
Not very worried • *Nie baie bekommerd nie*	2
A little worried • *'n Bietjie bekommerd*	3
Very worried • *Baie bekommerd*	4
REFUSED/NO ANSWER	8
NO ONE IS EMPLOYED/ALL UNEMPLOYED	9

Q.91 Have you or a member of your family become unemployed in the last 12 months?
• *Het u of 'n lid van u familie werkloos geraak in die afgelope 12 maande?*

Yes • *Ja*	36-1
No • *Nee*	2
DON'T KNOW/UNCERTAIN	8
REFUSED	9

Q.92 Thinking about the South African Parliament, would you say that you agree strongly, agree, are uncertain, disagree, disagree strongly with each of the following statements?
• *Dink nou aan die Suid-Afrikaanse parlement, sou u sê u stem sterk saam, stem saam, is onseker, verskil of verskil sterk met elk van die volgende stellings?*

INTERVIEWER: SHOW CARD 53

		AGREE STRONGLY	AGREE	UNCERTAIN	DISAGREE	DISAGREE STRONGLY	DON'T KNOW	REFUSED
1	If the South African Parliament started making a lot of decisions that most people disagree with, it might be better to do away with parliament altogether • *Indien die Suid-Afrikaanse Parlement begin om baie besluite te neem waarmee die meeste mense nie saamstem nie, sal dit dalk beter wees om heeltemal met die parlement weg te doen*	37-1	2	3	4	5	8	9
2	The South African Parliament can usually be trusted to make decisions that are right for the country as a whole • *Die Suid-Afrikaanse Parlement kan gewoonlik vertrou word om besluite te maak wat reg is vir die land in geheel*	38-1	2	3	4	5	8	9
3	The South African Parliament treats all groups who come before it – black, white, coloured and Asian – the same • *Die Suid-Afrikaanse Parlement behandel alle groepe wat voor dit kom – swart, wit, kleurling en Asiër – dieselfde*	39-1	2	3	4	5	8	9

ASK ALL:

Q.93 How likely is it that you will be living in South Africa 10 years from now (2010)? **(READ OUT)**
• *Hoe waarskynlik is dit dat u in Suid-Afrika sal bly 10 jaar van nou af (2010)?*

Extremely likely • *Uiters waarskynlik*	40-1
Quite likely • *Waarskynlik*	2
Not very likely • *Nie baie waarskynlik nie*	3
Highly unlikely • *Hoogs onwaarskynlik*	4
DON'T KNOW	8
REFUSED	9

PROJECT TOLERANCE III	- 46 -	CARD 8	DSI 14/2000

Q.94a) Do you or anyone else in your household own ..... ? **(READ OUT) (MULTIMENTIONS POSSIBLE)**
• *Besit u of enige iemand anders in u huishouding .... ?*

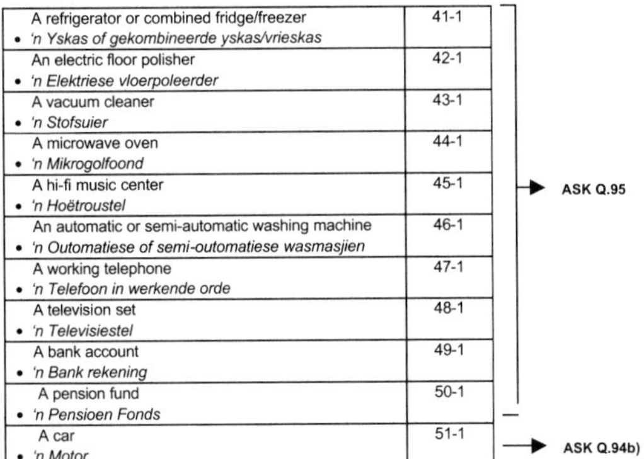

A refrigerator or combined fridge/freezer • *'n Yskas of gekombineerde yskas/vrieskas*	41-1	ASK Q.95
An electric floor polisher • *'n Elektriese vloerpoleerder*	42-1	ASK Q.95
A vacuum cleaner • *'n Stofsuier*	43-1	ASK Q.95
A microwave oven • *'n Mikrogolfoond*	44-1	ASK Q.95
A hi-fi music center • *'n Hoëtroustel*	45-1	ASK Q.95
An automatic or semi-automatic washing machine • *'n Outomatiese of semi-outomatiese wasmasjien*	46-1	ASK Q.95
A working telephone • *'n Telefoon in werkende orde*	47-1	ASK Q.95
A television set • *'n Televisiestel*	48-1	ASK Q.95
A bank account • *'n Bank rekening*	49-1	ASK Q.95
A pension fund • *'n Pensioen Fonds*	50-1	ASK Q.95
A car • *'n Motor*	51-1	ASK Q.94b)

INTERVIEWER: IF OWN A CAR, IN Q.94a), ASK:

Q.94b) How many cars do you own?
• *Hoeveel motors besit u?*

[ ][ ] 52-53

ASK ALL:

Q.95 Finally, we are interested in your experiences under the old system of apartheid. In general, how would you judge your life under apartheid compared with now? Would you say it was ..... ? **(READ OUT)**
• *Laastens, ons stel belang in u ondervindinge onder die ou stelsel van apartheid. Oor die algemeen, hoe sou u u lewe beoordeel onder apartheid in vergelyking met nou? Sou u sê dit was ..... ?*

A lot worse • *Baie erger*	54-1
A little worse • *'n Bietjie erger*	2
About the same • *Omtrent dieselfde*	3
A little better • *'n Bietjie beter*	4
A lot better • *Baie beter*	5
DON'T KNOW	8
REFUSED/NO ANSWER	9

ENG/AFR

Q.96a) People use many different words to describe their relationship with apartheid in the past. Which of the following best describes your role under apartheid? **(ONE MENTION ONLY)**
• *Mense gebruik baie verskillende woorde om hulle verhouding met apartheid in die verlede te beskryf. Watter van die volgende beskryf u verhouding met apartheid of hoe u deur apartheid beïnvloed is die beste?*

INTERVIEWER: SHOW CARD 54

Activist • *Aktivis*	55-1
Beneficiary • *Voordeeltrekker*	2
Bystander • *Bystander*	3
Collaborator • *Medewerker*	4
Hero • *Held*	5
Inactive opponent • *Onaktiewe opponent*	6
Slave • *Slaaf*	7
Victim • *Slagoffer*	8
Victor • *Oorwinnaar*	9
Spectator • *Toekyker*	56-1
Sellout • *Uitverkoper*	2
DON'T KNOW/UNCERTAIN	8
REFUSED	9

PROBE:
Q.96b) Do any of the other terms describe you as well?
• *Beskryf enige van die ander terme u ook so goed?*

____________________ 57-58 [|]

Q.97 Were you ever personally harmed or injured by apartheid?
• *Is u ooit persoonlik benadeel of beseer deur apartheid?*

Yes • *Ja*	59-1
No • *Nee*	2
DON'T KNOW/UNCERTAIN	8
REFUSED/NO ANSWER	9

Q.98 Here is a list of things that happened to people under apartheid. Please tell me which, if any, of these experiences you have had.
• *Hier is 'n lys van dinge wat met mense onder apartheid gebeur het. Sê asseblief watter van hierdie ondervindinge u gehad het, indien enige?*

		YES	NO	DON'T KNOW	REFUSED
1	Required to move my residence • *Nodig gehad om my woonplek te verskuif*	60-1	2	8	9
2	Lost my job because of apartheid • *My werk verloor as gevolg van apartheid*	61-1	2	8	9
3	Was assaulted by the police • *Was deur die polisie mishandel*	62-1	2	8	9
4	Was imprisoned by the authorities • *Was deur die owerhede in die tronk geplaas*	63-1	2	8	9
5	Was psychologically harmed • *Was sielkundig geskaad*	64-1	2	8	9
6	Was denied access to education of my choice • *Was toegang tot onderwys van my keuse geweier*	65-1	2	8	9
7	Was unable to associate with people of different race and colour • *Was nie by magte om met mense van verskillende rasse en kleure te assosieer nie*	66-1	2	8	9
8	Had to use a pass to move about • *Moes 'n pas gebruik het om rond te beweeg*	67-1	2	8	9
9	Profited from the system • *Het voordeel uit die sisteem getrek*	68-1	2	8	9

ENG/AFR

Q.99 Some people have told us that they benefited from the old system of apartheid. What about you – would you say you definitely benefited, probably benefited, probably did not benefit, or definitely did not benefit from ..... ?

• *Sommige mense het ons vertel dat hulle voordeel getrek het uit die ou sisteem van apartheid. Wat van u – sou u sê u het definitief voordeel getrek, moontlik voordeel getrek, moontlik nie voordeel getrek nie, of definitief nie voordeel getrek nie uit .... ?*

INTERVIEWER: SHOW CARD 55

		DEFINITELY BENEFITED	PROBABLY BENEFITED	PROBABLY DID NOT BENEFIT	DEFINITELY DID NOT BENEFIT	DON'T KNOW	REFUSED
1	The educational system under apartheid • *Die opvoedingsisteem onder apartheid*	69-1	2	3	4	8	9
2	Cheap labour available under apartheid • *Goedkoop arbeid beskikbaar onder apartheid*	70-1	2	3	4	8	9
3	Level of crime under apartheid • *Vlak van geweld onder apartheid*	71-1	2	3	4	8	9
4	Access to jobs under apartheid • *Toegang tot werk onder apartheid*	72-1	2	3	4	8	9

FOR THOSE WHO ANSWERED "YES" TO ANY OF THE ITEMS IN Q.98, ASK Q.100
FOR THOSE WHO ANSWERED "NO," "DON'T KNOW" OR "REFUSED" TO ALL IN Q.98, SKIP TO Q.101

Q.100 Would you say that you agree strongly, agree, are uncertain, disagree, disagree strongly with the following statements?

• *Sou u sê dat u sterk saam stem, saam stem, is onseker, verskil of sterk verskil met die volgende stellings?*

INTERVIEWER: SHOW CARD 56

		AGREE STRONGLY	AGREE	UNCERTAIN	DISAGREE	DISAGREE STRONGLY	DON'T KNOW	REFUSED
1	I can never reclaim what was taken from me under apartheid • *Ek kan dit wat van my weggeneem is onder apartheid nooit terugeis nie*	73-1	2	3	4	5	8	9
2	Those who harmed me deserve now to be forgiven • *Diegene wat my leed aangedoen het verdien nou om vergewe te word*	74-1	2	3	4	5	8	9
3	Those who say they had no knowledge of the human rights abuses committed under apartheid are not telling the truth • *Diegene wat sê dat hulle geen kennis gehad het van die menseregtskendings wat onder apartheid gepleeg is nie, praat nie die waarheid nie*	75-1	2	3	4	5	8	9
4	Supporting the National Party during the apartheid era was the same as supporting apartheid • *Om die Nasionale Party tydens die apartheid era te ondersteun het was dieselfde as om apartheid te ondersteun*	76-1	2	3	4	5	8	9
5	Those who created apartheid continue to benefit from it in numerous ways • *Diegene wat apartheid geskep het gaan aan om nog voordeel daaruit te trek in op baie maniere*	77-1	2	3	4	5	8	9
6	Apartheid is basically irrelevant to my life today • *Apartheid is basies irrelevant in my lewe vandag*	78-1	2	3	4	5	8	9

79 - 80 - 08

PROJECT TOLERANCE III — - 49 - — CARD 9 DSI 14/2000

ASK ALL:

Q.101 What kind of housing are you living in at the moment?

• *In watter soort huis woon u op die oomblik?*

House in suburb	7-1
House in township	2
Townhouse/cluster	3
Flat	4
Hotel/residential hotel	5
Hut	6
Room in backyard	7
Shack in backyard	8
Squatter camp	9
House on employer's property	8-1
Compound	2
Domestic accommodation room	3
Farm workers' house	4
Shack in rural area	5
Other (specify)	

INTERVIEWER NOTE:

DO YOU THINK THAT YOU WILL STILL BE LIVING AT THIS ADDRESS IN THE YEAR 2001? IF NOT, DO YOU KNOW HOW WE CAN CONTACT YOU?

YES	9-1
NO	2

ADDRESS: ____________________

____

TEL (H) ____________________

(W) ____________________

What is your relationship with the contact person?

• *Wat is u verhouding met die kontakpersoon?*

Parent	10-1
Child	2
Sibling	3
Other family member	4
Friend	5
Colleague	6
Employer	7
Other (specify)	8

THANK YOU VERY MUCH FOR YOUR EFFORT

ENG/AFR

PROJECT TOLERANCE III	- 50 -	CARD 9 DSI 14/2000

INTERVIEWER REMARKS
(TO BE COMPLETED AFTER THE SURVEY IS FINISHED)

A. Date of interview.

11-12	13-14	15-16
MONTH	DAY	YEAR

B. In general, what was the respondent's attitude toward the interview? **(CODE ONE)**

Friendly and interested	17-1
Cooperative but not particularly interested	2
Impatient and restless	3
Hostile	4

C. Did the respondent understand the questions? **[THE QUESTIONS IN THE MAIN QUESTIONNAIRE, NOT THE VIGNETTES)**

Well	18-1
Not very well	2
Poorly	3

D. Was the respondent able to read the showcards ..... ?

Without any apparent difficulty	19-1
With some difficulty	2
With a great deal of difficulty	3
Could not read the showcards	4

E. Compared to other respondents, how well did this respondent understand the stories (vignettes)?

	PHILLIP
Well	20-1
Not very well	2
Poorly	3
First interview so can't compare	4

F. Was the respondent ..... ?

About as clever as most respondents	21-1
Not as clever as most respondents	2
Somewhat more clever than most respondents	3
A great deal more clever than most respondents	4
First interview, so can't compare	5
Can't compare	6

G. Compared to other respondents, was the respondent ..... ?

About as honest and open as most respondents	22-1
Not as honest and open as most respondents	2
Somewhat more honest and open than most respondents	3
A great deal more honest and open than most respondents	4
First interview, can't compare	5

ENG/AFR

H. Were any other people immediately present who might be listening during the interview?

CIRCLE ALL THAT APPLY

No one else was present	23-1
The spouse of the respondent was present	24-1
Children of the respondent were present	25-1
Other adults were present	26-1

I. How would you evaluate the living quarters of the respondent?

Clearly much better off than most people	27-1
About as well off as most people	2
Clearly less well off than most people	3
Interview did not take place in living quarters of respondent	4

J. In what type of dwelling was the interview conducted?

House in suburb/township	28-1
House in township	2
Townhouse/cluster	3
Flat	4
Hotel/residential hotel	5
Hut	6
Room in backyard	7
Shack in backyard	8
Squatter camp	9
House on employer's property	29-1
Compound	2
Domestic accommodation room	3
Farm workers' house	4
Shack in rural area	5
Other (specify)	

K. What would you say is the socio-economic status of the respondent?

AB Upper, upper-middle class	30-1
C1 Middle, non-manual workers	2
C2 Manual workers – skilled, semi-skilled	3
D Manual workers – unskilled, unemployed	4

L. How well could the respondent read?

Was able to read without difficulty	31-1
Was able to read, but with some difficulty	2
Was able to read, but with great difficulty	3
Was not able to read	4
Could not judge	5

PROJECT TOLERANCE III	- 52 -	CARD 9	DSI 14/2000

M. In what language/languages was the interview conducted?

Afrikaans	32-1
English	33-1
North Sotho	34-1
South Sotho	35-1
Tswana	36-1
Tsonga	37-1
Venda	38-1
Xhosa	39-1
Zulu	40-1

N. Was it necessary to use a mixture of languages to conduct the interview?

1	Languages were often mixed	41-1
2	Languages were occasionally mixed	2
3	Languages were not mixed	3

INTERVIEWER DETAILS – NOTE YOUR DETAILS, NOT THE RESPONDENT'S:

MALE	42-1
FEMALE	2

RACE				
Black	Coloured	White	Indian	Other (specify) ....
43-1	2	3	4	

INTERVIEWER NAME: ______________________ INTERVIEWER No.: 44-46 [| |]

INTERVIEWER AGE: ______________________

LENGTH OF TIME OF INTERVIEW [| |] 47-49

79 - 80 - 09

ENG/AFR

Notes

Preface and Acknowledgments

1. Any opinions, findings, and conclusions or recommendations expressed in this material are those of the author and do not necessarily reflect the views of the National Science Foundation.
2. IJR has also published a version of the dataset on which this study is based, Gibson (2002a); available on its website and on CD.

Chapter 1

1. See chapter 2 for a brief overview of apartheid in South Africa.
2. In 2001 President Thabo Mbeki charged the TRC with producing additional volumes—a codicil to the original report. Volume 6 was published in March 2003, volume 7 in October 2002.
3. In 1985 four Cradock United Democratic Front activists were murdered by several security branch policemen. The policemen later sought amnesty before the Truth and Reconciliation Commission for their actions.
4. In general, no more important collection of essays about the TRC can be found than in Villa-Vicencio and Verwoerd (2000).
5. The defining characteristic of a liberal democracy is that all political movements have institutionalized opportunities to compete for political power, that is, to try to become a political majority. With Dahl (1971, 1, 2), I believe that democracy is a system that must grant unimpaired opportunities for all full citizens (1) to formulate their preferences; (2) to signify their preferences to their fellow citizens and the government by individual and collective action; and (3) to have their preferences weighed equally in the conduct of the government, that is, weighted with no discrimination because of the content or source of the preference. Democracies need not allow all political interests equal *influence* over public policies, but they must allow all political interests *equal opportunity to compete* for the control of public policies. Unless all political interests have the opportunity to persuade

the majority, the marketplace of ideas is unnecessarily constrained and competition among ideas cannot flourish. Without such competition, citizens may be denied the opportunity to support the political movements of their choice, political freedom may be lost, and democratic accountability may be undermined.

6. For a comparison of the South African and Latin American approaches to the truth and reconciliation process, see Valdez (1998); see also Hayner (1994, 2002). Priscilla Hayner (2000, 33) distinguishes the South African truth and reconciliation process in the following ways: "a public process of disclosure by perpetrators and public hearings for victims; an amnesty process that reviewed individual applications and avoided any blanket amnesty; and a process that was intensely focused on national healing and reconciliation, with the intent of moving a country from its repressive past to a peaceful future, where former opponents could work side by side."

7. For objections to the truth and reconciliation process, see Ngidi (1998). The spring 1998 issue of *Siyaya!* is devoted to the TRC and provides several interesting articles critical of the process.

8. On the motives of the Biko family in challenging the TRC legislation, see Biko (2000).

9. These volumes address the experiences of the victims and the work of the Amnesty Committee. Excellent accounts of the operation of the TRC have been published; see, for example, Orr (2000); Boraine (2000).

10. Actually, views toward the truth and reconciliation process are fairly complicated. For a full report on opinions in South Africa, see Gibson and Macdonald (2001).

11. See the widely popular and much discussed Krog (1998); see also Orr (2000). The father of Amy Biehl, a young American woman killed in South Africa, is one of the most poignant examples. A statement by Biehl's parents is included in the decision granting amnesty to her killers. See "Amnesty Decision: Vusumzi Samuel Ntamo (4734/97); Ntombeki Ambrose Peni (5188/97); Mzikhona Eazi Nofemela (5282/97); Mongesi Christopher Manqina (0669/96)," Truth and Reconciliation Commission, http://www.doj.gov.za/trc/amntrans/ct3/biehl01a.htm (accessed on October 13, 2003).

12. See Wilson (2001) for a very strong critique of the TRC for injecting religious overtones into its work.

13. In South Africa it is common to refer to "Coloured people." In this book the term has been conformed to American English spelling. When Americans speak of "colored people," they tend to refer to African Americans. These people generally would not be called "Coloured" in South Africa; instead, they would be called "black" or "African." The term "Coloured" has no analogue in the case of the United States.

14. For a major study of political tolerance in South Africa, see Gibson and Gouws (2003).

15. Institutions, of course, may be thought of as little more than a set of values, norms, and expectations. Nonetheless, those who study processes of democratization typically distinguish between formal institutions (such as constitutions) and the beliefs, values, attitudes, and behavior prevalent among ordinary people.

16. Throughout this book I avoid the use of "Black" (capitalized) to refer to the consolidated group of blacks, colored people, and Indians of Asian origin. When I refer to "blacks," I mean Africans.

17. For a most useful review of racial categorization under apartheid, see Posel (2001).

18. Stephen Graubard (2001, viii), the editor of a special issue of *Daedalus* on South Africa had this to say about the use of racial terms in the articles in the journal: "Many of the authors in this issue observe the South African convention of dividing the country's population into four racial categories: white (of European descent), colored (of mixed ancestry), Indian (forebears from the Indian subcontinent), and African. The official nomenclature for 'Africans' has itself varied over the years, changing from 'native' to 'Bantu' in the middle of the apartheid era, and then changing again to 'black' or, today, 'African/black.' All of these terms appear in the essays that follow."

19. Although many racial communities remained separate during the first part of the twentieth century, others developed into vibrant multicultural communities (such as District Six in Cape Town).

Chapter 2

1. Nor is politics immune to difficulties in assessing causality, as in President Mbeki's claim that the HIV virus does not cause AIDS.

2. That apartheid was a body of laws adopted through legal procedures by a parliament accountable to the white majority has long triggered debates about the meaning of the rule of law in a dictatorial political system (see, for example, Gibson and Gouws 1997).

3. The race of 0.9 percent of South Africans is listed as "unspecified/ other." The total population of the country is given as 43,685,699.

4. It is perhaps useful to offer some general comments about the statistical assumptions and methods employed in this research.

   The Pearson correlation coefficient, r, is a measure of the strength of association between two variables. In this book, the coefficient is treated as the *total* (linear) relationship between one variable and another. Except under some unusual circumstances, the *independent* effect of a variable will be smaller than the total effect. Hence, when a correlation is found to be zero, there is little reason to expect that the variable will have any influence within a multivariate equation (see Cohen and Cohen 1983).

   Eta (η) is a curvilinear correlation coefficient. Since this coefficient taps both linear and nonlinear effects, the relationship between two variables can never be larger than eta. Eta is equivalent to R-squared when an independent variable is nominalized (rendered into a set of dummy variables). Eta is a coefficient useful only for categorical independent variables (such as race).

   Statistical significance is not a very useful guide to understanding relationships in this dataset. The significance of a coefficient depends overwhelmingly on the number of cases. When subgroups (such as racial groups) have vastly different numbers of cases (as they do in this research), then exactly the same coefficient may be significant in one group but not in the other. When groups are large (black South Africans, for example), even coefficients that are trivial (indicating little relationship between variables) may be (and often are) statistically significant. Statistical significance is not the same thing as substantive significance.

   With survey data (and especially with fairly large numbers of illiterate respondents), a great deal of measurement error is present, which means that relatively small correlation coefficients are often treated as substantively meaningful. A rule of thumb employed in this research is that coefficients smaller than .10 (in absolute value) represent trivial relationships. Coefficients between .10 and .20 are usually described as weak relationships; coefficients between .20 and .30 are moderate relationships; and those greater than .30 are fairly strong relationships. The same standards would not be applied to other types of data, because survey data are notorious for including large quantities of random measurement error.

Racial dummy variables are not often used in this analysis. Instead, the results are presented separately by race. I adopt this strategy because racial dummy variables address only the issue of differences across races in intercepts, not slopes. A dummy variable approach assumes that the slopes across races are equal. Given the overpowering effect of race in South Africa, I consider it unwise to assume that the linkage between independent and dependent variables (for example, truth and reconciliation) is invariant across race.

5. The race variable to which I am referring here might reasonably be called "nominal race." Later in this chapter, and especially in chapter 6, I consider in some detail group identities and their influence on processes of truth and reconciliation.

6. Courtney Jung's classic book *Then I Was Black* (2000) makes this point quite powerfully.

7. To reiterate, throughout this book I refer to this consolidated group as "Blacks," capitalizing the term. When I refer to "blacks," I mean Africans.

8. The denominator for these figures is the total number of respondents in the sample, which includes some who are unemployed but have given up looking and many who are not part of the labor market (such as pensioners). Thus, these figures may diverge somewhat from official estimates of unemployment in the country.

9. Showcards are cards on which the possible responses to our questions are written. These cards are handed to the respondents, as appropriate, with the different questions asked during the interview.

10. The primary consequence of random measurement error is to attenuate correlation coefficients. Thus, where reliability is expected to be low, we must adjust our understanding of what constitutes weak, moderate, and strong relationships.

11. The follow-up question read: "Do any of the other terms describe you as well?"

12. This 9.9 percent figure may not be so small if we exclude people too young to have been imprisoned under apartheid. Though no reliable figures exist, there are probably few countries in the world in which a survey would discover that one in ten respondents had suffered some imprisonment at the hands of the authorities.

13. It should also be noted that in a general query preceding these specific questions, fully 68 percent of the black respondents claim not to have been injured by apartheid. This is an astounding figure.

14. The freedom of movement of black South Africans was restricted under apartheid by the Pass Laws Act. According to the TRC's *Final Report*: "The pass laws were a source of considerable anger. The most humiliating symbol of this control was the pass book (dompas) which all black persons over the age of sixteen had to carry, indicating whether they had the right to be in an urban area and for how long. Only those who qualified under section 10 of the Urban Areas Act of 1945 were allowed to stay in the urban areas for more than seventy-two hours. Those who did not could be arrested and deported to the homeland of their 'ethnic' origin. By 1972 the South African Institute of Race Relations (SAIRR) estimated that over one million people had been endorsed out of (ordered to leave) the urban areas" (Truth and Reconciliation Commission 1998, vol. 3, ch. 6, sect. 3, p. 528). The pass laws were abolished in 1986. However, since residents of the Bantustans were not considered citizens of South Africa, they were subject to a form of "passport control." On the pass system, see Savage (1986).

15. In the introductory, general question, only 7.1 percent of the white respondents claim any injury whatsoever from the apartheid system.

16. We asked a limited number of questions about the benefits of apartheid since the questionnaire pretest revealed very high correlations across specific benefits. This most likely indicates that some respondents were generally prepared to understand that they benefited from apartheid and others were not. The specific type of benefit may not be of much significance for the replies that South Africans give to these questions.

17. Very large majorities of South Africans of all races judge the seriousness of the crime problem in 2001 as "very important" (the most extreme point in the response set) when asked to rate various social, political, and economic problems in the country. The percentages range from 74.7 percent of Africans to 89.4 percent of whites.

18. On the vast economic inequality wrought by apartheid, see Nattrass and Seekings (2001).

19. The limits of these questions should be reiterated. The questions were asked long after apartheid ended and dealt with specific harms and benefits. In our focus groups, some participants spoke of reclaiming their "dignity" after the fall of apartheid; one participant described

what it is like not to be afraid anymore; and others were pleased that now they can walk into a store and expect to be served. Apartheid harmed people in myriad ways not captured by these questions.

20. For a moving account of some of these incidents, see Krog (1998).

21. On attitudes toward amnesty in South Africa, see Gibson and Gouws (1999) and Gibson (2002b).

22. Note that on the full four-point distribution of responses to this question, the black mean response is 2.38 while the white mean response is 2.32. This difference is entirely trivial.

23. The question read: "How likely is it that you will be living in South Africa ten years from now (2010)—extremely likely, quite likely, not very likely, or highly unlikely?"

24. For a useful, recent review of social identity theory, see Huddy (2001).

25. The term "African" is sometimes contested, as by whites who claim to be "Africans" by virtue of being born on the continent.

26. Table 2.9 reports the number of cases within each of these types of identity.

27. These questions were not asked in our 1996 survey.

28. Among all South Africans, willingness to claim an anti-identity has increased substantially since 1996.

29. Perhaps the imposed limitation of only two responses to the identity question was unfair to Colored people, many of whom are of mixed racial ancestry. Given the results of the closed-end questions, it seems likely that many Colored South Africans would have selected a national identity had they been given a third opportunity to respond to the group identity question.

30. The question read: "People have different sorts of feelings as a result of being a member of a group. Which of the following characteristics describes how you feel about being a [member of your group]?"

31. The results of the initial factor extraction are:

    Eigenvalue_1 = 2.34, variance explained = 38.9 percent
    Eigenvalue_2 = 1.07, variance explained = 17.9 percent
    Eigenvalue_3 = .79, variance explained = 13.2 percent

    The items in table 2.11 are ordered by the size of the factor loadings. The loadings on the first factor range from .43 to .64, and the loadings on the second factor are −.74 and −.60.

Chapter 3

1. Howard Schuman and Amy Corning (2000, 915) distinguish between research on collective memories at the "cultural" and "individual" levels, arguing that the latter focuses "directly on memories of past events that are shared to a greater or lesser extent by the individuals who constitute a representative sample of a larger population." My research is strongly in the individual-level tradition, which is also most faithful to Maurice Halbwachs's (1950/1980) original understanding of the concept.

2. Bischoping and Kalmin (1999, 505) is an interesting article because it appears to have been motivated by academic criticism of ordinary people for not accepting the view that the Holocaust was a unique historical event (for example, when "academics deplore" the comparisons that ordinary people make between the Holocaust and other events). The "academics" whom Bischoping and Kalmin cite are apparently united in the belief that there is only one correct historical understanding of the meaning of the Holocaust (but see Rummel 1994), and they also seem to assume that beliefs about the Holocaust derive from self-interested motives (for example, the desire to make one's own group appear to have been victimized). One important corrective provided by their analysis is to document that "self-interest is not the sole motivator" for "misunderstandings" of history.

3. Schuman and Corning (2000, 951) assert that, "although the term 'collective memory' is useful for conceptualizing the broad area in which our and other research falls, the term does not point unambiguously to particular phenomena at either the individual or the cultural level."

4. Some research exists that examines the effectiveness of media campaigns to change public attitudes and perceptions. For instance, Robert Donovan and Susan Leivers (1993) analyze an effort to change Australians' attitudes toward Aborigines through public service announcements in the media. A considerable body of literature has examined the effectiveness of media campaigns on a variety of social issues, especially health issues (see Rice and Atkin 1989; Ball-Rokeach, Rokeach, and Grube 1984). If we can assume that the truth and reconciliation process was analogous to a sustained "media campaign," which is probably a fair assumption, then this research is of direct relevance to my analysis here. Unfortunately, however, that

literature tells us little about individual differences in attentiveness to such campaigns.

5. In 1970, resolution 2671 of the General Assembly of the United Nations declared that the policies of apartheid were contrary to the charter of the UN and constituted a crime against humanity. Resolution 556 in 1984 of the UN Security Council declared the apartheid regime illegitimate. Many other such condemnations and resolutions were made not only by the UN but by other countries and organizations. According to Mads Vestergaard (2001, 25), the truth and reconciliation process "has been central to the creation of the new South Africa, as it affirms one of its fundamental premises—that apartheid was a 'crime against humanity.'" Kadar Asmal (2000, 1225) concludes: "Thus in South Africa, justice must necessarily include establishing a basis for a nation-wide acknowledgement of the illegitimacy of apartheid."

6. The TRC gives as evidence of its evenhandedness the fact that its final report was attacked by both de Klerk and the ANC leadership; see Villa-Vicencio and Verwoerd (2000, 287). Afrikaners tended to view the TRC as an "ANC witch hunt," and the Afrikaans-language press continuously vilified the commission. Villa-Vicencio and Verwoerd (2000, 284) describe this as a "sustained campaign to undermine the legitimacy" of the TRC and its work.

7. The TRC held hearings on the media, prisons, the faith community, the legal system, and the health sector, focusing on the stances taken by each of these institutions toward the apartheid system. The commission also held special hearings on compulsory military service under the apartheid regime and on the impact of apartheid on children and youth and women (Truth and Reconciliation Commission 1998, vol. 4).

8. The details of any given incident in South Africa's apartheid past are inevitably contested. See, for instance, Jeffery (1999), who takes the TRC to task for what she claims are specific historical inaccuracies in the findings of the commission. One can accept that people might disagree about what happened in specific incidents—especially since the state was so proficient at destroying records during the run-up to the transfer of power to the ANC (Harris 2000)—but the broad contours of South Africa's apartheid history are much less contestable. As an analogy, one might easily accept that millions of Jews were killed during the Holocaust, even though disagreement might exist about some of the details of any given massacre.

9. The commission made a moral judgment about the struggle—that it was a just cause—but it also "distinguished, in an even-handed way, between just and unjust *ways* of pursuing that cause" (Villa-Vicencio and Verwoerd 2000, 287, emphasis in original).

10. John Kane-Berman (1993, 43) quotes Alfred Nzo, an important ANC leader, as having said that "collaborators with the enemy must be eliminated," even if that included "necklacing." See Marks (2001, 98–99) for a discussion of some comrades' attitudes toward necklacing.

11. Intolerance—as in "liberatory intolerance"—is one consequence of confronting an enemy who is radically evil. As Pallo Jordan (1988), an ANC stalwart, noted, apartheid was a doctrine that was radically evil and that therefore could not be tolerated. Consequently, Jordan called for "liberatory intolerance." Through this theory, the liberal notion of tolerance is rejected: apartheid could not be viewed as just another idea in the marketplace of ideas. Liberatory intolerance divided supporters of apartheid and those struggling against it into categories of enemies and friends, evil and good, and lent a certain justification (if not imperative) to intolerance.

12. The term "accepting the veracity" is used to indicate accepting that the statement is either true or false, depending on the coding scheme reported in the text. These items were constructed in collaboration with Charles Villa-Vicencio, currently director of the Institute for Justice and Reconciliation, so obviously at least one of the leaders of the truth and reconciliation process considers these truths to be uncontroversial.

13. H. F. Verwoerd, the principal architect of modern apartheid, propounded the ideology of separate development. Defending the viewpoint in the 1960s, Prime Minister John Vorster spoke of "recognising the right of existence of distinct nations and colour groups" and of "providing each with opportunities to develop according to their ability and with the maintenance of their identity" (quoted in Giliomee and Schlemmer 1989, 64, citing *Die Burger*, May 18, 1968). Note that the ANC has always explicitly rejected the ideology of separate development, although other elements of the liberation forces were very much in favor of racial separation.

14. Note that 21.8 percent of Afrikaans-speaking whites believe that apartheid was a crime, but mainly owing to its implementation, while 7.5 percent assert that apartheid was not a crime and reject the

idea that the ideology was poorly implemented. I resist pursuing this analysis much further, however, since it is often difficult to discern the precise meaning of a "disagree" response to some of these statements.

15. It is useful to remember that the TRC had a legal mandate that required it to address individual human rights violations, not whether South Africa's history was good or bad. Many critics of the commission fault it for not doing tasks it was in fact not designed or commissioned to accomplish.
16. To produce a measure with more variance by taking advantage of intensity of beliefs, I also employ the average response to these items (after scoring each item such that a high score on the five-point scale indicates greater agreement with the TRC's truth). This measure is employed in the analytical portion of this research.
17. The last item is perhaps a bit ambivalent in the sense that the struggle may have been unjust owing to its ends (because apartheid was a crime against humanity) or owing to the means by which the struggle was fought.
18. Even a simple pre-TRC, post-TRC research design has some fairly serious limitations in terms of attributing causality to the truth and reconciliation process. On the strengths and weaknesses of experimental designs, see Campbell and Stanley (1966) and Cook and Campbell (1979).
19. Plausible arguments can be made for both directions of causality. For example, those more accepting of the truth about the past may have been more likely to attend to the activities of the TRC. The first step in understanding the nature of the relationship is to determine whether the two variables are in fact connected. The nature of the causal relationship is considered more fully later in this chapter.
20. The TRC hearings were in general highly salient within South Africa. For instance, Alex Boraine (2000, 89) has written: "Never in my wildest imaginings did I think that the media would retain its insatiable interest in the Commission throughout its life. Not a day passed when we were not reported on the radio. We were very seldom absent from the major television evening news broadcasts, and we were, if not on the front page, on the inside pages of every newspaper throughout the two and a half years of our work." The special reports on the TRC aired by the SABC every Sunday from April 1996 until March 1998 often scored as among the most popular on South African television. And TV exposure pales in comparison to radio ex-

posure, which is especially significant since radio is the most popular information medium for most South Africans.

21. The question was: "How much do you know about the activities of the Truth and Reconciliation Commission (TRC)—a great deal, some but not a great deal, not very much, or nothing at all?"

22. The respondents were asked to indicate how much confidence they have in the TRC: a great deal, quite a lot, not very much, or none at all.

23. Were one to have a great deal of confidence in the commission, it might not be necessary to pay careful attention to its actions. Confidence may reduce the need for strict scrutiny.

24. This conclusion is derived from the significance of the change in variance explained when the interactive term is added to the linear equation.

25. So as not to clutter the table, I have not reported the individual regression coefficients.

26. Note that this survey was fielded well after the TRC hearings had ended, and therefore any residual evidence of the influence of commission activities is unlikely to be very strong. Had this survey been conducted in 1998, for instance, these relationships would most likely have been more substantial.

27. Note that beliefs about the political relevance of groups are not related to age within any of the four racial groups.

28. Note that a correlation coefficient may be thought of as representing the *total* linear effect of one variable on another. The independent effect, discerned through multivariate analysis, is virtually always smaller than the total effect.

29. There are many reasons why the explained variance is not higher. As already noted, survey data inevitably contain large amounts of measurement error. But another factor is surely that beliefs about apartheid are to some degree idiosyncratic. For instance, one might accept that apartheid was a crime against humanity—because that has become the socially accepted view in South Africa—but nonetheless view apartheid as a crime of individuals, not institutions. The particular package of beliefs that an individual adopts varies considerably, making systematic explanation difficult. Perhaps this reinforces the view that feelings about apartheid are complex and not necessarily simply divisible into "pro" and "anti" camps.

30. For a complete discussion of interracial contact, see chapter 4.

Chapter 4

1. On stereotyping, see Bobo and Massagli (2001) and Gibson and Duch (1992).
2. See, for example, Horowitz (1991, 23–27). The white government under apartheid instituted a tricameral parliament in 1983, with chambers reserved for Colored people and those of Indian origin. Blacks were denied representation in the parliament under the theory that they were not full citizens of South Africa and therefore would be represented in their own Bantustan governments. This obvious ploy to split the liberation forces was apparently rejected by most Colored and Asian South Africans, although few rigorous empirical data on this score are available.
3. The TRC itself was more interested in relationships between whites and "Blacks," largely because it was addressing South Africa's past.
4. Uncertainty seems to be more common when the statements refer to the perceived characteristics of the opposite racial group and to be less common when the statement directly characterizes the respondent's own feelings. It seems reasonable that people are more likely to know how they feel than they are to have information about other groups.
5. An extensive literature on the value of multiple indicators of concepts exists (see, for example, Sullivan and Feldman 1980). Of course, any sophisticated analysis of the psychometric properties of measures requires multiple indicators of concepts.
6. Note that racial differences on each of the items reported in table 4.1 are highly statistically significant as well.
7. James Kuklinski has developed the so-called list experiment as a means of unobtrusively measuring racial attitudes among whites (see Kuklinski, Cobb, and Gilens 1997). These pressures favoring socially desirable replies are often treated by scholars as little more than an inconvenient artifact that make the measurement of racial attitudes arduous. But a society in which open racial animus is judged inappropriate must be considered to be more reconciled than a society in which few social pressures impede the expression of hostility toward other racial groups.
8. Though a focus group perhaps presents a different context than a personal interview, there was certainly no apparent reticence to express antagonistic, even fierce, views toward other racial groups during the focus-group discussions.

9. We gave careful consideration to any connotations that might be associated with the name of the fictitious group. "Mishlenti" was a figment of the imagination of Gennady Denisovsky, one of my Russian colleagues, and is derived from the names of several of the stops on the route that Gennady typically takes to work on the Moscow subway. "Mishlenti" has no particular subtle meanings or associations in any of the South African languages, nor does it sound jarring in any of the tongues.

10. Note as well that virtually all white respondents were interviewed by white interviewers.

11. See the appendix to this chapter for additional evidence on whether social desirability pressures influenced responses to these questions.

12. This lack of relationship between attitudes toward whites and acceptance of the truth among black South Africans should dispel any suspicion that the relationship between truth acceptance and racial reconciliation is tautological.

13. Multiple hypotheses are involved here (for example, that "truth" has a greater impact on young people since they did not live through the most repressive period of apartheid), but since none of the hypotheses was supported, I mention them only in passing and without much discussion.

14. For an analysis of the effect of the racial integration of churches on racial attitudes in the United States, see Yancey (1999).

15. Note that the frequency of church attendance was collected using a seven-category response set. For the three categories of low attendance (less than once a month), all standardized regression coefficients exceed +.10, and the coefficients are statistically significant for all except the 66 respondents who report that they attend church services two to three times per year. Among those attending church more frequently, only one of the coefficients is statistically significant. Among the 121 respondents who attend religious services about once a month, the standardized regression coefficient is −.19 ($p = .035$). Instead of trying to provide an explanation for this negative relationship among a fairly small number of respondents, I have decided to treat religiosity as a dichotomous variable for the purposes of this analysis.

16. Note that no differences exist between the two groups in acceptance of the truth about the apartheid past.

17. Among those I define as religious, the most common denominational affiliation is with the Zion Christian Church (256 respondents). The standardized coefficient linking truth and reconciliation is −.04. For Methodists, the coefficient is .07 (not significant), for Catholics it is .01, and for the mixture of charismatic religions the coefficient is −.13, significant at $p = .03$.

18. According to the *Statistics South Africa* midyear estimates in 2000, 77.6 percent of the South African population is African, 10.3 percent is white, 8.7 percent is Colored, and 2.5 percent is Indian/Asian (see Forgey et al. 2001, 49).

19. It is reasonable to suspect that these relationships may not be linear. In fact, all of them are, as demonstrated by the tiny differences between the linear correlation coefficient and the nonlinear coefficient, η.

20. For a study that examines the effects of contact with whites among African Americans, see Ellison and Powers (1994).

21. The literature on interracial contact often points to the difficult question of causal direction. That is, the central hypothesis in the literature is that contact influences racial attitudes. A legitimate contrary viewpoint is that more tolerant racial attitudes result in greater interracial contact. Some have considered this question empirically and support the conventional view that contact causes reconciliation (see, for example, Ellison and Powers 1994; Pettigrew 1997; Powers and Ellison 1995; Pettigrew and Tropp 2000), but with cross-sectional data this question of causality continues to nag. Positing that contact causes reconciliation, rather than vice versa, is ultimately based on an assumption, not empirical evidence. Additional consideration of the issue of causality is reported in the appendix to this chapter.

22. For a recent practical effort in Cape Town at creating reconciliation through meals, see Horner (2001). This program was apparently inspired by these statistical results, which were reported at a press conference in Cape Town in June 2001.

23. The intense antipathy focused *within* the black community in South Africa should not be overlooked. Most of the political violence in South Africa in recent times has been black-on-black violence, even if the root cause of such violence can be found in the instigations of the apartheid state.

24. Pumla Gobodo-Madikizela (2003, 26, 109), a member of the Human Rights Violations Committee of the TRC, concludes that it is plausible

that whites did not know of many of the reprehensible activities of the apartheid government. She refers to this as an "apartheid of the mind."

25. Because the information produced by the TRC was in part redundant, the effect of truth on reconciliation is probably weaker among blacks than among whites. This most likely accounts for the tiny correlation coefficient between truth and interracial reconciliation that I reported earlier for black South Africans.

26. As Shanto Iyengar and Adam Simon (2000, 156) observe, the image of President Gerald Ford attempting to eat a tamale without first shucking it was a very clear signal to Hispanics in the United States of the sensitivity of the president to this constituency. Subtle messages are often more effective at social persuasion than more explicit appeals to attitude change.

27. For an example of a well-respected cross-sectional study that makes clear claims about causality, without any empirical consideration of the alternative causal sequence, see Sigelman and Welch (1993). This type of research is extremely common in the literature on the contact hypothesis.

28. In a similar vein, Ellison and Powers (1994, 397) analyze cross-sectional data but argue that because they find that "*childhood* interracial contact predicts *adult* internal friendship" (emphasis in original), they are entitled to the causal inference that contact causes racial attitudes and not vice versa.

29. See, for example, Link and Cullen (1986). Much of the contact literature can be found in journals that political scientists do not often read.

Chapter 5

1. Analyses of cultural norms and values have a long and distinguished legacy within the social sciences (see, for example, Almond and Verba 1963). But this approach has also achieved great currency lately among economists and legal analysts, as in their concern with *social norms*. The sociologist Amitai Etzioni (2000, 159) writes of the importance of these norms: "It is widely held that strong social norms reduce the burden on law enforcement; that laws supported by social norms are likely to be significantly more enforceable; and that laws that are formulated in ways that are congruent with social norms are

much more likely to be enacted than laws that offend such norms." In essence, Etzioni and others are asserting that if we are to understand how law and politics operate within a polity, we need to look beyond institutions to examine the cultural norms and values that undergird the institutions and shape the behavior of individual citizens. That is precisely the purpose of this chapter.

2. When we speak of corruption, for instance, as antithetical to the rule of law, we often are referring to a set of norms and expectations about whether corrupt behavior is acceptable within a polity. This refers to "ways of doing business," which are in part institutionally determined but are in larger part cultural.

3. At least some observers of South African politics agree. Ronald Slye (2000, 170) defines a human rights culture in the South African context as "a political culture that values human dignity and the rule of law." He asserts that the creation of such a culture is one of two necessary conditions for reconciliation. (The other condition is accountability for past violations.)

4. For earlier research using a similar conceptualization of universalism and particularism, see Levin (1972, 1977), Wilson (1976), Gibson and Gouws (1997), and Gibson (2003).

5. Furthermore, the TRC's *Final Report* (vol. 5, p. 212) often refers to the state as a perpetrator, and the South African state is specifically indicted for gross human rights violations.

6. For a balanced view of whether the liberation struggle encouraged intolerance, see Seekings (2000, 322–24). Jeremy Seekings believes that the United Democratic Front played an important role in developing rights consciousness in South Africa, and that "most UDF leaders sought to promote non-racialism, an appreciation of rights and a tolerance of difference."

7. This survey, funded by the National Science Foundation and the National Council for Soviet and East European Research, was based on representative samples within each of these countries. For an earlier report based on these data, see Gibson (1998).

8. This statement, which seems so obviously true, in fact ignores some indirect processes of interpersonal persuasion. One might be influenced by an institution without having any awareness of that institution through a "two-step" flow of information. If the institution affects opinion leaders, and opinion leaders affect ordinary people (opinion followers), then the institution has had an influence on the

followers, perhaps without them knowing much about the institution itself.

9. Richard Wilson (2001, 209) asserts: "Because human rights [have] been seen by politicized Africans as at odds with the punishment of alleged apartheid collaborators, human rights are equated with weakness on issues of social order, as soft on criminals and apartheid-era murderers, and as pro-bail and pro-amnesty for perpetrators."
10. Heinz Klug (2000, 47) offers the contrary hypothesis that "it may be reasonable to believe that the victims of apartheid would support the introduction of a bill of rights in response to the massive denial of rights under apartheid."
11. Among some of the liberation thinkers, majoritarianism is closely associated with deep skepticism about minority rights and indeed with liberal democratic theory in general. See, for instance, the useful discussion of this tension in Horowitz (1991).
12. For very useful analyses of the constitution-making process in South Africa, see Spitz and Chaskalson (2000) and Klug (2000).
13. One of the focus groups we conducted as part of this research was held among Indian subjects living in KwaZulu Natal. It took very little prodding for the issue of tension between the Indian community and the IFP to surface. When one subject recalled an assertion by Mangosuthu Buthelezi to the effect that "all Indians must go back to India, this is no place for you here," virtually all of the focus-group participants claimed to have been aware of that statement. An important part of the collective memory of Indians in KwaZulu Natal is the recurrent conflict and violence with the black majority.
14. These are the independent variables from table 5.5 that have the strongest and most consistent influence on support for the rule of law.

Chapter 6

1. It is perhaps inaccurate to imply that only a single version of social identity theory exists, since different authors disagree about whether in-group sympathy is associated with out-group antipathy. The clearest statement of this connection can be found in Sumner (1906). Marilynn Brewer (1999, 430) asserts that the belief that sympathy and antipathy are closely connected is widespread among political psychologists: "Most contemporary research on intergroup relations,

prejudice, and discrimination appears to accept, at least implicitly, the idea that ingroup favoritism and outgroup negativity are reciprocally related." Brewer's own view that the connection between favoritism and negativity is conditional on a variety of factors is surely correct. Throughout this book, I attribute the sympathy-antipathy hypothesis to social identity theory, while recognizing that not all social identity theorists accept the plausibility of the linkages and that not all extant literature demonstrates the veracity of the hypothesis proposing a connection.

2. PAGAD is an organization that arose as a vigilante group on the Cape Flats. Many believe that the group evolved over time into a criminal cartel that was often more responsible for committing than policing and punishing criminal behavior. The U.S. Department of State identifies PAGAD as a terrorist group (see U.S. Department of State 2001).

3. We randomly varied the order of presentation of these groups, by means of a random entry into the list of groups. Though a few of the statistical tests indicate some response differences based on the order of presentation, none of the tests is significant at $p < .001$ (with over 3,700 cases), and in no instance does eta exceed .10. The strongest linear relationship between order of presentation and the responses is .05. Thus, the data allow me to conclude that the order in which the respondents heard these group names had little if anything to do with how they evaluated the groups.

4. The AWB is an Afrikaner nationalist group that many view as neo-fascist. See http://www.awb.co.za/english.htm (accessed December 7, 2002).

5. For purposes of this analysis, I score a response of 1 or 2 as "extremely disliked," responses of 3, 4, and 5 as "disliked," 6 as neutral, 7, 8, and 9 as "liked," and 10 and 11 as "extremely liked." This scoring system is compatible with the spatial representation of the response categories on the showcard presented to the respondents.

6. The IFP was part of the initial Government of National Unity formed after the 1994 election, and it remains a junior partner in the ANC government. For more on the IFP, see http:www.ifp.org/za (accessed December 7, 2002).

7. Note that Colored people are divided in their attitudes toward Muslims, with neither a majority opposing them nor a majority supporting them.

8. Though the respondents were allowed to supplement the list of groups shown in table 6.3, in fact very few did.

9. If the respondent names four disliked groups, the "other highly disliked group" is the fourth most disliked. If only three groups are named, it is the third most disliked, and if only two groups are identified, the second most disliked group was asked about.

10. Considerable variability exists in the perceived power of the various groups. For instance, among those naming the ANC as their most disliked group, 42.0 percent assign the highest score on the "powerful" continuum to the party. The next most powerful group is perceived to be the New National Party, which is given the highest power score by 16.4 percent of the respondents.

11. The eigenvalues of the first four factors extracted through common factor analysis are 2.86, 1.66, 1.21, and .98, respectively. The first three factors account for 26.0 percent, 15.1 percent, and 11.0 percent of the common variance, respectively. Oblique rotation was used, since there is no reason for postulating that these three factors are unrelated to each other.

12. One of the items, the predictability or unpredictability of the group, loaded on no factor. Note as well that these findings are compatible with the factor structure in 1996, except that the third factor did not emerge, since those three questions were not asked in the survey.

13. Perhaps one explanation of this finding is that an uncommonly large number of South Africans name mainstream political groups (such as the ANC) as their most disliked foe. Though these groups may be powerful, they are part of the legitimate institutional structure of South Africa and therefore are not especially threatening. Consequently, intolerance may take on different characteristics when it is focused on groups that are part of the governing coalition in a country, in contrast to groups considered to be "extremist."

14. For a thorough discussion of what democracies can and cannot ban, see Gibson and Gouws (2003).

15. According to the "false consensus" hypothesis, people generally are predisposed to perceive greater agreement with their views among others than in fact exists. Why there would be such a strong asymmetry between the perceptions of the tolerant and the intolerant, however, cannot be explained by the false consensus literature.

16. As Janet Cherry (2000, 140) notes: "It is probably true to say that it was the very effectiveness with which the security police managed to infiltrate the liberation movements that made the 'struggle' such an awful, secretive, intolerant, distrustful affair."

17. Differences across the ethnic and linguistic groups among blacks are highly statistically significant and fairly substantial ($\eta = .14$ for the most disliked group; $\eta = .23$ for the other highly disliked group).

18. This conclusion is reinforced by the results of regressing intolerance on each of the individual threat items. The strongest predictor is the variable measuring perceived threat from the group to society.

19. Note that when I examine the influence of the three types of threat perceptions on tolerance by whether the respondent knows a member of the least liked group, I find that sociotropic threat perceptions remain the strongest predictor of intolerance. Among those who know a member of the group, $\beta = -.14$ for egocentric threat perceptions; among those who do not know a member of the group, $\beta = -.07$ for egocentric perceptions. Thus, knowing a member of the group does have some influence on the threat-tolerance relationship, although sociotropic threat perceptions still dominate.

20. For details on the measurement of the various aspects of group identities, see chapter 2.

21. In these mini-figures (as in the tables), I use the following scheme to designate statistical significance: $***p < .001$; $**p < .01$; $*p < .05$.

22. To be judged to provide support for the hypothesis, a coefficient must be correctly signed and greater than or equal to .10.

23. Note that these data do not support the conditional hypothesis that the importance of sociotropic threat perceptions in producing intolerance grows with increasing commitment to the importance of group solidarity.

Chapter 7

1. For a useful discussion of the major characteristics of the South African transition, see de Lange (2000, 17–18). He asserts: "It is a widely held view, by serious commentators, that without [the compromise on amnesty], there would have been no settlement, no interim constitution, no elections, no democracy and a possible continuation of the conflicts of the past" (22).

2. As Mamphela Ramphele asserts (2001, 11): "The outcome, brutally stated, is that white South Africans got away with murder. They were not asked to give up any of their previous privileges. On the contrary, the settlement entrenched their privileges."

3. For a moving account of some of these incidents, see Krog (1998). The TRC's website also reports full details of the atrocities committed by those who sought amnesty.

4. I do not necessarily need to address the issue of whether the state *ought* to punish those found to have violated human rights. The normative questions are not nearly as simple as some seem to think. Clearly, in the minds of many South Africans, including those who negotiated the transition, the price of avoiding civil war was amnesty. Whether this is a "fair" price cannot be resolved by my research.

5. For a most useful review of the literature on distributive justice, see Hegtvedt and Cook (2001).

6. President Mbeki has asserted that the issue of reparations will be addressed after the Amnesty Committee of the TRC files its final report (in late 2001). The president also reported that 16,501 applications for urgent interim relief had been made and that 9,605 had been acted upon.

7. John Daniel (2000, 4), for example, complains about "the extraordinary meanness the government has displayed to the paying of the modest and affordable [for the state budget] financial reparations recommended by the Commission to those found to have been victims of apartheid abuse."

8. The basis of law in much of rural South Africa remains "customary law," and restorative justice is a central element in that system. The new constitution did not abolish customary law, even if it did subordinate it to civil law. For a useful recent analysis, see Chambers (2000); see also Bennett (1995). The TRC *Final Report* explicitly considered the importance of restorative justice; see Truth and Reconciliation Commission (1998, vol. 1, pp. 125–31).

9. For a quite strong and well-reasoned argument that ubuntu is a concept inimical to the development of democracy in South Africa, see Marx (2002).

10. Those who write about restorative justice typically refer to far more than apologies when they speak of restoring the dignity of the victim and the relationship between the victim and the perpetrator (see, for

example, Kiss 2000). Still, few would disagree that apologies are a central element of the concept.

11. For an excellent recent review of the literature on procedural justice, see Tyler and Lind (2001).

12. Despite the differences in the univariate frequencies, these fairness judgments all reflect a single underlying fairness propensity. When subjected to factor analysis, a sole dominant factor emerges. This is also true when the factor analysis is conducted within the racial groups.

13. Neil Vidmar (2001, 42) and others refer to third-party reactions to moral wrongs as "disinterested" justice judgments. People are concerned about the injustice done to others either through an identification with the victim or in terms of concern over violations of a "social contract." The latter refers to judgments that are grounded in concerns for social peace and order and in desires to reaffirm the community's consensus about right and wrong. Thus, in some respects the judgments that ordinary people make about amnesty are similar to the judgments people make about so-called victimless crimes. In neither case does the bystander experience a direct and tangible injury, but the lack of injury often does not mitigate the moral outrage over the act. Many South Africans (if not most) were outraged at the human rights abuses revealed by the truth and reconciliation process, and concern about unfairness to the victims and their families is essentially the same thing as concern about unfairness to the moral order in South Africa.

14. I use the term "vignette" to refer to a short story told to the respondent. Vignettes nested in surveys have been used widely in the social sciences; see, for example, Bachman, Paternoster, and Ward (1992), Hamilton and Sanders (1992, 1995), Marcus et al. (1995), Gibson (1997), and Gibson and Gouws (1999).

15. We expended considerable effort in finding a racially and ethnically neutral name. In South Africa, "Phillip" implies very little about the actor, and it is not uncommon to find men named Phillip within every racial or ethnic group. Note that we consciously decided not to vary the actor's gender, since a very large majority of the South Africans appealing to the TRC were male. For a study using a similar strategy in controlling actor gender, see Gonzales et al. (1995).

16. The distinction between internal and external validity was first made by Donald Campbell; for an explication, see Cook and Campbell (1979).

17. Though there is some ambiguity as to whether each of these manipulation exclusively represents these different types of justice—for instance, compensation might be considered by some to be a form of restorative justice—it is clear that all relevant forms of justice are included in the experiment. To avoid confusion, I tend to refer to the variables in more literal than conceptual terms.

18. Not all victims who wished to give public statements at the human rights violations hearings were in fact allowed to give them. The criteria for selecting who was allowed to speak and who was not allowed varied enormously and were largely determined by the leaders of the community where the hearings were held (Charles Villa-Vicencio and Paul Haupt, now at the Institute of Justice and Reconciliation but formerly of the TRC, personal communication, June 24, 2001).

19. For instance, Aryeh Neier (1990, 34) has argued that "to identify those responsible, to show what they did, is to mark them with a public stigma that is a punishment in itself."

20. One should not assume that manipulations routinely pass their "checks," since in fact many do not; see, for example, Gibson (1997).

21. In the pretest we also measured perceptions of how fair the outcome was from the respondent's own perspective rather than from the perspective of the families. Since responses to this question are very strongly correlated with responses to the family fairness question, we concluded that when respondents view an outcome as fair to the family, they are also asserting that they believe the outcome was fair from their own viewpoint. See also the evidence presented earlier in this chapter.

22. Not unexpectedly, these judgments of fairness to the families of the victim are not strongly related to general assessments of the fairness of amnesty. The strongest correlation is with perceptions of the fairness of amnesty to ordinary people, but that correlation is only .23. This suggests that context does indeed matter, since the conclusions that people draw when they have some details about amnesty are only modestly related to their attitudes toward amnesty in general. And of course in the vignettes the details heard varied across respondents according to the version of the vignette to which the respondent was assigned.

23. I created a five-category variable from the continuous fairness judgments as follows: 1 to 2—very unfair; 3 to 5—unfair; 6 to 8—fair; and 9 to 10—very fair.

24. Note that none of the interactions among the manipulations achieves statistical significance.

25. It should be clear that the four manipulation variables are, by design, orthogonal to each other, and that under this condition bivariate and multivariate results do not differ. The perceptual variables are not orthogonal; instead, they are weakly to moderately intercorrelated (average correlation = .18). For a study using similar analytical techniques, see Gibson and Gouws (1999).

26. Table 7.5 reports the results of testing the null hypotheses that each of the coefficients (individually) is indistinguishable from zero. Because I am testing for racial interactions with the experimental and perceptual variables, and because the primary finding is that few interactions exist, the most useful information to report in table 7.5 is the results of the various significance tests. Most coefficients achieving statistical significance are discussed in the text, where the actual regression coefficients (and their standard errors) are reported.

27. Indeed, South Africans of Asian origin are the only group for whom the addition of the perceptual variables to the experimental equation (model 2) does not result in a statistically significant increase in explained variance. This may indicate that the whole issue of amnesty is of little salience to those of Asian origin.

28. It is worth reiterating that racial differences in how fair amnesty is thought to be to people in general are trivial.

29. How one feels about amnesty apparently does not directly translate into satisfaction or dissatisfaction with the truth and reconciliation process. For example, most Africans oppose amnesty, but most also support the work of the TRC.

30. For instance, it seems unlikely that a simple apology for the evils of slavery would satisfy those seeking reparations for the damages done by the slave trade.

Chapter 8

1. In one of the most important books ever published on the psychology of political legitimacy, John Jost and Brenda Major (2001, 4) argue: "Legitimacy is, quite literally, the key to politics, and it therefore deserves a central place in any theory of political psychology."

2. As noted earlier, the *Final Report* (Truth and Reconciliation Commission 1998, vol. 4, p. 101) asserts: "Part of the reason for the longevity

of apartheid was the superficial adherence to 'rule by law' by the National Party (NP), whose leaders craved the aura of legitimacy that 'the law' bestowed on their harsh injustice." Embedded in this sentence is a theory of legitimacy quite similar to the one I pursue in this chapter.

3. Unfortunately, Wilson (2001) provides no rigorous empirical evidence to support the various assumptions and processes underlying his claims.

4. As observed in chapter 5, some of those who write about the legitimacy of human rights (for example, Sarkin 1998) focus almost exclusively on the institutions designed to address human rights claims.

5. When I refer to the Parliament I mean the National Assembly, not the National Council of Provinces. The country's legislature is typically referred to as the Parliament, not the National Assembly (which is a little-known moniker), and I have every confidence that when our survey questions asked about "the Parliament," the respondents had the National Assembly in mind.

6. My understanding of democratic theory comports entirely with that of Robert Dahl (1989). For a useful application of this theory of democracy to Africa, see the introduction to Bratton and van de Walle (1997).

7. One might argue that the clearest institution of majority rule is the presidency, since the president in South Africa is selected on the basis of a majority vote of the members of the National Assembly. This research chose not to focus on the presidency since it is so easy to conflate attitudes toward the incumbent (Thabo Mbeki at the time of the survey) and the institution itself. Moreover, a traditional source of the failure of African democracies is the aggrandizement of political power by presidents, typically at the expense of the parliament (see, for example, Bratton and van de Walle 1997); few scholars see *weak* African presidents as a major threat to the consolidation of democratic reform. I do not gainsay that the legitimacy of all political institutions is generally important to the consolidation of democratic change, but in the South African context establishing the legitimacy of the Parliament and the Constitutional Court is of tremendous practical political importance.

8. In an otherwise very valuable review article, Morris Zelditch (2001, 33) proclaims: "The definition I will use is . . . that something is legitimate if it is in accord with the norms, values, beliefs, practices, and

procedures accepted by a group." I do not find such a definition useful because it confuses the *definition* of legitimacy with the *sources* of legitimacy. Agreeing with the basic values represented in an institution (for example, the protection of minority rights), as Caldeira and Gibson (1995) have shown us, is one reason why people extend legitimacy to an institution. But there are other reasons as well. An institution has legitimacy when people accept that it has a right (or authority) to make binding decisions for a group. People may extend legitimacy to an institution despite fairly serious value conflicts (for example, American Catholics and the Vatican).

9. Moreover, the literature on distributive and procedural justice (see, for example, Lind and Tyler 1988; Tyler 1990) teaches us that those who lose on distributive issues often find losing palatable if the procedures leading to the decision are perceived to be fair (see, for example, Baird 2001). However, controversy exists in the literature on the causal relationships between perceived fairness, legitimacy, and compliance (see Gibson 1989; Tyler and Rasinski 1991; Gibson 1991; Mondak 1993).

10. "Legitimacy" tends to be used more often by those conducting macrolevel analysis, which is common among sociologists (for example, Stryker 1994) and philosophers (for example, Habermas 1979). Robin Stryker (1994, 856) refers to my approach—a microlevel analysis—as one of "attitudinal approval." She asserts: "In the attitudinal approval approach to legitimacy, attachment, loyalty, allegiance, and a 'favorable affective orientation' to the political and legal system are synonymous with legitimacy." See also Tyler (1990, 28).

11. Research on legitimacy sometimes addresses the legitimacy of regimes and states but at other times focuses on the legitimacy of specific institutions. This chapter obviously addresses the latter.

12. Comparativists (for example, Tsebelis 2000; Alivizatos 1995) have recently focused on courts as "veto players" (by which they mean institutions that have the ability to go against majority preferences) and have acknowledged that legitimacy is a necessary resource if courts are to play this role; see also Gibson and Caldeira (2003).

13. For example, Tom Tyler (1990, 4) makes this distinction: "Normative commitment through personal morality means obeying a law because one feels the law is just; normative commitment through legitimacy means obeying a law because one feels that the authority enforcing the law has the right to dictate behavior." Unless we distin-

guish between legitimacy and obeying the law, this hypothesis cannot be examined empirically.

14. As in the advertisement in the *New York Times* on January 13, 2001, by 585 law professors condemning the Court's decision as illegitimate. A copy of the advertisement, as well as much additional material and criticism, can be found at Law Professors for the Rule of Law, http://www.the-rule-of-law.com/ (accessed December 7, 2001).

15. For empirical evidence that the Court did *not* in fact expend its legitimacy in this decision, see Gibson, Caldeira, and Spence (2003).

16. An example from the United States of the way in which a single individual, perhaps a particularly well endowed individual, can shape public policy through access to the courts can be found in the crusade of Michael A. Newdow to remove the phrase "under God" from the American Pledge of Allegiance (*Michael A. Newdow v. U.S. Congress, et al.*, U.S. Court of Appeals for the Ninth Circuit, 00-16423, 2002. http://caselaw.lp.findlaw.com/data2/circs/9th/0016423p.pdf). (Accessed on October 13, 2003.) Were Newdow fighting in the court of public opinion, his cause would have gone nowhere. In a court of law, however, he has had some success (however temporary, since, as of mid-2003, the Ninth Circuit Court of Appeals ruling is under review by the Supreme Court).

17. I say "directly profit" because it is possible to argue that all South Africans profit from a set of institutions that satisfies the demands and expectations of people. Thus, minorities profit from majoritarian institutions because such institutions keep the majority happy (or rather, in the absence of such institutions the majority would be very unhappy), thereby contributing to system stability, from which whites profit. But care should be taken with such logic, since it can become Panglossian or tautological (one always profits in some way from everything). I could be said to profit from the murder of my wife because, by punishing the murderer, society reaffirms and reinforces the norm that murder is improper, thereby giving me solace and perhaps reducing the chances of murder—even my own murder—happening in the future, which is of course to my benefit.

18. I also asked the respondents to give their estimates of the racial composition of the justices of the Constitutional Court. The distribution of responses is as follows: 11.1 percent said all the justices are white; 37.7 percent said that most of the justices are white; 13.4 percent said that a few justices are white; and 37.7 percent said they did not

know. Thus, knowledge of the Court cannot be considered to be very substantial among ordinary South Africans.

19. This follows the convention established in our earlier work on institutional legitimacy. See, for example, Gibson, Caldeira, and Baird (1998) and Gibson and Caldeira (2003). As asserted in Gibson, Caldeira, and Baird (1998, 348): "The replies of those who claimed little or no awareness are most likely dominated by random variation. Excluding them may restrict somewhat the theoretical variation in the correlation coefficients (although not the empirical variance in the items, since these respondents tended overwhelmingly to give 'don't know' responses to our substantive questions), but we believe their exclusion is necessary when analyzing attitudes toward the national high courts."

20. For a full explication of the conceptual and theoretical meaning of this concept, see the discussion in Caldeira and Gibson (1992, 636–42). Here I provide only an overview of the conceptualization, since this is well-trodden territory.

21. Under apartheid, the independence of the Appellate Division of the Supreme Court was often under attack. For excellent examinations of that court, see Ellmann (1992) and Forsyth (1985). For contemporary analyses of the Court, see Haynie (1998, 1999).

22. When I refer to the attitudes that "South Africans" hold toward these institutions, I am referring, unless otherwise indicated, to the institution's "attentive public."

23. An important exception to this generalization concerns the old Communist systems of Central and Eastern Europe and the former Soviet Union. There the system of "telephone justice" under communism apparently did much to delegitimize the court systems (see Markovits 1995). Under apartheid, South Africa did not have such a patently and obviously subservient judiciary, even if the courts typically did the bidding of the apartheid regime. Unlike the Communist systems, there were very important and highly salient instances in South Africa in which courageous judges and lawyers battled apartheid in the courts (see, for examples, Abel 1995; Bizos 1998).

24. My colleagues and I have suggested that the legitimacy of courts such as the Constitutional Court grows only to the extent that people become cognizant of the activities of the institution (Gibson, Caldeira, and Baird 1998). We argue that as people become more aware of constitutional courts, they tend to take more notice of decisions of

which they approve, and that this contributes to institutional loyalty. Gregory Caldeira and I (Caldeira and Gibson 1995) have suggested that lack of support for a court may be largely a function of low levels of knowledge of the court and its policies. Thus, courts seem to profit from making themselves more visible.

25. In nearly all respects, these two surveys were highly comparable. For details and findings on the earlier study, see Gibson and Gouws (2003) and Gibson and Caldeira (2003). The questions about the Parliament were not asked in 1997.

26. Note that in our 1997 survey 15 percent of the respondents said they had never heard of the Court. This compares to 17 percent in 2001 (an insignificant difference). The decline in uncertain responses among those who have at least some awareness of the Court seems to indicate that the quality of information held by the institution's attentive public has increased since the earlier survey.

27. So as to make the indices comparable, I have excluded the replies to the item asked only about the Constitutional Court.

28. Klug (2000, 77) argues that the ANC acquiesced to a strongly rights-based constitution in part out of the strategic realization that the white minority would not accept the political transition without such guarantees. Whites seemed to believe at the time of the transition that constitutional rights and a strong and independent judiciary to enforce such rights were essential to the protection of their political freedom.

29. The logic here is that winners are typically satisfied with the institution granting them their victory, while losers do not blame the institution. Thus, over time support increases because there is always a winning party.

30. This is not just a matter of constraints imposed by the length of the interview. In actual disputes, especially over civil liberties, specific controversies are often submitted to the courts, not the legislature, to resolve. Thus, the court vignette profits from verisimilitude: a conflagration arises, a court intervenes and rules, and then people must decide whether to accept the judicial decision or challenge it.

31. Those who had no opinion about whether Phillip should be given amnesty were excluded from the acquiescence experiment.

32. I should note that some might object to referring to this as an "experiment," since the respondents were not—and should not be from the

point of view of theory—randomly assigned to the type of Constitutional Court decision. Those of this viewpoint might prefer instead to think of this as a "quasi-experiment." For a detailed defense of exactly this sort of research design, see Gibson, Caldeira, and Spence (2002).

33. Within each racial group a strong relationship exists between initial preferences (whether one would grant or deny amnesty) and the willingness to acquiesce to a Court decision.

34. Among those who would deny amnesty, however, the general relationship is that stronger attitudinal intensity is associated with less acceptance of the Court decision.

35. Nor do controls for the salience of the amnesty issue to the respondent affect any of these conclusions.

36. Moreover, the creation of the Court was enveloped in partisan controversy; see Spitz and Chaskalson (2000, ch. 11).

Chapter 9

1. For three of the four subdimensions of reconciliation, the metric of the index reflects the individual-item response set, which is a Likert scale varying from 1 to 5. The interracial reconciliation index can be readily transformed into a comparable scale. The assessments in table 9.1 are based on the following judgments of the average group scores on each of the subdimensions: 1.0 to 1.9—not at all reconciled; 2.0 to 2.9—not very reconciled; 3.0 to 3.9—somewhat reconciled; and 4.0 to 5.0—highly reconciled. For institutional legitimacy, I use the mean of the responses to questions about both the Constitutional Court and the Parliament.

2. It is beyond the scope of this analysis to assess the macrolevel factors that allowed the TRC to act impartially. Perhaps the fact that South Africa's transition was brokered, based on a political and military stalemate, has something to do with how the TRC functioned. Perhaps it is important as well that all sides in the struggle had to live together after the transition; partition of the country was viewed by nearly everyone as unacceptable (just as federalism was viewed by most as desirable). For an excellent macrolevel analysis of truth commissions, see Hayner (2002).

3. See Marx (2002) for an explication of this point. Christoph Marx is particularly concerned about the ways in which the African concept

of "ubuntu"—from the Xhosa expression "Umuntu ngumuntu ngabanye bantu" (People are people through other people)—and traditional African collectivism foster conformity and undermine the legitimacy of political conflict. The truth and reconciliation process, and Archbishop Tutu in particular, often referred to ubuntu as essential to the process of reconciliation.

Appendix A

1. The incentive was a magnetic torch (flashlight), with which the respondents were quite pleased. Singer, Van Hoewyk, and Maher (1998) show that providing incentives has few negative consequences for survey responses.
2. Following the practice of the American National Election Study (1998), we trimmed (recoded the bottom and top percentiles) the distribution of weights so as not to allow extreme weights to have disproportionate influence.

References

Abel, Richard L. 1995. *Politics by Other Means: Law in the Struggle Against Apartheid, 1980–1994*. New York: Routledge.

Alivizatos, Nicos. 1995. "Judges as Veto Players." In *Parliaments and Majority Rule in Western Europe*, edited by Herbert Doring. New York: St. Martin's Press.

Allport, Gordon W. 1954. *The Nature of Prejudice*. Reading, Mass.: Addison-Wesley.

Almond, Gabriel A., and Sidney Verba. 1963. *The Civic Culture: Political Attitudes and Democracy in Five Nations*. Princeton, N.J.: Princeton University Press.

American National Election Study. 1998. "Poststratified Cross-sectional Analysis Weights for the 1992, 1994, and 1996 NES Data." Ann Arbor, Mich.: University of Michigan, Institute for Social Research, Survey Research Center, Sampling Section Division of Surveys and Technologies. Technical Report 37 (April 1998). Available at: ftp://ftp.nes.isr.umich.edu/ftp/resourcs/techrpts/reports/Tch37.pdf (accessed on October 13, 2003).

Asmal, Kadar. 2000. "International Law and Practice: Dealing with the Past in the South African Experience." *American University International Law Review* 15: 1211–29.

Bachman, Ronet, Raymond Paternoster, and Sally Ward. 1992. "The Rationality of Sexual Offending: Testing a Deterrence/Rational Choice Conception of Sexual Assault." *Law and Society Review* 26(2, June): 343–72.

Baird, Vanessa A. 2001. "Building Institutional Legitimacy: The Role of Procedural Justice." *Political Research Quarterly* 54(2, June): 333–54.

Ball-Rokeach, Sandra J., Milton Rokeach, and Joel Grube. 1984. *The Great American Values Test*. New York: Free Press.

Bennett, Thomas W. 1995. *Human Rights and African Customary Law*. Cape Town: Juta & Co.

Berry, William D. 1984. *Nonrecursive Causal Models*. Newbury Park, Calif.: Sage Publications.

Biko, Nkosinathi. 2000. "Amnesty and Denial." In *Looking Back, Reaching Forward: Reflections on the Truth and Reconciliation Commission of South Africa*, edited by Charles Villa-Vicencio and Wilhelm Verwoerd. Cape Town: University of Cape Town Press.

Bischoping, Katherine, and Andrea Kalmin. 1999. "Public Opinion About Comparisons to the Holocaust." *Public Opinion Quarterly* 63(4, Winter): 485–507.

Bizos, George. 1998. *No One to Blame? In Pursuit of Justice in South Africa.* Cape Town: David Philip & Mayibuye Books.

Bobo, Lawrence D., and Michael P. Massagli. 2001. "Stereotyping and Urban Inequality." In *Urban Inequality: Evidence from Four Cities,* edited by Alice O'Connor, Chris Tilly, and Lawrence D. Bobo. New York: Russell Sage Foundation.

Boraine, Alex. 2000. *A Country Unmasked: Inside South Africa's Truth and Reconciliation Commission.* Oxford: Oxford University Press.

Boynton, G. R., and Gerhard Loewenberg. 1973. "The Development of Public Support for Parliament in Germany, 1951–1959." *British Journal of Political Science* 3(pt. 3, April): 169–89.

Bratton, Michael, and Nicolas van de Walle. 1997. *Democratic Experiments in Africa: Regime Transition in Comparative Perspective.* New York: Cambridge University Press.

Brewer, Marilynn B. 1999. "The Psychology of Prejudice: Ingroup Love or Outgroup Hate?" *Journal of Social Issues* 55(3, Fall): 439–44.

Brislin, Richard W. 1970. "Back-translation for Cross-cultural Research." *Journal of Cross-cultural Psychology* 1(3, September): 185–216.

Brookes, Edgar H. 1968. *Apartheid: A Documentary Study of Modern South Africa.* London: Routledge and Kegan Paul.

Business Day Reporter. 1998. "Most Believe Truth Body Harmed Race Relations, Survey Finds." *Business Day,* July 27. Available at www.doj.gov.za/TRC/Media/1998/9807/s980727a.htm.

Caldeira, Gregory A. 1987. "Public Opinion and the U.S. Supreme Court: FDR's Court-Packing Plan." *American Political Science Review* 81(4, December): 1139–53.

———. 1994. "Legitimacy, Compliance, and the Roots of Justice: A Strategic Plan for Global Research." Report. Alexandria, Va.: National Science Foundation.

Caldeira, Gregory A., and James L. Gibson. 1992. "The Etiology of Public Support for the Supreme Court." *American Journal of Political Science* 36(3, August): 635–64.

———. 1995. "The Legitimacy of the Court of Justice in the European Union: Models of Institutional Support." *American Political Science Review,* 89(2, June): 356–76.

Campbell, Donald T., and J. C. Stanley. 1966. *Experimental and Quasi-experimental Designs for Research.* Chicago: Rand McNally.

Caplan, Bryan. 2002. "Sociotropes, Systematic Bias, and Political Failure: Reflections on the Survey of Americans and Economists on the Economy." *Social Science Quarterly* 83(2, June): 416–35.

Chambers, David L. 2000. "Civilizing the Natives: Marriage in Post-Apartheid South Africa." *Daedalus* 129(4, Fall): 101–24.

Cherry, Janet. 2000. "Historical Truth: Something to Fight For." In *Looking Back, Reaching Forward: Reflections on the Truth and Reconciliation Commission of South Africa*, edited by Charles Villa-Vicencio and Wilhelm Verwoerd. Cape Town: University of Cape Town Press.

Chong, Dennis, and Anna-Maria Marshall. 1999. "When Morality and Economics Collide (or Not) in a Texas Community." *Political Behavior* 21(2, June): 91–121.

Choper, Jesse H. 1980. *Judicial Review and the National Political Process: A Functional Reconsideration of the Role of the Supreme Court*. Chicago: University of Chicago Press.

Christie, Kenneth. 2000. *The South African Truth Commission*. New York: St. Martin's Press.

Clawson, Rosalee A., Elizabeth R. Kegler, and Eric N. Waltenburg. 2001. "The Legitimacy-Conferring Authority of the U.S. Supreme Court: An Experimental Design." *American Politics Research* 29(6, November): 566–91.

Cloninger, C. Robert, Dragan M. Svrakic, and Thomas R. Przybeck. 1993. "A Psychological Model of Temperament and Character." *Archives of General Psychiatry* 50: 975–90.

Cohen, Jacob, and Patricia Cohen. 1983. *Applied Multiple Regression/Correlation Analysis for the Behavioral Sciences*. 2nd ed. Hillsdale, N.J.: Lawrence Erlbaum Associates.

Cook, Thomas D., and Donald T. Campbell. 1979. *Quasi-experimentation: Design and Analysis Issues for Field Settings*. Chicago: Rand McNally.

Corder, Hugh. 1995. "Establishing Legitimacy for the Administration of Justice in South Africa." *Stellenbosch Law Review* 2: 202–15.

Dahl, Robert A. 1957. "Decisionmaking in a Democracy: The Supreme Court as a National Policymaker." *Journal of Public Law* 6: 279–95.

———. 1971. *Polyarchy*. New Haven, Conn.: Yale University Press.

———. 1989. *Democracy and Its Critics*. New Haven, Conn.: Yale University Press.

Daniel, John. 2000. "Editorial: The Truth and Reconciliation Commission." *Transformation: Critical Perspectives on Southern Africa* 42: 1–8.

Darby, B. W., and Barry R. Schlenker. 1989. "Children's Reactions to Transgressions: Effects of the Actor's Apology, Reputation, and Remorse." *British Journal of Social Psychology* 28(4, December): 353–64.

Davenport, T. R. H., and Christopher Saunders. 2000. *South Africa: A Modern History*. 5th ed. New York: St. Martin's Press.

De Kock, Eugene. 1998. *A Long Night's Damage: Working for the Apartheid State*. Saxonwold, Republic of South Africa: Contra Press.

De Lange, Johnny. 2000. "The Historical Context, Legal Origins, and Philosophical Foundation of the South African Trust and Reconciliation Commission." In *Looking Back, Reaching Forward: Reflections on the Truth and Reconciliation Commission of South Africa,* edited by Charles Villa-Vicencio and Wilhelm Verwoerd. Cape Town: University of Cape Town Press.

Delli Carpini, Michael X., and Bruce A. Williams. 1994. "Methods, Metaphors, and Media Research: The Uses of Television in Political Conversation." *Communication Research* 21(6, December): 782–812.

Diamond, Larry. 1999. *Developing Democracy: Toward Consolidation.* Baltimore: Johns Hopkins University Press.

Donovan, Robert J., and Susan Leivers. 1993. "Using Paid Advertising to Modify Racial Stereotype Beliefs." *Public Opinion Quarterly* 57(2, Summer): 205–18.

Duckitt, John, and Thobi Mphuthing. 1998. "Group Identification and Intergroup Attitudes: A Longitudinal Analysis in South Africa." *Journal of Personality and Social Psychology* 74(1, January): 80–85.

Du Preez, Max. 2001. "Too Many Truths to Tell." *Sunday Independent* (June 24, 2001): 13, 15.

Du Toit, André. 2000. "The Moral Foundations of the South African TRC: Truth as Acknowledgment and Justice as Recognition." In *Truth v. Justice: The Morality of Truth Commissions,* edited by Robert I. Rotberg and Dennis Thompson. Princeton, N.J.: Princeton University Press.

Easton, David. 1965. *A Systems Analysis of Political Life.* New York: John Wiley.

———. 1975. "A Reassessment of the Concept of Political Support." *British Journal of Political Science* 5(4, October): 435–57.

Ellis, Stephen. 1998. "The Historical Significance of South Africa's Third Force." *Journal of Southern African Studies* 24(2, June): 261–99.

Ellison, Christopher G., and Daniel A. Powers. 1994. "The Contact Hypothesis and Racial Attitudes Among Black Americans." *Social Science Quarterly* 75(2, June): 385–400.

Ellmann, Stephen. 1992. *In a Time of Trouble: Law and Liberty in South Africa's State of Emergency.* New York: Oxford University Press.

Esterhuyse, Willie. 2000. "Truth as a Trigger for Transformation: From Apartheid Injustice to Transformational Justice." In *Looking Back, Reaching Forward: Reflections on the Truth and Reconciliation Commission of South Africa,* edited by Charles Villa-Vicencio and Wilhelm Verwoerd. Cape Town: University of Cape Town Press.

Etzioni, Amitai. 2000. "Social Norms: Internationalization, Persuasion, and History." *Law and Society Review* 34(1): 157–78.

Feldman, Stanley. 2003. "Enforcing Social Conformity: A Theory of Authoritarianism." *Political Psychology* 24(1, March): 41–74.

Forgey, Herma, Tamara Dimant, Terence Corrigan, Thabo Mophuthing, Jessica Spratt, Daniel Pienaar, and Nyanisile Peter. 2001. *South Africa Survey 2000/2001*. Johannesburg: South African Institute of Race Relations.

Forsyth, C. F. 1985. *In Danger for Their Talents: A Study of the Appellate Division of the Supreme Court of South Africa from 1950 to 1980*. Cape Town: Juta & Co.

Friedman, Lawrence M. 1977. *Law and Society: An Introduction*. Englewood Cliffs, N.J.: Prentice-Hall.

———. 1998. *American Law: An Introduction*. Revised and updated edition. New York: W. W. Norton.

Gevisser, Mark. 1996. "The Ultimate Test of Faith." *Mail & Guardian*, April 12.

Gibson, James L. 1989. "Understandings of Justice: Institutional Legitimacy, Procedural Justice, and Political Tolerance." *Law and Society Review* 23(3): 469–96.

———. 1991. "Institutional Legitimacy, Procedural Justice, and Compliance with Supreme Court Decisions: A Question of Causality." *Law and Society Review* 25: 631–35.

———. 1997. "The Struggle Between Order and Liberty in Contemporary Russian Political Culture." *Australian Journal of Political Science* 32(2, July): 271–90.

———. 1998. "Putting Up with Fellow Russians: An Analysis of Political Tolerance in the Fledgling Russian Democracy." *Political Research Quarterly* 51(1, March): 37–68.

———. 2002a. "Truth and Reconciliation Survey 2001." Compact disk. Institute for Justice and Reconciliation, Cape Town. http://www.ijr.org.za.

———. 2002b. "Truth, Justice, and Reconciliation: Judging the Fairness of Amnesty in South Africa." *American Journal of Political Science* 46(3, July): 540–56.

———. 2003. "The Legacy of Apartheid: Racial Differences in the Legitimacy of Democratic Institutions and Processes in the New South Africa." *Comparative Political Studies* 36(7, September): 772–800.

———. 2004. "Truth, Reconciliation, and the Creation of a Human Rights Culture in South Africa." *Law and Society Review* 38(1, March): 5–40.

Gibson, James L., and Gregory A. Caldeira. 1995. "The Legitimacy of Transnational Legal Institutions: Compliance, Support, and the European Court of Justice." *American Journal of Political Science* 39(2, May): 459–89.

———. 1996. "The Legal Cultures of Europe." *Law and Society Review* 30(1): 55–85.

———. 1998. "Changes in the Legitimacy of the European Court of Justice: A Post-Maastricht Analysis." *British Journal of Political Science* 28(1, January): 63–91.

———. 2003. "Defenders of Democracy? Legitimacy, Popular Acceptance, and the South African Constitutional Court." *Journal of Politics* 65(1, February): 1–30.

Gibson, James L., Gregory A. Caldeira, and Vanessa Baird. 1998. "On the Legitimacy of National High Courts." *American Political Science Review* 92(2, June): 343–58.

Gibson, James L., Gregory A. Caldeira, and Lester Kenyatta Spence. 2002. "The Role of Theory in Experimental Design: Experiments Without Randomization." *Political Analysis* (Special Issue on Experimental Methods in Political Science) 10(4, Autumn): 362–75.

———. 2003. "The Supreme Court and the U.S. Presidential Election of 2000: Wounds, Self-inflicted or Otherwise?" *British Journal of Political Science* 33(4, October): 535–56.

Gibson, James L., and Raymond M. Duch. 1992. "Anti-Semitic Attitudes of the Mass Public: Estimates and Explanations Based on a Survey of the Moscow Oblast." *Public Opinion Quarterly* 56(1, Spring): 1–28.

Gibson, James L., and Amanda Gouws. 1997. "Support for the Rule of Law in the Emerging South African Democracy." *International Social Science Journal* 152(2, June): 173–91.

———. 1999. "Truth and Reconciliation in South Africa: Attributions of Blame and the Struggle over Apartheid." *American Political Science Review* 93(3, September): 501–17.

———. 2000. "Social Identities and Political Intolerance: Linkages Within the South African Mass Public." *American Journal of Political Science* 44(2, April): 278–92.

———. 2003. *Overcoming Intolerance in South Africa: Experiments in Democratic Persuasion*. New York: Cambridge University Press.

Gibson, James L., and Helen Macdonald. 2001. "Truth—Yes, Reconciliation—Maybe: South Africans Judge the Truth and Reconciliation Process." Research report. Rondebosch: Institute for Justice and Reconciliation. http://www.ijr.org.za/pdfs/exec.pdf (accessed June 3, 2003).

Giliomee, Herman, and Lawrence Schlemmer. 1989. *From Apartheid to Nation-Building: Contemporary South African Debates*. Cape Town: Oxford University Press.

Gobodo-Madikizela, Pumla. 2003. *A Human Being Died That Night: A South African Story of Forgiveness*. Boston: Houghton Mifflin.

Goffman, Erving. 1971. *Relations in Public*. New York: Harper & Row.

Goldstone, Judge Richard. 2000. Foreword to *Looking Back, Reaching Forward: Reflections on the Truth and Reconciliation Commission of South Af-*

rica, edited by Charles Villa-Vicencio and Wilhelm Verwoerd. Cape Town: University of Cape Town Press.

Gonzales, Marti Hope, Margaret Bull Kovera, John L. Sullivan, and Virginia Chanley. 1995. "Private Reactions to Public Transgressions: Predictors of Evaluative Responses to Allegations of Political Misconduct." *Personality and Social Psychology Bulletin* 21(2, February): 136–48.

Graubard, Stephen R. 2001. Preface to the issue "Why South Africa Matters," *Daedalus* 130(1, Winter): v–viii.

Graybill, Lyn S. 1998. "South Africa's Truth and Reconciliation Commission: Ethical and Theological Perspectives." *Ethics and International Affairs* 12: 43–62.

Habermas, Jürgen. 1979. *Communication and the Evolution of Society.* Translated and with an introduction by Thomas McCarthy. Boston: Beacon Press.

Halbwachs, Maurice. 1950/1980. *The Collective Memory.* New York: Harper & Row.

Hamber, Brandon, and Hugo van der Merwe. 1998. "What Is This Thing Called Reconciliation?" Paper presented to the Goedgedacht Forum "After the Truth and Reconciliation Commission" (March 28). Goedgedacht Farm, Cape Town, www.csvr.org/za/articles/artcb&h.htm (accessed June 23, 2001).

Hamber, Brandon, and Richard Wilson. n.d. "Symbolic Closure Through Memory, Reparation, and Revenge in Post-Conflict Societies." Available at www.csvr.org.za/papers/papbh&rw.htm (accessed on October 13, 2003).

Hamilton, V. Lee, and Joseph Sanders. 1992. *Everyday Justice: Responsibility and the Individual in Japan and the United States.* New Haven, Conn.: Yale University Press.

———. 1995. "Crimes and Obedience and Conformity in the Workplace: Surveys of Americans, Russians, and Japanese." *Journal of Social Issues* 51(3, Fall): 67–88.

Hanushek, Eric A., and John E. Jackson. 1977. *Statistical Methods for Social Scientists.* New York: Academic Press.

Harris, Verne. 2000. "'They Should Have Destroyed More': The Destruction of Public Records by the South African State in the Final Years of Apartheid, 1990–1994." *Transformation: Critical Perspectives on Southern Africa* 42: 29–56.

Hay, Mark. 1998. *Ukubuyisana: Reconciliation in South Africa.* Pietermaritzburg: Cluster Publications.

Hayner, Priscilla B. 1994. "Fifteen Truth Commissions—1974 to 1994: A Comparative Study." *Human Rights Quarterly* 16(4, November): 597–655.

———. 2000. "Same Species, Different Animal: How South Africa Compares to Truth Commissions Worldwide." In *Looking Back, Reaching Forward: Reflections on the Truth and Reconciliation Commission of South Africa,* edited by Charles Villa-Vicencio and Wilhelm Verwoerd. Cape Town: University of Cape Town Press.

———. 2002. *Unspeakable Truths: Facing the Challenge of Truth Commissions.* New York: Routledge.

Haynie, Stacia L. 1998. "Ideology and Judicial Decisionmaking in the South African Appellate Division, 1950–1990." Paper presented to the 1998 meeting of the Midwest Political Science Association, Chicago (April 23–25, 1998).

———. 1999. "Courts and Revolution: Independence and Legitimacy in the New Republic of South Africa." *Justice System Journal* 19: 167–79.

Hegtvedt, Karen A., and Karen S. Cook. 2001. "Distributive Justice: Recent Theoretical Developments and Applications." In *Handbook of Justice Research in Law,* edited by Joseph Sanders and V. Lee Hamilton. New York: Kluwer Academic/Plenum Publishers.

Hibbing, John R., and Elizabeth Theiss-Morse. 1995. *Congress as Public Enemy: Public Attitudes Toward American Political Institutions.* Cambridge: Cambridge University Press.

———. 2001. "Process Preferences and American Politics: What People Want Government to Be." *American Political Science Review* 95(1, March): 145–53.

Hoffmann, Erik P. 1998. "Democratic Theories and Authority Patterns in Contemporary Russian Politics." In *Can Democracy Take Root in Post-Soviet Russia? Explorations in State–Society Relations,* edited by Harry Eckstein, Frederic J. Fleron Jr., Erik P. Hoffmann, and William M. Reisinger, with Richard Ahl, Russell Bova, and Philip G. Roeder. Lanham, Md.: Rowman & Littlefield.

Hogan, Robert, and Nicholas P. Emler. 1981. "Retributive Justice." In *The Justice Motive in Social Behavior: Adapting to Times of Scarcity and Change,* edited by Melvin J. Lerner and Sally C. Lerner. New York: Plenum Press.

Horner, Brett. 2001. "Making a Meal of Reconciliation." *Sunday Times,* South Africa, August 12, 2001.

Horowitz, Donald L. 1991. *A Democratic South Africa? Constitutional Engineering in a Divided Society.* Cape Town: Oxford University Press.

Horrel, Muriel. 1982. *Race Relations as Regulated by Law in South Africa, 1948–1979.* Johannesburg: South African Institute of Race Relations.

Huddy, Leonie. 2001. "From Social to Political Identity: A Critical Examination of Social Identity Theory." *Political Psychology* 22(1, March): 127–56.

Hyde, Alan. 1983. "The Concept of Legitimation in the Sociology of Law." *Wisconsin Law Review* (2): 379–426.

Ibhawoh, Bonny. 2000. "Between Culture and Constitution: Evaluating the Cultural Legitimacy of Human Rights in the African State." *Human Rights Quarterly* 22(3, August): 838–60.

Ignatieff, Michael. 1996. "Articles of Faith." *Index on Censorship* 25(5, September): 110–22.

Irwin-Zarecka, Iwona. 1994. *Frames of Remembrance: The Dynamics of Collective Memory.* New Brunswick, N.J.: Transactions.

Iyengar, Shanto, and Adam F. Simon. 2000. "New Perspectives and Evidence on Political Communication and Campaign Effects." *Annual Review of Psychology* 51: 149–69.

Jackman, Mary R., and Marie Crane. 1986. "'Some of My Best Friends Are Black . . .': Interracial Friendship and Whites' Racial Attitudes." *Public Opinion Quarterly* 50(4, Winter): 459–86.

James, Wilmot, and Jeffrey Lever. 2000. "South Africa—The Second Republic: Race, Inequality, and Democracy in South Africa." In *Three Nations at the Crossroad.* Beyond Racism: Embracing an Interdependent Future Series. Atlanta: Southern Education Foundation.

Jeffery, Anthea. 1999. *The Truth About the Truth Commission.* Johannesburg: South African Institute of Race Relations.

Jennings, M. Kent. 1996. "Political Knowledge Across Time and Generations." *Public Opinion Quarterly* 60(2, Summer): 228–52.

Jordan, Pallo. 1988. "Why Won't Afrikaners Rely on Democracy?" *Die Suid-Afrikaan* (February): 24–25, 29.

Jost, John T., and Brenda Major. 2001. "Emerging Perspectives on the Psychology of Legitimacy." In *The Psychology of Legitimacy: Emerging Perspectives on Ideology, Justice, and Intergroup Relations,* edited by John J. Jost and Brenda Major. New York: Cambridge University Press.

Jung, Courtney. 2000. *Then I Was Black: South African Political Identities in Transition.* New Haven, Conn.: Yale University Press.

Kane-Berman, John. 1993. *Political Violence in South Africa.* Johannesburg: South African Institute of Race Relations.

Kiss, Elizabeth. 2000. "Moral Ambition Within and Beyond Political Constraints: Reflections on Restorative Justice." In *Truth v. Justice: The Morality of the Truth Commissions,* edited by Robert I. Rotberg and Dennis Thompson. Princeton, N.J.: Princeton University Press.

Klug, Heinz. 2000. *Constituting Democracy: Law, Globalism, and South Africa's Political Reconstruction.* Cambridge: Cambridge University Press.

Krog, Antjie. 1998. *Country of My Skull.* Johannesburg: Random House.

Krygier, Martin. 1990. "Marxism and the Rule of Law: Reflections After the Collapse of Communism." *Law and Social Inquiry* 15(4, Fall): 633–63.

Kuklinski, James H., Michael D. Cobb, and Martin Gilens. 1997. "Racial Attitudes and the 'New South.'" *Journal of Politics* 59(2, May): 323–49.

Leatt, James, Theo Kneifel, and Klaus Nürnberger. 1986. *Contending Ideologies in South Africa*. Cape Town: David Philip.

Levin, Martin A. 1972. "Urban Politics and Judicial Behavior." *Journal of Legal Studies* 1: 193–221.

———. 1977. *Urban Politics and Criminal Courts*. Chicago: University of Chicago Press.

Lind, E. Allan, and Tom R. Tyler. 1988. *The Social Psychology of Procedural Justice*. New York: Plenum Press.

Link, Bruce G., and Francis T. Cullen. 1986. "Contact with the Mentally Ill and Perceptions of How Dangerous They Are." *Journal of Health and Social Behavior* 27(4, December): 289–303.

Lipset, Seymour Martin. 1994. "The Social Requisites of Democracy Revisited." *American Sociological Review* 59(1, February): 1–22.

Loewenberg, Gerhard. 1971. "The Influence of Parliamentary Behavior on Regime Stability." *Comparative Politics* 3(2, January): 177–200.

Macdonald, Helen. 2000. "IJR Report on Reconciliation Survey Research." Institute for Justice and Reconciliation, http://www.ijr.org/za/papers/report.html (accessed October 13, 2003).

Marais, Hein. 1998. *South Africa: Limits to Change: The Political Economy of Transition*. Cape Town: University of Cape Town Press.

Marcus, Georges E., John L. Sullivan, Elizabeth Theiss-Morse, and Sandra L. Wood. 1995. *With Malice Toward Some: How People Make Civil Liberties Judgments*. New York: Cambridge University Press.

Markel, Dan. 1999. "The Justice of Amnesty? Towards a Theory of Retributivism in Recovering States." *University of Toronto Law Journal* 49(3, Summer): 389–445.

Markovits, Inga. 1995. *Imperfect Justice: An East-West German Diary*. New York: Oxford University Press.

Marks, Monique. 2001. *Young Warriors: Youth Politics, Identity, and Violence in South Africa*. Johannesburg: Witwatersrand University Press.

Marx, Christoph. 2002. "Ubu and Ubuntu: On the Dialects of Apartheid and Nation-Building." *Politikon: South African Journal of Political Studies* 29(1, May): 49–69.

Minow, Martha. 1998. *Between Vengeance and Forgiveness: Facing History After Genocide and Mass Violence*. Boston: Beacon Press.

Mishler, William, and Richard Rose. 1994. "Support for Parliaments and Regimes in the Transition Toward Democracy in Eastern Europe." *Legislative Studies Quarterly* 19(1, February): 5–32.

Mondak, Jeffrey J. 1992. "Institutional Legitimacy, Policy Legitimacy, and the Supreme Court." *American Politics Quarterly* 20(4, October): 457–77.

———. 1993. "Institutional Legitimacy and Procedural Justice: Reexamining the Question of Causality." *Law and Society Review* 27: 599–608.

Nattrass, Nicoli, and Jeremy Seekings. 2001. "'Two Nations'? Race and Economic Inequality in South Africa Today." *Daedalus* 130(3, Winter): 45–70.

Neier, Aryeh. 1990. "What Should Be Done About the Guilty?" *New York Review of Books* (February 1, 1990): 32–35.

Ngidi, Sandile. 1998. "Bitter Pill of Amnesty." *Siyaya!* 3(Spring): 24–25.

Noelle-Neumann, Elisabeth. 1984. *The Spiral of Silence: Public Opinion—Our Social Skin*. Chicago: University of Chicago Press. (Orig. pub. in German in 1980.)

Ohbuchi, Ken-ichi, Masuyo Kameda, and Nariyuki Agarie. 1989. "Apology as Aggression Control: Its Role in Mediating Appraisal of and Response to Harm." *Journal of Personality and Social Psychology* 56(2): 219–27.

Omar, Abdullah M. 1996. Foreword to *Confronting Past Injustices: Approaches to Amnesty, Punishment, Reparation, and Restitution in South Africa and Germany*, edited by M. R. Rwelamira and G. Werle. Durban: Butterworths.

Orr, Wendy. 2000. *From Biko to Basson: Wendy Orr's Search for the Soul of South Africa as a Commissioner of the TRC*. Saxonwold, Republic of South Africa: Contra Press.

Pauw, Jacques. 1997. *Into the Heart of Darkness: Confessions of Apartheid's Assassins*. Johannesburg: Jonathan Ball.

Pettigrew, Thomas F. 1997. "Generalized Intergroup Contact Effects on Prejudice." *Personality and Social Psychology Bulletin* 23(2, February): 173–85.

———. 1998. "Intergroup Contact Theory." *Annual Review of Psychology* 49(1): 65–85.

Pettigrew, Thomas F., and L. R. Tropp. 2000. "Does Intergroup Contact Reduce Prejudice? Recent Meta-analytic Findings." In *Reducing Prejudice and Discrimination*, edited by Stuart Oskamp. Mahwah, N.J.: Lawrence Erlbaum Associates.

Posel, Deborah. 2001. "What's in a Name? Racial Categorizations Under Apartheid and Their Afterlife." *Transformation: Critical Perspectives on Southern Africa* 47: 50–74.

Powers, Daniel A., and Christopher G. Ellison. 1995. "Interracial Contact and Black Racial Attitudes: The Contact Hypothesis and Selectivity Bias." *Social Forces* 74(1, September): 205–46.

Ramphele, Mamphela. 2001. "Citizenship Challenges for South Africa's Young Democracy." *Daedalus: Journal of the American Academy of Arts and Sciences* 130(1, Winter): 1–17.

Ranulf, Svend. 1964. *Moral Indignation and Middle Class Psychology*. New York: Schocken Books.

Rice, Ronald E., and Charles K. Atkin. 1989. *Public Communication Campaigns*. Newbury Park, Calif.: Sage Publications.

Rose, Richard, William Mishler, and Christian Haerpfer. 1998. *Democracy and Its Alternatives: Understanding Post-Communist Societies.* Baltimore, Md.: Johns Hopkins University Press.

Rummel, R. J. 1994. *Death by Government.* New Brunswick, N.J.: Transactions Publishers.

Rwelamira, Medard R. 1996. "Punishing Past Human Rights Violations: Considerations in the South African Context." In *Confronting Past Injustices: Approaches to Amnesty, Punishment, Reparation, and Restitution in South Africa and Germany,* edited by Medard R. Rwelamira and Gerhard Werle. Durban: Butterworths.

Sanders, Joseph, and V. Lee Hamilton. 2001. "Justice and Legal Institutions." In *Handbook of Justice Research in Law,* edited by Joseph Sanders and V. Lee Hamilton. New York: Kluwer Academic/Plenum Publishers.

Sarkin, Jeremy. 1998. "The Development of a Human Rights Culture in South Africa." *Human Rights Quarterly* 20(3, August): 628–65.

Savage, Michael. 1986. "The Imposition of Pass Laws on the African Population in South Africa 1916–1984." *African Affairs* 85(339): 181–205.

Scheb, John M., II, and William Lyons. 2000. "The Myth of Legality and Public Evaluation of the Supreme Court." *Social Science Quarterly* 81(4, December): 928–40.

Scheler, Max. 1961. *Ressentiment.* New York: Free Press.

Scher, Steven J., and John M. Darley. 1997. "How Effective Are the Things People Say to Apologize: Effects of the Realization of Apology Speech Act." *Journal of Psycholinguistic Research* 26(1, January): 127–40.

Schuman, Howard, Robert F. Belli, and Katherine Bischoping. 1997. "The Generational Basis of Historical Knowledge." In *Collective Memory of Political Events: Social Psychological Perspectives,* edited by James W. Pennebaker, Dario Paez, and Bernard Rimé. Mahwah, N.J.: Lawrence Erlbaum Associates.

Schuman, Howard, and Amy D. Corning. 2000. "Collective Knowledge of Public Events: The Soviet Era from the Great Purge to Glasnost." *American Journal of Sociology* 105(4, January): 913–56.

Schuman, Howard, and Stanley Presser. 1981. *Questions and Answers in Attitude Surveys: Experiments on Question Form, Wording, and Content.* Orlando, Fla.: Academic Press.

Schuman, Howard, and Jacqueline Scott. 1989. "Generations and Collective Memories." *American Sociological Review* 54(3, June): 359–81.

Schwartz, Herman. 2000. *The Struggle for Constitutional Justice in Post-Communist Europe.* Chicago: University of Chicago Press.

Seekings, Jeremy. 2000. *The UDF: A History of the United Democratic Front in South Africa, 1983–1991.* Cape Town: David Philip.

Sibisi, C. D. T. 1991. "The Psychology of Liberation." In *Bounds of Possibility: The Legacy of Steve Biko and Black Consciousness,* edited by N. Barney Pityana, Mamphela Ramphele, Malusi Mpumlwana, and Lindy Wilson. Cape Town: David Philip.

Sidanius, Jim, Seymour Fechbach, Shana Levin, and Felicia Pratto. 1997. "The Interface Between Ethnic and National Attachment: Ethnic Pluralism or Ethnic Dominance?" *Public Opinion Quarterly* 61(1, Spring): 102–33.

Sigelman, Lee, Timothy Bledsoe, Susan Welch, and Michael W. Combs. 1996. "Making Contact? Black-White Social Interaction in an Urban Setting." *American Journal of Sociology* 101(5, March): 1306–32.

Sigelman, Lee, and Susan Welch. 1993. "The Contact Hypothesis Revisited: Interracial Contact and Positive Racial Attitudes." *Social Forces* 71(3, March): 781–95.

Singer, Eleanor, John Van Hoewyk, and Mary P. Maher. 1998. "Does the Payment of Incentives Create Expectation Effects?" *Public Opinion Quarterly* 62(2, Summer): 152–64.

Skapska, Grazyna. 1990. "The Rule of Law from the East Central European Perspective." *Law and Social Inquiry* 15(4, Fall): 699–706.

Slye, Ronald. 2000. "Amnesty, Truth, and Reconciliation: Reflections on the South African Amnesty Process." In *Truth v. Justice: The Morality of Truth Commissions,* edited by Robert I. Rotberg and Dennis Thompson. Princeton, N.J.: Princeton University Press.

Sniderman, Paul M., and Thomas Piazza. 2002. *Black Pride and Black Prejudice.* Princeton, N.J.: Princeton University Press.

Solomon, Peter H., Jr. 1992. "Legality in Soviet Political Culture: A Perspective on Gorbachev's Reforms." In *Stalinism: Its Nature and Aftermath: Essays in Honor of Moshe Lewin,* edited by Nick Lampert and Gabor T. Rittersporn. New York: M. E. Sharpe.

Spitz, Richard, and Matthew Chaskalson. 2000. *The Politics of Transition: A Hidden History of South Africa's Negotiated Settlement.* Johannesburg: Witwatersrand University Press.

Spriggs, James F., II. 1996. "The Supreme Court and Federal Administrative Agencies: A Resource-Based Theory and Analysis of Judicial Impact." *American Journal of Political Science* 40(4, November): 1122–51.

———. 1997. "Explaining Federal Bureaucratic Compliance with Supreme Court Opinions." *Political Research Quarterly* 50(3, September): 567–93.

Stryker, Robin. 1994. "Rules, Resources, and Legitimacy Processes: Some Implications for Social Conflict, Order, and Change." *American Journal of Sociology* 99(4, January): 847–910.

Sullivan, John L., and Stanley Feldman. 1980. *Multiple Indicators: An Intro-*

duction. Quantitative Applications in the Social Sciences, vol. 15. Thousand Oaks, Calif.: Sage Publications.

Sullivan, John L., James E. Piereson, and George E. Marcus. 1982. *Political Tolerance and American Democracy*. Chicago: University of Chicago Press.

Sumner, William G. 1906. *Folkways: A Study of the Sociological Importance of Usages, Manners, Customs, Mores, and Morals*. New York: Ginn and Co.

Theissen, Gunnar. 1997. "Between Acknowledgment and Ignorance: How White South Africans Have Dealt with the Apartheid Past." Johannesburg: Centre for the Study of Violence and Reconciliation.

Theissen, Gunnar, and Brandon Hamber. 1998. "A State of Denial: White South Africans' Attitudes to the Truth and Reconciliation Commission." *Indicator South Africa* 15(1): 8–12.

Thompson, Leonard, and Andrew Prior. 1982. *South African Politics*. Cape Town: David Philip.

Truth and Reconciliation Commission. 1998. *Truth and Reconciliation Commission of South Africa Report*. 5 vols. Cape Town: Juta & Co.

Tsebelis, George. 2000. "Veto Players and Institutional Analysis." *Governance* 13(4, October): 441–74.

Tutu, Desmond Mpilo. 1999. *No Future Without Forgiveness*. New York: Doubleday.

Tyler, Tom R. 1990. *Why People Follow the Law: Procedural Justice, Legitimacy, and Compliance*. New Haven, Conn.: Yale University Press.

———. 2001. "A Psychological Perspective on the Legitimacy of Institutions and Authorities." In *The Psychology of Legitimacy: Emerging Perspectives on Ideology, Justice, and Intergroup Relations*, edited by John J. Jost and Brenda Major. New York: Cambridge University Press.

Tyler, Tom R., and Robert J. Boeckmann. 1997. "Three Strikes and You Are Out, but Why? The Psychology of Public Support for Punishing Rule Breakers." *Law and Society Review* 31(2, June): 237–65.

Tyler, Tom R., Robert J. Boeckmann, Heather J. Smith, and Yuen J. Huo. 1997. *Social Justice in a Diverse Society*. Boulder, Colo.: Westview Press.

Tyler, Tom R., and E. Allan Lind. 2001. "Procedural Justice." In *Handbook of Justice Research in Law*, edited by Joseph Sanders and V. Lee Hamilton. New York: Kluwer Academic/Plenum Publishers.

Tyler, Tom R., and Gregory Mitchell. 1994. "Legitimacy and the Empowerment of Discretionary Legal Authority: The United States Supreme Court and Abortion Rights." *Duke Law Journal* 43(4, February): 703–815.

Tyler, Tom, and Kenneth Rasinski. 1991. "Legitimacy and the Acceptance of Unpopular U.S. Supreme Court Decisions: A Reply to Gibson." *Law and Society Review* 25(3): 621–30.

U.S. Department of State. Office of the Coordinator for Counterterrorism. 2001. "Appendix B: Background Information on Terrorist Groups." In

Patterns of Global Terrorism, 2000. Released April 30. http://www.state.gov/s/ct/rls/pgtrpt/2000/2450.htm (accessed December 7, 2002).

Valdez, Patricia. 1998. "Must the Victims Always Wait?" *Siyaya!* 3(Spring): 53–55.

Verwoerd, Wilhelm. 1997. "Justice After Apartheid? Reflections on the South African Truth and Reconciliation Commission." Paper delivered to the Firth International Conference on Ethics and Development: Globalization, Self-determination, and Justice in Development. Madras, India, January 2–9.

Vestergaard, Mads. 2001. "Who's Got the Map? The Negotiation of Afrikaner Identities in Post-Apartheid South Africa." *Daedalus* 130(1, Winter): 19–44.

Vidmar, Neil. 2001. "Retribution and Revenge." In *Handbook of Justice Research in Law*, edited by Joseph Sanders and V. Lee Hamilton. New York: Kluwer Academic/Plenum Publishers.

Villa-Vicencio, Charles. 2000. "Getting On with Life: A Move Towards Reconciliation." In *Looking Back, Reaching Forward: Reflections on the Truth and Reconciliation Commission of South Africa*, edited by Charles Villa-Vicencio and Wilhelm Verwoerd. Cape Town: University of Cape Town Press.

Villa-Vicencio, Charles, and Wilhelm Verwoerd. 2000. "Constructing a Report: Writing Up the 'Truth.'" In *Truth v. Justice: The Morality of Truth Commissions*, edited by Robert I. Rotberg and Dennis Thompson. Princeton, N.J.: Princeton University Press.

Weiner, Bernard, Sandra Graham, Orli Peter, and Mary Zmuidinas. 1991. "Public Confession and Forgiveness." *Journal of Personality* 59(2, June): 281–312.

Wilson, James Q. 1976. *Varieties of Political Behavior*. New York: Basic Books.

Wilson, Richard. 1995. "Manufacturing Legitimacy: The Truth and Reconciliation Commission and the Rule of Law." *Indicator SA* 13(1, Summer): 41–46.

———. 2001. *The Politics of Truth and Reconciliation in South Africa: Legitimizing the Post-Apartheid States*. New York: Cambridge University Press.

Wilson, Thomas C. 1996. "Prejudice Reduction or Self Selection? A Test of the Contact Hypothesis." *Sociological Spectrum* 16: 43–60.

Yancey, George. 1999. "An Examination of the Effects of Residential and Church Integration on Racial Attitudes of Whites." *Sociological Perspectives* 42(2, Spring): 279–304.

Yoo, John C. 2001. "In Defense of the Court's Legitimacy." In *The Vote: Bush, Gore, and the Supreme Court*, edited by Cass R. Sunstein and Richard A. Epstein. Chicago: University of Chicago Press.

Zalaquett, Jose. 1997. "Why Deal with the Past?" In *Dealing with the Past:*

Truth and Reconciliation in South Africa, 2nd ed., edited by Alex Boraine, Janet Levy, and Ronel Scheffer. Cape Town: Institute for Democracy in South Africa.

Zelditich, Morris, Jr. 2001. "Theories of Legitimacy." In *The Psychology of Legitimacy: Emerging Perspectives on Ideology, Justice, and Intergroup Relations*, edited by John J. Jost and Brenda Major. New York: Cambridge University Press.

Index

Boldface numbers refer to figures and tables.